THE BOOK OF THE
MINIATURE SCHNAUZER

by Anna Katherine Nicholas
with special sections by Gloria Lewis, Mrs. K.L. Church, and Joseph P. Sayres, DVM

0-86622-151-4

Distributed in the UNITED STATES by T.F.H. Publications, Inc., 211 West Sylvania Avenue, Neptune City, NJ 07753; in CANADA by H & L Pet Supplies Inc., 27 Kingston Crescent, Kitchener, Ontario N2B 2T6; Rolf C. Hagen Ltd., 3225 Sartelon Street, Montreal 382 Quebec; in ENGLAND by T.F.H. Publications Limited, 4 Kier Park, Ascot, Berkshire SL5 7DS; in AUSTRALIA AND THE SOUTH PACIFIC by T.F.H. (Australia) Pty. Ltd., Box 149, Brookvale 2100 N.S.W., Australia; in NEW ZEALAND by Ross Haines & Son, Ltd., 18 Monmouth Street, Grey Lynn, Auckland 2 New Zealand; in SINGAPORE AND MALAYSIA by MPH Distributors (S) Pte., Ltd., 601 Sims Drive, # 03/07/21, Singapore 1438; in the PHILIPPINES by Bio-Research, 5 Lippay Street, San Lorenzo Village, Makati Rizal; in SOUTH AFRICA by Multipet Pty. Ltd., 30 Turners Avenue, Durban 4001. Published by T.F.H. Publications Inc. Manufactured in the United States of America by T.F.H. Publications, Inc.

Dedication
To all the handsome Miniature
Schnauzers I have admired in the
show ring: and to all the many others
bringing happiness to their owners.

In Appreciation

We are deeply appreciative of the support our announcement that we were doing a new Miniature Schnauzer book has received. A great many people have generously contributed photos, information, and other important material which we have included. We thank them sincerely!

We are especially grateful to Dan Kiedrowski, editor-publisher of *Schnauzer Shorts,* the breed's excellent magazine, for the generosity with which he has supplied photos which would have otherwise been unavailable to us. He was extremely helpful, particularly in the historical background section of this book which reflects the assistance he gave us, both through use of photos and information about various dogs.

Mrs. K.L. Church has done what we think is a very valuable section on the rolling of the coat in a rough coated terrier. Read her ideas carefully; we think you will find them very useful.

Gloria Lewis has contributed much material on clipping, grooming, and the Schnauzer generally. She is another whose interest we appreciate.

There is also our Veterinarian's Corner, especially slanted towards Schnauzers, by Joseph P. Sayres, in which we also take pride.

To Marcia Foy, here at home, our thanks for many hours contacting the breeders, pasting up pictures, and generally helping to make the preparation of the book go smoothly.

To everyone who has participated in any way, our heartfelt appreciation.

Contents

About the Author

Since early childhood, Anna Katherine Nicholas has been involved with dogs. Her first pets were a Boston Terrier, an Airedale, and a German Shepherd Dog. Then, in 1925, came the first Pekingese, a gift from a family friend who raised them. Now her home is shared with a Miniature Poodle and a dozen or so Beagles, including her noted Best in Show and National Specialty winner, Champion Rockaplenty's Wild Oats, an internationally famous Beagle sire, who as a show dog was top Beagle in the nation in 1973. She also owns Champion Foyscroft True Blue Lou and, in co-ownership with Marcia Foy who lives with her, Champion Foyscroft Triple Mitey Migit.

Miss Nicholas is best known in the dog fancy as a writer and as a judge. Her first magazine articles were about Pekingese, published in *Dog News* magazine about 1930. This was followed by a widely acclaimed breed column, "Peeking at the Pekingese," which appeared continuously for at least two decades, originally in *Dogdom* and, when that magazine ceased to exist, in *Popular Dogs*.

During the 1940's she was Boxer columnist for the American Kennel Club *Gazette* and a featured East Coast representative for *Boxer Briefs*. More recently, many of her articles of general interest to the dog fancy have appeared in *Popular Dogs*, *Pure-Bred Dogs/American Kennel Gazette*, and *Show Dogs*. She is presently a featured columnist for *Dog World*, *Canine Chronicle*, and *Kennel Review* in the United States and *Dog Fancier* in Canada. Her *Dog World* column, "Here, There and Everywhere," was the Dog Writers Association of America selection for Best Series in a dog magazine which was awarded her for 1979. And for 1981 her feature article, "Faster Is Not Better," published in the *Canine Chronicle*, was one of four nominated for the Best Feature Article Award from the Dog Writers Association. She also has been a columnist for *World of the Working Dog*.

It was during the 1930's that Miss Nicholas' first book, *The Pekingese*, was published by the Judy Publishing Company. This book completely sold out two editions and is now an eagerly sought-after collector's item, as is her *The Skye Terrier Book*, published through the Skye Terrier Club of America during the early 1960's.

Miss Nicholas won the Dog Writers Association of America award in 1970 for the Best Technical Book of the Year with her *Nicholas Guide to Dog Judging*. Then in 1979 the revision of this book again won the Dog Writers Association of America Best Technical Book Award, the first time ever that a revision has been so honored by this association.

In the early 1970's Miss Nicholas co-authored with Joan Brearley five breed books for T.F.H. Publications. These were *This is the Bichon Frise*, *The Wonderful World of Beagles and Beagling*, *The Book of the Pekingese*, *This is the Skye Terrier*, and *The Book of the Boxer*. *The Wonderful World of Beagles and Beagling* won a Dog Writers Association of America Honorable Mention Award the year that it was published.

All of Miss Nicholas' recent releases from T.F.H. have been received with enthusiasm and acclaim; these include *Successful Dog Show Exhibiting*, *The Book of the Rottweiler*, *The Book of the Poodle*, *The Book of the Labrador Retriever*, *The Book of the English Springer Spaniel*, *The Book of the Golden Retriever*, *The Book of the German Shepherd Dog*, and *The Book of the Shetland Sheepdog*.

In another series, also from T.F.H., Miss Nicholas has written *The Maltese*, *The Keeshond*, *The Poodle*, *The Boxer*, *The Chow Chow*, *The Beagle*, *The Basset Hound*, *The German Pointer* and several other titles.

In addition to her four Dog Writers Association of America awards, Miss Nicholas has received the Gaines "Fido" as Dog Writer of the Year on two occasions, in the late 1970's and again in 1982; and she has received, on separate occasions, two "Winkies" from *Kennel Review* as Dog Journalist of the Year.

The great Ch. Hughcrest Hugh Hefner (Ch. Marcheim Poppin Fresh-Anna Rose) was bred by Rosemary and Harvey Morehouse; shown to the title under the Hughcrest banner, Chris and Judy Hughes; then sold to Kelly Hoskins for whom he was campaigned by Clay Coady (pictured). No. 3 Miniature Schnauzer in 1973; No. 1 in 1974 and 1975. During five years of showing, Hugh Hefner won 14 Specialty Shows (a record for a while), was Best of Breed on 131 occasions, 92 Group placements which included 29 times Best in the Terrier Group, and he had five Bests in Show among his credits. The sire of 15 champions, among them Top Producer Ch. Hughcrest Harvey Wallbanger.

CHAPTER ONE

Origin of the Miniature Schnauzer

From "way back when" these are two homebreds and an import which helped to shape the future of the breed in the 1920's. On the left, Ch. Hermoine of Marienhof, born October 1928; uncropped Primrose of Marienhof is from the next decade, born 1938; the import, Flieger Heinzelmannchen, born in 1929. Flieger was one of the breed's great foundation sires. All from Marienhof Kennels owned by Mrs. Marie Slattery. Photo courtesy of Dan Kiedrowski, *Schnauzer Shorts*.

There are three separate breeds of dog who come under the heading of "Schnauzer": the Giant Schnauzer, the Standard Schnauzer and the Miniature Schnauzer, all of whom originated in Germany. "Schnauzer" is a word which translated means "moustache," and all three of the Schnauzers are heavily moustached.

The Giant Schnauzer, largest member of the "family," was long known as the Munchener Dog, later becoming the Riesenschnauzer. History traces *its* origin to the highlands of Bavaria, where it was one of the types of dog used as a cattle or drover's dog, its appearance similar to that of the Bouvier des Flandres, a breed used for the same purpose. It is theorized, but unproven, that there may be Standard Schnauzer blood in the Giant Schnauzer. It is also possible that the early and now extinct Thuringian Shepherd Dog and the Great Dane were used as outcrosses; the former to bring in the wire coat and salt and pepper coloring, the latter for black coloring and erect ears. No actual proof of any of this exists.

The Standard Schnauzer ranks between the Giant and the Miniature Schnauzer in size, and is evidently the oldest of the three breeds. As far

back as the fifteenth century, pictures were painted of dogs of this type and evidence of their existence has been seen in tapestries and other artwork of this period. As in most breeds, differences of opinion and various theories exist regarding the origin of the Standard Schnauzer. One school of thought considers the early dogs to have been a cross between the Middle Ages 'Beaver Dog' and a rough-coated dog used as ratters. Another equally popular theory is that the Wirehaired German Pinscher and the Schafer Pudel (all of these refer to breeds long since extinct) formed the nucleus of early ancestry.

There seems to be general agreement that the Standard Schnauzer traces its background to Wurttemberg and Bavaria, where other cattle dogs also had their origins. Setting the Standard Schnauzer apart from the others was his considerable ability as a ratter, this leading some to feel that he was a terrier, an opinion with which others vehemently disagree.

The Miniature Schnauzer, the breed with which this book is concerned, was known in its homeland, Germany, as the Zwergschnauzer. He, like the Standard Schnauzer, was a proficient ratter. But he is not, as some fanciers

9

Some of Marie Slattery's original Miniature Schnauzers: *left to right,* Mehitabel of Marienhof, Ch. Lotte v d Goldbachhohe, Ch. Cuno von Burgstadt, and Ch. Moses Taylor. Photo courtesy of Dan Kiedrowski, *Schnauzer Shorts.*

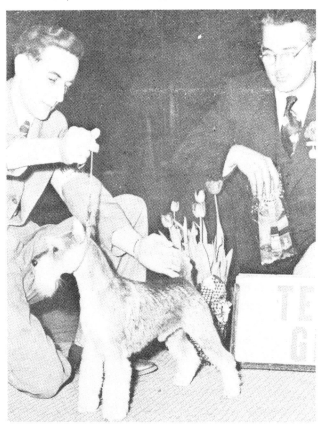

The most influential of all Miniature Schnauzers, Ch. Dorem Display, with George Ward handling on the historic occasion of his winning the Terrier Group at Westminster in 1947. Judge John Marvin. Display was bred by Dorothy Williams (Dorem), owned and campaigned by Mr. and Mrs. Phil Meldon, then retired to the ownership of Mrs. H. Weldon Angus (Benrook), under whose loving care he lived out the remainder of his lifetime. Photo courtesy of Dan Kiedrowski, *Schnauzer Shorts.*

evidently believe, merely a smaller-sized version of the Standard Schnauzer, although the latter obviously figures in his background. The most popularly accepted dog to have been combined with the Standard Schnauzer to produce the Miniature Schnauzer is the Affenpinscher, and pictures we have seen from early times clearly bear this out. Affenpinschers were popular in Europe as long ago as the seventeenth century. There have been many more elaborate theories than this one expounded; but when one considers the characteristics of both Affenpinschers and Miniature Schnauzers, it does appear that this theory is correct.

Speculation has been raised at various times that Miniature Pinschers, Pomeranians, Fox Terriers, and Scottish Terriers had some part to play. This may have been true in some cases, as, for example, we have read that a dog born in 1920 by the name of Michel Chemnitz-Plauen was registered as a Miniature Pinscher but sired by the Miniature Schnauzer Sieger Trumpf Chemnitz-Plauen from another Miniature Schnauzer, Resl Chemnitz-Plauen. Both of these parents were noted producers of Miniature Schnauzers! But considering the background physical characteristics and color ranges in both breeds, we do feel that the Affenpinscher tips the scales heavily as the breed most likely to have shared in the basic creation of Miniature Schnauzers.

Early German records provide the information that at least two early German breeders, both from Frankfurt, bred Affenpinschers and Miniature Schnauzers, the former under the Dornbusch banner (Georg Riehl) and the latter under Affentor (Heinrich Schott). Who is to say that these two gentlemen never experimented a bit with a litter or two, combining the breeds, which would have been possible at the beginning of the present century??

The three best known important German Miniature Schnauzer Stud Dogs between the early twentieth century and the end of World War I were Peter v. Westerberg, born in November 1902, owned by Werneberg Kennels, Herr Max Woch at Weimar; Prinz v. Rheinstein, born July 1903, owned by Herr Trampe of Berlin, bred by Herr Kissel of Frankfurt; and the dog who was known as Lord v. Dornbusch, Lord v. Riehl, and Horburg's Lord, bred by Herr Georg Riehl of Frankfurt, born November 1904.

Peter v. Westerberg was a solid black of unknown pedigree. He produced both black and yellow puppies, and is recorded as having sired 55 litters during his lifetime of 12 years. Peter also was shown successfully. It has been stated that he is probably to be found in the background of the majority of Miniature Schnauzers of the present day.

Prinz v. Rheinstein was a black dog with yellow-gray markings. He, too, was of unknown pedigree, said to have strongly resembled an Affenpinscher-Miniature Pinscher combination. He only lived to be a few years of age, during which time he sired some half dozen litters with at least several champions among his progeny.

Lord, again of uncertain breeding, was a very typical Schnauzer in appearance. He reached about eight years of age, and sired three memorable sons: Frick v. Dornbusch, Fritz v. Lohr, and Rauber v. Dornbusch.

Ch. Andrel's Romance winning Best of Breed at Devon Dog Show Ass'n. in 1970. One of the very handsome Miniature Schnauzers from the Andrel Kennels of Andrew O. and Elinor Czapski, so prominent around the 1960's. Bob Crews is handling.

Kismet of Marienhof, from Marie Slattery's famed kennel, sired two champion daughters.

Marienhof Kennels' Ch. Cockerel of Sharvogue, one of three brothers who were very famous in the Miniature Schnauzer world of the 1930's. Owned by Marie Slattery, Cockerel sired five American and two Canadian Champions. Cockerel was one of six producers from Ch. T.M.G. of Marienhof and Wild Honey of Sharvogue.

Ch. Phil-Mar Watta Lady was the first champion bred by Peggy Anspach Wolfe, Phil-Mar Kennels. Photo courtesy of *Schnauzer Shorts*.

Handful's Snow Flurry, by Ch. Diplomat of Marienhof ex Ch. Benrook Bona, was foundation bitch for Trayhom Kennels. Photo courtesy of Dan Kiedrowski, *Schnauzer Shorts*

Ch. Handful's Pop Up from Miss Gene Simmonds' kennels. Photo courtesy of Dan Kiedrowski, *Schnauzer Shorts*.

Ch. Boomerang of Marienhof, by Ch. Blythewood Ricochet of La May ex Ch. Hansel's Prudence of Marienhof, owned by Mrs. Ruth Ziegler. Photo courtesy of *Schnauzer Shorts.*

Ch. Handful's Pheasant, one of the Miniature Schnauzers from Handful Kennels, Miss Gene Simmonds. Photo courtesy of Dan Kiedrowski.

Ch. Mankit's Signal Go, son of Ch. Mankit's Moon-shot, owned by Mankit's Kennels. Photo courtesy of *Schnauzer Shorts.*

Ch. Mankit's Moon Shot, sire of Ch. Mankit's Signal Go, owned by the Emanuel Millers, Mankit Kennels. Photo courtesy of *Schnauzer Shorts,* Dan Kiedrowski, editor and publisher.

Salisbury, Maryland in 1959. Andrew and Elinor Czapski's Ch. Andrel Adjutant, Winners Dog and Best of Winners; Ch. Handful's Pepper, Best of Breed; and Ch. Andrel's Argenta, Winners Bitch and Best of Opposite Sex. William Ackland is the judge. Photo courtesy of Tom and Kay Gately who played a very active part in early Schnauzer history in this country.

CHAPTER TWO

Three "pillars of the breed." Ch. Handsome of Marienhof, *left*, with Ch. T.M.G. of Marienhof and Ch. Kubla Khan of Marienhof. These are all from the kennels of the late Marie Slattery. T.M.G. (named for Thomas Michael Gately) was the leading sire of his day, a son of the great importation Ch. Marko v Beutenberg, who was sired by Mrs. Slattery's still earlier import, Ch. Cuno v Burgstadt who came to her from Germany in 1927. Photo courtesy of Dan Kiedrowski, *Schnauzer Shorts* magazine.

Miniature Schnauzers in the United States

It was not until the 1920's that the first Miniature Schnauzers appeared in the United States. The earliest of them arrived here in 1923, imported by W.D. Goff of Concord, Massachusetts. These were a dog and a bitch who left no progeny, and a bitch named Hella v.d. Goldbachhohe who was registered several years later and who did eventually produce two or more litters, the first of them in 1927, but whose offspring failed to reproduce.

It was in 1924 that Rudolph Krappatsch, the same gentleman who had exported those mentioned above to Mr. Goff, again sent some Miniature Schnauzers to this country. These were imported by Mrs. Marie E. Lewis, at South Lincoln, Massachusetts, who as Mrs. Marie Slattery, was to become a lady of tremendous importance in the American history of this breed owner of the famed Marienhof Kennels, which were a leading force in the Schnauzer world for close to five decades. During that period the Marienhof Kennels must have produced well over a hundred champions. At the time of her earliest imports, Mrs. Slattery, as Mrs. Lewis, owned the Zeitgest Kennels, changing the kennel identification to Marienhof following her

marriage to J.W. Slattery.

It was three bitches, Amsel v.d. Cyriaksburg and her two daughters, Lotte and Lady v.d. Goldbachhohe, who became the true foundations of the breed here. Lotte and Lady, born in 1924, were sired by Fels v.d. Goldbachhohe (who also was the sire of Mr. Goff's Hella) from Amsel, who had been born in 1921. Historians have stated that without a doubt there are very few American-bred champions in the records who do not trace back their ancestry to Amsel and these two daughters. It was Amsel who produced the first American-bred litter of Miniature Schnauzers, on July 15th 1925, of which Champion Affe of Oddacre, originally named Affe v. Zeitgeist, was a member.

In the beginning, Standard Schnauzers were known as Wire-haired Pinschers here in the United States, and Miniature Schnauzers did not receive separate recognition as a breed until late 1926 when registration was granted them, the same year that the name was officially changed to Schnauzers. Prior to recognition they were shown for a short period in the same class as the Standards, and separate classes were provided for the first time at the Combined Terrier

The great Ch. Dorem Display, background of the modern Miniature Schnauzer world. During the 1940's-1950's this fabulous dog set exciting records in the show ring and as a stud dog, making him the most influential individual dog in the history of this breed. Bred by Miss Dorothy Williams. Owned during most of his show career by Mr. and Mrs. Phil Meldon, later owned by Benrook Kennels. Photo courtesy of *Schnauzer Shorts.*

Ch. Cunning Asta of Bambivin, a 1936 champion who completed title by winning third in Group at Santa Cruz K.C. She was the breed's first black champion in the U.S.; the first American-bred and Bred-by-Exhibitor black champion, probably the first California-bred champion; and the first Miniature Schnauzer to win Best in Match All Breeds. Bred and owned by Mrs. Willis N. Maguire, she lived to be 16 years and eight months of age.

Clubs Specialty Show in 1927. All Schnauzers were originally shown in the Working Group but Standards and Miniatures were transferred from there to the Terrier Group in 1927. Until 1931 awards were made for Best Standard Schnauzer and Best Miniature Schnauzer, each of them being represented in the Group. Then, through an American Kennel Club rule change, they competed together with only one "Best" selected; but in the Spring of 1933 a change again took place, restoring separate awards for the Miniatures and Standards.

Borste v. Bischofsleben, an imported bitch owned by Monson Morris, was the first Miniature Schnauzer registered with the American Kennel Club. She left no champion descendants. Even though Miniatures had been registered as such since 1926, the American Kennel Club suddenly ordained that a Specialty Club could cover only one breed. As the Schnauzer Club of America included both Standards and Miniatures, this ruling made them all Schnauzers without distinction, which would have opened the door to inter-breeding of the two varieties. This had been done in Germany during the early years of development, but did not seem feasible at that time from the point of view of Miniature fanciers. And so two separate clubs were formed to replace the original Schnauzer Club of America (which in the beginning had been known as the Wire-haired Pinscher Club of America). Thus, in 1933, the Miniature Schnauzer Club of America and the Standard Schnauzer Club of America were founded, two separate Specialty Clubs each involved with its own breed.

The American Miniature Schnauzer Club was officially founded on August 19th, 1933. Its Officers were President, Mrs. Isaac W. Jeanes (Mardale Kennels); Vice-President, Monson Morris (Woodway Kennels), who also served as American Kennel Club Delegate; and Secretary,

Ch. Cosburn's Esquire was Winners Dog at the Associated Terrier Club Specialty in New York in 1954 owned by John Graziano of Mount Vernon, New York. Sired by Cosburn's Admiration (litter brother to Ch. Cosburn's Aristocrat) Esquire had an outstanding record in the United States, and was the first Canadian-bred Schnauzer to so distinguish himself here. He was purchased by Mrs. Priscilla Deaver who won well with him, then went to Edward Marshall Boehm who co-owned him with Mr. and Mrs. William Moore. After Mr. Boehm's death, he became the sole property of the Moores and he helped to found the Travelmor Kennels. Photo courtesy of *Schnauzer Shorts*.

Miss Anne FitzGerald (Anfiger Kennels). Twelve members made up the Board of Directors, three of them elected annually to serve four years. 32 members were active in the club at that time, including Mrs. J.W. Slattery of Marienhof; Mrs. Leda B. Martin of Ledahof; Mrs. R.N. Pierson of Edgeover; Mrs. Dodge Sloane of Brookmeade; Mrs. Joseph Sailer, Twells Kennels; Richard A. Kerns, Wollaton Kennels; and Mrs. Anne F. Eskrigge of Anfiger. Two former Standard Schnauzer fanciers later also joined the American Miniature Schnauzer Club, Mrs. H.L. Woehling and Mr. G. Harrison Frazier.

Mrs. Slattery and Mrs. Dodge Sloane (who was still a member of the American Miniature Schnauzer Club at the time of her death in 1964) were both exhibitors at the first Terrier Breeds Specialty in 1927. Mr. Frank Brumby handled Miniature Schnauzers for Mrs. Sloane back in 1927, continuing to do so over a goodly number of years.

At the first Terrier Specialty Show just mentioned, Best of Breed was awarded to Sieger and American Champion Don v. Dornbusch, belonging to the Hitofa Kennels, owned by Frank Spiekerman.

The first Miniature to complete championship in the United States was Siegerin Lenchen v. Dornbusch owned by Mrs. Sloane. This bitch was the dam of Don v. Dornbusch, and was also the oldest of the breed to come to America since she was whelped in October 1920, eight months prior to the arrival here of Amsel.

Champion Moses Taylor, owned by Mrs. Marie Slattery, was the first American-bred of the breed to gain title here by Champion Affe of

Ch. Perci-Bee's First Impression, the sire of Ch. Phil-Mar's Lugar, was a successful winner in his own right, handled by Peggy Anspach Wolfe for owner. Photo courtesy of *Schnauzer Shorts*.

Ch. Phil-Mar Lugar, by Ch. Perci-Bee's First Impression (Ch. Dorem Favorite-Ch. Phil-Mar Lady Be Good) from Ch. Phil-Mar's Lucy Lady (Ch. Dorem Tempo-Ch. Phil-Mar Watta Lady) was the breed's top winner in 1959-1960. Lugar had an all-breed Best in Show during each of those years and compiled a record of 70 times Best in Breed, which included the American Miniature Schnauzer Club and the Paul Revere Specialties plus 40 Group placements which included 12 Group Firsts. The 26 A.K.C. champions he sired have also played an important role in Miniature Schnauzer history. Photo courtesy of *Schnauzer Shorts*.

Oddacre, from the first litter born in the States. Moses was a double grandson of Champion Amsel v.d. Cyriaksburg.

Don v. Dornbusch and Moses Taylor were tied for first male champion of the breed since both finished on the same date, at different dog shows, in 1927.

It was in 1928 that Miniature Schnauzers made their first Group win. This honor was accorded Champion Dolf v. Feldschlosschen, imported from Czechoslavakia by J.M. Brown. The first American-bred and first bitch to win a Group was Champion Aennchen v. Marienhof, in October 1930 at the North Carolina State Fair, one of Marie Slattery's great homebreds. This excellent bitch was quite a trail-blazer for her sex, as, sold to Mrs. Jeanes (Mardale Kennels), she became the only bitch to take Best Miniature Schnauzer at Westminster prior to 1938 and she was the Best Miniature over an entry of 52 at Morris and Essex in 1934 at past six years of age, thus becoming the only Miniature

prior to Champion Dorem Display to take Best of Breed honors at both these prestigious shows.

Aennchen was a member of a very distinguished family, being a full sister to Champion Cuno v. Wollaton and Champion Mardale Rudi. Like their sister, Aennchen, these two were Best of Breed winners at Westminster: Cuno became the first American-bred to attain this award and Rudi, on the occasion of his victory, also defeated the Standard Schnauzer. These triumphs were in 1930 and 1931 respectively.

No resumé of the 1930's would be complete without paying tribute to Mrs. Richard Kerns and her Champion Jeff of Wollaton, who won the Annual Trophy of the American Miniature Schnauzer Club in 1934 and 1935 which was subsequently retired the following year by Mrs. Kerns with Champion Wollaton Sheik. Mrs. Joseph Sailer was the second person to win the trophy outright, her "legs" on it having been awarded in 1940 to Champion Wingless Victor of Sharvogue, in 1942 to Champion Cockeral of Sharvogue, and in 1944 to Champion Neff's Luzon.

Ch. Rik-Rak Regina, C.D., by Ch. Delfin James ex Can. and Am. Ch. Rik-Rak Rebel's Banner. A Canadian and American C.D., she was campaigned to conformation title by Mr. and Mrs. William B. Austin, Jr., then was re-acquired by her breeder in 1961. Regina gained her C.D. in the spring of 1962, at the same time becoming the breed's only third generation obedience titled champion.

It took awhile for Miniature Schnauzers to make the breakthrough to Best in Show, but in 1946 that wonderful little dog whose influence on the breed has been so tremendous, Champion Dorem Display, did so. He went on to win a total of five Bests in Show at all-breed events during his ring career, plus four Specialty Show Bests of Breed and numerous Terrier Group wins and placements, including Best Terrier at Westminster.

The first all-breed winning Best in Show bitch at a dog show held in the United States was Champion Forest Nod of Mandeville, one of three Best in Show winning Miniature Schnauzers during 1952. The other two were Champion Meldon's Ruffian and Champion Kalenheim Arno. Nod and Ruffian each added a second Best in Show the following year.

Other distinguished winning Miniature Schnauzers of the 1950's included Champion Hit Parade's Lamplighter, Champion Charlena Sho Nuff, Champion Bursche v. Hessen, Champion Phil Mar's Mister John, Champion Phil

Ch. Meldon's Ruffian, owned by Mr. and Mrs. George Hendrickson and handled by Larry Downey was a consistent and important winner from the 1950's. He was the second Miniature Schnauzer to go Best in Show in the United States, following right along in the pawprints of his sire, Ch. Dorem Display, who had been the first Best in Show Miniature Schnauzer here. Ruffian was the sire of 26 champions. Photo courtesy of Mrs. Alice Downey.

Ch. Benrook Brandy was Best of Breed at the American Miniature Schnauzer Club Specialty in New York in 1957 under judge Alva Rosenberg, followed up by a string of Bests of Breed including Eastern and Chicago International in 1957. In 1958 he repeated at Eastern and Chicago (adding a Group placement at the latter), won the Terrier Group at Detroit, and won the Penn-Ohio Specialty. Bred by Mrs. H. Weldon Angus, Benrook Kennels, Swansea, Massachusetts.

Mar's Gay Lady, Champion Phil Mar's Gay Knight, and Champion Phil Mar's Lucy Lady, the latter four all homebreds from this highly important and successful kennel owned by the Anspachs. Lucy Lady was Top Winning Miniature Schnauzer for 1953.

Since "firsts" are always interesting to look back upon, here are some others for you. Champion Hit Parade's Blacksmith Blues was the first to celebrate a weekend with back-to-back Group Firsts when doing so in 1953.

Champion Dodi's Dimitri was the first Miniature Schnauzer to win Best in Show at Montgomery County in 1955, Champion Mankit's To The Moon the second, and the first Miniature Schnauzer to do so TWICE.

Handful Kennels, owned by Miss Gene Simmonds, was the first to win Best Team in Show for the breed at Westminster and Boston, in 1955.

But returning to the 1930's, the Westminster Kennel Club catalogue for 1937 lists the following among the Miniature Schnauzer exhibitors there: Marienhof Kennels with four individual entries plus a brace and a team; Gene Simmonds

Mr. Dean Jagger and his daughter with Florence Bradburn's Eric v Elfland, an M.G.M. photo from 1955. Eric was the litter brother to Ch. Edel v Elfland.

Bob Hope in 1974 on NBC Television has as a guest Walter's Enchanted Echo (Ch. Blythewood Mr. Sandman ex Walter's Strutabout Tempest). Dolores Walters, owner, Gas Light Kennels, Burbank, California.

Ch. Winposa Arch Rival, owned by Kansho Kennels, Clyde and Margaret Brown, Levelland, Texas. Shown sparingly, Rival was third among Miniature Schnauzers in 1961, among his wins four Terrier Groups, two of them from the classes.

Ch. Fancy Filly of Elfland with Florence Bradburn, Elfland Kennels, Temple City, California.

with Handful of Marienhof, a puppy then (born 1936) by Champion Porgie of Marienhof ex Champion Hope of Marienhof; Jack Crockett with some puppies and, in Specials, Champion Opal Heinzelmannchen, by Balzar v.d. Zwick ex Carmen Heinzelmannchen, born 1933; Mrs. J. Montgomery Deaver with littermates by Champion Wollaton Sheik ex Heidi of Mardale and a dog, Shortstop of Mardale, by Champion Urian Thuringia ex Waffe Heinzelmannchen. Mrs. James A. Sailor had Mardale Chief. Dorothy S. Williams was competing with Dorem Dilettante and Doren Diva, these two being littermates. Edgeover Kennels were represented, as were Normack, Sharvogue, Wollaton, and more. The total Miniature Schnauzer entry that year was close to 40.

Coming back to the 1950's we find the handsome and important little dog, Champion Perci-Bee's First Impression, who was the 1958 Westminster Best of Breed, winner of four American Miniature Schnauzer Club Specialty

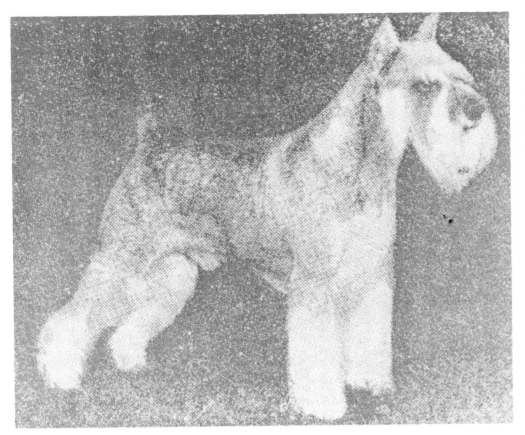

Ch. Luvemal's Master Copy, born September 1959, by Ch. Phil Mar Lugar ex Ch. Luvemal's Carbon Copy, bred and owned by Charlotte L. Stacy. An outstanding winner of Eastern Specialties in 1961, Master Copy gained his championship in three weeks at only 11 months of age, finishing with five majors including an important Specialty. He was among the Top Ten for 1961, and had multiple Specialty wins to his credit.

Ch. Orwina Anfiger, co-owned by Anfiger Kennels, Mrs. Anne F. Eskrigge, Needham, Massachusetts, and by Kolohof Kennels, Chicago, Illinois. A winner during the early 1960's she had Group Firsts to her credit. A daughter of Ch. Dorem Original Darwina Anfiger, who is a daughter of Ch. Dody's Dimitri.

Am. and Braz. Ch. Helarry's Dark Victory, born November 1958, by Ch. Meldon's Ruffian ex Helarry's Delsey. Bred and owned by Mrs. Helen C. Wiedenbeck, handled by Larry Downey. This dog, No. 10 in the Terrier Group for 1960, Dark Victory was a multiple Best in Show and Group winning dog. As a sire he accounted for more than two dozen champions.

Ch. Alpine Baby Ruth winning a Best in Show in 1970, handled by Dick Cooper for the Lou Auslanders, Lake Forest, IL. Sired by Ch. Alpine Great Scott. Photo courtesy of *Schnauzer Shorts*.

This marvelous photo of Tom Gately shows him with Ch. Porgie or Marienhof, Hope of Marienhof, Ch. Charity of Marienhof, and Ch. Mehitabel of Marienhof, from Marie Slattery's famed kennels in the 1930's-1940's period. Photo courtesy of the Gatelys.

Shows, and the top Best of Breed winner of 1956, who had to his credit 53 Best of Breed and 25 Group placements. Perci-Bee gained further prestige as the sire of Champion Phil-Mar's Lugar, bred and owned by Mr. and Mrs. Philip Anspach, from Champion Phil-Mar's Lucy Lady. Mrs. Anspach (now Mrs. Wolfe) handled Perci-Bee for owner Mrs. Emmett Shelley.

Champion Marwyn Pitt-Penn-Pirate was a Best in Show winner of the 1950's. Champion Benrook Randy had two Bests in Show and many Bests of Breed. Champion Bursche v. Hessen had several Bests in Show.

Pitt-Penn Pirate sired 44 champions. He was a son of Champion Asset of Ledahof ex Marwyn S.D. Comet, and was born February 15, 1954; his breeder was Marion Evashwick, Marwyck Kennels. He was raised by Cathryn and Walter Francis (Pitt-Penn), started his show career with Mrs. Evashwick, then became co-owned with Jean and Glenn Fancy.

Tom Gately Reminisces about Some Schnauzers

Recalling the strong involvement of both Kay and Tom Gately with the Miniature Schnauzers of the early days, we contacted them for photos and comment. They were exceedingly generous with both, which we are proud and happy to present to our readers. In speaking of "the old days" in Schnauzers, Tom Gately states:— "Champion Yankee Pride Colonel Stump, known as 'Stumpy' was considered to have been the most outstanding in the Gatelys' Schnauzer past. This remarkable little dog had five all-breed Bests in Show, which was a goodly number in those days when shows were far less numerous, plus many Specialties. Among his notable successes, he also won the breed three years consecutively at Westminster." Tom sometimes handled him, but due to his commitments to other terrier clients, it was Kay who actually showed 'Stumpy' most frequently. They were a terrific team, chalking up wins and friends for the breed wherever they appeared.

Another dog whom Tom regarded highly was Champion Mehitabel of Marienhof II, of whom Tom says, "She was at least thirty years ahead of her time. Despite a horrible ear-crop, she swamped all competition."

Sieger Marko von Butenberg was sent directly to Tom Gately from Germany. Tom's comment on this dog is that he was ". . .different from any Miniature we had seen. He was truly an undersized Standard. We made him a champion quickly, and he was mated to Champion Mehitabel of Marienhof II. This was the 'golden cross' that revolutionized the breed, changing such things as little round skulls, big, poppy eyes, monkey faces, bantam bone. And it improved temperament."

It was from this litter that Champion Marko of Marienhof was produced, who became Tom Gately's first Westminster Kennel Club Best of Breed winning Miniature Schnauzer back in the mid-1930's. Marko was breeder-owned by Mrs. Marie Slattery, and was the first home-bred Miniature Schnauzer to gain the Best Miniature Schnauzer award at this most prestigious of all American dog shows. Tom Gately tells us that, in handing him the ribbon, judge Frank Addyman commented loud and clear, "This breed has really improved!", which was a well-deserved compliment to a fine little dog.

We appreciate the time Tom has taken to send us photos and opinions on these important early Schnauzers.

Champion Dorem Display was, as is well-known, the Miniature Schnauzer "star" of the 1940's. His breeder-owner, Dorothy Williams, who had been actively breeding some excellent Schnauzers since the early 1930's, really hit the jackpot with this dog. He was everyone's ideal; his show career made all sorts of "firsts" for the breed; but most of all, he was a sire whose impact on the breed has been inestimably influential.

One of Display's outstanding sons was Champion Meldon's Ruffian who went Best in Show on his first showing and to which award he added as his career continued. Both Ruffian and his son, Brazilian and American Champion Helarry's Dark Victory, lived with Alice Downey and her late husband Larry Downey from puppyhood to their old age, 13 years and 14 years respectively. Larry Downey managed both their show careers and their breeding programs. To quote Alice Downey, who has so kindly loaned us photos of these two for this book, "Of all the fine dogs we showed, these were very high on the list of GREAT ones."

Champion Helarry's Dark Victory, during 1960, made the impressive sweep of Best in Show on three successive days from the classes (what a way to gain a title!) plus winning first in nine Terrier Groups and 15 Bests of Breed out of 17 times shown. Champion Helarry's Har-

Braz. and Am. Ch. Helarry's Dark Victory, sire of 35 champions, was owned by Joe Obstfeldt and Larry Downey and breeder Helen Wiedenbeck. Handled by Larry Downey, he finished his championship in the early 1960's by winning three Bests in Show on three consecutive days during the Florida Circuit. Sired by Meldon's Ruffian, he was this dog's greatest producing son. Photo and comment courtesy of Alice Downey, Libertyville, Illinois.

Tom and Kay Gately share this photo with us. *Left to right*, Priscilla of Marienhof, granddaughter of Ch. Yankee Pride Colonel Stump; Fanciful of Marienhof, the sire of Colonel Stump; Francine of Marienhof, a Fanciful daughter from a German-bred bitch; and Betsy Bop of Marienhof, a Fanciful daughter. Marie Slattery is the owner of Marienhof Schnauzers, America's oldest kennel of the breed.

Ch. Gladding's Bie Bie winning Best of Breed at the 1958 Chicago International under judge William L. Kendrick. Bred by Mrs. Mary Seamans, Winchester, New Hampshire, Bie Bie was the last champion daughter sired by Ch. Dorem Display, and his top producing daughter. This was also the foundation bitch at Mankit's Kennels, owned by Mr. and Mrs. Emanuel Miller by whom she was purchased in 1957. Photo courtesy of *Schnauzer Shorts*, Dan Kiedrowski, editor and publisher.

Fanciful's Noel of Marienhof, owned by Kathleen and Norbert Kanzler, was a winner in the early 1960's. Barbara Humphries, handler.

Ch. Yankee Pride Ringmaster, photo courtesy of Kay and Tom Gately.

Ch. Dorem Tempo, *left*, handled by R. Stephen Shaw taking Best of Breed at the Morris and Essex K.C., May 1952. Harry Lumb judging. Ch. Forest Nod of Mandeville, *right*, handled by Larry Downey, Best of Opposite Sex. Nod was a two-time Best in Show winner at all-breed events, the first Miniature Schnauzer bitch in the U.S. to gain a Best in Show. Nod was owned by Ed Jenner whose kennels have housed so many famous winners in various breeds. Photo courtesy of *Schnauzer Shorts*, Dan Kiedrowski, editor and publisher.

Judging the Terrier Group at Westminster 1959. Caught by the camera, Kay Gately is moving Mrs. Joseph Sailer's noted Miniature Schnauzer, Ch. Yankee Pride Colonel Stump. Photo courtesy of Tom and Kay Gately.

mony, Dark Victory's son, won a total of five Bests in Show, thus in 1964 becoming the first Miniature Schnauzer to equal Champion Dorem Display's Best in Show winning record. It is interesting that Display, Ruffian, and Dark Victory were part of a four generation Best in Show winning record, the fourth generation having been shared by Harmony's two sons, Champion Blue Devil Sharpshooter (in 1966 from the classes) and Champion Franzel's Quick Silver.

It was full sister to Champion Dorem Display, Champion Dorem Shady Lady, C.D., who was the foundation bitch at Phil-Mar Kennels, owned in the beginning by the Philip Anspachs, now by Peggy Wolfe who is the former Mrs. Marguerite Anspach. Shady was purchased in whelp to Dorem Dominant, arriving at the Anspachs' in March 1949. She was the ONLY bitch upon whom Marguerite Anspach Wolfe's famous line was founded; a kennel which has produced around 40 champions in about 35 years.

In her first litter, Shady Lady produced seven puppies. Among them were the future Champion Phil-Mar Watta Lady, along with two who earned obedience degrees.

Next Shady was bred to her uncle, Champion Dorem Tribute, again producing seven puppies. Of these, two bitches were retained, one was future champion Phil-Mar Gay Lady.

For her third breeding, the sire selected was Champion Dorem Tempo, son of Champion Delegate of Ledahof, this time producing Champion Phil-Mar Lucky Lady.

Now plans turned towards the next generation, that which would be produced from Shady's daughters. Watta Lady, from the first litter, was bred to Champion Dorem Tempo, owned by Muriel and Jack Ainley in Connecticut. From this came the first Best in Show winner; (and a homebred for icing on the cake) from Phil-Mar, Champion Phil-Mar Lucy Lady, who was the breed's top winner in 1954 and in winning her second Best in Show became the first of only four bitches with "multiple" all-breed Bests in Show! She also was one of the few bitches to go Best of Breed at Westminster. Bred to Champion Perci-Bee's First Impression, a dog whom Peggy was handling, Ch. Phil-Mar Lucy Lady also became the dam of the great Champion Phil-Mar Lugar in 1956 when she produced her first litter. The sire was a son of Ch. Dorem Favorite and Ch. Phil-Mar Lady Be Good.

Gay Lady was the second of Shady's daughters to be bred, this one also to Tempo. This was obviously a wise choice as the progeny included two Best in Show brothers, Champion Phil-Mar Gay Knight and Champion Phil-Mar Mister John.

Gay Knight sired nine champions, including Champion Phil-Mar Dark Knight who in turn was the sire of 19 champions.

The magnificent Champion Phil-Mar Lugar was the breed's top winner in 1959 and 1960. Among the show honors he gained, Lugar scored a record 70 times Best of Breed (including two Specialties), two all-breed Bests in Show, and 40 Group placements including first on about a dozen occasions. He sired 26 American champions, plus numerous title-holders in other parts of the world. Among six champions he sired for Joan Huber at Blythewood was Champion Blythewood's Main Gazebo, the sire of 31 champions. He produced two champions each for Dorem, Luvemal, Mankit and Phil-Mar. His son, Champion Mankit's Eager, is behind all of the Mankit Best in Show winners. His daughter, Champion Dorem Symphony II, was the dam of Champion Helarry's Harmony, who has 21 champions on the credit list.

Miss Gene Simmonds founded Handful Kennels in the early 1930's with two Schnauzers who became American and Canadian Champion Handful of Marienhof, for whom the kennel was named, who was the first Canadian Champion Miniature Schnauzer; and Champion Nosea of Marienhof, who was uncropped. These two lived to be 16 years and 17 years old respectively, and were Miss Simmonds's house pets until their death in 1951.

As she had done originally all those years ago, Miss Simmonds went to Marienhof for two puppies following the loss of her old dogs. These puppies became Champion Diplomat of Marienhof and Champion Handful's Me Too of Marienhof. Then, needing a bitch from which to breed and give Handful Kennels a new start, Miss Simmonds selected Benrook Bona, by Champion Dorem Display ex Champion Meldon's Manana, whom she purchased from Shirley Angus, Benrook Kennels' owner,.

In due time Bona was bred to Me Too, her first puppies born in July 1952. Two males and four bitches made up the litter, from which Handful's Ruddy Duck and Handful's Teal finished.

From 1952 until 1956 there was tremendous activity at Handful, with many breedings, good dogs produced, and some sold to excellent homes. Among these were Champion Handful's Bantam and Champion Handful's Wren to California and Champion Handful's Quail to Florida, thus taking new blood into these areas. Then, in 1956, illness forced her to offer Handful for sale. Handful's Snow Flurry and Champion Handful's Pop Up went to Trayhom Kennels and, combined, helped to start the Mankits and the Winsomors in Indiana and Ohio. Champion Handful's Popper and Handful's Doll provided a foundation for the Czapskis and their Andrel Kennel in Connecticut. Handful's Petunia and Handful's Periwinkle started Crown Post Kennels in New Jersey. Handful's Ragula, Raguletta, Snowstorm and Bull Cochin started the Pfulhans in Virginia. Champion Handful's Corbo, Handful's Bantam, Handful's Fashion and Handful's Wren went to Windy Hill in California and helped to start Belleve in Denver; Handful's Thrush went to Denver; Champion Handful's Tanter settled in Salt Lake City; the Fancys in California and the La Mays in Nevada completed the Bona line.

Champion Handful's Bantam sired ten champions, among them the Best in Show winning Champion Brausestadt's Terry Dee. He is also the maternal grandsire of Champion Windy Hill Defiance who has 15 or more champions to his credit. His own show record was 25 Bests of Breed with numerous Group placements.

In total, the Handful breeding program produced 25 American Champions and two Canadian Champions. From the Handful dogs and bitches came the background, as noted, of numerous highly successful lines in all parts of the United States.

Miss Simmonds passed away towards the mid-1980's. In recent years she had become keenly interested in Smooth Foxterriers, breeding and showing many good ones. She also had a few Schnauzers still.

The top producing daughter of Champion Dorem Display was Champion Gladdings' Bie Bie, bred by Mrs. Mary Seamans, who became foundation bitch for the so very famous Mankit Kennels owned by Mr. and Mrs. Emanuel Miller of Indiana. Bie Bie won her first two points at a dog show in Marion, Ohio, then went on to the Chicago International where, from the American-bred class, she swept through to Best of Winners and Best of Opposite Sex, completing title three weeks later in three shows in Ohio.

Returning to the International the following year, Bie Bie took Best of Opposite Sex again there. Between these two appearances she had been busy producing a litter by Champion Dorem Favorite. There was one male along with five bitches in this litter, and that male, Mankit's Adam, became the first champion homebred by the Millers. Three of his sisters quickly followed Adam to the title, they being Champions Mankit's Ada, Alfreda, and Augusta. The last was a marvelous producer, and attained such honors as Top Producing Terrier Dam at one point in her lifetime.

Bie Bie did not just rest on her laurels following that first litter, but again produced a litter of six, this time by the Snow Flurry son Champion Trayhom Talleyrand. Champion Mankit's Countess Talleyrand was the most notable from this litter, going to Trayhom Kennels for whom she produced those two noted sires, Champion Mankit's Xerxes (21 champions) and Moon Shot (five champions).

Returning to Augusta, Champion Phil-Mar Lugar was selected as the first dog to whom she was bred—and what an ideal choice this was! The litter produced Champion Mankit's Eager, enabling the Millers to linebreed on Bie Bie, thus starting a dynasty of Best in Show winners, Champion Mankit's Signal Go, Champion Alex of Dunbar, and culminating in Champion Mankit's To The Moon.

Signal Go was a champion by ten months of age, and in a five-year Specials career (1964-1968) won three Bests in Show, eight Specialty Show Bests of Breed, 24 Terrier Groups, and 48 additional Group placements. His handler throughout his career was Wayne Miller, of Trayhom Kennels.

Mankit's To The Moon, a sixth generation Mankit dog, came out soon after Signal Go's retirement and picked up the gauntlet where it had landed. Again handled by Wayne Miller (Trayhom) for Emanuel and Kitty Miller (Mankit), Miniature Schnauzer history was about to be made! To The Moon came to Montgomery County weekend 1968 just out of the puppy class, having one "major" and a few single points. Trotting into the ring at Devon, he left with Winners Dog for a 5-point "major," then watched his uncle, Mankit's Xerxes, take Best of Breed. At the American Miniature Schnauzer Specialty the following day, To The Moon swept through the breed clear to the top award, then gained Best in Show under the late

Ch. Phil-Mar Lucy Lady handled by Peggy Anspach Wolfe, winning at Westminster in 1955 under judge Miss Dorothy Williams of the famed Dorem Kennels, breeder of Display. Lucy Lady won two all-breed Bests in Show among many other honors during her show career. Photo courtesy of *Schnauzer Shorts.*

Ch. Yankee Pride Colonel Stump winning Best in Show at Monmouth County in 1959. Kay Gately handling.

Ch. Phil-Mar Lugar winning one of his all breed Bests in Show, owner-handled by Peggy Anspach Wolfe. The judge here is noted Schnauzer authority Richard Kerns, co-owner with Mrs. Kerns of the Wollaton Kennels where so many outstanding Miniature Schnauzers were raised. Photo courtesy of *Schnauzer Shorts*.

Kay Gately has the lead on Ch. Yankee Pride Colonel Stump, gaining the approval here of judge Dr. Mitten. This fabulous little dog also went on to Best in Show that same day in 1959. Photo courtesy of Tom and Kay Gately.

James A. Farrell, Jr. The following year To The Moon returned to make further history by taking a SECOND Best Miniature Schnauzer award at Montgomery County in a then record entry, 115 including 14 Specials, and then went on to his second Montgomery Best in Show.

By the time of To The Moon's retirement, he had gained 12 Specialty Bests of Breed, seven of them in 1969; two all-breed Bests in Show; and an imposing total of points under the Knight System.

Along with To The Moon, Champion Mankit's Alex of Dunbar was sharing honors in the show ring, both being campaigned during this period. In 1969 Alex led the breed in Knight System points, and during his career he amassed a total of seven Bests in Show. A pair of Schnauzers to look upon with pride!

Wayne Miller and his wife Twilla, the handlers for Mankit dogs and good friends of Emanuel and Kitty Miller over the years of Mankit's tremendous success, retired in 1970. The Emanuel Millers cut back their breeding program sharply at this time. They were certainly well content with the 32 champions bearing the Mankit prefix, their impact on the breed, and their excellent results.

The Wayne Millers' own kennel was Trayhom. Among the fine Miniature Schnauzers they bred was Trayhom Truly Fair, C.D., who became the backbone for the breeding program at Barclay Square Kennels when Trayhom was dispersed. She will long be remembered by

Ch. Dorem Tempo in 1953 winning Best of Breed at the American Miniature Schnauzer Club Specialty Show. The judge is Mrs. Marie Slattery of Marienhof Kennels. Tempo handled by R. Stephen Shaw. This son of Ch. Delegate of Ledahof ex Ch. Doren Silverette was used by Peggy Anspach Wolfe as the stud for her Display sister, Ch. Dorem Shady Lady, and for a daughter and a granddaughter of Shady Lady, producing champions in all three litters, including three Best in Show winners. He was the sire of Ch. Phil-Mar's Gay Knight, sire of nine champions, among others. Photo courtesy of Schnauzer Shorts.

Ch. Asset of Ledahof, by Ch. Diplomat of Ledahof ex Annabelle of Ledahof with handler Ben Burwell. One of the Ledahof homebreds, Asset sired ten champions. Photo courtesy of Schnauzer Shorts, Dan Kiedrowski, editor and publisher.

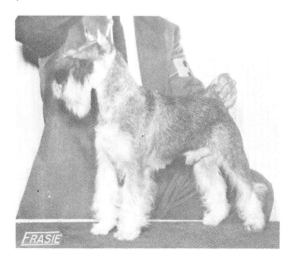

Schnauzer fanciers as the dam of Barclay Square Brick Silver, sired by Champion Winsomer Dubbl Y Money (a double grandson of Champion Mankit's Adam). Truly Fair was by Champion Handful's Pop Up ex a Pitt Penn Pirate daughter. Although not herself a show bitch, Brick Silver was a producer par excellence. She had six litters, the first and last consisting of just one puppy apiece, but the others ranging from two of nine puppies each to one of seven and one of eight. Among her offspring were three champions and four Top Producers.

Two from Brick Silver were the littermates, Champion Barclay Square Becky Sharp and Champion Barclay Square Brickbat, these sired by Champion Mankit's Signal Go. Brickbat, owned by Barbara Harvill, sired nine champions, eight of which carry the Archway kennel prefix of this lady. Becky Sharp in her first litter produced four puppies, all of whom became champions, sired by Champion Mankit's Signal Go. These included the Best in Show winner Champion

Ch. Marwyck Pitt-Penn Pirate was bred by Dorothy Whitton, Buffalo, New York, by Ch. Asset of Ledahof ex Ch. Marwyck S.D. Comet. Shown to the title under ownership of Mrs. Marion Evashwick, he started his career going from the puppy class to Best of Breed at the Michigan Specialty for five points, finishing at 11 months. Sold to Dr. Rod King and handled by Thomas Lenfesty, Pirate continued his successful career as a Special. Later Glenn and Jean Fancy became his co-owners. He sired a total of 44 champions. Photo courtesy of *Schnauzer Shorts.*

Barclay Square Be Grand owned by the Allen Starks of St. Louis. The same breeding combination was repeated on three occasions which produced 19 puppies, 12 of them champions.

Harry and Patsy Laughter and their family, now busy and popular dog show superintendents, owned the Miown Miniature Schnauzers which produced 21 champions during the 1960's to the mid-1970's. Their foundation sire was Miown Erich von Brach, by Champion Budhof's Stylist of Multi-Lakes (American and Canadian Champion Benrook Beau Brummel – the Champion Dorem Display daughter, Dorem My Play) ex Eniva's Shane (Champion Handful's Pop Up—Yankee Pride Sonia). All but four of the champions bearing the Miown kennel prefix and descendants of Erich.

Champion Miown Exotic Poppy was a bitch in whom the Laughters took particular pride. Her tragic death at only a year's age was certainly a tremendous loss. She gained her title as a puppy, then scored the exciting victory of Best of Opposite Sex to Champion Mankit's To The Moon under a highly respected judge, the late Alva Rosenberg, these wins being repeated for both Schnauzers at Westminster the following day. Poppy was breeder-owner-handled by P. Laughter, a teenager at the time, then to be campaigned by Joanne Trubee during 1969 to two all-breed Bests in Show, 13 Group placements, and Best of Breed for the second time at the Michigan Specialty.

The Laughters bred five generations of champions during their breeding program which, as mentioned above, ended in the mid-1970s. Among the descendants of the Miown stock one thinks of Champion Miown Society Charmer, dam of three champions, owned by the Postillion Kennels of Charles and Jane Post, formerly in the East, now located in California.

Ledahof Kennels have been a force in the Miniature Schnauzer world over several decades; Leda Martin was among the most successful pioneer breeders, and many are the honors which have gone to her dogs over the years, not to mention their impact on the breed as producers! Although it was not in the United States, it was a bitch from this kennel, Champion Sorceress of Ledahof, who was the first of her sex to win a Best in Show on this continent, at Quebec, in Canada, during 1948. Then there were the full brothers, Champion Delegate of

Ch. Benrook Bona, daughter of Ch. Dorem Display ex Ch. Meldon's Manana, born April 1950, is the bitch Miss Simmonds selected to go with her two Marienhof males, renewing the Handful breeding program in 1951. Photo courtesy of *Schnauzer Shorts.*

Ch. Yankee Pride Colonel Stump winning the American Miniature Schnauzer Club Specialty in 1958. Handled by Kay Gately for Mrs. Joseph Sailer.

Ledahof and Champion Diplomat of Ledahof, son of Champion Enchantress of Ledahof ex Ch. Dorem Display. Diplomat was widely used at stud and became the sire of 29 champion offspring plus 90 champion grandchildren. Delegate was less widely publicized, but sired five champions, among them Champion Dorem Tempo (from Champion Dorem Silverette), Champion Rannoch's Rampion (from Rannoch's Nutmeg), Champion Clairedale Lady Luck (from Champion Havahome Freshie), and Champions Marwyck Prinz Vellhelm and Marwyck Princess Juno (from Champion Lady Gildae).

By 1954, Ledahof had produced 14 champions at its New Brunswick, New Jersey, kennels. Mrs. Martin was breeding for more than a decade after that, adding further names to the list. The pages of this book attest time after time to the number of outstanding Schnauzers who, even today, trace their beginnings back to these splendid dogs. Ledahof's first champion, Abner of Marlou, was born in 1930.

Anfiger Kennels, owned by Anne Paramour Eskrigge, began breeding in 1928, and Mrs. Eskrigge was active in the breed from 1924 to 1939. Then, in 1952, she again became involved with her favorite breed, and wrote a splendid book about it. Mrs. Eskrigge passed away in 1984.

In retrospect, some facts become very clear. As one looks back over Miniature Schnauzer history, one is impressed with the Marienhof influence on this breed, and with Mrs. Marie Slattery's constant interest and devotion to it over so many decades. That in itself speaks volumes in these days of such rapid turnover among members of our Fancy. Just see in how many places one meets the Marienhof identification on dogs of importance! Not just in the United States, but in all parts of the world. There must be at least 100 champions bearing the Marienhof prefix, not to mention those of her breeding which carry kennel names apart from her own. This lady passed away early in the 1980's, truly marking the end of an era of success and contribution to the breed that stands second to none.

As far as individual dogs are concerned, Champion Dorem Display has been influential to an almost incredible extent, though it is really not so incredible when one considers the PRODUCING quality of his background. This was a great producing dog, bred almost entirely from great producing dogs back to the earliest part of his pedigree. Who can wonder, then, that his impact on future generations has been so notable?

Display's breeder, Miss Dorothy Williams, was active with her Dorem Kennels from 1935, the year in which her first homebred champion, Dorem Dilletante, was born. She seemed to have a true "green thumb" in breeding Schnauzers, as her strain quickly established a type and were known for outstanding quality even prior to Display.

Dorem Dilletante was by Champion Jeff of Wollaton from Jill of Wollaton II. As a producer, in her first litter for Dorem, there was also a bitch, Dorem Diva, who produced Champion Dorem Dubonnet, by Flieger of Edgeover and Champion Dorem Escapade, by Timothy of Sharvogue. Champion Dorem Dubonnet produced a handsome litter of seven puppies by Champion Stylobate of Sharvogue, which included Dorem Spotlight, sire of six champions: Champion Dorem Highlight, dam of four champions and granddam of 15 champions; and Champion Dorem Searchlight, dam of three champions, one of which was Champion Dorem Display.

Champion Dorem Escapade, bred to Champion Sandman of Sharvogue (littermate to Champion Stylobate of Sharvogue) produced Champion Dorem Parade, the paternal grandsire of Display, carrying down the male line from Champion T.M.G. of Marienhof. Parade was not used often at stud, which is, indeed, a pity when one considers that a dog sired by him who never gained championship, Dorem Cockade, became the sire of Champion Dorem Display!

Display was born in April 1945 and lived to be 14 years of age. During his lifetime he sired 42 champions, among them 26 males, 16 of them sires of at least one champion. A total of ten dogs by Display sired four or more champions each. The leading three were: Champion Dorem Tribute, sire of 41 champions; Champion Diplomat of Ledahof, sire of 29; and Champion Meldon's Ruffian, sire of 26 champions. Champion Dorem High Test had 15 champions to his credit; and Champion Benrook Beau Brummell had 13. Others include Champion Meldon's Merit, nine champions; Champion Gengler's Drum Major, seven champions; Champion Delegate of Ledahof, five champions; Champion Benrook Zorra, six champions; and Dorem Chance Play, four champions.

Display was sold to the Phil Meldons of Meldon Kennels, for whom he did the greatest part of his winning.

More Handful Schnauzers, owned by Miss Gene Simmonds, a breeder from the early 1930's until the 1980's.

Ch. Delegate of Ledahof, by Ch. Dorem Display ex Ch. Enchantress of Ledahof, sired Ch. Dorem Tempo, Ch. Rannoch Rampion, Ch. Clairedale Lady Luck, and Marwyck Prinz Vellheim and Marwyck Princess Juno. A full brother to Ch. Diplomat of Ledahof. Photo courtesey of *Schnauzer Shorts*.

Ch. Handful's Pheasant owned by Miss Gene Simmonds, Joppa, Maryland, whose famous Handful Kennels were founded in 1930 and continued until the time of her death in the early 1980's.

Ch. Yankee Squadron Leader in January 1964 handled by Olive Moore to Best of Breed at Miami. This was one of the early winners from Travelmor Kennels owned by William and Olive Moore at Trenton, New Jersey, a kennel still very much in the limelight. Mrs. Kay Hoos is judging on this occasion.

Ch. Mankit's To The Moon was Best in Show at Montgomery County in 1968 under James A. Farrell, Jr. and in 1969 under judge John Marvin, pictured. An unprecedented victory in the Miniature Schnauzer world. Handled by Wayne Miller. Photo courtesy of *Schnauzer Shorts*, Dan Kiedrowksi, editor and publisher.

Miniature Schnauzer Clubs in the U.S.A.

The Miniature Schnauzer Club of America is the Parent Club for this breed in the United States. The club was founded in August 1933, as mentioned in the historical chapter, with an original membership of 32.

It is the responsibility of the Parent Club to deal with matters pertaining to the standard, where changes over the years have been mostly pertaining to size. In the beginning the height limit was 12 inches but gradually raised over the years to the present, and more realistic, 14 inches.

Throughout its years of activity, the membership of the Miniature Schnauzer Club of America has grown into the 500 persons area, with a very wide distribution of interest from all parts of the United States as well as other countries. A goodly number of regional clubs have also been founded, providing educational programs and an opportunity to participate in and benefit by club activities almost everywhere around the country.

The oldest of the regional clubs, the Potomac Miniature Schnauzer Club, held its first Specialty Show in 1945. This has now been replaced by the Mount Vernon Miniature Schnauzer Club, which had started life back in 1953, going on to hold its first match in 1955 in preparation for its Specialty Shows, which have since become important events.

The Penn Ohio Miniature Schnauzer Club was founded in 1946, its original membership numbering 46. This is a good-sized club, open to local and non-local members, which issues a monthly news sheet and which holds very memorable Specialty events.

Chicago Miniature Schnauzer Club's first Specialty Show was in April 1954. The Miniature Schnauzer Club of Michigan joined the ranks in 1954; Paul Revere was a year earlier than these, in 1953; the Miniature Schnauzer Club of California was formed in 1956. These were the early ones! Their numbers have grown quite steadily until now there are several in various parts of California; Florida has at least two; there is one in Alabama, Colorado, Georgia and Missouri. All these clubs have very important functions, and serve their purpose well. While one should always belong to the PARENT Club in one's breed, also joining the nearest of the regional clubs reaps its reward in the information provided, interesting events in which to participate, and the pleasure of meeting others whose interests are compatible with your own.

The Educational Committee of the Miniature Schnauzer Club of America has some excellent pamphlets available to those who request them. A note to the American Kennel Club, 51 Madison Avenue, New York, N.Y. 10010 will bring the name and address of the Parent Club's secretary to you, who will be pleased to help you if you request information about either the parent or any of the regional clubs.

Ch. Irrenhaus Bluet, by Ch. Irrenhaus Blueprint ex Ch. Rockaplenty's Winsome, completed title owner-breeder-handled by Jacqueline Hicks. This lovely bitch is the dam of nine champions including the Top Schnauzer Male in England for 1982, Ch. Irrenhaus Impact of Risepark. Photo by Sue Baines.

CHAPTER THREE

Important Miniature Schnauzer Kennels in the United States

Ch. Frevohly's Best Bon-Bon, U.D., dam of five champions, was the breed's first Champion and Utility Dog combination. Owned by Mrs. Ruth Ziegler, from the first Allaruth litter. Photo courtesy of *Schnauzer Shorts.*

Allaruth

Allaruth Miniature Schnauzers was started back in the 1950's by Mrs. Ruth Ziegler, and continues today, a recent acquisition having been Valharra's Magic Melody, a granddaughter of Champion Allaruth Daniel.

As we have mentioned in the obedience chapter, Mrs. Ziegler's first homebred litter was from her Doman Mehitabel, C.D.X., whom she had purchased from Frederick von Huly, then bred to Blinken of Mandeville, litter brother to Best in Show winning Champion Forest Nod of Mandeville. This litter produced Champion Frevohly's Best Bon Bon U.D., the first Champion Utility Dog, who became the foundation bitch for Allaruth's future.

Bon Bon produced five champions (the first western Miniature Schnauzer bitch to do so), and was the West Coast's top producing bitch throughout her lifetime.

Bred to Champion Marwyck Pitt Penn Pirate, sire of 44 champions, Bon Bon produced Champion Allaruth's Jorgette, Champion Allaruth's Joshua, and Allaruth Jolly Anne. Joshua sired Champion Allaruth's Jericho, from Cookie v. Elfland, who was a consistent winner of the early

1960's, under Ric Chashoudian's handling. He won the Northern California Specialty twice, and sired seven linebred champions. Champion Allaruth's Jasmine, by Jericho from Champion Allaruth's Dinah Mite (daughter of Champion Dorem Original) was the dam of Champion Landmark's Masterpiece, owned by Gloria Wiedlein, who has sired 32 champions.

Two other daughters of Jericho have particularly distinguished themselves. One is Champion Orbit's Mach Meter, by Jericho from Fran Cazier's top producing bitch Minchette Maier (dam of six champions), who herself became a Top Producer with three champions to her credit. A litter sister, Champion Allaruth's Jemima, became the foundation for Janhof Kennels (Dr. Jeanette Schulz) as dam of two champions including the Top Producer, Champion Janhof's Bon-Bon of Adford. She was the dam of four champions including still another Top Producer, Champion Orbit's Agena B, in addition to Champion Orbit's Lift Off, C.D.X., foundation for Carol Parker, Skyline Kennels.

During the latter part of the 1960's, Mrs. Ziegler wanted an outcross for the Allaruths, so Boomerang of Marienhof was purchased from

Marie Slattery. Boomerang finished in short order and met with success as a Special, but most important of all, he became the sire of ten champions, four of them for Arador, two for Orbit, and two at Allaruth, the latter including Champion Allaruth's Daniel. His eight champion progeny include the Best in Show winner and noted sire Champion Valharra's Dionysos, who has sired more than 30 champions, owned by Enid Quick at Valharra.

Mrs. Ziegler, in the late 1960's, purchased Champion Gaea of Arador and Champion Kerith of Arador from Arador Kennels. Both were finished by her, and both have given her champions.

The lovely winning dog, Champion Allaruth's Mama's Boy, son of Allaruth Hang Up, won Best of Breed from the Bred-by Exhibitor Class at Westminster in 1972, going on to many further honors. Mama's Boy sired five champions, including Champion Country Squire Soot N Cinder, sire of five champions.

Alpine

Alpine Miniature Schnauzers are owned by Seme and Louis Auslander and since the mid-1960's have carried on a highly successful Miniature Schnauzer breeding program at their home in Lake Forest, Illinois.

The purchase of Champion Dansel Dutch Treat in 1965 was the start of their activities, and the 14 or more champions who bear the Alpine prefix include, among others, the Best in Show bitch, Champion Alpine Baby Ruth.

Dutch Treat was an already proven producer when purchased by the Auslanders. Bred to Champion Phil-Mar Lugar she produced Champion Dansel Erda das Hundlein, sold to California, and Dansel Dutch Maid, who was retained by the Dansel Kennels.

Dutch Treat produced just one litter at Alpine, which resulted in two champion bitches. From these, 11 additional champions were bred.

Another foundation bitch at Alpine was Champion Lougin's Charm, the daughter of two non-champion top producers, Mankit's Hector (sire of six champions) and Trayhom Tu Tu, dam of two who gained the title. Charm, as Dutch Treat had done, came to the Auslanders as a proven producer, being the dam of Champion Lougin's Gad-A-Bout. Bred by the Auslanders to Champion Mankit's Signal Go, Charm became the dam of Champion Alpine Patent Pending, sold to Charles and Marlene

Ch. Dansel Dutch Treat, the bitch behind the breeding program of Alpine Kennels owned by Mr. and Mrs. Lou Auslander, Lake Forest, Illinois. Photo courtesy of *Schnauzer Shorts.*

Congdon in California, where she produced their Champion Marcheim Helzapoppin (by Champion Marcheim Poppin' Fresh) who became the sire of seven champions.

In the early 1970's, the Auslanders turned their attention to some of the other breeds they admire, principally Whippets. During this time, their best producing Schnauzer bitches were carefully placed, and have brought the bloodlines back up to the present. Champion Alpine Double Dutch went to the Edward Harveys in New Jersey and has produced four champions there. Alpine Ultra Violet has gone to the Robert Rains in California, producing four champions there, among the latter Champion Rainbou's Tornado, a Best in Show winner, while Champion Alpine Ol' King Cole also sired another champion for the Rains.

Lou Auslander is busy these days as a judge with a very full schedule and as show chairman for the International Kennel Club of Chicago. Nevertheless, both his and Seme's interest in Schnauzers continues, and Lou also remains active in the Parent Club for Miniature Schnauzers. As we go to press Mr. Auslander has been made a Director of the American Kennel Club.

Andrel

Andrel Kennels were highly successful from the 1950's until the death of their owners, and disbanding of the kennel, in the early 1980's. Andrew and Elinor Czapski, who lived at Westport, Connecticut, were both much involved with the dogs, showing homebreds of excellent quality.

Champion Andrel's Viceroy, by Champion Cosburn's Esquire ex Hollow Ridge's Pandora, was the first purchase as a foundation for future breeding, followed shortly thereafter by littermates Champion Andrel's Argenta and Champion Andrel's Adjutant, they, in turn, by Champion Yankee Pride Colonel Stump ex Sandown's Career Girl.

The first homebred Andrel litter came from two Schnauzers purchased from Miss Gene Simmonds's Handful Kennels. From them was produced Champion Andrel's Aladdin (Champion Handful's Popper-Handful's Doll). Aladdin's dam, Doll, became the Czapskis' first Top Producer, giving them, in addition to Aladdin, Champion Andrel's Debonair by Adjutant and Champion Andrel's Importance and Champion Andrel's, the latter littermates by Viceroy.

More than a dozen homebred champions followed these early ones, all based on various combinations of the Doll, Argenta, and Viceroy progeny. These included Champion Andrel's Importance, a 1965 Best in Show winner, who along with his sire, Viceroy, was part of a Best in Show winning brace in 1967.

The last champion bred at Andrel was Champion Andrel's Satellite whelped in 1972, who sired two puppies, Andrel's Triumph and Andrel's Tenderness, in 1981.

Probably (to the Count and Countess Czapski) the most memorable of all their dogs were the littermates Champion Andrel's Reliance and Champion Andrel's Romance. Certainly they made the great Terrier weekend, Montgomery County, in 1970 an unforgettable event. Romance, already a champion, took Best of Opposite Sex at the American Miniature Schnauzer Club National Specialty at Montgomery, while Reliance was awarded Winners Dog and Best of Winners, the breed entry 117. The previous day, Romance had topped a sizeable entry at Devon, and, a week later, she won the Mount Vernon Specialty. For that year and the following one, Romance was among the breed's top winning bitches.

Andrel's Tenderness, sister to Meina Random Sketches, handled by Robert L. Crews for owner, Elinor Czapski.

Best of Breed, Ch. Andrel's Romance, *right* and Best of Opposite Sex, Ch. Andrel's Reliance, *left*. Both owned by Elinor and Andrew O. Czapski. Handled by Robert L. Crews, at Del-Otse-Nango in 1971.

Ch. Richlene's Top Billing, born August 19th 1980, bred by Richard and Arlene Smith, Fort Wayne, Indiana. Owned by Barbara A. Hall and Carol Nagengast, Uncasville, Connecticut. Owner-handled, as he was throughout his career. Specialed on a very limited basis, he nonetheless attained many Best of Breed honors and Group placements. Topper has now been retired in favor of his children and grandchildren. He was named a Top Producer for 1983 with four champions published.

Angler's

Angler's Miniature Schnauzers are owned by Daniel and Sandra Nagengast, at Uncasville, Connecticut. This is a small hobby kennel that breeds a litter every year or so. The Nagengasts have had Schnauzers since 1966, when they started out in obedience, from where they moved into the breed ring in the late 1970's.

The foundation bitch and first champion at Angler's came from the Richlene Kennels of Richard and Arlene Smith at Fort Wayne, Indiana. It was decided to go to the Smiths for the purpose of selecting their foundation show stock as the Nagengasts had noted that they were both breeding and finishing their own dogs, which was their own goal. Thus, they were especially anxious to obtain sound Schnauzers from top-producing lines. Richlene was founded on Penlan, their two foundation bitches having been Champion Penlan Paragon's Exceptional and Champion Penlan Perfect Choice, half-sisters out of the great producing bitch, Penlan Cadet Too.

The Nagengasts' first three champions were Champion Richlene's Linette, Champion Richlene Angler's Keepsake, and Champion Richlene's Top Billing. Linette is the dam of Champion Angler's Allure of Ansu and of Champion Richlene's Nutcracker, littermates sired by Champion Penlan Checkmate. Keepsake is the dam of Champion Angler's Top Drawer. Top Billing is the sire of Champion Angler's Top Drawer, Champion Webber's Forever and Ever, Champion Wyndwood Back Packer, and Champion Wyndwood Big Spender.

Sandra Nagengast and Barbara A. Hall co-own a very special Miniature Schnauzer in Champion Richlene's Top Billing, who was bred by Richard and Arlene Smith and is handled by Sandra. This fantastic little dog, mentioned above as one of the first three champions at

Angler's Kennels, completed his championship very quickly. Shown only a few times as a puppy, he won his first "major" at seven months of age, after which he was kept home for awhile to gain more maturity. At a year old he made his debut in the open classes, taking Winners Dog on six of the seven times he was shown, and Reserve on the other occasion. He finished at the prestigious Westchester Kennel Club, climaxing just three weekends of showing, and the following month, October 1981, scored the memorable victory of Best of Breed at the American Miniature Schnauzer Club Specialty held in conjunction with Montgomery County—OWNER-HANDLED in the midst of all those leading terrier professionals! He was after that Specialed on a limited basis, winning Best of Breed and Group placements a satisfying number of times. He was then retired to permit his children their turn in the ring. As we write this, he has already qualified as a Top Producer for 1983.

It was an exciting win at Montgomery County on many counts, not the least of which was the winning of the Best of Breed Medallion. This, the American Miniature Schnauzer Club's 104th Specialty, was dedicated to the memory of Emanuel Miller, who, with his wife, owned Mankit Miniature Schnauzers.

Ch. Richlene's Top Billing with some of his puppies bred by the Wyndwood Kennels of Barbara Hall.

Ch. Bandsman's Prophecy owned by Carole Luke, Bandsman's Miniature Schnauzers, Silver Springs, Maryland.

Bandsman

The Bandsman Miniature Schnauzers began with the purchase of a Champion Jadee's Jump Up daughter, Jadee's Wild Flower. This excellent bitch produced two champions, American and Canadian Champion Bandsman's Sky Rocket in Flite (who became the sire of five champions), by Sky Rocket's Uproar; and Canadian Champion Bandsman's Herald Trumpet, who died prior to earning his second American "major" when only two and a half years old.

For two years Bandsman was inactive for personal reasons and due to several re-locations.

Then, in 1978, Carole Luke, owner of the kennel, purchased Repitition's Renaissance from Kurt and Carol Garmaker. "Poppy" finished her title quest with a Group 1st, having been shown sparingly in open (only four times) and undefeated. As a Special she earned 24 Bests of Breed in tough competition over well-known males, along with numerous Group placements.

"Poppy" has raised four litters, the first two of which were sired by Champion Dardane Wagonmaster. These produced four champions with two others pointed. Among them are Champion Bandsman's Legacy, who is a multiple Group, Specialty, and all-breed Best in Show winner, among the Top Ten Minis two years running; Bandsman's Prophecy, a top contender for No. 1 in 1983 and a Group and Specialty winner; and Champion Bandsman's Ringside Gossip, Best of Opposite Sex at Montgomery County in 1982 and dam of two champions including the 1984 Westminster winner; and Bandsman's Barrage, a multiple group placer. Also Bandsman's Sonata, who took time out for a litter and should by now have picked up her final "major" to have earned her title.

The third breeding of "Poppy" was to Champion R-Bo'a Victory Flash. From this, three champions have finished, all bitches, two of whom are currently being Specialed. Two more from this litter are currently pointed.

Then, in 1983, "Poppy" was bred to her son, Prophecy, and produced two pups, the male making his debut soon after these notes were written. Her final breeding took place not long ago, to Jackie Heck's new dog, Irrenhaus Sensation, whose litter was anticipated with excitement and high hopes.

Currently Bandsman Kennels, located at Silver Spring, Maryland, house several 'Poppy' grandchildren and a young great grandchild who

Ch. Bandsman's Bouquet gaining points at Middleburg in 1983. Carole Luke, owner.

is growing up for future shows.

Carole Luke has some provocative comments to make along with her kennel resume which we think bear repeating for our readers. She says, "When I look back on pictures of dogs shown only twenty years ago, I am astonished at the transformation the breed has undergone. In many ways the changes have been for the better. Certainly over-all movement has improved. And of course, an apple-headed dog is the exception rather than the rule. Not as acceptable to me is the growing trend towards larger, more "impressive" specimens—more noticeable in the group, but closer and closer to the limit of the Schnauzer Standard. I also mourn the loss of the good, harsh wire coat that was always the hallmark of the breed. As we concentrate more and more on producing 'Cocker Spaniel' type of leg furnishings, we are naturally getting soft, wavy coats that accompany them." Feeling that opinions from breeders are valuable to others, we thank Carole Luke for sharing her thoughts with us on the breed.

Ch. Ruedesheim's Creme de la Creme, or "Cinder" to friends, is another splendid winner owned by W.A. Arnold, III, Bark Kennels, Greenwich, Connecticut.

Bark

Bark Kennels, whose name was coined from the words *B*ill *Ar*nold's *K*ennel, is owned by William A. Arnold, III, at Greenwich, Connecticut. This is the home of that well-known and handsome Best in Show winner, Champion Tel-Mo's Top Cat, known as "Topper" to his friends, who gained the Best in Show award at Leavenworth Kennel Club in Kansas under judge Alfred E. Treen. Topper is, as well, a Specialty Best of Breed winner and has numerous group placements to his credit. He is co-owned by Mr. Arnold with Lynda Lucast.

Topper is a son of Champion Charmar Copy Cat (Champion Penlan Paper Boy—Champion Charmar Checkenberry) from Carolane's Annie Get Your Gun (Champion Penlan's Peter Gunn —Carolane's Heaven Sent.)

At Bark there is also the lovely champion, Ruedensheim's Creme de la Creme, bred by Anne Lockney in Oklahoma, a show bitch of excellent quality.

Baws

Baws Miniature Schnauzers are owned by Violet and Robert Baws at Rosemead, California. This, since 1980, has been the home of the well-known and very handsome Champion Valharra's Double Extra, or "Marvin" to his friends, who has the impressive show record of four times first in the Terrier Group and a Specialty Best in Show at the Miniature Schnauzer Club of Southern California in February 1982. Now, in 1985 "Marvin" is to be shown as a "veteran" occasionally at Specialty events.

As a sire this lovely dog has certainly done himself proud with nine champions to date and some very promising youngsters soon likely to join them. He is a son of Champion Valharra's Extra (Champion Valharra's Trade Mark—Valharra's Annie Fanny) ex Champion Valharra's Touch of Magic (Champion Valharra's Max Pax-Champion Valharra's Dubarry), thus representing the finest of Enid Quick's Valharra strain.

The Baws are active breeders with a number of lovely Schnauzers in their kennels, to whom "Marvin" has proven himself a most welcome addition.

Ch. Log Cabin's Blue Skies. This daughter of Ch. Sky Rocket's Victory Bound ex Ch. Pine Needles Tara of Log Cabin was the foundation bitch of Blue Skies Kennels, Marilyn Cooper owner, St. Louis, Missouri. Bob Condon handling.

Blue Skies Barnstormer at the Gateway Miniature Schnauzer Specialty in June 1982. Bred and owned by Mrs. Marilyn Cooper. The judge pictured is Mrs. Alice Gough.

Blue Skies

Blue Skies Miniature Schnauzers are owned by Marilyn Cooper at St. Louis, Missouri, and are based on the foundation bitch, Champion Log Cabin's Blue Skies, for whom the kennel also was named. Her bloodlines are a combination of Sky Rocket, Mankit and Blythewood, being a daughter of Champion Sky Rocket's Victory Bound ex Champion Pine Needles Tara of Log Cabin.

Bred four times to dogs descended from the Sky Rocket line, this bitch has produced several pointed offspring in the United States and Canada. Her two sons from her last litter, Blue Skies Barnstormer and Blue Skies Trailblazer II, are currently being shown.

Bobette's

Bobette's Miniature Schnauzers are owned by Mrs. Bobette Gowan Tomasoff at Glendale, California, who started with the breed in 1967 when Baron Von Stobo was presented to her as a gift. Bobbie was interested in obedience, and trailed "Kelly," then took him through to his C.D.

Shirley's Charade came into the picture after Bobbie had met Shirley and Dick Willey, owners of the Shirley's dogs, during 1969 at an obedience match. Charade was one year old then, and it was mutual love at first sight between Bobbie and this little Schnauzer. Charade was trained in obedience and had her C.D. before her first litter was born. The latter consisted of three puppies by Baron Von Stobo, of which one female remained with Bobbie. This one, Bobette's Milady, when old enough, followed right along in her parents' paw prints, becoming Bobette's Milady C.D.

Shirley's Charade, C.D.X., and Baron Von Stobo, C.D.X., were both actively participating in the Hollywood Dog Obedience Club's Top Dog Team and in the Miniature Schnauzer Club of Southern California's Top Dog Team. Before being bred to Shirley Willey's Champion Mankit's Bang Bang of Dunbar, Charade obtained her C.D.X.

From the Bang Bang-Charade litter came Champion Bobette's Go Go Boy, C.D. and Bobette's Morning Star, C.D.

Again Bobbie and a Miniature Schnauzer fell in love, the latter being Shirley's September Morn, who was in the conformation ring and

Bobette's Schnauzers flying away to a dog show. Bobette Gowan-Tomasoff, owner.

had points towards her championship. Bobbie and Shirley Willey co-own Ember, and when they decided not to have her continue her quest for championship, she went into obedience with Bobette, her trainer-handler. So far she has completed her C.D.X.

Ember took time out to have one litter, sired by Champion Bobette's Go Go Boy, C.D. From this breeding came Champion Bobette's Mona Lisa, who was the only puppy in the litter.

During this period Bobette became Mrs. John Tomasoff, and immediately instructed John in obedience. It was he who trained and handled Bobette's Mona Lisa to her C.D. title.

Champion Bobette's Mona Lisa, C.D., bred and owned by Bobette Gowan Tomasoff and Shirley Willey, was bred to Champion Carolane's Fancy That, owned by Shirley to produce Champion Bobette's Bang Bang.

Bobette has been a member of the Hollywood Dog Obedience Club and the Miniature Schnauzer Club of Southern California for 20 years, and has been an obedience trainer for the Hollywood Dog Obedience Club for the past ten years. She has bred five litters during the time that she has been in Schnauzers, and is happy that they are living up to the standard of beauty and brains for the Miniature Schnauzer.

Bo-Nanza

Bo-Nanza Miniature Schnauzers had their beginning through an anniversary gift to Bob and Nancy Berg, Excelsior, Minnesota, of a seven-month-old dark salt and pepper male, bought from a pet owner with a stud right retained by the breeder. The retained stud right led the Bergs to becoming acquainted with the breeders, and thence to membership in the local Schnauzer Club. Six months later they had the good fortune to purchase Pickwicks G.W. Honey on breeder's terms. Honey, sired by Best in Show winning American and Canadian Champion Gough's Silver Franchise, was bred to the Bergs' pet male, presenting the couple with their first Miniature Schnauzer litter.

The Bergs became especially interested in the blacks, and therefore bred Honey to Goughs Ebony Knight Longleat. From this mating came Bo-Nanza's Black Beauty and Goughs Black Honey of Knight. Black Honey produced Champion Goughs Black Shadow of Knight, Champion Kellys Ebony-Dyn-O-Mite, and Champion Goughs Bi-Centennial Black, C.D.X. Black Beauty produced American and Canadian Champion Bo-Nanza's Black Bulletin, who led all black Schnauzers in the Top Fifty Knight System from 1976 through 1978. He also

In the Miniature Schnauzer Club of Southern California Top Dog Team, October 1975, Bobette and Shirley's Charade, C.D.X., are third from left. Bobette Gowan Tomasoff, Shirley's owner.

This is the famous producing bitch Bo-Nanza's Black Beauty (sitting) with her litter brother at about 12 weeks of age. Black Beauty, by Goughs Ebony Knight Longleat ex Pickwicks G.W. Honey (daughter of Best in Show winning Am. and Can. Ch. Goughs Silver Franchise) was the dam of such important winners as Am. and Can. Ch. Bo-Nanza's Black Bulletin. Bred and owned by Bo-Nanza Kennels.

became the first black Miniature Schnauzer to hold both an American and a Canadian Championship title.

Beauty's next champion, Bo-Nanza's Black-eyed Susan, finished her title at the Milshore Specialty. Beauty's influence continues as the granddam of three black and silvers of special note. These are Champion Bo-Nanza's Frosty City Slicker, Champion Bo-Nanza's Frosty Lone Ranger, and Champion Bo-Nanza's Frosty R Jr. While in blacks Champion Bo-Nanza's Black Baby Doll is one of special merit. Beauty also is the granddam of two Canadian, a Finnish, and two International champions.

Beauty was the first black Schnauzer ever shown by the Bergs. It is notable that despite their being novices in the show ring and beginners with this color, Beauty did extremely well in competition, hurdling with ease the obstacle of very few blacks being in competition at that period. At a year and a half, and with her needing only a "major" to finish, the Bergs

elected to breed Beauty, thus ending her brief show career. Now over 11 years old as we write, Beauty is enjoying herself as a real companion, having done her job well not only of building a strong foundation at Bo-Nanza for blacks and blacks and silvers alike, but also of helping to provide breeders in the United States, Canada, Switzerland, Belgium, and Finland with foundation stock with which to develop their own strains.

Looking to maintain and improve good quality coats in the black and silvers, and to avoid cross-breeding with the salt and peppers, the Bergs are importing a black and silver female Schnauzi's Melissa, who is an International and Scandinavian Champion and has been, over the males, the top producer of any color in Scandinavia. She also has successful progeny throughout Europe.

Melissa is owned by Soile Bister, Ytixer prefix, of Helsinki, Finland.

Another source of pride and pleasure to the Bergs is that of having been the breeders of Obedience Trial Champion Bo-Nanza's Miss Dark Shadow and Bo-Nanza's Sann's Mirandi, C.D.X. Both are owned and handled exclusively by Eunice Revsbech. Mirandi has earned the *Dog World Award* for having completed her C.D.X. requirements in three consecutive shows.

Ch. Bo-Nanza's Frosty Lone Ranger, grandson of Bo-Nanza's Black Beauty, owned by Bo-Nanza Miniature Schnauzers, Bob and Nancy Berg, Excelsior, Minnesota.

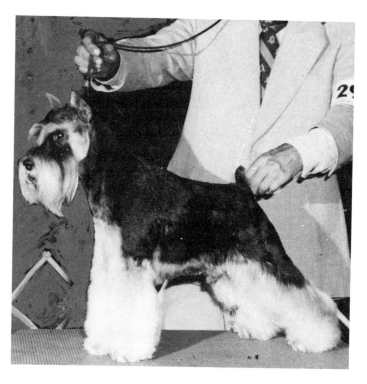

Am. and Can. Ch. Britmor Sunnymeade Frost, Am. and Can. C.D. is demonstrating correct Schnauzer action. Karen Brittan, Britmor Kennels, owns this very handsome little dog.

Britmor

Britmor Kennels are owned by Karen J. Brittan at St. Louis Park, Minnesota, who has been going great guns with a very handsome male, American and Canadian Champion Britmor Sunnymeade Frost, American and Canadian C.D. Ms. Brittan is one of the exhibitors who has had great success with the rolled coat method of which Mrs. Church has written elsewhere in this book, having begun rolling Sunny's coat in November 1980, at which time he had been in a 14 week show coat. A couple of weeks later he earned his second 4-point "major," bringing his point total up to 14. He earned his final point in March 1981, taking two Bests of Breed that weekend.

Later in 1981 Sunny was shown in Canada, finishing his Canadian title with five Bests of Breed and two Group 4's. As a class dog, he was always entered in the Bred-by Exhibitor class.

In the spring and summer of 1982, Sunny was shown to both his American and Canadian Companion Dog degrees with a high score of 198 and six class placements while being shown in Novice. Two of his obedience class placements were earned at shows where he also went Best of Breed. He was Specialed on a limited basis in Canada in 1982, earning 12 Bests of Breed, a Group 3 and a Group 4.

The following year Sunny was Specialed more heavily, mainly in Canada, and his record for 1983 was 28 Bests of Breed, two Group 4's, five Group 3's, one Group 1, and one Best in Show, the last on August 1st in Winnipeg at the Manitoba Canine Association under judge Eugene Phoa, making Sunny the FIRST black and silver Miniature Schnauzer to win a Best in Show. Sunny has always been breeder-owner handled.

Carolane

Carolane Miniature Schnauzers, at Brookville, New York, had their start in May 1963 when Carol and Carl Beiles purchased an eight-week-old female puppy from Leda Martin of Ledahof Kennels in Somerset, New Jersey. She was a very happy puppy of most outgoing temperament and endless enthusiasm with a constantly wagging tail. Thus her name became Ledahof Frederika Fantail. She was to be the housepet of her new owners, the Beiles, and was their constant companion for the next 15 years. She was also destined to produce the first two Carolane champions from two litters. In addition, she contrived to mother each and every puppy born at Carolane thereafter during her lifetime. Carol and Carl Beiles are quick to pay tribute to this lovely bitch with the words, "Our love and enjoyment of Miniature Schnauzers was due in large part to how we felt about her." From Fantail's first litter by Champion Ledahof Ambassador, the late Nicholas Daks, a Schnauzer judge whom the Beileses had met when they joined the Miniature Schnauzer Club of New York, chose a puppy bitch for them to keep. This puppy became Champion Carolane's Amanda in 1966.

The Beileses' change of address in 1965, due to Carl's military service plus a great deal of good luck, introduced this couple to Betty and Edward Bracey. Within three weeks of his taking her to show, Ed Bracy handled the bitch, Amanda, to her championship at the early age of 11 months old, this in the spring of 1966.

Fantail's next breeding was to the Bracy's Best in Show winning Champion Helarry's Harmony, a dog Carol and Carl had seen being shown and whom they admired immensely. From this breeding a male was kept, future Champion Carolane's Clarion, who turned out to be the first stud dog and second homebred champion at "Carolane." Clarion was owner-handled to a Group 1st award after being shown to a quickly completed championship by Ed Bracy. Clarion was used almost exclusively as a stud dog at home, where he produced the Beileses' Champion Carolane's Lucy In The Sky and Helen Werber's Clearview's Bright Future. He was also the sire of Carolane's Pixie Princess, owned by Philip Emden, Winners Bitch at Montgomery County in the "year of the flood," 1971. Her novice owners decided to discontinue showing her when she had a total of 14 points including both "majors."

Ch. Penlan Peter Gunn winning Best in Show at Tuscaloosa, Alabama, in Nov. 1977. Judge, the late Miss Gene Simmonds. Owners, Carol and Carl Beiles.

Ch. Penlan Peter Gunn winning Best of Breed in the big Miniature Schnauzer entry at Devon in 1977 on Montgomery County weekend. Owned by Carl and Carol Beiles, Brookville, New York. The Top Producing Miniature Schnauzer Dog in history!

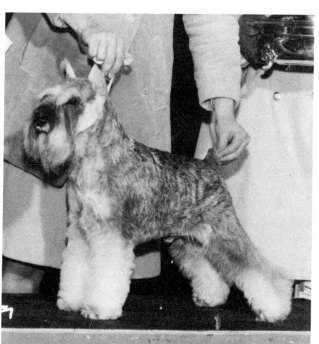

A litter of puppies at six weeks of age sired by Ch. Penland Peter Gunn. Note black puppy in the center. Owners, Carl and Carol Beiles, Carolane Kennels.

When Champion Carolane's Amanda was just one year old, she was bred to the Top Producing Champion Fancway's Pirate, Jr. of La May, this on the recommendation of Leda Martin. No champions resulted from this breeding, but one of the offspring, Carolane's Dark Delight, produced Champion Carolane's Lucy In The Sky when bred to Clarion. Amanda herself was next bred to Clarion, her half brother. From this breeding, two non-champion bitches were kept which were to become dams of champions:— Carolane's Ideal, dam of Champion Carolane's Odette (sired by Champion Phil-Mar Dark Knight); Carolane's Image von Clarion, dam of champion producing Carolane's Victoria, when bred to Champion Carolane's Bright Knight. Victoria produced Champion Carolane's Gangbuster when bred to Champion Penlan Peter Gunn. When bred to Champion Sky Rocket's Uproar she produced Champion Blue Snow's Something Special, sire of several champions for Arlene Parascandola.

As long-time admirers of the multiple group and Best in Show winning Champion Helarry's Harmony, in 1967 the Beileses purchased a puppy bitch from Betty Bracey which was a double Harmony granddaughter. She became Champion Harga's Terri, handled by Peggy Anspach. Terri was an extraordinary brood bitch and Carolane's first Top Producer. The seven Carolane champions by Champion Harga's Terri were Champion Carolane's Bright Knight and Champion Carolane's Royal Rogue sired by Champion Phil-Mar Dark Knight; Champion Carolane's Fantasy, Champion Carolane's Fantasies, Champion Carolane's Fancy Free, sired by Champion Penlan Paragon's Pride; Champion Carolane's Tess Trueheart and Champion Carolane's Christy Love sired by Champion Penlan Peter Gunn.

All of Terri's champions were themselves destined to produce champions, and several of them compiled top show records as well. Champion Carolane's Bright Knight bred to Carolane's Image von Clarion, sired Carolane's Victoria, a multiple-champion producer as mentioned previously. Bright Knight also sired Champion Ledahof My Fair Lady, owned by Ledahof Kennels, who became the dam of champions. Then there was Champion Carolane's Royal Rogue, handled by his breeder, Carol Beiles, to his championship and to a Group win and, most exciting of all, to Best in Show at the American Miniature Schnauzer Club Specialty Show in New York in February 1973. Although owned by non-doggy people, Royal Rogue produced three champions among them Champion Carolane's Crown Royal, whose dam was Carolane's Ultra, she by Carolane's Majestic Prince (an offspring of the Carolane's Dreamwitch breeding to Champion Carolane's Clarion). Dreamwitch was the offspring of Champion Fancway's Pirate Jr. of La May and Champion Carolane's Amanda. Ultra's dam was the original Ledahof bitch, Fantail. Another Royal Rogue champion was Carolane's Heritage, the first of nine champions produced by Carolane's Heaven Sent.

Another from Terri, Champion Carolane's Fantasy, handled by Claudia Seeberg, was the Top Winning Miniature Schnauzer Bitch in the United States in 1974, and was the dam of two champions plus several non-champions who themselves produced champions. Royal Rogue was also the sire of Champion Tomellee's Dixie Romance.

Fantasy, mentioned above, was the dam of Champion Carolane's Conquering Hero and Champion Carolane's Sky Walker, littermates sired by the Champion Penlan Peter Gunn son, Champion Carolane's Flying High. Bred to Peter Gunn himself, Fantasy produced Carolane's Classic of Mojean, purchased by Ramona Fleming of Cincinnati, who became the

Ch. Carolane's Royal Rogue taking Best of Breed at the American Miniature Schnauzer Club Specialty at Associated Terrier Clubs in New York City during February 1973.

Ch. Carolane's Fantasy was Top Miniature Schnauzer Bitch for 1974. Owned by Carl and Carol Beiles.

dam of Champion Mojean's Classic Rag Doll and Champion Mojean Country Dandy.

Still another of Terri's offspring, Champion Carolane's Fancy Free, was the dam of Champion Carolane's Golden Boy and Champion Carolane's Fancy That, the latter purchased by Shirley Willey of California after going Best in Sweepstakes and Best of Winners at Montgomery County in 1976 at 11 months of age. At that same show, his half sister, Champion Carolane's Christy Love, was Winners bitch and Best of Opposite Sex while another by Peter Gunn, Champion Penlan Peter's Son, was Best of Breed.

Champion Carolane's Fancy That is now the sire of Group and Specialty winners himself, with five champion offspring including his first champion sired at Carolane prior to his departure for the West Coast, Champion Carolane's Royal Fancy, who is owned by Lowell Hudson.

Champion Carolane's Fantasies, again Terri's offspring, was the Top Producing dam of three champions, Carolane's Magic Moment and The Wizard of Carolane sired by Champion Paxon's Magic Factor; and Carolane's Warlord, sire of several Canadian champions, by Champion Penlan Peter Gunn.

The Terri daughter, Champion Carolane's Tess Trueheart, was the dam of Champion Carolane's Swordsman sired by Champion Shorlaine Top Flash; and Champion Carolane's Christy Love, Winners Bitch and Best of Opposite Sex at Montgomery County the same year that her two half brothers were Winners Dog and Best of Breed respectively, has done her bit as a Terri daughter, too, being the dam of Carolane's Surprise Package, on the way to her title as this is being written.

Terri deserves credit, too, as the dam of Carolane's Optimism, who, although not a champion, is the dam of the Peter Gunn sired Champion Carolane's Orion.

1973 will probably go down in history as Carolane's most important year, for during it two Schnauzers were born who have contributed in a truly remarkable manner not only to this kennel but to the Schnauzer world in general. These two were the bitch, Carolane's Heaven Sent (by Champion Sky Rocket's Uproar ex Shorlaine Jeanie Jump Up), who was an extremely exaggerated dark bitch of decidedly terrier type, who was to become Carolane's Top Producing Bitch. The other was the dog, Champion Penlan Peter Gunn, who is owned by Carolane Kennels and has become the Top Miniature Schnauzer Sire in the history of the breed. Heaven Sent produced nine champions for Carolane. Peter Gunn has sired more than 60 champions at the time of writing, including eight from Heaven Sent. These latter are Champion Carolane's Galaxie; Champion Carolane's In Orbit; Champion Carolane's Flying High; Champion Carolane's Scandal of Seacrest; Champion Carolane's Light Up The Sky; Champion Carolane's Moonraker; Champion Carolane's Starburst; and Champion Carolane's Starfire.

The above Peter Gunn—Heaven Sent champions in their turn have produced Schnauzers of extraordinary quality, carrying on the family tradition. Galaxie, bred to her half brother Champion Penlan Pistol Packer, produced Carolane's Annie Oakley, dam of Champion Carolane's Topspin sired by Champion Paxon's Pacesetter. Topspin completed her championship going Winners Bitch at the Associated Terrier Club Specialty in 1982. Champion Carolane's Scandal of Seacrest is the dam of Champion Seacrest Subtle Suggestion. Champion Carolane's Flying High, a Specialty and Group winner, sired Champion Carolane's Conquering Hero, Champion Carolane's Sky Walker, and Champion Carolane's Star Warrior, the latter Best of Breed from the puppy class at the South Florida Miniature Schnauzer Specialty in 1978 and Best in Sweepstakes at the American Miniature Schnauzer Club Specialty, held with the Associated Terrier Specialties the following February. The combination of Heaven Sent and Peter Gunn also produced a non-champion Top Producer, Carolane's Annie Get Your Gun, owned by Linda Lucast (Tel-Mo Kennels). Annie was the dam of Best in Show winning Champion Tel-Mo's Top Cat and four other Tel-Mo champions from two breedings to Champion Charmar Copy Cat.

Champion Penlan Peter Gunn was born in October 1973, and purchased as a 15-month-old dog while still a non-champion. He completed his championship, handled by his breeders, Lanny and Penny Hirstein, during which he was undefeated in Open and took Winners Dog, then Best of Winners, at both the American Miniature Schnauzer Club Specialty and Westminster. Between 1975 and 1978, conditioned and handled by Claudia Seaberg for Carolane, he compiled an extraordinary show record, his wins having included two all-breed Bests in Show, 15 Specialty Bests in Show (a breed record) plus innumerable Group placements which included at least two dozen Group firsts. Peter Gunn came to Carolane as an addition to their stud force which included home-bred Group winning males. But the Beileses liked what had been produced in some of their previous breedings of their good bitches to Phil-mar and Penlan studs. A study of their pedigrees reveals that, several generations back, Carolane, Phil-Mar and Penlan had similar Helarry and Dorem ancestry. Therefore, Peter Gunn was purchased to breed this extreme and sound-moving linebred male, from a line obviously compatible to theirs, to the finest of their females. The results have been exciting. Peter Gunn has lived up to—and even beyond—their expectations as a producer!

Daland Coast to Coast, one of the splendid winning Schnauzers from David J. Kirkland's Daland Kennels, East Brunswick, New Jersey.

Daland

Daland Miniature Schnauzers are owned by David J. Kirkland and located at East Brunswick, New Jersey. David's breeding program started with a lovely bitch he purchased from Peggy Dunner, who is no longer active in the breed. This bitch represented the finest of bloodlines, being a daughter of Champion Sky Rocket's Uproar from a champion daughter of Champion Blythewood His Majesty, thus tracing back to Sky Rocket on her dam's side as well. David bred her to Champion Jadee's Jump Up, which combination produced his first homebred champion, Daland Dazzling Debut. The record she made in the show ring was an enviable one for a Schnauzer bitch, highlights consisting of a Group First, two Group fourths, and two Specialty Bests of Breed, these from the classes, plus an American Miniature Schnauzer Club Best in Sweepstakes, twice Best of Opposite Sex at American Miniature Schnauzer Club Specialty Shows, a total of ten times Best of Breed, and the grand climax-attaining No. 3 Schnauzer bitch for 1980.

Dazzling Debut for her first litter was bred to Champion Skylines Blue Spruce, Carol Parker's dog who is a Top Producer with more than 40 champions to his credit. This litter produced David's second home-bred to gain the title, Champion Daland Disco Dancer. Major-pointed from the puppy class, this bitch finished on one adult coat with a 5-point "major" and two Bests of Breed from the classes, owner-handled. She has a litter just starting to grow up as we are writing, this being the third generation in David's breeding program, and he is eagerly awaiting the reaching of show age for these promising youngsters.

The second litter from Champion Daland Dazzling Debut was sired by Champion Regen-

Ch. Daland Dazzling Debut, a Group and Specialty winner , #3 Schnauzer bitch in the U.S. for 1980, bred, owned, and handled by David Kirkland, Daland Kennels.

cy's Right On Target (grandson of Blue Spruce), from which David has kept a bitch, Daland Day Dreamer, who was already "major" pointed at ten months: a Specialty Sweepstakes winner; and Reserve Winners Bitch at both Delaware Valley Miniature Schnauzer Club and Montgomery County from the puppy classes.

The bloodlines with which David has chosen to work are basically dogs that have descended from the Sky Rocket bloodlines, or to pinpoint a bit more specifically, dogs who have descended from Blue Spruce and Uproar.

Due to space limitations and commitments to his occupation, David has deliberately en-

deavored to keep his breeding program small in quantity. He breeds a litter or two each year, sells a lot of his finishable dogs as pets, and keeps only a select few for breeding and showing. For the past few years, Daland has had a commitment to quality, never quantity, with bitches bred two or three times and offspring being kept only if superior to the parents. By this method, he brings into the ring only what he considers to be a tribute to the breed and "distinctly Daland." His breeding program has not drastically affected the breed as yet, but he is very justly proud of his accomplishments during the short time of his involvement.

Dor-Ru

Although primarily breeders of Lakeland Terriers, Dorothy and Ruth Anderson, owners of Dor Ru Kennels at Santa Ana Heights, California, are the owners as well of some very excellent Miniature Schnauzers.

Included among the latter are Champion Bokay Dandy Lion, who did some notable winning for his owners, handled by Clay Coady. Then there is Champion Blue Echo of Dor-Ru. And at the present time much interest centers around Champion Johnny O of Dor-Ru who took Best of Breed at nine months under Jon Cole at Santa Clara, to finish at 13 months, again going Best of Breed, under Mrs. Margaret Young. Johnny is preparing now for his Specials career, which from these early indications should be successful.

Ch. Blue Echo of Dor-Ru owned by Ruth and Dorothy Anderson, Dor-Ru Kennels, Santa Ana Heights, California.

Ch. Samos of Elfland, Best in Show at the Santa Ana Valley K.C., 1964, in an entry of 1850 dogs, handled by Jimmy Butler for Florence Bradburn, Elfland Kennels, Temple City, California. By Ch. Melmar's Jack Frost ex Polly of Elfland.

Elfland

Elfland Miniature Schnauzers were established by Miss Florence Bradburn, Temple City, California, back in the 1940's, and the interest of their owner in her breed still continues right up to the present day. This Schnauzer kennel is one of the oldest of any in the United States, dedicated to the breed which has lasted over more than four decades.

The original bitch at Elfland was Vanessa Anfinger, by Champion Amour zum Schlagbaum ex Heidy Anfinger, who was bred by another

Ch. Adam v Elfland, by Ch. Tribute v Elfland ex Ch. Benrook Jewel, littermate to Ch. Annabelle v Elfland. Florence Bradburn, owner, Elfland Miniature Schnauzers.

famous lady in this breed, the late Anne Fitzgerald Eskrigge, with several others coming to Elfland from this same source.

Florence Bradburn and the famed professional handler, Ben Burwell, became acquainted when Ben was on the Pacific Coast showing dogs. Ben (who is now retired from handling and lives at St. Croix in the Virgin Islands) obviously admired the Elfland dogs, and especially took an interest in the lovely small bitch, Champion Bitsi v Elfland, a daughter of Champion Seigmund v Nibelheim—Elli v Elfland, whom he suggested should be bred to Champion Dorem Tribute, a son of Champion Dorem Display. Champion Tribute v Elfland was a result of this breeding, who became an imported, highly regarded sire in his own right.

During this same period, again at Ben's suggestion, Miss Bradburn contacted the Benrook Kennels here in the East with the result that from them she purchased two splendid bitches, Benrock Vogue (Ch. Dorem Display—Meldon's Mariel) and Benrock Jewel, II, by Ch. Benrock Buckaroo ex Benrock Brilliantine. Jewel was handled by Ben Burwell to a five-point "major" her first time shown on the west Coast, then quickly completed her title owner-handled by Miss Bradburn. Both of these bitches were descended from Champion Dorem High Test.

Champion Tribute v Elfland was chosen to be the sire of Jewel's first litter for Miss Bradburn, and from the combination came Champion Adam v Elfland, U.D. Adam was used on Vogue for her first Elfland litter, and the results in-

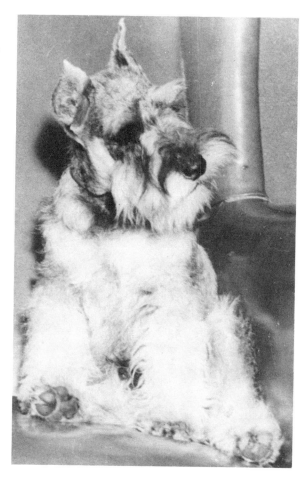

Ch. Annabelle of Elfland, owned by Florence Bradburn, Elfland Kennels.

cluded Champion Eve v Elfland. It was on the descendants of these Schnauzers that Elfland has continued its breeding program.

Champion Samos v Elfland represents Elfland breeding at its best. He is a magnificent dog who won an important all-breed Best in Show in an entry of 1,850 at Santa Ana in April 1964, handled to this honor by Jimmy Butler.

It was largely through Florence Bradburn's concern for and interest in the subject that the American Miniature Schnauzer Club formed its Committee on Eye Problems, initially headed effectively by Dr. Schulz of Janhof. During the 1950's rumors of blindness in Miniature Schnauzers started to appear, which unfortunately turned out to be fact rather than rumor. Miss Bradburn, some of whose dogs were among those affected by the appearance of cataracts, lost no time in helping organize research on the subject. Miss Bradburn approached knowledgeable people and asked for their help. Other serious breeders backed her up in supporting the program. The result was that by the beginning of the present decade, an impressive number of Miniature Schnauzers had been test-bred successfully for congenital cataracts, in a program which is continuing. If the considerable number of tested dogs continue to dominate breeding programs, the complete eradication of this defect is entirely possible. Miss Bradburn deserves the thanks of all who love Miniature Schnauzers for her efforts in this matter!

Florence Bradburn with her first litter of Miniature Schnauzers in 1941. This kennel has been continuously active for more than 40 years, and has been extremely influential in the progress of Miniature Schnauzers in the United States, particularly on the Pacific Coast.

Cindy Fancy, daughter of Jean and Glenn Fancy, with Ch. Fancway's Voodoo Doll in 1964. A Top Producer in the breed.

Fancway

The owners of Fancway Miniature Schnauzers, Jean and Glenn Fancy, were best known during the late 1940's for their Fancway Boxers. Then in 1952 they acquired their first Miniature Schnauzer, and soon their principal interest started centering around this breed.

In 1953 the Fancys had their first Miniature Schnauzer litter, producing in it two champions, Fancway's Blue Magic and Fancway's Blue Volt.

In 1954 the immortal American, Canadian, and Mexican Champion Marwyck Pitt-Penn Pirate was acquired by the Fancys. Pirate became Top Sire in the breed, a position he held over many years, with 48 A.K.C. champions plus numerous Mexican and Canadian champions.

Pirate is credited with having completely changed the style of Schnauzers for the Fancys, enabling them to breed both outstanding winners and outstanding producers. Between 1953 and 1968 their kennel produced 39 American champions. Since then they have bred only an occasional litter, the last of which was in 1973.

Pirate sired American, Canadian and Mexican Champion Fancway's Pirate Jr., a sire of 30 or more champions, among them Champion Faerwynd of Arador, the Top Producing Dam in the breed. Faerwynd's dam was Champion Fancway's Vampira, a Group winner and dam of seven champions, who was by Champion Fancway's Tom Terrific, also a Top Producer and top breed winner. The Fancway bloodlines have produced top show winners and producers alike with consistency.

Jean and Glenn, due to their worldwide judging commitments, are no longer active today as breeders. However, their contribution to great show and breeding stock and to truly magnificent Miniature Schnauzers will always be part of the heritage of this breed.

Giminhof

Giminhof Kennels, owned by Garry and Karen Clausing, are at Coffeyville, Kansas, and have been the home of Miniature Schnauzers since 1965, with Giant Schnauzers being added in 1971, and around 1980, Miniature Pinschers. By now these fanciers have bred champions in all three breeds, and have obedience titles on the Giant and Miniature Schnauzers.

Giminhof's Miniature Schnauzer lines are from the black Joninus line, from Sky Rocket and from Helarry. Later Blythewood was added, in the form of the excellent dog, Champion Blythewood Rocket Man. Mrs. Clausing describes him as being a breeder's dream, stamping his wonderful temperament and good type on his offspring and on their offspring.

Bred to a black bitch, Rocket Man produced his salt and pepper daughter, Champion Giminhof Ruffles and Flourishes, owned by Susan Atherton. Mrs. Clausing believes that Ruffles is headed towards becoming a top producer, as in her first two litters she has two group winning champions, one group placing puppy bitch, and others with "majors."

Rocky, bred to the salt and peppper Uproar daughter, gave the Clausings an outstanding litter that included a youngster who at his first show went from puppy class to first in the Terrier Group. That was Champion Giminhof Super Trooper, who now himself has a champion son, while Champion Rocky has three.

The Clausings are extremely pleased that these dogs are not only doing well in the ring, but are producing well, too. It is their plan to continue linebreeding in order to produce, hopefully, black Schnauzers with the looks of Trooper and Rocky.

Ch. Giminhof Super Trooper winning the Terrier Group at St. Joseph, Missouri K.C. in February 1983. Garry and Karen Clausing, owners, Coffeyville, Kansas. Handler, Priscilla Wells.

Haybrook

Haybrook Miniature Schnauzers are located at Springfield, Illinois, where they are breeding some excellent quality.

At the time of writing, their current "star" in the show ring is a young dog named Haybrook's Jumping Cidd who has been making a good impression on the judges. He is the result of Jadee's Jump Up having been bred to a Kazel's Favorite daughter, thus combining the bloodlines of a top producer and a top winner's daughter.

As "JC" needed only a point to finish in the mid-summer of 1984, we are sure that he must have completed title by this time.

Haybrook's Jumping Cidd, by Ch. Jadee's Jump Up ex Haybrook's Maiden Mary, born in 1982. Breeder-owners J.S. Hayden and R.E. Lashbrook. Best of Winners at the Columbia, Missouri, Kennel Club, July 1984, under judge Ric Chashoudian, handled by Judy Smith.

Ch. Irrenhaus Stamp of Approval, by Ch. Imperial's Stamp O'Kharashal ex Ch. Irrenhaus Flights of Fancy, is a multiple Group winner and a Specialty winner including Montgomery County. Owned by Jacqueline Hicks, handled by Sue Baines.

Irrenhaus

Irrenhaus Miniature Schnauzers are owned by Jacqueline Hicks at Woodford, Virginia. This kennel is the home of the noted Champion Irrenhaus Blueprint, sire of more than 16 champions, and of such impressive bitches as Champion Irrenhaus Flights of Fancy and her dam, Champion Irrenhaus Fancy Finish.

Flights of Fancy set a new breed record as a producing bitch in the early 1980's with her ALL CHAMPION litter of SIX! Since then she has added at least two more from subsequent litters, with probably more to follow. The all-champion litter was sired by Champion Imperial Stamp of Kharasahl, and consisted of Champions Irrenhaus Devil's Playmate, Flight Pattern, Pretty Boy Alfie, Replica, Stamp of Approval and Stand Out. Her other two champions are Champion Irrenhaus Mistletoe and Champion Irrenhaus Saint Nicholas, both by Champion Kharasahl Blue Chips.

Champion Skyline's Blue Spruce is the sire of Flights of Fancy. Her dam is Champion Irrenhaus Fancy Finish, also a Top Producer, whose total of champions was five when this was written.

Irrenhaus dogs are handled in the show ring by Sue Baines, and they have made some splendid achievements in this area, too, as a check of our illustrations shows clearly.

Ch. Irrenhaus Monogram, by Ch. Skyline's Blue Spruce ex Ch. Irrenhaus Fancy Finish. Bred and owned by Jacqueline Hicks, Irrenhaus Kennels. Handled by Sue Baines.

Ch. Jadee's Junebug, a Top Producer, owned by David W. Williams, DOW, pictured finishing handled by Judy Smith.

Jadee's

Jadee's Miniature Schnauzers (which identification stands for the initials of Judy Ann and Donald Lee Smith) is located at Bettendorf, Iowa and was founded in the early 1970's. Actually the groundwork started with a pet by the name of Shatzi in 1966, a son of Champion Gay Cavilier of Silver Oaks, a dog who had done some modest winning in the mid-West. After combing his mats out for four years, the Smiths took him to the local conformation class to see if he was indeed a show dog, since he was extremely well bred. He was four years old, over-muscled, with level bite, and no hair. The instructor very nicely, and tactfullly, convinced the Smiths to buy a young bitch "since you can't teach an old dog new tricks." This started them off with Heather's Windy Weather (named by the Smiths' daughter, Heather), later to become a top producing bitch of 1976, and the foundation of Jadee's.

Windy was purchased from Jean Lindell of York, Nebraska, and was from the popular Helarry line. After a bucket of yellow ribbons and 13 points including one "major," it was decided that the time had arrived to move on to the next step. As Judy says, "We had learned a lot of 'don'ts' in three years, but we did learn a lot!"

In 1971 the Smiths met the Fergusons, of Skyrocket fame, whom they had admired from afar, (as they also had done the Hirsteins and their Penlans). They purchased a four-month-old puppy by the name of Skyrocket's Upswing from the Fergusons, and Frank and Judy Ferguson showed them how easy winning can be! Swinger's first outing, at six months, was at the Montgomery County Terrier Specialty. He went Best Puppy in Sweepstakes, then, under the late Gene Simmonds, on to Winners Dog and Best of Winners for five points. This was the well-remembered "year of the mud" at Montgomery, but a day of triumph for these exhibitors. The Fergusons also took Best of Breed with Swinger's half-brother, Champion Skyrocket's Uproar, 1971's No. 1 Miniature Schnauzer.

Since the breeding was well suited to her bloodlines, it was decided to breed Heather's Windy Weather to Uproar, then try the puppies from that combination with Swinger.

Meanwhile, the Smiths continued learning from the Fergusons the art of presentation. Uproar proved to be prepotent with their first

66

Heather's Windy Weather, dam of six champions, is a Top Producer and has 12 points, including a major towards her title. Owned by Don and Judy Smith, Jadee's Miniature Schnauzers, Bettendorf, Iowa.

litter which produced the Smiths' now very famous Champion Jadee's Jump Up, who was the only puppy saved from Windy's litter of seven. Jump Up also possessed his sire's magical prepotency for style, soundness, movement and showmanship, with a plus on the latter. Jump Up made the Smiths be noticed, as he was truly a "natural" in the show ring. At the age of ten, they took him to the Milwaukee Specialty, where they found him to be still competitive and admired, still with all his teeth, strong topline, and true terrier temperment. As Judy says, "To this day he still loves dog shows."

The Smiths give full credit for their learning about dog showing to the Fergusons—Frank for the grooming and Judy for the handling. From these two they also learned how to help the newcomer in the breed. The Smiths are known for their encouragement of novice members of the Fancy, and on many a day have helped groom the competition and given their owners handling instructions only to be beaten by them in the ring later that day. And they are very quick to say that they found out how much such encouragement and friendliness means to those just joining our dog show world from the helpfulness extended to them by the Fergusons when they themselves started out.

Judy loves showing the dogs, and does so with expertise. Don, who is an architect by profession, enjoys the grooming aspects of showing, since grooming is a form of designing and sculpturing, thus right up his alley.

The foundation of Jadee's has remained a mixture of Helarry and Skyrocket bloodlines. With this combination, the Smiths have succeeded in producing a line that is foundation for many of today's winners. Some of these are Bandsman owned by Carol Luke, Repetition owned by Kurt and Carol Garmaker, Mariah owned by Doug and Ruth Dempster, and DOW owned by David Williams. Dalend owned by David Kirkland, and Dargo owned by Doug and Margo Reed are others to have included both Upswing and Jump Up in their breeding programs.

Upswing, sire of 16 champions, has among them the breed's noted producer, Champion Skyline's Blue Spruce, who is owned by Carol Parker and of the outstanding top producing bitch Champion Jadee's June Bug, owned by David Williams. Jump Up is also one of the breed's top producing sires with a record year in 1977 of 11 champions in a single year; his total number will soon top 40!

At Jadee a limited breeding program has been conducted, the emphasis on quality. By helping to cultivate or show the dogs from each litter, on many occasions they have finished the entire litter.

The Smiths' interest in dogs is not limited to the breeding and showing of their Schnauzers. Don is a past board member of the Nebraska Kennel Club. Judy and Don started the Omaha Miniature Schnauzer Club with a group of

American Miniature Schnauzer Club (February 10, 1974), Best of Opposite Sex in the Puppy Sweepstakes won by Sky Rocket's Travel More, by Ch. Jadee's Jump Up ex Ch. Sky Rocket's Upstart. Bred by Frank Ferguson and William J. Hoehne. Photo courtesy of owner, Judy Smith.

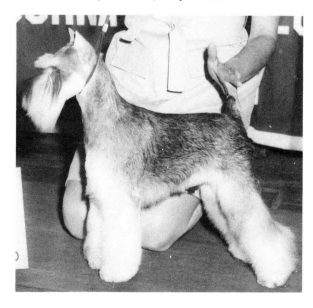

friends. And Don has served as Nebraska State Chairman for the Morris Animal Foundation for several years.

Now living in Iowa, the Smiths plan to continue with their program of quality breeding. They have a new young Special out, Champion Jadee's Royal Super Shot, who is the first stud dog they have kept and specialed since the loss of Upswing. Super brings in the Regency line owned by Bev Vernon, and goes back to Upswing on both sides of his pedigree. Since Swinger was the sixth generation of Best in Show dogs, the Smiths hope to continue with Super, whom they finished proudly from the Bred-by-Exhibitor Class.

Jilmar

Jilmar Miniature Schnauzers belong to Lisa M. Grames at Winter Springs, Florida, who purchased her first of the breed from the Gough Kennels in Minnesota. Her name was Gough's Silver Shining Star, and she was a daughter of the then top winner Champion Valharra's Dionysos, sire of more than 30 champions. While Lisa was showing her, she also wanted to have a litter, so she leased Shining Star's dam from the Goughs. Her name was Gough's Silver Starshine.

Starshine was already the dam of one champion, so Lisa was delighted at being able to make this arrangement. She was bred to Champion Bly-

Ch. Jilmar's Stardust owned by Lisa Grames, Winter Springs, Florida. Shown here with Claudia Seeberg.

thewood Ricochet of La May, and on November 2nd, 1973 Lisa Grames had her first litter. From this a lovely male was retained, who was to become her first champion, Jilmar's Big Wally.

With the success of the breeding of Starshine and Ricochet, it was decided to also breed Starshine's daughter, Shining Star, to Ricochet. One female was kept from the litter of three girls, Jilmar's Star Image, who was shown for a while but really did not care for being in the ring. Thus it was decided to retire her to maternal duties, and another top sire was selected, Champion Moores Max Derkleiner, from Valharra Kennels, with a pedigree reaching back into Mankit and Dorem. This produced two bitches so outstanding that the two of them were kept. One is Jilmar's Stardust; the other, Jilmar's Starlet. Stardust went on to become a champion and has produced two champions. Starlet, although a top quality bitch, did not like showing, so was kept for breeding. She more than proved herself in the whelping box, and was recently added to the list of top producing bitches with three champions and another son close to the title.

Starlet was bred to Champion Blythewood's National Acclaim who is a top Best in Show dog, the feeling being that his superior movement and other qualities would complement the bitch. He also is a grandson of Champion Valharra's Dionysos and great-grandson of Max Derkleiner. This litter produced Starlet's most noteworthy son, Champion Jilmar's Allstar, who was whelped in December 1979. Allstar's quest for the title was swift. Making his ring debut at six months, he completed his championship in four weekends of showing, finishing on the day he turned seven months, thus setting a new record of being the youngest male Miniature Champion to gain the title Champion.

All of Allstar's wins were from the puppy class, and on all occasions he was breeder-owner-handled. Allstar was specialed in 1981, ending the year as No. 5 Miniature Schnauzer in the country and the top homebred owner-handled by an amateur Miniature Schnauzer for that year. Allstar is a multiple Group winner and a multiple champion producer, despite being a young sire whose potential has not yet been reached.

Lisa Grames is still showing and breeding, although her breeding program is a small one, usually about one litter a year, aimed at quality rather than quantity.

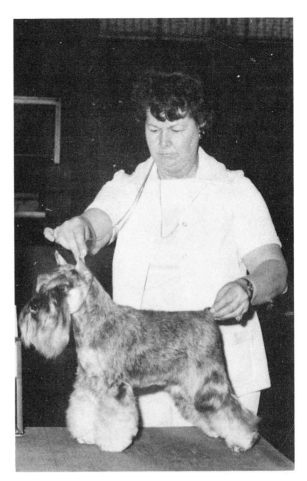

Kazels Spectaculaire, by Ch. Kazel's Favorite, owned and handled by Mrs. K. L. Church, Imperial, Missouri.

Kazels

Kazels Miniature Schnauzers are a very highly respected kennel owned by Mrs. K.L. Church and her daughter, Leslie Church, who reside at Hillsboro, Missouri. The Churches are breeders of some extremely notable Schnauzers, led by the handsome and extremely successful International, Mexican, Canadian, and American Champion Kazels Favorite, or "Bronco" to his friends. This lovely dog was born in February 1970, and at last report is still going strong.

Bronco was sired by Champion Abingdon Authority, owned by George and Edna Hendrickson, whom I understand holds the breed Best in Show record in the continental United States with nine Bests in Show. Cinder von Kirche, C.D.X., Bronco's dam, was a top producer and the dam of an all-champion litter. Bred three times to Authority (the combination which produced Bronco) she whelped eight pup-

Ch. Kazel's Pretty Cute, C.D., one of three in an all-champion litter. Mrs. K.L. Church, owner, Kazel Schnauzers.

pies by this sire of which seven were pointed. In addition to Bronco, Cindy also did herself proud with the daughter Kazels Omega who was Best of Winners at Westminster.

Cinder was quite a "star" in obedience, earned a Top Scoring Terrier award and had a leg on her utility title prior to the start of her breeding career. Cinder was by way of being the "official puppy lead trainer" at Kazels, in which she excelled. Mrs. Church has greatly missed her since her death in January 1984.

Champion Kazels Favorite set a new Best of Breed record for Miniature Schnauzers when he took this award for the 132nd time, and the author feels honored at having been the judge to make the selection that day. A memorable dog in every way! Among the roles in which he has starred has been that of Junior Showmanship Dog, as it was he who helped his young co-owner gain Best Junior Handler at Westminster. He also was campaigned successfully in Mexico and in Canada. Elsewhere in this book appears a chapter on rolled coats written by Mrs. Church. It is interesting to note that Bronco had a rolled coat for at least ten years before Mrs. Church permitted it to get blown.

Mrs. Church is a great student of pedigrees and breed characteristics involving her Schnauzers. She comments that, in researching their personal heritage, she was very surprised to discover that Favorite is only 12 generations from an original breeding which used the Standard Schnauzer to create the Miniature Schnauzer breed. Information on the bitch used is not available, to Mrs. Church's regret, as she is fascinated at being this close to history right there at home!

The breeding program at Kazels has been heavily inbred, as Mrs. Church has used Favorite back to his own daughters successfully through three generations. Kazels Artful Dodger is one of the results of this. Now that Favorite is past 12 years, Dodger will be used, possibly with a full sister from another breeding.

Favorite is the winner of five all-breed Bests in show and four Specialty Bests of Breed, the latter including two American Miniature Schnauzer Club Specialties.

Int., Mex., Can., and Am. Ch. Kazel's Favorite here is receiving his 132 Best of Breed, thus setting a new record for the breed. Judge, Anna Katherine Nicholas. Favorite went on to Group 4th that day. Owner, Mrs. K.L. Church, Kazel Miniature Schnauzers.

Kelly's

Kelly's Miniature Schnauzers, owned by Richard and Geri Kelly at North Falmouth, Massachussetts, have attained an admirable level of excellence in their breeding of blacks, which are Geri Kelly's special favorites of the Schnauzer world.

Pride of place at this kennel goes to the little dog who is Top Winning Black Miniature Schnauzer of the Decade, American, Canadian, and Bermudian Champion Kelly's K.E. Ebony Show Stopper. Among his honors, Stopper has an all-breed Best in Show, was Best of Breed at a National Specialty, and achieved his title when only seven months of age. An interesting fact about him is that he is a black who has sired all three colors; Geri Kelly believes he is the only one of whom this can be said.

Stopper's sire, Champion Kelly's Black Onyx, is another distinguished member of the Kellys' Schnauzer family. Also included are such well-known dogs as Champion Kelly's Flam-Boy-Ant Black, Champion Kelly's Jolee's Top of the Mark, Champion Kelly's Im-pec-able Black, Champion Kelly's Ebony's Dyn-O-Mite, and other well-known winners.

Geri Kelly breeds and handles the majority of her dogs. A number of them have won and placed consistently in Terrier Group competition, and their style and quality have attracted much favorable attention to the blacks in the New England area.

Ch. Kelly's Top of the Line Black Dee finished at ten months of age. Winning the Terrier Group here with owner-handler Geri Kelly at Albany Kennel Club in 1983. By Ch. Kelly's Im-Per-Ial Black ex Ch. Kelly's Flam-Boy-Ant Black.

Ch. Landmark's Masterpiece, bred and owned by Gloria Weidlein, is the sire of 31 champions. He finished at Montgomery County when only eight months old, and among his many exciting wins he was Best of Breed at Westminster during the late 1960's.

Landmark

Landmark Kennels are owned by Gloria Weidlein, located at Sun City, California, and have earned a position of high esteem in the Miniature Schnauzer world as the home of that great dog Champion Landmark's Masterpiece.

"Willie," as Masterpiece was known to friends, was by American and Canadian Champion Mutiny Master Spy ex-Champion Allaruth's Jasmine, and he was owner-bred by the Weidleins. At age six months and one day old, he made his show debut by going, from the puppy class, to Best of Breed and Group 2, completing his title in six shows at Montgomery County. Ric Chashoudian handled Masterpiece, as he did all of Gloria Weidlein's dogs for 13

years. His other commitments with the Wires and the Lakelands led to his never taking Masterpiece personally into the Groups, but Barbara La Bounty (later Butler), who finished him, was the one who handled him in Group competition, gaining a Group first and many placements on him. Masterpiece was always a housedog and pet, Gloria traveling with him wherever he went.

Masterpiece sired 31 champions, and himself had titles in both Canada and the United States.

The Weidleins always had a small kennel, about ten dogs at a time, which got down to only a couple following the deaths of Gloria's husband, Al and of Masterpiece during 1978. Among the champions bred by the Weidleins, in addition

Ch. Landmark's Masterpiece posing naturally. Five and a half years of age, and all set to go! Gloria Weidlein, owner, Sun City, California.

Am. and Can. Ch. Mutiny Master Spy, sire of Ch. Landmark's Masterpiece, finishing at San Diego, handled by Ric Chashoudian for owner Gloria Weidlein, Landmark Kennels.

to Masterpiece, were Champion Landmark's The Hustler, also a dog, and the four bitches Champion Landmark's Terrific Twist, Champion Landmark's Allaglow, Champion Landmark's Jezebel, and Champion Landmark's Charlie.

Other champions which Gloria has owned and finished are Champion Fancways Tom Terrific, Champion Allaruth's Jasmine, Champion Starfire Criterion Landmark, Champion Bon-Ell Upstart (co-owned), Champion Mutiny Master Spy, Champion Mutiny Uproar, and Champion Brag About of Hansenhaus (co-owned).

Recently Gloria Weidlein attended a Beverly Hills Kennel Club dog show, where she saw a lovely black bitch, Champion Gretchen's Black Tulip, whom she purchased. So, as she says, "Here we go again!", as she has now become interested in the blacks, and is trying her luck with just two or three of them to see how it goes. Her young Landmark's Black 'n' Blue, by Champion Skyline's Blue Spruce, is well on the way to the title, and her many friends in the Fancy wish Gloria much success with this new venture.

Ch. Janhof's Merry Maker with offspring at ten weeks. Puppy on *right* became Ch. Merry Maker's Dyna-Mite. Mrs. Mabel (Jinx) Gunville, owner, Deerfield, Illinois.

Am. and Can. Ch. Amigo of Merry Makers, owned by Mrs. Mabel M. Gunville, is in the pedigree of many of today's Miniature Schnauzers. By Ch. Helarry's Dyna-Mite ex Ursafell Blossomtime.

Merry Makers

Merry Makers Miniature Schnauzers at Deerfield, Illinois, were established when Mrs. Mabel (Jinx) Gunville and her late husband Paul Gunville purchased their first of the breed during 1957. Their kennel name has always been "Merry Makers," and Mrs. Gunville has always been a hobby breeder, producing about one litter each year and, on average, keeping and finishing one puppy from each of these litters.

Top winning Schnauzer here was Champion Merry Maker's Dyna Mite, also known as "Topper," who is still alive and frisky at 14 years of age. This memorable homebred dog, by Champion Penlan Paragon's Pride ex Champion Janhof's Merry Maker, was named for his grandsire, Champion Helarry's Dyna Mite, who spent his autumn years at Merry Makers and who passed away during the week that "Topper" was whelped. The present Dyna Mite is described as a truly elegant, sturdy little guy who keeps himself in very hard, trim condition by "zooming" around his large backyard. He is completely square, measuring 13½ inches at the shoulder, and has exceptionally sound movement, with a "Well, here I am attitude" in the ring according to the descriptions of him we have read. At home he is a fun-loving pet who is everyone's friend. Truly a dog to be enjoyed, who has brought much pleasure to his breeder-owner over the years!

"Topper" represents many years of selective, well-planned breeding, not only at Merry Makers but also at Penlan where his Group winning sire was produced; and at Janhof from where his Specialty winning dam came. Helarry and Allaruth also played an important role in the background of his pedigree.

When "Topper" retired from show competition, he had amassed the striking total of three all-breed Bests in Show, 12 Terrier Group Firsts, and as a sire had produced 15 champions.

One of the first homebreds which was successful for the Gunvilles was American and Canadian Champion Amigo of Merry Makers, a Group winner who carried the black and silver gene. Many of the current black and silver Miniature Schnauzers trace back to him in their pedigrees.

Other of Mrs. Gunville's favorites whom she has bred include Champion Merry Maker's Tempest and Champion Merry Maker's Bo Kay. Two bitches who have contributed well to the breeding program have been Champion Janhof's Merry Maker (the dam of both Dyna Mite and

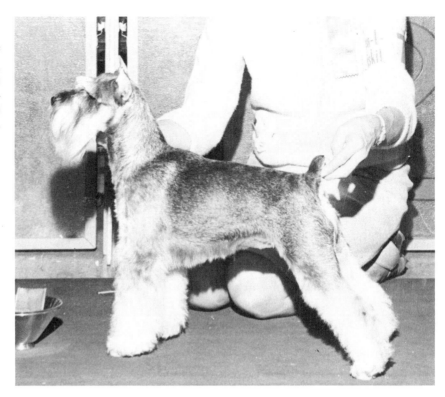

Ch. Janhof's Merry Maker, dam of Ch. Merry Maker's Dyna-Mite, was a Specialty winner and finished with three 5-point majors, owner-handled. By Am. and Can. Ch. Amigo of Merry Makers ex Ch. Allaruth's Jemima.

Tempest) and Champion Bardon Dear Abby.

Mrs. Gunville has served on the Board of Governors of the American Miniature Schnauzer Club, as Treasurer, and currently she is serving her fifth term as President of the American Miniature Schnauzer Club. She is, as well, an A.K.C. judge of the Working Group, about half of the terrier breeds, and several of the herding breeds.

Mi-Sher

Mi-Sher Miniature Schnauzers are at Clackamas, Oregon, where they are owned by Sheryl Stump.

With the exception of their first champion, Mi-Sher's Dynamic Destiny, this kennel's limited breeding program has been based on one dog, Champion Walters' Tradewinds. A multiple Group and Specialty winner, this lovely Schnauzer is the sire of five champions of which three are owned by Sheryl. These are Champion Linalee's E Z Loven' of Mi-Sher, Champion Mi-Sher's Windsong, and Champion Mi-Sher's One and Only.

Champion Linalee's E Z Loven' of Mi-Sher is the dam of two champions as we write, these being Champion Mi-Sher's One and Only and Champion Mi-Sher's Mystic Moment, the latter finishing title with three "majors" at just nine months of age from the puppy class.

Ch. Walter's Tradewinds, owned by Sheryl Stump, Clackamas, Oregon. The dog behind Mi-Sher's Kennels.

Penlan

Penlan Miniature Schnauzers, owned by Landis and Penny Hirstein at Washington, Illinois, are among the most distinguished and prestigious in the history of this breed. The breeding program here has produced something in the area of 60-70 champions since the Hirsteins first became active in the Schnauzer world back in the early 1960's.

The Hirsteins started out with the very sound theory that the best way to start a successful breeding kennel was with the purchase of the finest possible bitch they could obtain—which they did. Helarry's Lolly was purchased by them from Mrs. Helen Wiedenbeck, owner of Helarry Kennels, and on this bitch, her children and her grandchildren, the Penlan bloodline has been developed.

Lolly's own show career was cut short by the arrival of the Hirsteins' first daughter. But the wealth of quality she has contributed to the breed through future generations of her descendants speaks eloquently of her quality. She had been whelped on January 28, 1961, having been tightly line bred back into one side of her pedigree. From her first litter came the Hirsteins' leading foundation—producing bitch Penlan Cadet too, whose sire was Champion

Penlan Cadet Too, from the first litter of Helarry's Lolly, Hirstein's foundation bitch. Cadet, never shown, produced ten champions for Penlan Kennels and had two more offspring pointed. The ten champions are Ch. Penlan Mystic Bowman, *Ch. Penlan Paragon, *Ch. Penlan Paramour, *Ch. Penlan Paragon's Pride, Ch. Penlan Paragon's Joy, *Ch. Penlan Prelude to Victory, *Ch. Penlan Paragon's Exceptional, Ch. Penlan Perfect Timing, *Ch. Penlan Perfect Choice, and Ch. Penlan Play Girl. Each of these produced at least one champion; those marked * were Top Producers.

Ch. Penlan's Promissory, by Ch. Penlan Pride's Promise ex Ch. Penlan Powder Puff. "Rebel" completed his championship with two Bests in Show from the classes. Out of five Group Firsts he now has four Bests in Show. He is a National Specialty winner as well as multiple winner at other Specialty events. Not yet three years old, he has several offspring with points, plus a number more standing in the wings. Owned by Penny and Lanny Hirstein, Penland Miniature Schnauzers. Pictured going Best in Show at Greater Naples K.C. in May 1982.

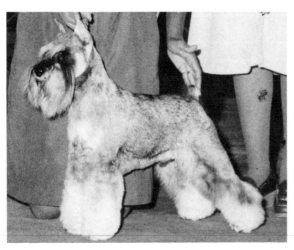

Helarry's Danny Boy. Interestingly, Cadet measured more than 14 inches, thus was ineligible to be shown. But the Hirsteins appreciated her quality and her pedigree nonetheless and she was kept by them for breeding—a wise decision, as Cadet produced a champion in each of her litters, all of whom were Best of Breed winners from the classes and/or Specialty point winners. The quality of her progeny remained consistent whether she was linebred of tried with an outcross, which speaks well for her dominance as a producer.

The earliest Penlan champions were handled professionally by Richard and Joanne Trubee, until the time of Dick Trubee's very unexpected death in 1968. Champion Penlan Proud Knight, this kennel's first Specialty winner, was handled by him, as were the littermates Champion Penlan Paragon and Champion Penlan Paramour. She gained her title with great success, taking Winners Bitch and Best of Opposite Sex at the

Ch. Penlan Pacesetter (Ch. Penlan Pistol Packer ex Penlan Picture Please) was owned throughout his show career by Miss Gene Simmonds, of the famous Handful Kennels in Maryland. No. 1 winning Miniature Schnauzer in 1981, a multiple Group winner and Specialty winner, this dog is also the producer of champions. From the Penlan Kennels, handled by Landis Hirstein.

Ch. Penlan Powder Keg, the dam of Ch. Penlan Pistol Packer, is by Merry Makin Dynamite ex Ch. Penlan Prim Miss. This lovely bitch established two "firsts" for Penlan Kennels; producing their first all-championship litter and finishing her own championship after the puppies were whelped, when the latter were eight weeks old. She is a Top Producer with five champions by three sires and with another daughter who has produced champions. Powder Keg's champions are, in addition to Pistol Packer, Ch. Penlan Percussion, Ch. Penlan Powder Puff, Ch. Penlan Pampered Lady, and Ch. Penlan Paragon's Music Maker. Penlan Schnauzers, Landis and Penny Hirstein, Washington, Illinois.

Ch. Penlan Checkmate, by Ch. Penlan Paragon's Fanfare ex Orlane's Middle Maid, was a stud fee puppy who came to live at Penlan at the age of four months. Sold to the Charles Krieghauns at seven months of age, became a Group and Specialty winner and a Top Producing sire with 29 Champions. Handled here by Landis Hirstein.

American Miniature Schnauzer Club National Specialty at Montgomery County in 1968.

Probably the most important Cadet offspring was Champion Penlan Paragon, who was sired by Champion Phil-Mar Dark Knight. He quickly obtained his title, his victories including a Group first from the classes and points at the South Florida Specialty, further distinguishing himself by becoming the sire of eleven champions, all from Penlan bitches. Among these was Champion Penlan Paragon's Pride, following in his sire's pawprints by finishing with a Group first from the classes, and had also been Best of Winners at the Chicago Specialty, these triumphs when less than nine months of age.

Pride was an extremely popular stud, both for his looks and for his pedigree, winding up with 29 champions to his credit, including Champion Penlan Paper Boy (producer of 35 champions) and Champion Merry Makers Dyna-Mite, (producer of 15 champions).

For her next breeding, it was decided that Cadet should go to Champion Helarry's Dark

Victory for a second time, from which came just one puppy. She was future Champion Penlan Prelude to Victory, becoming a puppy champion in the family tradition by earning one of her majors at a Specialty, that of the 1969 American Miniature Schnauzer Club event.

It was in 1975 when the Hirsteins brought the year old Peter Gunn to the New York American Miniature Schnauzer Club Specialty, accompanied by a homebred bitch puppy who became Champion Penlan Pin-Up of Wolffcraft for James Wolff and Paul Reycraft. Gunner made his initial Eastern appearance by taking Best of Winners, which he repeated the following day at Westminster. Pin-Up did well for herself, too, winning Best in Sweepstakes at the Specialty. "Gunner" completed his title undefeated in the classes.

By the time the mid-1970's were here, Penlan was producing its fourth and fifth generation homebreds, all thoughtfully bred down from the original produce of Helarry's Lolly. By then the Hirsteins were able to contemplate with pleasure the fact that they had bred about a dozen Group and Best in Show winners, had won Bests in Show from the classes, and were constantly in the "winners circle" at Specialty events. Lanny, meanwhile, had been building a strong following as a highly successful professional handler, which, of course, meant that his own dogs now must take in fewer shows in deference to the dogs owned by clients. Champion Penlan Paper Boy did manage, in 1973, to get shown in two coasts, just missing the Top Ten listing by 15 points.

As breeders of Miniature Schnauzers, Penlan Kennels in 1976 saw Peter Gunn and his son, Peter's Son, both become National Specialty winners. The following year, Champion Penlan Pistol Packer, joined these two in the Top Ten listing. Then, in 1977, Peter Gunn led all of the breed rating systems with two Bests in Show, eight Groups, and six Specialty Bests in Show, as 16 of his offspring became champions! Claudia Seeberg was in charge of "Grunner's" Specials career, which must have been a very exciting period for his owners, Dr. and Mrs. Carl Beiles (Carolane Kennels) as well as for the Hirsteins. Outstanding among Peter Gunn's successes are his record number of Specialty wins, 15, which still stands unsurpassed and his record as the sire of more than 60 champions, making him top sire in the breed.

Following Peter Gunn's achievements, a Paper Boy son was shown by the Hirsteins to No. 1 Miniature Schnauzer, Knight System, in

This is the unforgettable Ch. Penlan Peter Gunn winning Best in Show at Jupiter-Tequesta K.C., 1977. Owned by Carol and Carl Beiles, Brookville, New York Peter Gunn was sent to the Beiles after his championship, the Hirsteins finished him with Best of Winners at the American Miniature Schnauzer Club and Westminster. Peter Gunn's sire was Ch. Penlan Checkmate; his dam Ch. Penlan Proud of Me.

Ch. Penlan Paragon, one of the superb Penlan Miniature Schnauzers belonging to Landis and Penny Hirstein.

1978. Then, in 1980, another handled by them, Champion Bardon Bounce Hunter (Checkmate ex a Peter's Son daughter) took over the No. 1 spot. No. 2 that same year, 1980, was Champion Penlan Pride's Promise, and Penlan Pacesetter was gaining points towards his title. This latter dog was purchased while a puppy by the late Gene Simmonds of "Handful" fame. Shown by the Hirsteins at the 100th Anniversary American Miniature Schnauzer Club Specialty, he went Best in Sweepstakes. The following year he led the Schnauzer winners in the Knight System ratings by a wide margin, having to his credit several Specialty victories including the National, plus becoming a Best in Show (all-breed) winner.

Champion Penlan Promissory followed Pacesetter to the Best in Show circle, the fifth to reach these heights for the Hirsteins.

Numerous important kennels have started out with foundation stock from Penlan. Among them Richlene (owned by Richard and Arlene Smith, Ft. Wayne, Indiana), Liebchen (Mrs. Jeanne Lindell), Busy (Pat and Gary Pigott), Ardicia (Richard and Patricia Roozen), Charmar (F. Joseph Williams), Ayre Acres (Mrs. Marie Voss), and many others. We salute the Penlan Miniature Schnauzers, and pay special tribute to their stud dogs, including the six who have alone sired well over 150 champions!

Regency

Regency Miniature Schnauzers are owned by Beverly J. Verna at Santa Clara, a small operation which nonetheless has the very nice number of 15 homebred champions to its credit.

Regency Schnauzers are all homebred. Beverly Verna started the kennel in 1975, since which time they have averaged one or two litters annually. Five years ago (1979) Ms. Verna started handling professionally, but doing so only for dogs she has bred or who have been sired by one of her studs.

The breeding program got under way with the foundation bitch, Jana PD, and her litter by Champion Skyline's Blue Spruce. This combination was repeated twice, producing a total of seven champions amongst the three litters. Included among them was Champion Regency's Rosy Glow, a multiple Group winning bitch, and Champion Regency's Right On, a leading show dog, No.4 Miniature Schnauzer in the country for 1979 and a Top Producer, having 21 champion offspring to date and still actively used at six years of age.

Ch. Regency's Right On Target, the Nation's No. 1 Miniature Schnauzer for 1982, is an all-breed Best in Show winner, a multiple Specialty winner, has ten Group Firsts to his credit, along with many placements. At three years of age, he has already produced ten champions. Owned by Beverly J. Verna, Santa Clara, California.

Ch. Regency's Equal Rights, by Ch. Regency's Right On, is the uncropped Schnauzer who made history as the first of her kind to gain the title here since 1934. Owner-handled and bred by Beverly J. Verna.

Among the champions sired by Right On are two of whom Beverly Verna is most proud. These are a bitch, Champion Regency's Equal Rights, the first uncropped Miniature Schnauzer to finish an American championship since 1934; and Champion Regency's Right On Target, who became the National No.1 Miniature Schnauzer for 1982, winning an all-breed Best in Show, Multiple Specialties (including a National), 10 Groups, and many placements.

There are two others from the same litter which produced Right On Target who have also brought honor to the kennel. These are Champion Regency's Dusty Rose and Champion Regency's Rose Blossom V B-Major, both bitches. This excellent litter was by Champion Regency's Right On from his full sister, Champion Regency's Rosy Glow.

The feeling is that Target is destined to become a cornerstone sire in the breed. Being so tightly bred, he is extremely prepotent, and has been used with outstanding results on bitches from all across the United States with a wide range of pedigree lines.

Royalcourt

Royalcourt Miniature Schnauzers are owned by Mrs. Gloria Lewis of Closter, New Jersey, who has been a highly successful breeder but who is now cutting back on this activity as she is so involved in the handling and breeding of her clients' dogs. Gloria is a first rate professional handler whose schedule is always full.

As is so often the case, the best producing bitch at Royalcourt was not a champion, just a beautifully bred bitch with the talent for producing tremendous quality in her litters. She was Tare-Royalcourt Happy Hooker, with 11 points towards the title, who produced three champions. One son of hers, Champion Royalcourt Ballplayer, went on to sire three champions, and one of his sons, Champion Royalcourt Name of the Game, also became a champion producer.

Champion Royalcourt Get Up and Go has been one of Gloria's important winners. How unfortunate that this most gorgeous bitch was

Ch. Royalcourt Get Up and Go, owned by Mrs. Gloria Lewis, Closter, New Jersey.

Ch. Royalcourt Ballplayer, sire of three champions, with Mrs. Gloria Lewis, Royalcourt Kennels, in 1978.

never able to conceive, thus was finally spayed!

Gloria is a familiar figure in our Schnauzer rings at all the prestigious shows, with dogs who are turned out to perfection. We feel most fortunate in being able to bring you, elsewhere in this book, some comments from her on correct grooming as well as on the various colors in the breed.

Shirley's

Shirley's Schnauzers are owned by Shirley and Dick Willey who now reside at Simi, California, and began, as our readers will note in the obedience section of this book, with the acquisition of Shirley's New Beau in July 1965 at age 10½ weeks. There is a discussion of the obedience activities of the kennel in the obedience chapter as this is a very important part of the Willeys' interest and involvement with Schnauzers.

The first litter of the Willeys was born on April 14th, 1968, the first and only litter sired by Shirley's New Beau, C.D.X., and the first of five litters for the dam, Shirley's Sugar 'n' Spice, C.D. The three puppies in this litter became Champion Shirley's Show Off, C.D.; Shirley's

Charade, C.D.X.; and Champion Shirley's Sir Prize Package, C.D.X. All three of them produced champions and obedience title-holders.

Shirley's Sir Prize Package, C.D.X., was the sire of Champion Shirley's Sporting Chance, C.D. There was only the one puppy in this litter, giving Sir an average of 100% as the sire of champions as this was his only pup ever. Sporting Chance, in his turn, is the sire of Shirley's Scheherazade, the foundation bitch for Debaru's Schnauzers owned by Ruth Pederson. Scheherazade is the granddam of champions in both America and Japan.

Charade, owned by Bobette Gowan-Tomasoff, produced an obedience titlist when bred to Baron Von Stobo, C.D.X. For her second litter she was bred to Champion Mankit's Bang Bang of Dunbar, owned by Shirley's Schnauzers, producing Champion Champion Bobette's Go Go Boy, C.D. and Bobette's Morning Star, C.D. These were the only two litters for Shirley's Charade, C.D.X.

In January 1970, Champion Mankit's Bang Bang of Dunbar, at 18 months of age, was adopted from Emanuel and Kitty Miller of the famed Mankit's line. Bang Bang was handled to his championship by Ric Chashoudian and then went on to become one of California's top winning Specials in 1971 and 1972. Bang was a small dog, but exciting to watch in the ring. He produced seven American champions, two Japanese champions, and the holders of four obedience titles, two of these being conformation champions as well.

Champion Shirley's Show Off, C.D., bred to Champion Mankit's Bang Bang of Dunbar, gave the Willeys four champions, one from each litter. These were Champion Shirley's So Bang, C.D.; Champion Shirley's Straight Shot; Champion Shirley's Sword of Lancelot; and Champion Shirley's Show Time. In the same litter with Show Time also was Japanese Champion Shirley's Show Biz.

Shirley's Sugar 'n' Spice, C.D. was bred to Champion Mankit's Bang Bang of Dunbar in May of 1970, producing five puppies, two of which were Champion Shirley's Siren of the Mini Set and Shirley's Sugar Pop, C.D., who

Ch. Shirley's Strike My Fancy at eleven months, winning the Sweepstakes at the Portland Miniature Schnauzer Club, January 1983. Owned by Shirley's Schnauzers, Dick and Shirley Willey.

Ch. Shirley's Show Off, C.D. taking Winners Bitch, Best of Winners and Best of Opposite Sex in August 1968 at Klamath Falls, handled by Ric Chashoudian for owners, Shirley and Dick Willey.

had conformation points as well. Her next litter, in March 1972, was of four babies, including Shirley's Sunday Matinee who was highly pointed but withdrawn from comformation competition short of her title in order to be bred to Champion Landmark's Masterpiece in 1974.

This breeding produced his 30th champion for Masterpiece, Champion Shirley's String of Pearls, another of the Willeys' leading producing bitches.

Another lovely dog was added to the Shirley's

Schnauzer clan in September 1976. This was Carol Beiles's puppy dog, Carolane's Fancy That, who made a memorable show debut by going Winners Dog and Best of Winners from the puppy class over 90 dogs at Montgomery County. "Hank" was sent to the Willeys on the West Coast to be handled by Eddie Boyes. A very typical and beautiful dog, he completed his championship with ease, then went on to become one of California's top winning Specials in 1977 and 1978.

When Champion Shirley's String of Pearls gained her championship in May 1977, she stepped into the role of motherhood. Bred to Champion Shirley's Show Time for two litters, she produced Champion Shirley's Spring Fever and Champion Shirley's Sunday Cowboy in the first, born March 1978; and Champion Shirley's Spectacular Bid along with Shirley's Somebody Special who is becoming an excellent producing dam.

Champion Shirley's Spring Fever bred to Champion Carolane's Fancy That had but two puppies, one of which is the Willeys' latest champion, Shirley's September Morgan. The repeat breeding, however, has produced three little girls.

Champion Shirley's Sunday Cowboy bred to Debaru's Dyna-Mite Doll (Shirley's Scheherazade is Doll's dam) produced Champion Shirley's Spurs That Jingle in the second litter, and Japanese Champion Shirley's Sky Rocket from the first. Sky Rocket was a Best in Show winner. Cowboy produced another Japanese champion when bred to Debaru's Bangerette, this one also a Best in Show winner. Her name, Japanese Champion Bar-Be's Benn A Truckn.

Champion Shirley's Spectacular Bid has granddaughters in the ring and winning and will soon be the granddam of champions.

Shirley's Somebody Special, who has points towards her championship, was pulled from the show ring to be bred to Champion Carolane's Fancy That, which proved to have been the right move as they produced the Willeys' Champion Shirley's Strike My Fancy who, in 1983 and 1984, has proven himself to be an outstanding Special; he seems destined to become a good producer as well.

In May of 1975 the Willeys purchased Kar-Sim's If Only from Karen Simmons. "Iffie" was a Best of Breed winner from the classes, including the Miniature Schnauzer Club of San

Diego 1975 Specialty. Upon completion of her championship, she was bred to Champion Shirley's Show Time, in which litter she produced Champion Shirley's September Song, American and Japanese Champion Shirley's September Rain, and Shirley's September Morn, C.D.X.

Champion Shirley's September Song had but one litter and one puppy, who proved to be a good one, Champion Shirley's Solo by Champion Carolane's Fancy That, being a Group winner from the classes at one year old.

American and Japanese Champion Shirley's September Rain went to Japan at five years of age, having been out of competition for more than two years. He made his Japanese Championship handled by Tomai Fujimata, who co-owns him with Shirley Willey.

Shirley's September Morn, C.D.X., co-owned by Shirley Willey with Bobette Gowan-Tomasoff, produced but one puppy, who is Champion Bobette's Mona Lisa, C.D. After John Tomasoff put a C.D. on Mona Lisa, she was bred to Champion Carolane's Fancy That, producing the close-to-championship Bobette's Bang Bang.

At present, Champion Shirley's Show Time is the Willeys' top producing dog, with seven American Champions to his credit, one of them a Japanese Champion as well. He has four champion grandchildren, and three generations of his progeny presently have points in conformation competition.

The Willeys look forward eagerly to their next generation of both show dogs and obedience dogs, and to continuing to breed happy, healthy, intelligent Miniature Schnauzers for others as well as themselves to enjoy.

Ch. Mankit's Bang Bang of Dunbar winning the breed at Kern County K.C. in 1971. Handled by Ric Chashoudian for owners, Shirley's Miniature Schnauzers, Simi, California.

Skyline

Skyline Miniature Schnauzers, Carol A. Parker's very famous kennel at Vail, Arizona, have become tremendously influential and important in this breed since their inception, in 1969, with the purchase of Orbit's Lift Off from Fran Cazier of Orbit Kennels, a successful West Coast bloodline. Lift Off was breeder-owner-handled to her championship as well as obedience degrees through C.D.X. She made a leg on her U.D., and had some preliminary training towards tracking as well, but the conformation ring was Carol Parker's first love, and soon all efforts were going in that direction. Lift Off was bred to Champion Laddin of Arador to produce her first litter, and Skyline Kennels' first champion.

This was Champion Skyline's Silver Lining, shown only in the Bred-by-Exhibitor Class; from which she won several Bests of Breed while on the way to her title. She became Skyline's true foundation bitch, producing six champions, five of which themselves became multiple champion producers. Today the number of champions directly descended from her number is close to two hundred, which is indeed impressive.

Over the past 13 years, Skyline has bred and/or owned over 30 champion Miniature Schnauzers, many of them top winners and top producers. The most famous of these is Champion Skyline's Blue Spruce, a Silver Lining son sired by the Best in Show winner, Champion Sky Rocket's Upswing. Spruce is still alive and healthy and producing additional show quality puppies to add to his record of 48 champion offspring, numbering among them many Group winners, Best in Show winners, and Top Producers. Many splendid bloodlines have been founded on this outstanding dog.

Skyline's breeding program blended two highly successful lines, the noted West Coast breeding of Fran Cazier's Orbit and Arador with the mid-Western Sky Rocket bloodlines. The resulting blend is what Carol Parker has been building on over the generations.

Returning to the subject of Blue Spruce, who is unquestionably one of the breed's all time "greats," he was the 2nd Top Producing Sire in breed history in 1984. In 1976 he was campaigned by his breeder-owner to No. 1 Miniature Schnauzer in the United States, winning six Specialties including the American Miniature Schnauzer Club National at Montgomery County. His offspring include numerous group and Best in Show winners, as well as many other Top Producers.

Champion Skyline's Signature, by Blue Spruce ex Champion Skyline's Frostflower, as a nine-month-old puppy won Best in Sweepstakes

Am. and Can. Ch. Skyline's Blue Spruce, by Ch. Sky Rocket's Upswing ex Ch. Skyline's Silver Lining. Born Nov. 1973. Currently the 2nd Top Producing sire in breed history. Campaigned in 1976 by his breeder-owner to No. 1 Miniature Schnauzer in the United States. Many Group and Best in Show winners included among his offspring. Carol A. Parker, owner, Vail, Arizona.

This magnificent Schnauzer bitch is Ch. Skyline's Silver Lining, by Ch. Aladdin of Arador ex Ch. Orbit's Lift Off, C.D.X. the foundation and first champion at Carol Parker's Skyline Kennels. It is interesting to note that Fran Cazier, owner of the Orbit Miniature Schnauzers, was for a number of years editor of *Kennel Review* magazine, and is now holding that position for a leading women's magazine.

at the Delaware Valley Miniature Schnauzer Club Specialty under breeder-judge Anne Kaeppler, the same weekend earning a 5-point "major" from the junior puppy class at the American Miniature Schnauzer Club National with Montgomery County. In 1983, "Dodger" was a top contender for No. 1 Miniature Schnauzer in the United States until late in the year, when his record was eclipsed by his spectacular young son, Champion Skyline's Storm Signal. The latter, from Skyline's Valley Forge, was born in April 1982. It is felt that "Thunder" should have a significant impact on the breed. He finished his championship during the summer of 1983 at the American Miniature Schnauzer Club Specialty during June, then debuted as a Special in September. Within two short months he had skyrocketed into the position of No. 1 Miniature Schnauzer in the United States for the entire year, this record aided considerably by his winning all four days of the Montgomery County weekend, entries of more than 100 each day, a feat unheard of in the breed prior to that time. He is being campaigned widely in 1984, and has already been accepted by breeders nationwide.

Champion Valharra's Extra Allaruth, by

Champion Valharra's Extra Valharra's Magic Melody, was whelped in April 1979, bred by Enid Quick of Valharra and Ruth Ziegler of Allaruth, and purchased by Carol Parker after earning title in 1981. During 1982 he was heavily campaigned by Clay Coady and ties as the No. 1 breed winner for that year, his successes including six Specialty Show Bests of Breed, and Best of Breed at Westminster. "Bentley" was added to the Skyline breeding program to provide an outcross to the dam's side of the pedigree of their foundation bitch, Champion Skyline's Silver Lining.

Another of Carol Parker's very famous winners is the Blue Spruce son, Champion Skyline's Star Spangled Banner, from Champion Skyline's Little Britches. This one completed championship while still a puppy, winning Specialty Bests of Breed from the classes, and finished his first coat by winning Best of Breed at the American Miniature Schnauzer Club Specialty in New York in 1976. That year he wound up No. 2 Miniature Schnauzer in the U.S. behind his sire, and the following year, breeder-owner-handled, he swept through to No. 1 Miniature Schnauzer. His wins that year included nine Specialty Shows, a breed record in one year. His total Specialty Show wins stand at 13, including all three of the American Miniature Schnauzer Club Nationals (Montgomery County where he went

Ch. Skyline's Fern of Winrush, by Ch. Skyline's Blue Spruce ex Ch. Skyline's Little Britches, born November 1976. She is the dam of three champions and full sister to Ch. Skyline's Star Spangled Banner. Carol A. Parker, owner.

Ch. Skyline's Sonora, by Ch. Skyline's Blue Spruce ex Ch. Skyline's Frostflower, born Sept. 1979. One of three champions from this breeding, he is the sire of Ch. Skyline Scorcher, currently the Top Winning Miniature Schnauzer of all time in Japan. Sonora is owned by Florence Flood of Gulfside Miniature Schnauzers.

Ch. Skyline's X-Rated, by Ch. Valharra's Extra Allaruth ex Ch. Skyline's Fern of Winrush, born Sept. 1981. "Angela" finished easily including this 5-point major at the American Miniature Schnauzer Club Specialty at Great Western in June 1983. Carol A. Parker, owner, Vail, Arizona.

Ch. Skyline's Star Spangled Banner, by Ch. Skyline's Blue Spruce ex Ch. Skyline's Little Britches, enjoyed a spectacular show career. Breeder-owner-handled by Carol A. Parker.

on to Group 2, Great Western, and Associated Terrier Clubs). He was a multiple Group and all-breed Best in Show winner as well.

Carol Parker ventured into showing an uncropped bitch in 1976, Skyline's Fallen Angel, who earned 12 points including three "majors" owner-handled, as well as reserve at the National in June of that year, but never completed her title. She is a litter sister to Champion Skyline's Sally Forth. Then, in the early 1980's, a second venture was made with natural ears, and this time Champion Skyline's Seventh Heaven (Champion Regency's Right On ex Skyline's Summer Rainbeaux) finished in short order, charming everyone with her personality and beauty. She is the second uncropped Miniature Schnauzer to have completed championship in the United States, the first of whom was her half sister, Champion Regency's Equal Rights.

Skyline Miniature Schnauzers have had considerable impact on the breed in Japan, where Champion Skyline's Scorcher, by Champion Skyline's Sonora ex Champion Regency's Reward, born in 1981, has been exported. He finished in the States in just ten shows, including the American Miniature Schnauzer Club Specialty in New York in February 1983, and in Japan has become the Top Winning Miniature Schnauzer of all time, with Bests in Show and other exciting wins to his credit.

Sole Baye

Sole Baye Miniature Schnauzers originated in 1962 when owner, Yvonne B. Phelps of El Monte, California, acquired one very special little female, Hilda V. Yvonne and she too also attended her very first dog show that year. After watching these great little dogs perform, Ms. Phelps was immediately "hooked," and the mental decision was reached there and then to breed her own champion Schnauzers. What followed, of course, was much discussion, research, many questions, all of which eventually led this new fancier to Gloria Weidlein of Landmark Kennels and to Hilda V being bred to the great American and Canadian Champion Landmark's Masterpiece. The resulting litter consisted of three pups, two of which became Champion Sole Baye's Charlie Boots and Champion Sisterce of Sole Baye.

The next decision was the selection of a kennel name. Being from England, Yvonne's thoughts returned to her home town there, and again, after much discussion, one day Yvonne's husband said, "How about Sole Baye?" So Sole Baye Charlie Boots and Sisterce were registered and Sole Baye

Ch. Sole Baye's Bold Impulse at Silver State K.C., owner-handled to Best of Winners for a 4-point major by Yvonne B. Phelps.

Ch. Sole Baye's Mira Femme and Sole Baye's Sound Off, handled by Berget Coady and Yvonne Phelps respectively making a "clean sweep" of the Schnauzer awards. Sole Baye Schnauzers, El Monte, California.

Schnauzers began. Sole Baye as a point of interest, are the names of historical landmarks of some variety in Yvonne Phelps' home town. There is a Sole Baye Lighthouse, a Sole Baye Inn, etc. And now there are Sole Baye Schnauzers.

Sisterce, upon completion of her championship, was bred to Fancways Daktari, a highly pointed dog bred by Jean Fancy and owned by Mrs. W.W. Clark. From that mating came two champions: Champion Jo-Jak's Fancy Dan, owned by the Battaglias, and the Phelps' own Champion Manta of Sole Baye, along with Sole Baye's Short Stop who is pointed.

A second breeding of Sisterce, this time to Champion Starfire Criterion Landmark (then owned by Gloria Weidlein), produced the Phelps' Patrice of Sole Baye who, when bred back to her grandsire, Champion Landmark's

Masterpiece, produced Champion Sole Baye's P.K. Esquire, American Miniature Schnauzer Club Sweepstakes winner at six months and a few days old. He then went on to complete his championship which included Best of Breed wins, a Group placement, and the Miniature Schnauzer Club of Northern California Specialty, owner-handled all the way. As Yvonne says, "a high point in my life, and a very special dog to me." P.K. himself sired several quality offspring, but for various and sundry reasons they remained "pointed" instead of "finished."

Going in a different direction for the moment, Yvonne bought a puppy from Bob Davis, BJ Kennels, who became B.J. of Sole Baye. She just did not care for the show ring at all, so even though "B.J." was major pointed she was retired to the whelping box, which she liked much bet-

Ch. Sole Baye's Happy Talk owned by Yvonne B. Phelps.

Ch. Sole Baye's Miss Musket, completing her title taking Winners Bitch and Best of Opposite Sex at Beverly Hills K.C. for a 4-point major. Yvonne B. Phelps, owner, Sole Baye Kennels.

ter as caring for puppies seemed to her the main purpose in life—her own or anybody else's. Truly an excellent mother!

Bred to Champion Sky Rocket's Bound To Win, owned by the Homer Grafs, "B.J." presented her owners with five puppies. One became Canadian Champion April of Sole Baye, also major pointed in the United States. Another was the Phelps' own Champion Sole Baye's Bold Impulse, and one other very important little male, Sole Baye's Ambassador, who was in turn bred to Champion Manta of Sole Baye. This bitch seemed to specialize in small litters, giving just one or two pups at a time. Fortunately for the Phelps, one of these pups was to become Champion Sole Baye's Miss Musket who bred to Champion Sunshine Sounder, owned by K. Dumble produced what proved to be a truly exciting litter, consisting of six puppies. Two were sold as pets, to quote Yvonne "a mistake on my part, as both were easily finishable as I discovered later to my regret." The other four became Champion Sole Baye's Mira Femme, owned by Mr. Watanabe, who finished in three weekends and included the Miniature Schnauzer Club of Southern California and the American Miniature Schnauzer Club back-to-back Specialties. Then there was Champion Sole Baye's Sound Off, who was sold to Senor Jose Machline who left him here to become an American champion, which he began by taking reserve at the Miniature Schnauzer Club of Southern California Specialty as a puppy, then followed with a 5-point "major" at Devon, whence he finished in short order prior to leaving for his new home in Brazil and his Brazilian championship with multiple Group Firsts and Bests in Show to his credit.

Still another from this litter is the Phelps' own Champion Sole Baye's Sundowner who en route to his title won an impressive Best of Breed from the classes with an equally impressive Group 3rd at the prestigious Santa Barbara Kennel Club in tough competition, from which the Terrier Group winner went Best in Show that day. Needless to say, "Sunny" also finished in short order, with his career as a Special already on the books. He enjoyed multiple Specialty wins and multiple Group placements (first through fourth) bringing him to top rating in California dogs.

Then there is, also from this litter, Champion Maizelle of Sole Baye, co-owned with Linda Ramsey, another giving a good account of herself by finishing fast and with wins including a Best of Breed from the classes.

Yvonne repeated this obviously highly successful breeding, and second time around Miss Musket presented her with six bitches. Three were very small, but the remaining three became Champion Sole Baye's Sound of Music, co-owned with Linda Mooney; Marmac's Icon of Sole Baye, major pointed as a puppy and owned by Ralph Martin; and Sole Baye's Sunbeam, owned by Dr. Nagatomo in Japan. Sunbeam was Reserve Winner at her first show in Japan, and went Best in Show at her second.

A third mating of Miss Musket and Sounder resulted in a smaller litter of four, from which Sole Baye's Landoluce is already pointed and two more young hopefuls are awaiting their turn. This extremely successful sire/dam combination has put Miss Musket on the "top producers" list. However, Yvonne Phelps did want to see how she would produce if bred in a different direction, so for her fourth and final litter she was bred to Mr. Watanabe's Champion Tomei Super Star, and there are more very nice puppies here as well to watch for in the future. Needless to say, the Phelps take tremendous pride in Miss Muffet and her accomplishments, and she has earned a very special place in her family's hearts.

Getting back to Sundowner, his first litter has produced two champions. The first is Champion Musket von Yasmar, owned by Mr. and Mrs. Gordon, who began with a Best of Breed from the junior puppy class for a 4-point "major." An accident which nearly proved fatal, caused by poisoning, almost cost him his life. This was followed by a six-month recovery period, plus new furnishings as his legs had been shaved to accommodate intravenous injections. He came through with flying colors, though returning to the ring to complete his championship with three more "major" wins, finishing at age 18 months—not bad for a little dog who had spent several days in a coma, and who was not expected to live! His litter-mate, Champion Yasmar's Sunchant, owned by Mr. and Mrs. Ramsay, recently completed his championship with two back-to-back "major" wins.

Returning to B.J. of Sole Baye she was bred to Sole Baye's Short Stop, and from that breeding came another special *little* dog. Standing 12¾ inches at the withers, Champion Sole Baye's Happy Talk became a Miniature Schnauzer Club of

Ch. Sole Bay's P.K. Esquire owner-handled by Mrs. Yvonne B. Phelps.

Ch. Sole Baye's Sound of Music owned by Yvonne B. Phelps.

Ch. Sole Baye's Sundowner, Best of Breed and Group First in April 1983. Owned by Yvonne B. Phelps, Sole Baye Schnauzers.

Southern California Sweepstakes winner and breed winner. He, in his turn, was bred to a Champion Playboy Blockbuster daughter who produced Fabel's Little Lacy, in her turn bred to Champion Sole Baye's Bold Impulse, which produced the top winning Champion Hudson's Bold Decision, owned by the Luther Hudsons. Multiple breed wins, group placements, and a Miniature Schnauzer Club of Southern California Specialty were on this one's list of credits, along with being the sire of other pointed progeny.

Another littermate was Sole Baye's Redi-To-Win, who was the dam of two champions, sired by Champion Baws Strait Shot v Hansenhaus. Then there is also Canadian Champion Karussel of Sole Baye, owned by Mr. and Mrs. McDonnell; and the Phelps' own Champion Sole Baye's

Modus Vivendi. Regretfully, Redi was lost at far too early an age. However, Vivendi has recently been bred to Sundowner, and the Phelps are looking forward to seeing the results of that mating and Redi's grandkids.

Yvonne Phelps classifies herself as a "small breeder," usually holding the limit to one litter a year or, at most, three litters in two years. She breeds only one bitch at a time, in order to spend more time with the puppies, and starts working with and training them at as early an age as is possible. She takes great satisfaction from planning the breedings, selecting the "hopefuls," making sure that the others end up with suitable owners, then proceeding with the "hopefuls" and when they are old enough, seeing how competitive they will be against their peers.

Spring-Along

Spring-Along Miniature Schnauzers consist of about 20 dogs, mostly old timers living out their lives peacefully, owned by Mary Spring and her daughter, Kim, at Good Hope Farm in Landenberg, Pennsylvania. Once a working farm, Good Hope is an historic place.

The few breedings done there each year have given the Springs some top quality dogs.

The Springs' first Miniature Schnauzer champion was Spring-Along's So Happy, who finished with four "majors" and was a double grandson of Champion Helarry's Dark Victory, a top producer. So Happy was the Springs' foundation dog and still is behind almost every dog at Spring-Along. His dam was Eden Martine, a Dark Victory daughter, who became the Springs' foundation bitch when the kennel was founded in 1963.

Ch. Spring-Along Happy Gunner finishing his championship with a 4-point major at the supported entry of the Western Pennsylvania Kennel Ass'n. Gunner is owner-handled by Mary E. Spring, Good Hope Farm, Landenberg, Pennsylvania.

Spring-Along Black Pony, by Ch. Aljamar Rabbit Punch ex Spring-Along Black Jasmine. Taking points en route to the title at Lackawanna in 1981. Bred owned and handled by Mary E. Spring.

So Happy's son, Champion Spring-along Happy Gunner, finished easily including Winners Dog from the Bred-by-Exhibitor Class at Montgomery County in 1973, then as a "special" won many Group placements, always owner-handled.

Gunner's daughter, Champion Spring-Along Dark Lily, finished with two Specialty "majors," including the American Miniature Schnauzer Club in New York in 1979, where she completed her title going Best of Winners over approximately 100 Schnauzers in competition.

Although the Springs have had many winners, both before and since Lily, her accomplishments were a source of very special pride to Mary Spring. As she says, "Winning with a homebred, owner-handled, at a Specialty is the icing on the cake." I am sure we all agree!

Ch. Spring-Along Happy Gunner going Winners Dog from the Bred-by Exhibitor Class at Montgomery County in 1973. He was a homebred and owner-handled by Mary E. Spring.

In 1977, the Springs bred their first all-black litter, and the grandson of one of those puppies needs just three single points to finish as we write. Spring-along Black Pony is a Champion Aljamar Rabbit Punch son, out of a Champion Dufferton Mack the Knight daughter, combining the famous Gough and Aljamar black lines. Recently two more were added, a dog Spring-along Midnight and a bitch, Spring-along Black Violet, sired by the beautiful California dog Champion Haig's Black Renaissance. These puppies look excitingly promising at nine months of age.

Also, two children of Champion Penlan Peter Gunn have lately been acquired, Peter Gunn being the breed's all time top producing sire. The dog, Champion Carolane's Gangbuster, finished in 11 shows, and is already the producer of champions. The bitch, Carolane's High Society, has produced three near-champions in two litters, winning from the puppy classes. These are Spring-along Country Cheer, Spring-along Sweet Daisy, and Carolane's Ode To Spring, the latter belonging to Carol Beiles.

Mary Spring comments, "To say that we love the breed is, of course, an understatement, as we have lived with and loved Schnauzers for some twenty years. Kim crawled in her diapers with my early puppies. It's amazing that she handles so many sighthounds." Kim Spring is a highly successful and very talented professional handler who has obviously loved dogs from an early age.

Tel-Mo

Tel-Mo Kennels, at Shakopee, Minnesota, are owned by Lynda Lucast, who is a "second generation" Miniature Schnauzer breeder, being a daughter of Leslie Maudsley who has raised and exhibited the breed since 1960.

Tel-Mo has already owned or bred some very distinguished Schnauzers: Champion Blythwood Grand March, a Group winner; Champion Tel-Mo's Am I Something, another Group winner; Champion Mutiny Thunderation, Champion Tel-Mo's Sonny Boy (Group winner), Champion Carolane's Skywalker, Champion Tel-Mo's Top Cat (Best in Show and Specialty winner), Champion Tel-Mo's Likely Lover (Group winner), Ch. Tel-Mo's Dominating, Champion Tel-Mo's Peachie Keen, and Champion Tel-Mo's Fancy Free.

The Top Producing Schnauzer bitch for 1983, Carolane's Annie Get Your Gun, is also one of the Tel-Mo family, four of her offspring having finished during that year.

The foundation stock for Tel-Mo's breeding program was provided by Blythwood, Phil-Mar, and Mutiny breeding. Later Carolane and Penlan were added.

Tomlen

Tomlen Miniature Schnauzers are owned by Mrs. Helen Clifford at Clearfield, Pennsylvania. This is the home of the handsome and well-known bitch Champion Sercatep's Sweet Melody; another lovely winning bitch, American and Canadian Champion Tom Len's Sassy Sissy; and the very promising youngster Tom Len's Ka Ka Ka Katie.

Mrs. Clifford has, as well, some striking "young hopefuls" in the kennel, who it is hoped, will follow in the successful winning footsteps of the aforementioned three.

This is the noted Top Producer bitch, Carolane's Annie Get Your Gun, daughter of Ch. Penlan Peter Gunn ex Carolane's Heaven Sent, bred by Carol Beiles, owned by Lynda Lucast, Tel-Mo Kennels, Shakopee, Minnesota.

Ch. Sercatep's Sweet Melody taking Best of Opposite Sex at Trumbull County in 1982 for owner Mrs. Helen Clifford, Clearfield, Pennsylvania.

Travelmor

Travelmor Miniature Schnauzers are the hobby of those two great enthusiasts, William and Olive Moore, and have brought many honors home from the shows to their kennel at Trenton, New Jersey.

The story of Travelmor begins in 1957 when Bill received from Olive a Christmas gift in the form of Yankee's Dark Drama, purchased from the famed bird sculptor Edward Marshall Boehm, who was also a dog breeder and judge. Then with the Boehms one day at Tom Gately's kennel, the Moores first saw the handsome Champion Cosburn's Esquire, a linebred grandson of American and Canadian Champion Benrock Beau Brummell, and it was decided that the Boehms and the Moores would own him together. Esquire, a leading winner of that period, was a Top Producing Sire, and had been bred at Cosburn Kennels, owned by William and Ethel Gottschalk in Ontario, where he sired 14 champions. He had been owned by John Graziano, from whom he was purchased by Mrs. Priscilla Deaver, winning well for her Sparks Kennel. It was from Mrs. Deaver that this mighty little dog was purchased by the Boehms for Yankee Kennels and by the Moores for Travelmor.

Edward Marshall Boehm passed away in 1960, at which time the Moores become sole owners of Esquire and also most of the Boehms' breeding stock with dispersal of that kennel. Included among the Schnauzers was the son of Esquire, Yankee Pattern Maker, who was the Moores' first owner-handled champion.

The first homebred champion at Travelmor, Beach Boy, also gained his title owner-handled with some prestigious wins including Best of Winners at the October American Miniature Schnauzer Club Specialty and at the Mount Vernon Specialty. Several other champions followed along swiftly, and Travelmor was on its way.

Then came Champion Travelmor Witchcraft, who combined three crosses to Esquire in his pedigree. I think it quite safe to say that "Crafty" right from the beginning was "the" dog so far as the Moores were concerned. It was feared that Witchcraft's career might have been ended without ever starting when he suffered a

Headstudy of Ch. Cosburn's Esquire, foundation sire at Travelmor, owned by Olive and Bill Moore.

A delightful "at home" scene from Travelmor Kennels. Bill and Olive Moore surrounded by a group of their champions. Travelmor is located at Trenton, New Jersey.

broken leg at age five months, leaving him hobbling in a cast for three weeks as the Moores worriedly considered the possible consequences. "Crafty" came out of it just fine, though and owner-handled won 64 Bests of Breed and 25 Group placements. Included in his record was Best of Breed at the American Miniature Schnauzer Club Specialty Show under the late famed authority Percy Roberts.

Five champions sired by Witchcraft included a dog, Champion Travelmor's Fantazio, who was exported to England where he was widely used at stud. He and his son, English Champion Buffel's All American Boy of Deansgate, stand behind a number of noted champions successfully carrying the Travelmor banner through both England and Sweden. Another of Witchcraft's offspring was the important producing bitch, Travelmor's Tattle Tale.

Recently another export has gone from Travelmor to England, appropriately named Travelmor's From Us To You. This daughter of Champion Sky Rocket's Travel More ex Champion Reflections Lively Image, was the Challenge Certificate winning bitch at her first show there when still less than a year old, where she

went on to Best of Breed in an entry of 128.

After several years of breeding tightly within their original line, the Moores felt the need of a dominant outcross. In judging the American Miniature Schnauzer Club Sweepstakes at Montgomery County in 1973, where Olive awarded Best in Sweepstakes to a daughter of Champion Sky Rocket's Uproar (sire of 35 champions) and the 6-9 Month Dog class to a son, future Champion Sky Rocket's Bound To Win, Olive decided that this would be the way to go in their future breeding program. Thus it was that during the following year future Champion Sky Rocket's Travel More joined the Schnauzer family at the Moores, where he has made an excellent record as the sire of champions.

A very happy day in the lives of Bill and Olive Moore was March 16th, 1971 when Jennifer Allen came to take charge of the Travelmor Kennels. The Moores had advertised in *Dog World*, and Jennifer, who was 19 years of age at the time, had replied. She was working then in a veterinary clinic and had her own grooming business, so was certainly well qualified for the sort of help the Moores needed. She came to Travelmor for an interview, returned to spend

Two champion offspring of Ch. Travelmor's Gay Blade; *left,* Ch. Travelmor's Witchcraft, handled by Olive Moore, taking Best of Breed; *right,* Ch. Travelmor's Mirage, Best of Opposite Sex. The show, Queensboro Kennel Club, 1966. Gay Blade was the fourth champion from Ch. Travelmor's Witch's Brew; Mirage the fifth from Ch. Travelmor's Witchcraft.

three weeks at home, and since that time has been at Travelmor to stay. Jennifer was adopted by the Moores, and it would be impossible to find a more congenial and happy trio than these three people make. Jenny does most of the grooming and handling of the Travelmor homebreds, taking particular pride in their American Miniature Schnauzer Club Sweepstakes record in recent years.

Olive Moore has earned tremendous respect as a Terrier judge, having officiated at Specialty events from coast to coast including Montgomery County.

Valharra

Valharra Miniature Schnauzers, owned by Mrs. Enid Quick of Dixon, Illinois, are a classic example of the benefit of starting one's breeding program with the right bitch. Of course, everyone cannot find what they would really like to have at the time needed. But in the case of Mrs. Quick, good fortune was very much on her side when she was able to purchase Champion Faerwynd of Arador and when, to go with her, she chose a young dog she had acquired specifically

for that purpose, to be bred to "Winni." This was Champion Allaruth's Daniel.

"Winni" had produced two litters, each including three champions, when she arrived at Valharra. Bred by Margaret Haley, she was a daughter of Champion Fancway's Pirate Jr. of LaMay (Champion Marwyck Pitt-Penn Pirate—LaMay's Little Goldilocks) from Champion Fancways Vampira (Champion Fancway's Tom Terrific—Hit Parades The Twist).

Champion Allaruth's Daniel was by Champion Boomering of Marienhof (Champion Blythewood Ricochet of LaMay—Champion Hansel's Prudence of Marienhof) from Allaruth's Bebe (Champion Landmark's Masterpiece—Champion Allaruth's Jade).

The Winni-Daniel combination well lived up to expectations. This litter produced a dog who will never be forgotten, and who goes down in history as one of the truly GREAT Miniature Schnauzers. This was Champion Valharra's Dionysos, who became a multiple Best in Show, Terrier Group and Specialty winner and the sire of 30 champions. He was, truly, an unforgettable dog, who was 15 years of age at the time of his death in 1984.

Winni, in her lifetime, produced a total of 16 champions, making her the top producing Miniature Schnauzer Bitch and the second top-producing Terrier bitch of all time. Her last champion daughter is Champion Valharra's Melba Moore, C.D., who is not only Valharra's only champion bitch to have earned a C.D. title in obedience but also one of the very few to have done so for this breed.

The dog whom Enid Quick is quoted as considering the best Valharra has ever bred is Champion Valharra's Extra, who is a widely admired multiple Best in Show winner.

Another splendid producing bitch at Valharra is the daughter of Champion Moore's Max Derkleiner, Valharra's Alexis, who became the Top Producing Bitch of 1974 as the dam of Champions Valharra's Dardanella, Diplomat, and Champion Moore's Deebarra of Valharra sired by Dionysos, who had nine of his progeny finish in that year alone.

It is interesting to note that Dionysos was a third generation Top producer (Vampira to Winni to him), which once again proves the fact that from a producing line one gets producers!

The top producing Miniature Schnauzer bitch of all time, Champion Faerwynd of Arador, dam of 16 champions including Ch. Valharra's Dionysos, the sire of 30 champions. This was the foundation bitch at Valharra, the famous kennel owned by Mrs. Enid Quick.

One of the Wa-Han-Ka Miniature Schnauzers with Labrador friend. Mr. and Mrs. George H. Roberts, take pride in the excellent temperament of their dogs.

Wa-Han-Ka

Wa-Han-Ka Kennels at Hornell, N.Y. are long established and owned by Mrs. George H. Roberts. Foundation bloodlines here came from Mr. Higgins' Geelong Kennels in New Jersey, from Mrs. Leda Martin's Ledahof dogs, from Champion Dorem Display descendants and from Blythewood. Dogs from this kennel are to be found in Germany, Brazil, Canada, Japan, Italy, and in all parts of the United States including Hawaii. Mrs. Roberts takes special pride in the good disposition and personality of her dogs, who are true family dogs in every sense of the word.

The multiple Best in Show winning Ch. Valharra's Dionysos, sire of 30 champions, was bred and owned by Mrs. Enid Quick, Valharra Kennels, Dixon, Illinois. Here winning Best in Show at Lake Shore in 1972.

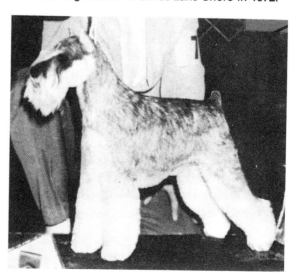

Walters' Ebony Snowman at four and a half months old. By Ch. Walters' Black Bonus ex Cynder Cone. Owned by Dolores Walters.

Walters

Walters Miniature Schnauzers, at Burbank, California, belong to Dolores Walters who bought her first of the breed, a salt and pepper puppy, in about 1960, when the major portion of her time was devoted to the raising of her two small boys, who were later followed by another boy and a girl.

Despite the demands of this growing family, Dolores became greatly interested in the Schnauzer, which she had bought as a pet with a complete lack of knowledge of the breed. As she says, "I soon learned fast, as she knit and purled in the front and rear and when shown did not look at all like the others." This bitch was bred to some nice dogs, but was just not a brood bitch, either. Despite all this, Dolores loved her every moment until the end of her 13 years. She had been bought as a "family dog," and at that she was entirely satisfactory! This bitch taught Dolores many things, and served as her "guinea pig" for learning about grooming, etc., while her

puppies paid for the grooming equipment. Thus the learning process was under way!

Dolores next fell in love with a black and silver, deciding that was what she wanted. Again she had a lot to learn, this being a recessive gene. She finally got a lovely "doggy" bitch who was a double Champion Melmar's Jack Frost granddaughter, and from her produced some outstanding puppies. She was bred to black and silver, and became the foundation bitch for Walters' Schnauzers. Her name, Pat-Je's Country Bumpkin. Out of a litter of nine, two sisters finished, Champion Mio's April Showers and Ch. Melmar's Christy Lee. This bitch stands behind all of the present day Walters' Schnauzers. She was bred to dogs selected to complement her, and produced several champions and others highly pointed, but Dolores, being so involved with her children, feels that she really did not have the time to do those early Schnauzers full justice, including not knowing how to place them advantageously as future show prospects.

A grandson of this bitch, Champion Walters' Irish Coffee (by Champion Landmark's Masterpiece), started Dolores Walters into the blacks. She had a call for a breeding to a black bitch, and bought two bitches from the puppies, both black —so there she was! At the time she was not terribly thrilled with the color, but felt that the timing was good for someone to work to improve them as the blacks were not too outstanding in those days. So she accepted the challenge! As owner of a good foundation salt and pepper stock, and not afraid of the "trial and error" method, she was not swayed by the warnings that she would never win with a black, accepting it rather as a challenge which she set out to disprove. Things fell in place for her just right as far as type was concerned, so now she was really "hooked." To date she has produced four black champions and others who are pointed. So she now is working on producing that long-awaited black and silver, using her excellent blacks. Since it was necessary to do so, she has created her own bloodline.

Walter's Miniature Schnauzers have been shipped to Taiwan, Mexico, Canada, Sweden, Norway, Denmark, Belgium, and Japan. They have won in all three colors, with Japanese and Danish champions among them and others who are pointed. Champion Walters Dazzling Black is the only champion who can boast of titles in

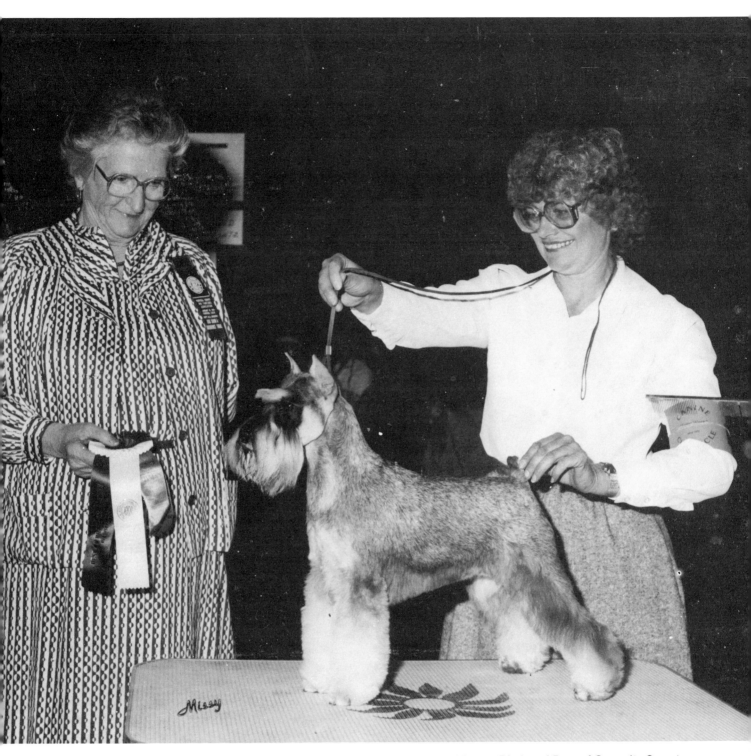

Tomei Jus-Me-Too of Walters, litter sister to Ch. Tomei Super Star, takes Winners Bitch and Best of Opposite Sex at Ventura K.C. in 1983. Handled by Barbara Wysocki for owner Dolores Walters.

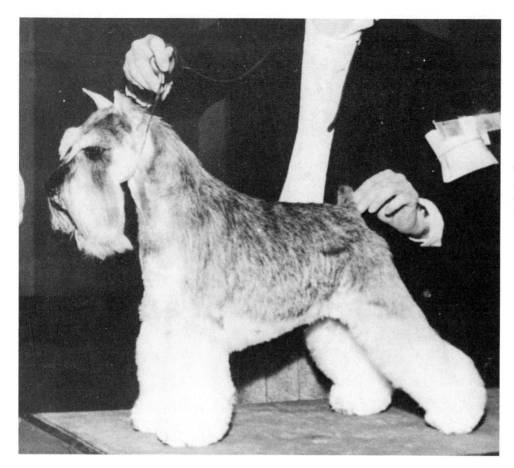

FOUR countries. Interestingly, he gained his American championship after having gone to Japan where he gained Japanese Kennel Club Grand Champion honors, then was shipped back to the States where he finished in one coat. He made the third generation black champion for Mrs. Walters.

As hers is a very small kennel, Dolores Walters feels quite rightly that she has done well, and her hopes are high for doing still better in the future. She comments on the fact that increasingly more breeders are becoming involved with the black Miniature Schnauzer. In less than ten years with blacks, she has achieved quality which she hopes to maintain, and she still loves and owns salt and peppers, too. She is a lady who has devoted close to 25 years to breeding splendid Miniature Schnauzers successfully.

Wyndwood

Wyndwood Miniature Schnauzers, owned by Barbara A. Hall, Amston, Connecticut, are the result of a family pet having been purchased back in 1969 who was so delightful to own that she completely "hooked" her owners on the breed. Barbara started attending dog shows, after which she purchased a three-month-old puppy as a show prospect, a new venture for her as he was her first show dog and he went on to complete his title. This was Champion Tare Rear Admiral, who combined the Blythewood and Sky Rocket lines.

In 1981, in partnership with Sandra Nagengast, Barbara purchased a six-month-old puppy from Arlene and Richard Smith, Richlene Kennels, who became Ch. Richlene's Top Billing. The Smiths' dogs are from the Penlan line. This new boy finished his championship in short order, and gained the notable distinction of winning the breed at Montgomery County when only 14 months of age. This is a super show dog and a top producer. Barbara is especially thrilled with the results she has attained in combining the Penlan and Sky Rocket lines, citing Champion Wyndwood Big Spender and Champion Wyndwood Back Packer as two good examples of what she has accomplished with this combination.

Over the years, Wyndwood has developed from a small to a medium sized hobby kennel, showing and breeding, striving for excellence of the breed.

Future Ch. Tare Rear Admiral, at four months of age, takes a few moments off from playing. Barbara A. Hall, owner.

Wyndwood Sweeter Than Honey, the dam of Ch. Wyndwood Big Spender, owned by Barbara A. Hall, Amston, Connecticut.

Miniature Schnauzers just after pet grooming. Owned by Barbara Hall.

Wy-O's

Wy-O's Miniature Schnauzers at Boise, Idaho, are the result of Wyoma and Owen Clouss having purchased a breeding quality pet puppy in 1974, only to have friends tell them she was show quality. As novices, they had not really understood that her sire, Champion Hughcrest Hugh Hefner, had been a Top Miniature Schnauzer for several years! They got together with well-known handler Paul Booher, and soon found themselves the proud owners of Champion Pine Needles Playboy Bunny. To the Clousses' knowledge, she was the only Miniature Schnauzer bitch to win a Group First in the United States during the year 1975. They next bought her half-sister, and soon had their second champion, Champion Vintage Hobo's Wife.

Meanwhile disaster struck as the Clousses discovered that certain Schnauzers in both their bitches' pedigrees were suspected to be carriers of congenital cataracts. Time out for test breeding! Bunny "had not been a very successful mother, so we spayed her and test-bred her daughter, Liz," Wyoma Clouss tells us. Hobo's Wife produced the Clousses' first homebred champion in that litter, Champion Wy-O's Tough Little Cookie, from their first cross to the Sky Rocket line. Their third purchase was a line-bred Sky Rocket male to use as a stud in the development of their breeding program. This was Champion Jadee's Hush Up. When he completed his title, Wyoma decided to handle him

Ch. Wy-O's Tough Little Cookie at ten months in her owners' back yard. Not yet being shown at that time, she is certainly eye-catching with the excellence of her reach and drive. Wyoma and Owen Clouss, Boise, Idaho.

Ch. Jadee's Hush Up owned by Owen and Wyoma Clouss, Boise, Idaho. Listed as a Top Producer, Hush Up has sired five American Champions and a Canadian Champion.

herself in the ring as a Special, and even though as a novice handler she dropped his lead the first day they appeared together in the ring, he placed in the Group and Wyoma was hooked!

Specialing Hush Up on a limited basis, Wyoma learned a lot while Hush Up won two Group Firsts and multiple placements. As a producer, Hush Up well fulfilled his owners' hopes right from the beginning, now being the sire of five American Champions and a Canadian Champion. He was also the sire of their two Bunny granddaughters through Liz, now well on their way to their titles, and grandsire of their third champion. It was especially thrilling for Wyoma to show the youngest bitch, Wy-O's Right Answer, to win Group First from the 6-9 puppy class in the fall of 1983.

It is the Clousses' plan to continue breeding in the Sky Rocket line, as they are well pleased with the basic type and quality they have found and anxious to continue tightening their pedigrees. Movement and soundness have been of prime importance to these breeders right from the first, and they are working to stamp in the style and outline they also admire.

Since the fall of 1982, the Clousses have enjoyed a home computer purchased specifically to keep their dog records—everything from pedigrees to show records and expenses to writing letters. The computer, Wyoma notes, has made record keeping interesting rather than a chore.

All the Clousses' Schnauzers are housedogs. Though they sleep at night in airline crates, there is no "kennel."

Can. Ch. Sylva Sprite Snowy Mittens, handsome winning Miniature Schnauzer owned by Sylva Sprite Kennels, Dr. Dorothy Griggs and Mrs. Joanna Griggs, Guelph, Ontario.

CHAPTER FOUR

Miniature Schnauzers in Canada

Am. and Can. Ch. Cosburn's Aristocrat was the first Canadian-bred to complete championship in the United States. He was Best of Breed at the Canadian Specialty in 1952 and in 1954. Owned by Cosburn Kennels, Mr. and Mrs. W. Gottschalk, Ontario. Full brother to Ch. Cosburn's Admiration, the sire of Ch. Cosburn's Esquire. Photo courtesy of *Schnauzer Shorts,* Dan Kiedrowski.

Morle v.d. Ludwigshohe, a German-bred male Miniature Schnauzer, went to Canada in 1927, to Mr. MacLimont; the dog evidently was not shown. So far as can be ascertained, the German-bred Nette v. Mumlingtal who was owned by Anfiger Kennels in the United States, was the first breed member to appear at Canadian dog shows. Nette was sired by Ari v. Schillerberg, older brother to Bodo v. Schillerberg, from from Siegerin Heidy v.d. Hermansburg, and she completed her championship there in 1933. No Nette progeny was left in Canada, although some generations later some of her American-bred descendants appeared, among them Champion Sorceress of Ledahof, who won a Canadian Best in Show at Quebec in 1948. This bitch produced a number of champions in the United States and a Canadian Champion. Other Canadian winners tracing their heritage back to Nette include Champion Dorem Delegate and Champion Marwyck Penn Hurst. Dorem Delegate was owned for a while in Toronto, later returning to the United States.

Canadian Champion Bendigo of Clearbrook, bred by the Misses Cluff, was the first Canadian-bred to gain the title of champion. The Cluffs had purchased Cora of Wollaton from Mrs. Kerns during 1935, breeding her to noted Kerns' winner Champion Rudy of Wollaton.

Four Miniature Schnauzers were entered for the Canadian National Show in September 1937. Then, as in later years, Ontario was the principal area for activity in the breed, although interest by now has spread from coast to coast.

Mr. Walter Reeves, a highly respected all-rounder judge in both the United States and Canada, acquired a Marienhof bitch in 1936, which we understand was either a black or black and silver.

It is interesting to learn that Miniature Schnauzers were originally shown in the Toy Group at Canadian Dog Shows.

American and Canadian Champion Handful of Marienhof, winning titles in both the United States and Canada within a brief length of time, did so prior to World War II. Champion Drossel of Furstenhof, an American-bred, became the first Canadian-owned bitch Miniature Schnauzer champion. She was a Handful daughter from Asta of Fuerstenhof, and was owned by Audrey Firman. American Champion Kathie of Marienhof added Canadian Champion

Can. Ch. Sensation Tribute to Frontenac, by Can. Ch. Frontenac's Cannon ex Can. Ch. Frontenac Cleopatra's Pearl, several times Best Puppy in Group and winner of many Group placements. She was Best of Breed at the Rideau Terrier Specialty in Ottawa in 1983 beating some very famous winners. Born November 1982, she is 13½ inches tall, was bred by I. Wessler and is owned by J. Gratton, Frontenac Kennels, Les Cedres, Quebec.

to her titles in 1944. A full sister to this bitch, Champion Kathie Khan of Marienhof, from Edwin Wright's quite active kennel in Montreal became the dam of Canadian Champion Winwel Love in Bloom, the first Canadian Champion from both Canadian Champion parents and the second Canadian-bred to gain the title.

Thomas C. Wylie was a gentleman who had good dogs, making notable wins in the 1940's, and he had chalked up some impressive credits when he was forced by poor health to give up breeding and return to England. He owned Champion Silvermist of Marienhof, who was the sire of the aforementioned Love In Bloom, who also sired Mr. Wylie's own homebred Champion Strathburn MP Alpha Cath (from Canadian Champion Princess Pat of Marienhof, the latter by Champion Cockerel of Sharvogue from Bubbi of Marienhof). Silvermist also sired, inbred to his daughter Cath, Strathburn MC Alpha Ann, the dam of American Champion MacMar Miniature Model, giving Ann the ap-

parent honor of having been the first Canadian-bred to produce an American champion.

Another prominent dog owned by Mr. Wylie was American and Canadian Champion Neff's Luzon, by Champion Kubla Khan of Marienhof from Rosel v. Neff II. Luzon was a consistent Best of Breed winner in both the States and Canada, and earned the American Miniature Schnauzer Club Annual Trophy for 1944. Luzon sired four American champions for the Schaumberg Kennels in California, then after coming to Mr. Wylie, sired Canadian Champion Strathburn JP Beta Misty.

By the time of closing his kennel, Mr. Wylie had owned two American and Canadian Champions, four Canadian Champions, and among them two homebred champions, making him unquestionably one of the IMPORTANT early fanciers. As an added note, Champion Strath-

Can. Ch. Frontenac's Franc Pirate, by Can. Ch. Fritzlar Carl ex Can. Ch. Postillion Pirate's Pearl, bred by J. and A. Gratton, owned by J. Gratton and L. Cote. This is Frontenac's top producing bitch with eight champions to her credit. 13½ inches, born in May 1976.

Can. Ch. Fronsen Gypsy, one of the many splendid Schnauzers from Frontenac Kennels, Armand and Jacline Gratton, Les Cedres, Quebec.

Can. Ch. Frontenac's Cannon taking the Best Terrier Award at Quebec for owners Armand and Jacline Gratton, Les Cedres, Quebec.

burn JP Beta Misty was the first Miniature Schnauzer to win the Group in Canada, this during 1948.

Cosburn Kennels, owned by William and Ethel Gottschalk, became the home of one of the truly important dogs to come to Canada from the United States, American and Canadian Champion Benrook Beau Brummell, who arrived in Ontario in 1951, just in time to win Best of Breed at the Miniature Schnauzer Club of Canada's first Specialty Show. Beau Brummell is in the background of at least 14 champions bred by the Gottschalks, five of them American Champions, eight Canadian Champions, and one South African Champion. These include the noted producing bitches Canadian Champion Cosburn's Deborah (five champions), the foundation bitch at Brittanhoff Kennels; American and Canadian Champion Cosburn's Beau Brummell's Honey (four champions); and American and Canadian Champion Cosburn's Sweet Tribute (three champions). One must also mention the memorable sire Champion Cosburn's Esquire, sire of 12 champions, who has contributed significantly to breed progress through Andrel, Miown and Travelmor Kennels in all of whose backgrounds he appears.

Champion Dorem Delegate is another fine American-bred who was brought to Canada by the Gottschalks.

Ch. Sylva Sprite Twilight Blue winning Best in Show from judge Doris Wilson. The only Miniature Schnauzer *bitch* to have won a Canadian Best in Show during the past 25 years. Owned by Sylva Sprite Kennels, Dr. Dorothy Griggs and Mrs. Joanna Griggs, Guelph, Ontario.

Can. and Am. Ch. Caldora's Returning Ace, the sire of ten or more champions, was an important Miniature Schnauzer in that breed's Canadian history during the 1960's. Owned by Mrs. Doris Hayes.

The Cosburn Miniature Schnauzers are also represented in Great Britain, Appeline Cosburn's Pickwick Peppers having gone to the Appletons there in the 1960's. He was an Esquire son from Canadian Champion Cosburn's Noranda.

The Miniature Schnauzer Club of Ontario was founded on September 26, 1951, its name subsequently changed four years later, to the Miniature Schnauzer Club of Canada. This is an active organization holding Annual Specialty Shows for the breed. Founder members were President, W. Harry McKendrick; First Vice-President, E.B. Reid; Second Vice-President, W. Gottschalk; Secretary-Treasurer, Mrs. Gottschalk.

Miniature Schnauzers in Western Canada

Our thanks to Mrs. Jean Fletcher for some background information on Miniature Schnauzers in Western Canada, and how the breed developed there. Mrs. Fletcher tells us that the person most responsible for the success of the breed in this area was the late Mrs. Doris Hayes of Burnaby, British Columbia. It was back in the 1950's when Mrs. Hayes started to finish homebred Schnauzer champions, and in September, 1958 her American-bred dog, Marwyck Hi-Hi, completed title.

The first Schnauzer owned by Caldora (from *CAL*, Mrs. Hayes' husband, and *DOR*is from her own first name) Kennels was a bitch imported from Missouri, who was bred to a dog from Chicago. From that litter came a bitch who founded an outstanding line of champions.

Most famous of the Hayes' dogs was Champion Caldora Returning Ace, who was Top Miniature Schnauzer in Canada over a period of four years. 1960 was a year of great triumph for this kennel and for Ace who was "Schnauzer of the Year" for the first time then, winning the Canadian Miniature Schnauzer Club award by an accumulation of points gained in 12 shows

Mrs. Doris Hayes, Caldora Kennels, Burnaby, Canada, was no stranger to the Best in Show spot some years back as a pioneer Canadian breeder of Miniature Schnauzers. Here she is with her Can. and Am. Ch. Caldora's Returning Ace.

Can. Ch. Postillion Pirate's Pearl, foundation bitch at Frontenac Kennels, by Am., Can., and Mex. Ch. Fancway's Pirate, Jr. of LaMay ex Helarry's Sweet Charity. Owned by Frontenac Schnauzers, the Grattons, Les Cedres, Quebec.

during it. His total was 1320 points, that of his closest rival, 512. That same year Ace's parents won the "Best Dam of the Year" and the "Best Sire of the Year" awards (both also owned by Mrs. Hayes), and she herself won her sixth "Breeder of the Year."

In addition to Ace, the kennel was also home of Canadian and American Champion Caldora's Van-Tell, Canadian Champion Caldora's Replacement II, Town and Country Nomad of Caldora, and others.

Another early breeder of Miniature Schnauzers in Western Canada was the late all-breed judge, Mark Gordon.

Mrs. Fletcher also owns and breeds some excellent Miniature Schnauzers, although Dachshunds are her principal canine love and the breed with which she is most closely associated.

On *left* of picture, with Armand Gratton, Ch. Onontio Scout; on *right*, with Jacline Gratton, Ch. Postillion Pirate's Pearl. Scout was the Grattons' first Canadian Champion; Pearl their foundation bitch and the dam of eight champions. These are the Schnauzers behind Frontenac's present day winners.

Frontenac

Frontenac Miniature Schnauzers, at Les Cedres, Quebec, in Canada, had their beginning when owners Armand and Jacline Gratton purchased the bitch who was to become Canadian Champion Postillion Pirate's Pearl from the Posts' Postillion Kennel, then located in New York, now established in California. Pearl had the Helarry bloodline behind her, which the Grattons wanted and which is also the foundation line behind the Hirsteins' Penlan Kennels. Her sire was one of the top producers of his time, American, Canadian, and Mexican Champion Fancway's Pirate Jr. of La May. Champion Postillion Pirate's Pearl is a half sister to one of the top producing bitches of all time, Champion Faerwynd of Arador.

Pearl was 8½ months old when the Grattons purchased her, and in show coat. She was shown the following month in Canada, making her new owners proud as she completed her Canadian title in two weekends. Twice Pearl was shipped back to her breeder for breeding, but unfortunately failed to conceive in both cases. So then it was decided to try her with an outcross, the Grattons' own male, Canadian Champion Onontio Scout, that time with better results. From this litter the Grattons have kept a female, Champion Frontenac's Pirate Gris-Sel. The following year she was shipped to Dale Miller (Barclay Square Schnauzers) to be bred to Champion Valharra's Big Sir. This dog was a son of one of the "best producing male in the United States," to quote Mrs. Gratton, and was, as well, a double grandson of Champion Faerwynd of Arador. From that litter of seven puppies one male was kept who is now American, Canadian, Bermudian Champion Frontenac's

Big Foot, the sire of six champions, and one female. Canadian Champion Frontenac's Big Deal, the dam of Champion Frontenac's Cannon and Champion Frontenac's Small Caliber, both sired by American Champion Penlan Peter Gunn, now top producing Schnauzer male of all time in the United States.

Sadly, Champion Postillion Pirate's Pearl met with an accident when only 6½-years-old, having whelped only four litters from which eight dogs were shown to their titles. One of her daughters, however, is doing a good job of "carrying on," Champion Frontenac Franc Pirate, having proven as good a producer as her dam, having also given the Grattons eight champions. While another daughter of Pearl, Champion Frontenac Cleopatra's Pearl, who was sired by Champion Frontenac Footstep, a Big Foot son, is also carrying on the family tradition with four champions already sired by four different dogs. This latter bitch is co-owned by Jacline Gratton with Irene Wessler of Toronto.

Jacline Gratton notes that Canadian Champion Postillion Pearl is in the pedigree of 40 of the 45 Frontenac champions, being either the dam, granddam, great-granddam or great-great-granddam. Thus her memory will live forever in the hearts of her owners.

Massawippi

Massawippi Miniature Schnauzers began, as is so often the case, with the purchase of a pet, in this case by Mr. and Mrs. S.I. Clark from Hillsburgh, Ontario, Canada. The pet did not have a distinguished background; however, the Clarks subsequently discovered that her dam, an import from Scotland, had an excellent British pedigree, featuring a number of British champions and top kennel names. Their pet's grandsire was British Champion Roundway Applejack, a British all-time top sire.

Thus it was decided to breed "Buffy," which the Clarks did twice, to a friend's Miniature Schnauzer purely to produce pets for their friends. They enjoyed raising the puppies, and became intrigued with the idea of contributing to the breed, by raising the very best possible. It was decided right from the outset that if they were going to raise and show Miniature Schnauzers they wanted to do it as breeders, not as purchasers, and they wanted to do it every step of the way themselves, including breeding, grooming, handling, etc. Fortunately their son,

Murray, became interested, too, making it a three-person family hobby ever since.

Starting out, casting about for a dog to breed to, the Clarks were extremely fortunate in meeting Joan Morden, owner of the outstanding Tannenbaum Kennel in Milton, Ontario. Her advice and help at that time and since have been of inestimable value to the Clarks, who began breeding to Joan Morden's excellent dogs, and two generations later they had their first champion and their real foundation bitch. Champion Massawippi Sunday Best, by Champion Tannenbaum Sunday Punch ex Massawippi Sam I Am.

Feeling the need to go further afield in their breeding program, the Clarks selected two American lines they particularly admired, these being the Fergusons' Skyrocket line (going directly back to Ruffian) and the Quick's Valharra line of splendid dogs. They bred their Sunday Best three times as follows: first, to Champion Blockley Knight of Mischief (linebred Skyrocket) producing Champion Massawippi Miss Mischief, from which breeding they are still pursuing various crosses and subsequent generations from this combination are looking very good; next to Champion Valharra's Dionysos, Sunday's grandfather, producing the beautiful Champion Massawippi Kiss Me Kate, now being crossed with the Skyrocket line; for the third litter, to the Grafs' Champion Skyrocket's Bound To Win, producing Massawippi In For A Penny. This last breeding has been the most spectacularly successful.

Penny has never been shown (except going Best in Match at an early sanctioned event) as the Clarks considered her too exaggerated in some ways. Pursuing the Skyrocket line, they bred her to the Abelov's Champion Skyrocket Victory Bound (this on Judy Ferguson's advice), producing three champions. The latter were Champion Massawippi Miss Conduct (Pippin) who finished in eight shows with four Bests of Breed and a Group second from the classes; Champion Massawippi Dancing Shoes (Jill), shown 20 times, who racked up two Group Firsts, nine other Group placements, 14 Bests of Breed including a Specialty, and who became Canada's No. 1 Miniature Schnauzer bitch in 1983; and Champion Massawippi Troubedour (Patrick), Canada's all time Top Winning Miniature Schnauzer—all systems—at only three years old. To date he was Canada's Top Schnauzer in 1981 and 1982, rising to No. 3 Terrier in 1982.

Ch. Massawippi Dancing Shoes, shown 20 times, the winner of two Group Firsts, nine other Group placements, and 14 Best of Breed which include a Specialty Show. Canada's No. 1 Miniature Schnauzer Bitch in 1983. Owned by Mr. and Mrs. S.I. Clark.

He retired with three all-breed Bests in Show, 35 Group firsts, about 70 other Group placements, and a string of 63 consecutive Bests of Breed, including Specialties, against the stiffest of competition. Patrick is a balanced, 'typy,' medium-sized dog who loves to show. To date he has sired three champions, two of which are Group winners from the classes, and he has beautiful puppies at home and elsewhere whom the Clarks are looking forward to seeing in the ring.

The Clarks are continuing to breed to dogs in the lines of their own, although they have recently begun to experiment a bit, slowly and cautiously, in a small way with other lines. As they remark, "one cannot linebreed forever" which is certainly true.

Currently there are five puppies of various ages at home with the Clarks. All, hopefully, are future champions, better than average examples of the breed. The kennel remains a small one as the owners like to watch carefully the progress and development of each litter, keeping the best, and only the BEST of the best for breeding. They have, in fact, sold two champions as pets as they were not quite what they wanted in their breeding program.

Sylva Sprite

The Sylva Sprite Miniature Schnauzers are owned by Dr. Dorothy Griggs and Mrs. Joanna Griggs, located at Guelph in Ontario. The kennel was established in 1959. A few years later the Griggs imported their first black and silver, Canadian Champion Walsh's Frosty Charmer, C.D. from Mrs. Jackie Walsh in Lombard, Illinois. This was during 1963, when black and silvers rarely were seen in the show ring. Frosty Charmer became the sire of Best in Show Canadian Champion Sylva Sprite Tonquin and the sire of Canadian Champion Sylva Sprite Benjamin, the latter the first black and silver to go Winners Dog at a Specialty Show in the United States, which he did at the Paul Revere Miniature Schnauzer Club Specialty in 1967, the only occasion on which he was ever shown in the States.

Frosty Charmer was the sire of Sylva Sprite Pyewacket who was shipped to Switzerland to become foundation for the black and silver line in Miss Frieda Steiger's "Schnauzi" Kennels during 1967.

The first black and silver dual (Canadian and America) champion was the Griggs's homebred Canadian and American Champion Sylva Sprite Snowy Mittens. The sire of Snowy Mittens was an English import, the small 12½ inch male who became Canadian Champion Eastwight Sea Voyager, C.D. and who had been bred by Miss Pamela Morrison-Bell. Snowy Mittens has not only enjoyed an exciting show career, but he is the sire of numerous champions, among them the Best in Show winning Canadian Champion Sylva Sprite Extra Dry.

Canadian Champion Sylva Sprite Twilight Blue, who was the only Miniature Schnauzer bitch to win a Best in Show in Canada during the past 25 years, is another of their memorable dogs to whom the Griggs point with pride.

So far, Sylva Sprite has finished 75 Canadian Champions, of which 20 have been black and silver. May there be lots more of the same for the Griggs in the future!

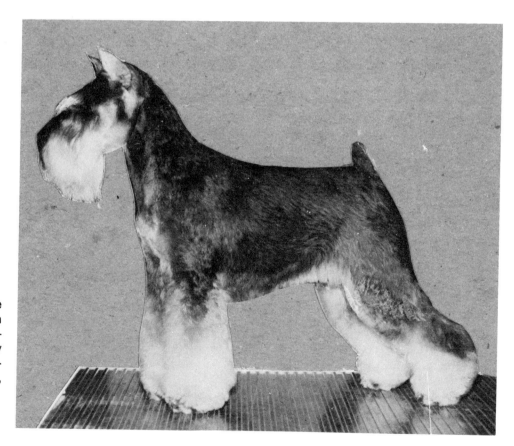

Can. Ch. Sylva Sprite Twilight Blue, born 1979 . Sylva Sprite Kennels. Dr. Dorothy Griggs and Mrs. Joanna Griggs, Guelph, Ontario.

Aust. Ch. Schonhardt Signature, noted Australian winner owned by Ms. Marelyne MacLeod-Woodhouse, Erskineville, New South Wales. Photo by Terry Dorizas, Sydney, Australia.

CHAPTER FIVE

Miniature Schnauzers in Australia

Australian Ch. Guadala Greta, owner-handled by Jeanette Tiltman, co-owner with Steve Tiltman, Cockatoo Valley, South Australia.

The more we learn about the Australian dog fanciers and their activities, the more greatly we admire their dedication and the quality of dogs being produced there.

Considerable rapport exists between the Australian fancy and ours here in the United States. It is quite usual nowadays for at least several judges each year from here to go there to officiate, and vice versa. This is good both ways, as it enlarges our true scope of what is taking place worldwide within the breeds of interest to us as individuals, and the exchange of ideas and opinions is certainly beneficial to all concerned.

The Australian standard for Miniature Schnauzers is based upon the English one. You will note that cropping of ears does not take place in that country either, and I personally find the expression and heads of the uncropped dogs to be attractive.

Australian breeders are using bloodlines from both England and the United States in their breeding programs, combining them judiciously and advantageously with their own.

The Casa Verde Kennels in New South Wales, owned by Mrs. Rees, are the earliest on record as having brought imported Miniature Schnauzers into Australia. English Champion Gosmore Wicket Keeper was the first to reach those shores from England, a son of American Champion Sternroc Sticky Wicket from Gosmore Peaches and Cream. Wicket Keeper only lived to become five years of age (1960-1965). Behind him in England he left a son, Lichstone Chasseur, who, although never a champion himself, became the sire of two English Champions, Lichstone Pacemaker and Sceptre of Settnor.

Wicket Keeper proved immediately successful in Australia, making his Australian title with ease and siring Champions Casa Verde Zipper, Casa Verde Mannequin and Casa Verde Diamond Jim, the latter two from Pickwick Buttons.

Australian Champion Deltone Deldario, owned by Mrs. C.V. Cerini, was a son of Wicket Keeper, bred in England, and a Challenge Certificate winner there before going to Australia. This little dog was the Best of Breed winner at the first championship Specialty Show held by the Australian Miniature Schnauzer Club in 1967. This Specialty was quite a clean sweep for Wicket Keeper offspring, as it was his daughter, Australian Champion Casa Verde Zipper, who

Guadala Gabrielle, owner-handled by V. Baron, is representative of the beautiful quality Schnauzer from Guadala Kennels owned by the Tiltmans, Cockatoo Valley, South Australia.

gained the award of Best Bitch.

The earliest Miniature Schnauzer Companion Dog Degree winner in Australia is said to have been Champion Casa Verde Handsome, by Champion Gosmore Trump Card ex Gosmore Spinners Wicket. Thus Casa Verde Schnauzers were obviously strong in working talents as well as conformation excellence.

During the 1960's, the first black to have been imported into Australia, Champion Jovinus Rigoletto, arrived there. He contributed well as a sire, his progeny including Koniglich Jason, C.D.

Champion Dorem Display is to be found behind the majority of the foundation stud dogs of Australia's early Miniature Schnauzers. The black dog, Rigoletto, by English Champion Jovinus Malya Swanee ex Jovinus Risotto, is of a German background, actually tracing back to Prinz v. Rheinstein.

Guadala

Guadala Kennels, breeders of Miniature Schnauzer, owned by Steve and Jeanette Tiltman, are situated in South Australia's picturesque Barossa Valley, which is Australia's foremost wine-making area. Initially the Tiltmans bred and exhibited Chihuahuas and, to a lesser degree, Rottweilers. But in May 1980 they took delivery of their foundation bitch in Schnauzers, Eastdon Aurora Belle, from Mrs. Rayma Ritzau. During an interrupted show career, Belle won 20 consecutive Challenge Certificates and 18 Bests of Breed. Four of the challenges have been Royal Show Challenges, one being at the Melbourne Royal Show, which is the largest dog show in Australia, and three at the Adelaide Royal Show.

Aurora Belle to date has produced three litters. From her first, of three puppies sired by English and Australian Champion Dengarse Take By Storm (imported from the United Kingdom) came an all-breeds Best in Show winner, Australian Champion Guadala Werewolf; and Australian Champion Guadala Greta, an Opposite Sex in Show winning bitch at the Schnauzer Club of Victoria, all varieties.

The second litter from Aurora Belle was equally successful. Bred to Australian Champion Schonhardt Copy Boy, she produced four puppies. These included another Best in Show all-breeds winner, Australian Champion Guadala Brunhilde; Guadala Siegfried, an outstanding young dog tragically killed in a vehicular accident when only seven months old en route to a show in Sydney; and Guadala Gabrielle, a multiple in-group and in-show winning bitch sparingly shown by her owners.

Champion Guadala Brunhilde has undoubtedly been the most successful Miniature Schnauzer in Australia during 1983 from what the Tiltmans tell us, having to her credit an all-breeds Best in Show at South Australia's most prestigious show, The South Australian Canine Association's Autumn Festival. "Hilde" was awarded Best in Group by Mrs. M. Boyd of New Zealand and awarded Best Exhibit in Show by Mrs. Michelle Billings from the United States. Hilde also achieved one runner-up to Best in Show and four Best Exhibit in Group awards. She won the 1983 Melbourne Royal Challenge Certificate and was Best of Breed at Sydney's popular 1983 Spring Fair under Schnauzer specialist Dr. Jan Nesvadba of

Switzerland. Hilde was also awarded the Best South Australian Bitch in Show at the Royal Adelaide Show, along with Best of Breed.

For her third litter, Aurora Belle was bred for the second time to English and Australian Champion Dengarse Take By Storm. A puppy bitch from this litter, Guadala Madchen, is currently making her presence felt in Specialty shows and all-breed show circles, with 13 in-group and four in-show awards to her credit.

Aurora gained her Australian championship title in 1981 after her first litter, and has been defeated only once for challenge points. She is the only Miniature Schnauzer bitch in Australia to have produced two all-breeds Best in Show winners. Upon Aurora's retirement from the show ring, Werewolf and Greta enjoyed success after success, taking out Best Miniature Schnauzer Dog and Bitch respectively at the Schnauzer Club of Victoria's Championship Show in 1982. Both Greta and Werewolf gained their Australian championship titles at this show, and have not looked back since. Also they have reproduced their fine quality in their progeny. Australian Champion Penfillan Siegerhund, who must be the youngest Miniature Schnauzer champion in Australia, is a son of Werewolf who completed title at only ten months of age. Previously the "youngest champion" distinction had been held by Brunhilde. Siegerhund is, to date, undefeated for challenge points and has won numerous group and show awards. His important wins include Challenge Dog at this year's Adelaide Royal, and Best of Breed at the Melbourne Royal. Werewolf has also sired other winning dogs in Victoria and in New Zealand.

Australian Champion Guadala Greta's progeny, sired by Brynsmor Joker are still very young, but had a major success at their first show, Guadala Sorceress winning Best Baby Puppy in Group and runner up to Best Baby Puppy in Show at an all-breed championship event.

The Tiltmans' breeding philosophy has been both simple and successful. They breed from only the very best of their bitches and they do a great deal of careful research on dogs they intend using at stud. Their kennel is numerically small, but has achieved a proven record of success in its short history. In their breeding program, major emphasis is placed on temperament. No matter how splendid a specimen may be in physical conformation, it is not, in these people's opinion, a breeding prospect unless it displays an

Aust. Ch. Guadala Brunhilde, well-known winner owner-handled by Jeanette Tiltman, Cockatoo Valley, South Australia.

outgoing and alert personality.

The Tiltmans tell us of an exciting annual canine spectacular which takes place in South Australia called the Battle of the Champions. This formal "black tie" affair is restricted to dogs who have achieved the supreme award of Best in Show at all-breed Championship Shows, and entry is by invitation only. Up until 1983 no Miniature Schnauzer ever had competed, but this year not only one but TWO Miniature Schnauzers had the honor, along with 25 other Best Dogs from South Australia and other states. These two Schnauzers were Champion Guadala Brunhilde and Champion Guadala Werewolf. Both of these dogs are true champions in every sense of the word, and both have made breed history in Australia. They are two of only four Miniature Schnauzers to have ever won all-breed Best in Show honors in Australia.

Guadala Madchen at the Adelaide Royal Show in 1983. Owner-handled by Steve Tiltman, co-owner with Jeanette Tiltman, Guadala Kennels, Cockatoo Valley, South Australia.

Schonhardt

The Schonhardt Miniature Schnauzer Kennels were established in 1974 by Ms. Marelyne MacLeod-Woodhouse, Erskineville, New South Wales, Australia.

The bloodlines at this kennel are predominantly Eastwight, those of Miss Pamela Morrison-Bell, for although Ms. Woodhouse did not herself import Eastwight stock, she had access to stock imported from there already in Australia.

English and Australian Champion Eastwight Sea Lord, who had come from the British kennel, has been successfully used by Ms. Woodhouse in her breeding program, following her first purchase of one of his daughters who, while still a puppy, became Australian Champion Thornor Suchi and did so on one coat! Among her wins were Best Exhibit in the Non-Sporting Group at an all-breeds Championship Show (with more than 1200 entries) where Suchi competed at only eight months old. And yes, lest any of our United States readers wonder if they have misread, Miniature Schnauzers ARE classified in the Non-Sporting Group in Australia.

Mr. N.A. Champion, of Thornor Kennels where Suchi had been bred, repeated the breeding from which Ms. Woodhouse obtained another exciting bitch, this one becoming Australian Champion Thornor Kakak Kechil. Not only did Kechil obtain her title of champion, but she proved an excellent producer, and in her second litter became dam of Ms. Woodhouse's Australian Champion Schonhardt Copy Boy, to date one of Australia's outstandingly consistent winning dogs.

Copy's wins to date are Challenge Dog at the Specialty Show for three consecutive years, going Best in Show on one of these occasions and runner up (after being beaten out by the Standard for the Best in Show) and Best Miniature in Show. At the most recent Specialty, before we received this material, Copy's seven-month-old puppy daughter, Schonhardt Signature, took Reserve Challenge and Best Minor in Show.

Copy retired at the last Specialty at age three-and-a-half years. His total show victories by then included one Best in Specialty Show, two Reserve Bests in Show (Specialty and All Breeds), seven times Best Exhibit in Group, five times Runner-Up Best Exhibit in Show, four Royal Show Challenges (three Bests of Breed) and Puppy of the Day, one Champion Sweepstakes and seven out of seven Puppy Sweepstakes' first place, and 54 Group placements. Copy was shown at fewer than 70 shows for the above wins.

Australian Ch. Schonhardt Copy Boy, well-known winner owned by Ms. Marelyne MacLeod-Woodhouse, Erskineville, New South Wales, Australia.

From three litters sired by Copy two Best in Show winning puppies were produced, one of whom is the bitch Champion Guadala Brunhilde who gained Best in Show at a mere 14 months of age. Copy is an extremely dominant sire who produces puppies similar to himself even in cases of complete outcross. He has also sired several black and silver puppies.

Arbey Dyna-Mite, imported from the U.K., is a bitch who was bred especially for Ms. Woodhouse by Mrs. Betty Fletcher of Arbey Kennels in England. This bitch combines the Eastwight and the Barclay Square (U.S.A.) bloodlines and Ms. Woodhouse especially wanted her as she represented not a complete outcross but, all the same, some new lines with which to work. Dyna-Mite was mated to English Champion Arbey Mistique who also combined the Eastwind-Barclay Square combination.

Then the dog was imported by her from the U.K., Rimmick Ricardo sired by English Champion Irrenhaus Impact at Risepark who had gone to England from the United States. Also a Barclay Square bred bitch again, to go with her Arbey bitch plus the puppies. Arbey Dyna-Mite whelped seven puppies in Australian quarantine, two of them males and five females.

Hi-Crest Triumph of Schonhardt was bred for Ms. Woodhouse by Mr. Arnold Hirahara, Hi-Crest Kennels in Hawaii. This one is by Sun-shine Indego and a Hi-Charge of Hansenhaus daughter, Hi-Crest Classy Chassy. Also she has added a bitch by the same dog from a different dam (a great-granddaughter of Charger). All of these go back to Skylines Blue Spruce, who is also behind Rimmick Ricardo.

Copy Boy to the time of writing has sired six Australian champions, all of whom have won multiple Group placements and Group firsts, or, as they put it in Australia, "Best Exhibit in Group," plus his Best in Show winners. In 1983 Copy retired after taking out Top Dog of the Year in the Schnauzer Club Points Score, and progeny from Copy and others in her kennels took Dog/Bitch Challenge at Brisbane Royal in 1982 and 1983; Bitch Challenge Adelaide Royal and Melbourne Royal in 1983; Dog Challenge in Hobart Royal 1983; and in Sydney Royal 1983, all of which have brought Ms. Woodhouse well merited pride as a breeder. Copy Boy now has progeny in Japan, Hong Kong, New Zealand, and Houston, Texas.

Schonhardt Signature attained her title while still a puppy on one coat, along the way gaining numerous Sweepstakes placements, Group and In Show placements, plus a C.K.A. Guinneas placement as well. She has been frequently complimented by the judges on her excellence, quality and balance. A bitch who is a true asset to the kennel.

CHAMPION MAXIMIN GRABEN OF DEANSGATE

Sire **BRYNSMOR JOKER**	Ch. Eastwight Sea-Goblin	Ch. Eastwight Sea-Gnome
		Ch. Eastwight Sea-Fantasy
	Tripaloe St. Opal	Rimmick Acapulco
		Dartvale Lusandra
Dam **SWEDISH & FINNISH CH. BARCLAY SQUARE MAXIMIN MINX**	Am. Ch. Skyrockets Uproar	Am. Ch. Skyrockets First Stage
		Tessie Tigerlily
	Am. Ch. Barclay Square Bugle Call Rag	Am. Ch. Valharras Big Sir
		Am. Ch. Barclay Square Bugle Ann

Engl. Ch. Maximin Graben of Deansgate, by Brynsmor Joker ex Swedish and Finnish Ch. Barclay Square Maximin Minx, owned by P. McLaren and E. Cooke, Deansgate Kennels, Rotherham, England.

CHAPTER SIX

Miniature Schnauzers in Great Britain

Eng. Ch. Risepark Toreador, by Ch. Risepark Bon-Ell Taurus ex Roundway Anklet, owned by Peter Newman, Risepark Kennels, England. Photo by Lewsby.

It was not until May of 1935 that Challenge Certificates were offered for Miniature Schnauzers at dog shows in Great Britain. Two years earlier the British Miniature Schnauzer Club had been established, but the breed was quite weak at that time both numerically and in breeder support, and the withdrawal, owing to illness of some of the largest and most important supporters of that time, forced liquidation of that Specialty Club in 1936, only three years after its beginning.

The original background fanciers of the Miniature Schnauzer in England had been the Hancocks, owners of Enstone Kennels, followed by Mrs. Simmons and her Crowsteps Kennels (who imported no less than 20 Miniature Schnauzers during the mid-1930's) and by Mrs. Rachel Firth, importer of the American-bred Dorem Domino who won the Challenge Certificate at 1937 Crufts. The loss of fanciers and kennels such as these was a hard blow for a "new" breed just earning its place in the Fancy. Yet that is what happened, and it was a difficult situation to be overcome. The breeders who remained, then, were Mrs. Langton Dennis, owner of Offley Kennels, and R.T. Colbourne with his Reden-

halls. Unfortunately, Mrs. Dennis died shortly thereafter, and then World War II had its devastating effect on the pure-bred dog world.

Reviewing the pre-wartime successes, it was in 1928 that Mr. Hancock imported a black Dutch bitch, Enstone Gerti van Duinslust. Two years later, in 1930, she was followed by the German-born Dutch Champion Enstone Ador v. Rheinstolz and Enstone Barbel von Dingshaus. All of these can be found way back in the pedigrees of many of today's British-bred winning Miniature Schnauzers. These Enstone dogs produced three of the first four Miniatures to gain championship honors.

From 1929 until May 1932, the Miniatures were registered with the Standard Schnauzers, delaying the granting of Challenge Certificates as three years of separate registration was necessary plus a total registration of no less than 80 of the breed. This number had been considerably exceeded when, at last, the Challenge Certificates were first made available to the breed in 1935.

It was also in 1935 that Great Britain officially changed the name of the breed to "Affenschnauzer," making its Specialty Club the British Affenschnauzer Club. Loud and clear

English Ch. Castilla Diamante, by Ch. Irrenhaus Impact at Risepark ex Ch. Castilla Zambra, is owned by Pam Radford and Dori Clarke in England. Photo by Radford.

breeding, with some very outstanding individuals among them. The offspring of two of these, Crowsteps Hasty, was the winner of two Challenge Certificates prior to World War II and he sired Quarrydene Hans, the sire of Offley Gray Shadow, one of the important producers of prewar days. Also three other Heinzelmannchen bitches from this breeding left their mark on future generations.

About the only Miniature Schnauzer breeding of the pre-war period to weather the storm and resume her Schnauzer activities following World War II was Mrs. Milsom of Quarrydene Kennels. This lady had started with the breed back in 1936, gained a championship title on Quarrydene Gretchen in 1939, and bred several postwar champions from Quarrydene Gelda who was herself a Challenge Certificate winner. Mr. Colbourne of Redenhall Kennels still occasionally bred a litter but no longer exhibited. To his Redenhall stock and to Mrs. Langton Dennis and her Offleys credit must go for the British postwar champions carrying pre-war bloodlines. Mrs. Dennis died during the war.

In postwar days a new group of Miniature Schnauzer fanciers were starting to appear, and bringing to Great Britain some excellent stock to use combined with their own from the Continent and from the United States. These include Mrs. Doreen Crowe with her Deltones. This lady's Champion Deltone Doughboy became the first to equal the show record of pre-war Champion Enstone Cito with the gaining of a total of eight Challenge Certificates. Doughboy was sired by the American-bred Rannoch Dune Randolph of Appeline who had been imported uncropped from the United States by Mr. Douglas Appleton for his Appeline Kennels. Doughboy did much to further the interests of show Miniature Schnauzers with the attention attracted to him at the shows, and his dominance as a stud has been tremendous. He is descended from the great Dorem Display.

Mr. H.D.P. Becker owns Dondeau kennels, where 15 or more champions were owned or bred in postwar years, including champions in Italy and South Africa.

The Miniature Schnauzer Club of Great Britain which was founded in 1953 has been an active organization in promoting the breed. The Schnauzer Club of Great Britain also welcomes Miniature fanciers as members. In keeping with the British Kennel Club's ruling, the standard

came the protests from Germany, and in August, 1936, the British Club, bowing to the German Klub, again became the British Miniature Schnauzer Club. In 1936, the British Club was disbanded, as we have noted earlier in this chapter. It was not revived as a separate organization until 1953. For the intervening time Miniature breeders belonged to and were committee members of the Schnauzer Club of Great Britain, which included Miniatures beginning in 1946.

We have already mentioned that Mrs. Simmons had imported twenty Miniature Schnauzers to her Crowsteps Kennels in the early 1930's. Dispersal came in 1936. Such a tremendous loss to the breed! The majority of these importations were of Heinzelmannchen

for both breeds is the same, apart from size, and the Miniature breed standard was reworded in 1954 to conform to this requirement. This is unlike the practice in the United States, where the Standard and Miniature Schnauzers are considered to be entirely independent breeds, each breed club making its own decisions with regard to the breed standard.

Deansgate

Deansgate Miniature Schnauzers are owned by Pamela McLaren and Elisabeth Cooke of Rotherham, South Yorkshire, England. We understand that this is England's largest kennel of Miniature Schnauzers and, as Pamela McLaren remarks, "we seem to have had a lot of first evers."

A very famous and widely admired dog in this kennel is Champion Maximim Graben of Deansgate, who won Best Dog and gained his title at the Miniature Schnauzer Club Championship show 1981. He also has numerous reserve certificates and Best in Show honors to his credit. He is a son of Brynsmor Joker (Champion Eastwight Sea Goblin ex Tripaloe St. Opal) from Swedish and Finnish Champion Barclay Square Maximim Minx (American Champion Sky Rockets Uproar ex American Champion Barclay Square Bugle Call). He is making his presence felt as a sire in a truly impressive manner. His son, Deansgate Truey Nuff, was Best in Show at Blackpool Championship Show as well as having gained two Challenge Certificates and his Junior Warrant for Mrs. Webster. Another son, Gildorwil Hans Kuff, won another Challenge Certificate and Reserve C.C., while a daughter, Gildorwil Fair Cop, won a C.C., these two being from Deansgate Ophelia Collar.

Then Maximim Graben's son, Deansgate Mister Again, owned by Mr. Weatherley and from Deansgate Mrs. Nothing, added some splendid wins to an already good record with Reserve C.C. on two occasions and Best in Show at the Northern Schnauzer Club Specialty. Zodene Mythical King, by this same sire, was Reserve C.C. at Richmond.

Champion Brynsmor Brainstorm at Deansgate, a half-sister to Maximim Graben, also gained her title in 1981 at 15 months of age and now holds half a dozen or more Challenge Certificates. Their mother, Swedish and Finnish Champion Barclay Square Maximim Minx, gained her titles with ease for Benny Blid in Sweden.

Deansgate I Am Mai has a long list of wins, including Bests in Show, as of early 1984. She was Best in Show at the Midland Schnauzer Club open show and the Derby K.A. all-breed open show; reserve Best in Show at the Halifax Open Show; Challenge Certificate at Blackpool; reserve C.C. at Windsor; and Best in Show at two successive Chapeltown shows. A daughter of Deansgate Honest Joe, she belongs to Deansgate Kennels, Pamela McLaren and Elizabeth Cooke, Rotherham, S. Yorks, England.

Deansgate I Am Mai, sporting her Institute of Advanced Motorists badge with her initials as their mascot, represents the Deansgate Kennels owned by Pamela McLaren and Elizabeth Cooke. Photo by Garwood.

Deansgate Truey Nuff, Best in Show, Blackpool Championship event, 1983. Photo by J.K. and E.A. McFarlane. Owners, Deansgate Kennels, Pamela McLaren and Elizabeth Cooke.

Italian, Int. and World Ch. Deansgate Mister President is a very distinguished representative of the Deansgate Kennels in England, P. McLaren and E. Cooke, Rotherham, Sheffield.

This is, so far as is known, a record-size litter for Miniature Schnauzers—11 puppies. Bred and owned in England by Deansgate Kennels, P. McLaren and E. Cooke, Sheffield. Photo courtesy of the South Yorkshire and Rotherham Advertiser.

Champion Buffel's All-American Boy of Deansgate is described by Pamela McLaren as "the top sire ever in the breed" in Britain, with hardly a Schnauzer in that country not having him somewhere in their pedigree. His bloodlines have produced leading winners abroad by virtue of bitches in whelp to him being exported to Australia and South Africa. His offspring include Champion Short and Sweet of Deansgate, her brother Italian, World and International Champion Hugo Furst of Deansgate; Champion Deansgate Mr. President; Champion Eastwight Sea Yank, Champion Eastwight Sea Spirit, and numerous others.

International Champion Deansgate Heir Apparant gained his South African title quicker than any dog. In that country, five Challenge Certificates are required, not three as in England. He left for his new home there the day after winning the Crufts' Challenge Certificate, certainly going out to his new owners with a bang! Obviously he is continuing in the same vein in South Africa.

Deansgate I Am Mai is mascot of the Institute of Advanced Motorists at Sheffield. She started her show career in June 1982, winning numerous first prizes, plus reserve C.C. honors under leading Schnauzer experts. She is by Deansgate Honest Joe from Deansgate Elsa Poppin.

Another proud representative of Deansgate Kennels is Nosbod Daniel of Deansgate, the first ever Miniature Schnauzer to have qualified for the Spillers—Dog World Pup of the Year Competition, where he was one of the 24 finalists from over 8,000 puppies! Daniel already has won Best Puppy in Show All Breeds and at breed Specialty Shows, and Best in Show in the record entry at the Sheffield open show. He is by Champion Castilla Linajudo ex Champion Castilla Real Quatro of Nosbod and, as his wins show, has received considerable acclaim from Schnauzer judges.

Eng. Ch. Catalanta True Luck of Risepark, by Ch. Jid-jis Min Cato at Risepark ex Catalanta Little Sparkle, owned by Peter Newman, Risepark Kennels, Hinxworth, Herts, England. Photo, sent by owner, courtesy of Sally Ann Thompson.

Risepark

Although Miniature Schnauzers have been the first and principal interest there, Risepark Kennels, owned by Peter Newman, Hinxworth, Herts, England, have also been associated with champions in the Hound, Terrier and Toy Groups.

Peter Newman had his first Miniature Schnauzer in 1955, starting off with two Champion Deltone Appeline Doughboy puppies. These were Deltone Delouisiana and Champion Deltone Delaware, the latter destined not only to make his title but also to win enough points to gain a Junior Warrant, only the second Miniature Schnauzer to do so. These two when mated together produced Risepark Ha'Penny Breeze, the dam of two champions.

With showing and breeding always somewhat limited, it is more through the stud dogs that the Risepark affix was to play a significant part in the breed's history. Interestingly the studs who have been available at Risepark from the very first homebred, Champion Risepark Happy Fella, all have sired champions and champion producers. The majority of champions and top producers in the breed in Great Britain all carry Risepark in their pedigrees.

Imports, too, have featured strongly over the years. The first was the Canadian-bred Appeline Cosburn's Pickwick Peppers, a son of U.S.A. Champion Cosburn's Noranda, with a background of Benrook, Dorem, Marienhof and Ledahof breeding. Imported by Douglas Appleton in 1960, Pepper was to tie in well with the bloodlines being developed in Britain. Possessing a delightful temperament, which he passed on to all his progeny, Pepper did not quarantine particularly well and was never shown, but lived out his life at Risepark, siring three champions all from Eastwight bitches, as well as others who became champion producers.

A son of Pepper, Risepark Northern Cockade, who was out of the Champion Delaware—Delouisiana daughter Risepark Northern Lass, sired four champions, three of them out of the breed's top producing bitch in Britain, Roundway Anklet, and one out of the Champion Risepark Happy Fella daughter, Risepark Penny Luck. Anklet, the result of a brother-sister mating, traced back to Champion Deltone Deldiablo and two Americans, Champion Wilkern Tony from America, sent over to Mrs. Josephine Creasy of Roundway Terrier fame by Tom and Kay Gately and Phil-Mar Ritzy Lady, a daughter of the American Champion Dorem Tribute and Phil-Mar Lucky Lady. Anklet also was the dam of three of the five champions to the credit of the American-bred Champion Risepark Bon-Ell Taurus, two of them, the littermates, Champion Sonshea Silver Bullette, owned by Sonny and Sheila Daws, and Champion Risepark Torreador proving especially successful. Champion Taurus, a son of American Champion Mutiny I'm Grumpy Too, blended well with the British stock and proved an influential stud.

Champion Bullette was the dam of Champion Sonshea Sweet Talk of Risepark, while the third champion from the Taurus—Anklet combination, Champion Risepark The Leading Lady, was the dam of Mr. and Mrs. Day's Champion Risepark

Crown Prince, winner of Best Puppy in Show, all-breeds, at Leicester Championship Show in 1976. Champion Toreador sired Pam Radford's and Dori Clarke's homebred Champion Iccabod Chervil out of Iccabod Solitaire, a daughter of Champion Risepark Happy Fella. Champion Chervil, in turn, sired six champions which included Fred and Phyl Morley's homebred Champion Castilla Zambra, out of Castilla Golosina, another from the Taurus—Anklet mating.

Champion Zambra was the dam of the breed's current top winner in Great Britain, Champion Castilla Lina Judo, as well as Champion Castilla Diamante owned by Pam Radford and Dori Clarke, the first bitch champion for Champion Irrenhaus Impact at Risepark.

Another import to Risepark who was to become a top producing sire was Champion Jidjis Min Cato at Risepark, bred in Sweden by Mrs. Furst-Danielson from her American Champion Starfire Criterion Landmark, an American Champion Landmark's Masterpiece son, and the Champion Toreador daughter,

Eng. Ch. Sonshea Sweet Talk of Risepark, by Sonshea Talk of the Town ex Ch. Sonshea Silver Bullette. Owner, Peter Newman, England. Photo, submitted by the owner, made by Anne Roslin-Williams.

Eng. Ch. Risepark The Leading Lady, by Ch. Risepark Bon-Ell Taurus ex Roundway Anklet, owned by Peter Newman, Risepark Kennels, England. Photo from the owner, done by Anne Roslin-Williams.

Catalanta Miss Lissette, sent out to Sweden by Sid and Gill Saville. Champion Min Cato was to sire eight champions in all from bitches of varying backgrounds. A son, Champion Catalanta True Luck of Risepark (out of Catalanta Little Sparkle, sister to Lissette) was to carry on the good work, giving three champions and other top producers. These included Mr. and Mrs. Dobson's Champion Castilla Real Quatro at Nosbod, the dam of the 1983 Pedigree Petfoods "Pup of the Year" finalist, Nosbod Daniel of Deansgate, a son of Champion Lina Judo.

The latest stud at Risepark is the royally-bred American import Champion Irrenhaus Impact at Risepark, who quickly made his mark with four champions and other good winners from his first crop of puppies. With his splendid pedigree, that complements other recent imports, as well as the fact that he has been joined by Irrenhaus Aims To Please Risepark, an American Champion Regency's Right On Target daughter, the future holds promise for Risepark to build upon the past and continue to play a progressive part in the British Miniature Schnauzer story.

Litter sisters Enriqueta and Catalina de C'an Jack at 10 months. Enriqueta is owned by Mr. J. Soler Segoviano and Catalina by Mr. J. Martinez-Solano, Madrid, Spain, the breeder of both.

CHAPTER SEVEN

Miniature Schnauzers in Europe

Sylva Sprite Pyewacket was shipped to Switzerland in 1967 to start the black and silver line in Miss Frieda Steiger's "Schnauzi" Kennels. By Can. Ch. Walsh's Frosty Charmer, C.D. Bred by Sylva Sprite Miniature Schnauzers, Dr. Dorothy Griggs and Mrs. Joanna Griggs, Guelph, Ontario, Canada.

Miniature Schnauzers in Germany and Belgium

Miniature Schnauzers are tremendously popular little dogs throughout Europe, with active Specialty Clubs for the breed in many countries there. Of course, their stronghold is in Germany, where Miniature registrations have gained numbers at an astronomical rate over the years.

One significant fact is that the American breeders are no longer finding it necessary to turn to Europe for breeding or show stock in this breed. In fact, to the contrary, dogs from the United States are more likely being exported to the continent to improve the type and quality there. This is, indeed, a compliment to the American breeders, who have used well the excellent dogs who came over during the early days, bringing Germany's finest bloodlines here where they were obviously used to best advantage.

Among the dogs from Germany who had an important impact on the breed here were Champion Cuno v Burgstadt, Mack v.d. Goldbachhohe, Champion Marko v. Beutenberg, Champion Don v. Dornbusch, Champion Viktor v.

Dornbusch, Champion Flieger Heinzelmannchen, Jorg v. Dornbusch, Champion Amor zum Schlagbaum, Herzbub Heinzelmannchen, Champion Urian Thuringia, Champion Fels Heinzelmannchen, and Heliaster v. Abbagamba.

Among the imported bitches, Champion Amsel v.d. Cyriaksburg heads the list, followed by Lotte v.d. Goldbachhohe, Lady v.d. Goldbachhohe, Christel v.d. Fallerburg, Sn. Gaudi Baltischhort, Pia van den Zonnenheuvel, Hadrosa v. Abbagamba, and, among the others, Canadian Champion Nette v. Mumlingtal, American Champion Mucke Heinzelmannchen and Champion Walkure Heinzelmannchen.

Champion Hupp v. Schonhardt, a black importation from Germany, was a dog of importance soon after World War II. And a black bitch, Dirndl v. Schloss Helmstedt, completed title in America in 1950.

Miniature Schnauzers in Germany are being shown in all three colors, with special classes for each—Salt and Pepper Classes, Black and Silver Classes, and Black Classes. Entries at important shows there run in the area of 100 Miniature Schnauzers.

Int. and Scandinavian Ch. Schnauzi's Melissa. Photo courtesy of Bob and Nancy Berg, Bo-Nanza Miniature Schnauzers.

We have read with interest of the Miniature Schnauzer Valharra's Extravagant Erik, bred by Enid Quick, who made a triumphant tour of European dog shows in 1981, taken there by his owner Erika Kalogeras. These two competed at Specialty Shows, the World Dog Show in Dortmund, Germany, and International Shows in France, Belgium and Germany. Erik won his class at each of the ten shows in which he was entered, was Best of Breed at two shows, and for frosting on the cake, at the World Dog Show, he gained the title of World Youth Champion (Welt-Jugendsieger), his age of only one year old having relegated him to the Jugend (Youth) Class.

There is considerable activity in Belgium, Mme. S. Theunis and Mr. and Mrs. Louis Huwaert being among those showing the breed there. Mme. Theunis owns Erikal's Foxy Nick and Erikal's Christel Postillion, both well-known winners. The Huwaerts have a black and silver dog and two black and silver bitches purchased from United States breeders.

A Short Note on Miniature Schnauzers in Spain
by Javier Martinez-Solano of Madrid

Although some Miniature Schnauzers of good quality were shown occasionally prior to 1970, the first Spanish breeder to bring in English and American bloodlines was Mr. A. Madueno, of Madrid, who imported English Champion Dengarse Pirates Treasure and his dam, Rosehill Pirates Silver in the early 1970's, and later two English-bred bitches, Eastwight Sea Ballet and Eastwight Sea Gem. All of them became Spanish Champions and did very well in the Show ring. From these dogs he bred several Spanish Champions, among them Champions Sami Kilimanjaro (now owned by Mr. Bollo de Brito), Nica Kilimanjaro (owned by Mr. J. Soler), and, most famous of all, International and Spanish Champion Miky Kilimanjaro, who was campaigned by his owner, Mr. F. Martinez Guijarro, to a total of 14 Best in Show plus many Group firsts, and

Enriqueta de C'an Jack, by Tono del Escarambrujo ex Ch. Beauty of Maidenhead, at the age of eight months. Bred by J. Martinez-Solano. Owned by J. Soler Segoviano, Spain.

who is undoubtedly the most famous Spanish Miniature Schnauzer of all time.

Another English-bred dog who has also done a lot of winning is Risepark Super Duper, bred by Mr. P. Newman and campaigned to his Spanish title by his owner, Mr. M. Zalduendo in 1979. That same year Mr. Guijarro, who is at present the leading Miniature Schnauzer breeder in Spain, imported Dengarse Pirates Silver in whelp to Dengarse Yankee Spinoff. From this mating came my foundation bitch, Champion Beauty of Maidenhead, who was Best of Breed at the first Championship Show of the Schnauzer Club of Spain in December 1982, under judge Heinz Holler, President of the German Pinscher-Schnauzer Klub.

All the above dogs were shown uncropped, as all the original English imports had excellent ear carriage, and generally passed it on to their progeny. Now the trend is reversed, and most dogs are cropped American-fashion (i.e. short pointed ears, as opposed to the longer crop favored in Germany and Continental Europe).

Recently a young dog, Champion Don Pedrin del Escarambrujo (by Champion Miky Kilimanjaro bred by Mr. Guijarro and owned by Mr. A. Lacoma), has also scored some spectacular wins, including several Best Puppy and Junior in Show awards, and also some Group firsts. A full

brother to this dog, Tono del Escarambrujo, bred also by Mr. Guijarro and owned by Miss Saizar, was Best of Breed at the 2nd Championship Show of the Schnauzer Club of Spain last December, and finished up Res. Best in Show (The Club caters to all three sizes of Schnauzers). A son of Tono and my own Champion Beauty of Maidenhead, Blas de C'an Jack, was Best Miniature Puppy and Reserve Best Puppy in Show.

The top sire in the breed has been for several years the afore-mentioned Champion Miky Kilimanjaro, with at least two champions at the time of writing [—not bad for Spain—] and many winning children. Mr. Guijarro is at present campaigning a son of his, Panda del Escarambrujo, who has scored some excellent wins, as has another daughter of Miky's, Spanish and Portuguese Champion Agar do Taramouco, owned by Mr. Fernandez Maquieira.

The breed's popularity has increased steadily over the last few years and there is some nice young stock currently starting their Show careers. However, there is considerable controversy regarding the "correct" type of Miniature Schnauzer, as there are people who feel that only the "Continental" (i.e. German) type is acceptable, while many others (among whom I count myself) much prefer the Ameri-

Catalina de C'an Jack, home-bred owned by Javier Martinez-Solano, Madrid, Spain. At 10 months of age. By Tono del Escarambrujo ex Ch. Beauty of Maidenhead.

Spanish Ch. Nica Kilimanjaro, by Eng. and Int. Ch. Dengarse Pirates Treasure ex Ch. Rosehill Pirates Silver. Bred by Mr. A. Madueno. Owned by Mr. J. Soler Segoviano, Spain. Photo at nine years of age.

Panda del Escarambrujo, by Int. and Sp. Ch. Miky Kilimanjaro ex Somni Dolc dels Segadors. Breeder-owner, F. Martinez Guijarro, Spain.

with greater force now that a male American Champion, Marmac Pretorian, has been imported into Spain by Mr. A. Pons, a well-known Dobermann breeder; this dog has already been shown over here with much success, and should prove a welcome addition to our stud force, bringing in new bloodlines which are certainly needed at present, since most of today's Miniature Schnauzers in Spain are pretty closely related, as practically all go back to Mr. Madueno's imports.

The advocates of the "German" type have so far bred very few litters (if any), at least as far as Salt and Peppers are concerned. Black and Silvers are currently much in vogue, and some stock has recently been imported from Germany and Switzerland. There are also some blacks, and even some whites!

A Black and Silver, French-owned Coppelia of Baccara won Best of Breed at the Madrid International Championship Show last November, while a Black, Champion Sambo von der Steinhager Heide, owned by V. and J. Giner Barat, also won Best of Breed at the Special Schnauzer Show held in conjunction with the Alicante International Championship Show last December.

can/British type, not only because they are far more attractive to look at, but because they are much better in general conformation, and have greater substance and quality. I personally find German-bred dogs usually lacking quality, with very little bone, poor heads with appledomed skulls and short, pointed muzzles, and round, sometimes light, eyes. (This applies especially to Salt and Peppers; Black and Silvers are usually much better, as, of course, most of them have American/Canadian bloodlines not far behind in their pedigrees.)

This controversy is naturally reflected in Show results; for example, Herr Lyon, the German judge who officiated at the 1983 FCI World show, held in Madrid last June, consistently put down all American-type dogs, claiming that their furnishings were "too white," that their hair was "too long," and, in fact, that their color was all wrong, as Miniature Schnauzers should be the same color all over! The net result was that some very poor specimens won, although the World Champion Title was not awarded in males.

The controversy will no doubt flare up again

Sp. Ch. and Sp. Schnauzer Club Ch. Don Pedrin Del Escarambrujo, by Int. and Sp. Ch. Miky Kilimanjaro ex Somni Dolc Segadors. Bred by F. Martinez Guijarro. Owned by Mr. A. Lacoma.

A magnificent headstudy of Ch. Skyline's Blue Spruce. Carol A. Parker, Vail, Arizona.

CHAPTER EIGHT

The Standards of the Breed

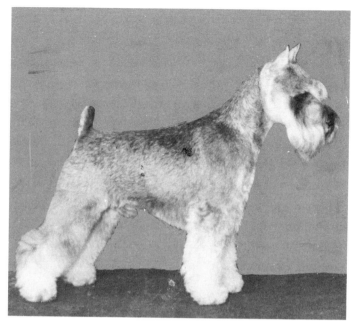

Ch. Walters' Irish Coffee, by Ch. Handmark's Masterpiece ex Walters' Rare Edition, taking Winners Dog and Best of Opposite Sex at Ventura County, June 1974. Bred and owned by Dolores Walters, Burbank, California.

The standard for a breed of dog is a detailed description of the ideal specimen of that particular breed—a word picture intended to describe in minute detail exactly how this dog should look, act, and gait. This standard outlines in detail, each and every feature of the specific breed, both in physical characteristics and in temperament, minutely describing the dog literally "from whisker to tail," creating for the reader a complete word picture of what is to be considered correct and what is not; the features comprising "breed type"; and the probable temperament and behavior patterns of typical members of the breed.

The standard is the guide for breeders endeavoring to produce quality dogs and for fanciers wishing to learn what is considered beautiful in these dogs; and it is the tool with which judges work in evaluating and reaching their decisions in the show ring. The dog it describes as ideal is the one which we seek as we look at and compare individuals.

Prior to the adoption of a breed standard, or any revisions of same, endless hours have been spent by dedicated fanciers selected from among the most knowledgeable and respected members of the parent club for the task of studying the background of the breed, searching out the earliest histories and breed descriptions from the country of origin and along the way throughout the breed's development. This committee's recommendations then come before the entire membership of the parent Specialty Club for further study, review and discussion, after which they are presented to the American Kennel Club from which approval must be granted prior to the standard or its revisions becoming effective.

American Standard for the Miniature Schnauzer

General Appearance: The Miniature Schnauzer is a robust, active dog of terrier-type, resembling his larger cousin, the Standard Schnauzer, in general appearance, and of an alert, active disposition. He is sturdily built, nearly square in proportion of body length to height, with plenty of bone, and without any suggestion of toyishness. *Faults:* Type—Toyishness, raciness or coarseness.

Temperament: The typical Miniature Schnauzer is alert and spirited, yet obedient to command. He is friendly, intelligent, and willing to please. He should never be over-aggressive or timid. *Faults:* Temperament—Shyness or viciousness.

Head: Strong and rectangular, its width diminishing slightly from ears to eyes, and again to the tip of the nose. The forehead is unwrinkled. The topskull is flat and fairly long. The foreface is parallel to the topskull, with a slight stop, and is at least as long as the topskull. The muzzle is strong in proportion to the skull; it ends in a moderately blunt manner, with thick whiskers which accentuate the rectangular shape of the head. *Faults:* Head coarse and cheeky. *Teeth:* The teeth meet in a scissors bite. That is, the upper front teeth overlap the lower front teeth in such a manner that the inner surface of the upper incisors barely touches the outer surface of the lower incisors when the mouth is closed. *Faults:* Bite—Undershot or overshot jaw. Level bite. **Eyes:** Small, dark brown and deep-set. They are oval in appearance and keen in expression. **Faults:** Eyes, Light and/or large and prominent in appearance. **Ears:** When cropped the ears are identical in shape and length, with pointed tips. They are in balance with the head and not exaggerated in length. They are set high on the skull and carried perpendicularly at the inner edges, with as little bell as possible along the outer edges. When uncropped, the ears are small and V-shaped, folding close to the skull.

Neck: Strong and well arched, blending into the shoulders, and with the skin fitting tightly at the throat.

Body: Short and deep, with the brisket extending at least to the elbows. Ribs are well-sprung and deep, extending well back to a short loin. The underbody does not present a tucked-up appearance at the flank. The topline is straight; it declines slightly from the withers to the base of the tail. The over-all length from chest to stern bone appears to equal the height at the withers. *Faults:* Chest too broad or shallow in brisket. Sway or roach back.

Forequarters: The forequarters have flat, somewhat sloping shoulders and high withers. Forelegs are straight and parallel when viewed from all sides. They have strong pasterns and good bone. They are separated by a fairly deep brisket which precludes a pinched front. The elbows are close, and the ribs spread gradually from the first rib so as to allow space for the elbow to move close to the body. *Faults:* Loose elbows.

Hindquarters: The hindquarters have strong-muscled, slanting thighs; they are well bent at the stifles and straight from hock to so-called heel. There is sufficient angulation so that, in stance, the hocks extend beyond the tail. The hindquarters never appear overbuilt or higher than the shoulders. *Faults:* Bowed or cow-hocked hindquarters.

Feet: Short and round (cat foot) with thick, black pads. The toes are arched and compact.

Movement: The trot is the gait at which movement is judged. When approaching, the forelegs, with elbows close to the body, move straight forward, neither too close nor too far apart. Going away, the hind legs are straight and travel in the same planes as the forelegs. *Note:* It is generally accepted that when a full trot is achieved, the rear legs continue to move in the same planes as the forelegs, but a very slight inward inclination will occur. It begins at the point of the shoulder in front and at the hip-joint in the rear. Viewed from the front or rear, the legs are straight from these points to the pads. The degree of inward inclination is almost imperceptible in a Miniature Schnauzer that has correct movement. It does not justify moving close behind, toe-ing in, crossing, or moving out at the elbows. Viewed from the side, the forelegs have good reach, while the hind legs have strong drive, with good pick-up of hocks. The feet turn neither inward nor outward. *Faults:* Single tracking. Sidegaiting. Paddling in front, or high hackney knee action. Weak rear action.

Tail: Set high and carried erect. It is docked only long enough to be clearly visible over the topline of the body when the dog is in proper length of coat. *Faults:* Tail set low.

Coat: Double, with hard, wiry, outer coat and close undercoat. Head, neck and body coat must be plucked. When in show condition the body coat should be of sufficient length to determine texture. Close covering on neck, ears and skull. Furnishings are fairly thick but not silky. *Faults:* Too soft or too smooth and slick in appearance.

Size: From 12 to 14 inches. Ideal size 13½ inches (See disqualifications).

Color: The recognized colors are salt and pepper, black and silver and solid black. The typical color is salt and pepper in shades of gray; tan shading is permissible. The salt and pepper mixture fades out to light gray or silver white in the eyebrows, whiskers, cheeks, under the throat, across chest, under tail, leg furnishings, under body, and inside legs. The light under-body hair

Ch. Valharra's Extra Allaruth, by Ch. Valharra's Extra ex Valharra's Magic Melody, whelped April 1979. Bred by Enid Quick of Valharra and Ruth Ziegler of Allaruth, purchased by Carol A. Parker following completion of his championship in 1981.

Ch. Fancway's Tom Terrific, famous top winner and top producer owned by Fancway Miniature Schnauzers, Jean and Glenn Fancy, La Canada Flintridge, California. Tom Terrific was born May 3rd 1962.

is not to rise higher on the sides of the body than the front elbows.

The black and silvers follow the same pattern as the salt and peppers. The entire salt and pepper section must be black.

Black is the only solid color allowed. It must be true black with no gray hairs and no brown tinge except where the whiskers may have become discolored. A small white spot on the chest is permissible.

DISQUALIFICATIONS

Dogs or bitches under 12 inches or over 14 inches. Color solid white or white patches on the body.

Approved March 13th, 1979.

Ch. Cyngar's Ultimatum, No. 1 Miniature Schnauzer, *Knight System,* for 1978. Bred and owned by Cynthia C. Garton, Lincoln, Nebraska. Handled by L.A. Hirstein.

English (Kennel Club) Standard for the Miniature Schnauzers

General Appearance: The Miniature Schnauzer is a powerfully built, robust, sinewy, nearly square, dog (length of body equal to height at shoulder). His temperament combines high spirits, reliability, strength, endurance and vigour. Expression keen and attitude alert. Correct conformation is of more importance than colour or other purely "beauty" points.

Head and Skull: Head strong and elongated, gradually narrowing from the ears to the eyes and thence forward toward the tip of the nose. Upper part of the head (occiput to the base of the forehead) moderately broad between the ears —with flat, creaseless, forehead and well muscled but not too strongly developed cheeks. Medium stop to accentuate prominent eyebrows. The powerful muzzle formed by the upper and lower jaws (base of forehead to the tip of the nose) should end in a moderately blunt line, with bristly moustache and chin whiskers. Ridge of the nose straight and running almost parallel to the extension of the forehead. The nose is black and full. Lips tight and not overlapping.

Eyes: Medium sized, dark, oval, set forward, with arched, bushy eyebrows.

Ears: Neat and V shaped, set high and dropping forward to temple.

Mouth: Scissor bite, slightly overlapping from the top; with strongly developed fangs; healthy and pure white.

Neck: Moderately long, nape strong and slightly arched, skin close to throat, neck set cleanly on shoulders.

Forequarters: Shoulders flat and sloping. Forelegs straight viewed from any position. Muscles smooth and lithe rather than prominent; bone strong, straight and carried well down to the feet; elbows set close to the body and pointing directly backward.

Body: Chest moderately broad, deep, with visible strong breast bone reaching down to at least the height of elbow and slightly rising backward to loins. Back strong and straight, slightly higher at the shoulder than at the hindquarters, with short, well developed loins. Ribs well sprung. Length of body equal to height from top of withers to ground.

Hindquarters: Thighs slanting and flat, but strongly muscled. Hindlegs (upper and lower thighs) at first verticle to the stifle, from stifle to

143

The black and silver Jet Set Snowy Knight owned by Florence Creasap. Photo courtesy of Bob Crews.

barrel-shaped ribs; slanting crupper; elbows turned out; heels turned in; hindpart overbuilt (too steep). Toes spread open; paws long and flat (hare). Coat too short and sleek, or too long, soft or curled. All white, spotty, tigered or red colours. Small white breast spot of marking is not a fault. Among other serious faults are cow hocks, sunken pasterns, or any weakness of joint, bones, or muscular development.

Note: Male animals should have two apparently normal testicles fully descended into the scrotum.

Australian Standard for the Miniature Schnauzer

Miniature Schnauzers in Australia are judged by a standard identical to that of the Kennel Club's Standard for the Miniature Schnauzer.

Aust. Ch. Guadala Brunhilde winning Best in Show under Mrs. Michelle Billings from the U.S.A. Owner-handler, Jeanette Tiltman, Guadala Kennels, Cockatoo Valley, South Australia. Brunhilde, to her owner's knowledge, is the only Schnauzer of any Variety to have won Best in Show at both an all-breed event and a Specialty in Australia.

hock, in line with the extension of the upper neck line, from hock, verticle to ground.

Feet: Short, round, extremely compact with close-arched toes (cat's paws), dark nails and hard soles. The feet also deep, or thickly padded, pointing forward.

Tail: Set on and carried high, cut down to three joints.

Coat: Hard and wiry and just short enough for smartness, clean on neck, shoulder, ears and skull, plenty of good hard hair on front legs. Good undercoat is essential.

Colour: All pepper and salt colours in even proportions, or pure black.

Height: The ideal height for bitches shall be 33 cm (13″) and for dogs 35.6 cm (14″). Too small toyish-appearing dogs are not typical and should be penalised.

Faults: Too heavy or too light; too low or high on the leg. Head too heavy or round, creased forehead, sticking-out, or badly carried, ears; light eye, with yellow or light grey rings; strongly protruding cheek bones; flabby throat skin; undershot or overshot jaw. Muzzle too pointed or too small. Back too long, sunken, or roached;

Aust. Ch. Eastdon Aurora Belle, owner-handled by Jeanette Tiltman, Guadala Kennels, Cockatoo Valley, South Australia. Co-owner with Steve Tiltman.

Can., Den., Ger., and Int'l Ch. Frontenac Pierre D'Asterix, by Am. Ch. Valharra's Peter Piper ex Can. Ch. Frontenac Pirate's Beaute, was Best puppy in Show at Chateauguay Valley K.C. in 1978, finishing his Canadian title at nine months of age. Exported to Denmark, to Mr. and Mrs. Henry Carlsen, he quickly became a European winner, and has a Best in Show in France. Bred by Frontenac Kennels in Canada.

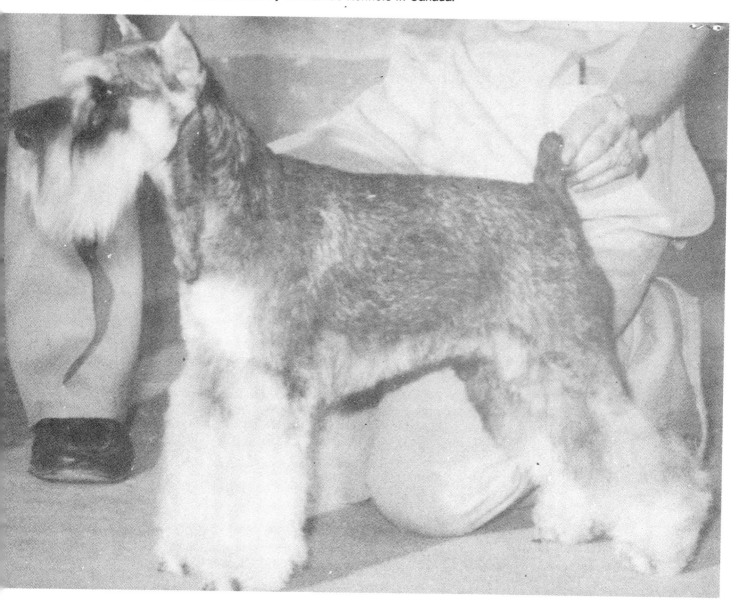

This was the first homebred champion at the very famous Richlene Kennels owned by Rich and Arlene Smith. Pictured here is Ch. Richlene's Whiz Kid, who is descended from the Mankit bloodlines.

Ch. Blythewood National Acclaim, photographed in full suspension, showing the reach in front, drive behind, and level topline with perfect tailset. Best of Breed twice at Westminster, he was the winner of six Terrier Group Firsts, sire of 18 champions at the close of 1983. Mrs. Joan L. Huber, Blythewood Kennels, Green Lawn, Pennsylvania.

Judging the Ideal Miniature Schnauzer

It is not always easy to picture in one's mind exactly what a breed standard is attempting to describe. There are some which do it well, clearly and specifically outlining what should be looked for in that breed. There are others which are quite the opposite, failing miserably in the function they should be performing, lost in too many vague adjectives, leaving the reader in a state of confusion rather than with a better knowledge of that breed of dog.

The Miniature Schnauzer is among the more fortunate breeds in this respect, for it has a standard which is specific regarding each and every feature of the breed. Familiarizing oneself with its words, paying attention to what they are SAYING not just to how they read, can and should give one a very clear picture of the correct Miniature Schnauzer.

The modern Miniature Schnauzer is a beautifully proportioned, squarely built solid little dog with good bone and substance, a short straight back which slopes slightly downward from the withers (point of shoulder) to the tail, and an overall appearance of solidity. This is a squarely built dog, length of body from chest to stern being equal to the height at the withers. Chest should be deep, coming to the point of elbow, ribs well sprung, the loin short and taut but with no apparent or exaggerated tuck up. Too broad a chest, or shallow a brisket, are undesirable faults.

Miniature Schnauzers have strong, rectangular heads which taper slightly in width from ears to eyes to tip of nose. The skull is flat on top and moderately long, the foreface parallel to the skull, of *at least* equal length, with a slight stop. The muzzle should never be too pointed, or "snipy", but ends rather like a blunt wedge in appearance. Remember, too, that only a scissors bite is acceptable, not level, NEVER undershot nor overshot. The incisors should meet in the manner of scissors, which is considered by many to be the most efficient of all bites.

Nothing can ruin a head more quickly than a large, round eye. So demand that they be small, dark brown and deep set. Light eyes are as unattractive and atypical as those which are too large. Also, note with care the ear set and placement. Remember, too, that natural ears are becoming increasingly popular, so learn to appreciate them and do not penalize a dog merely because he or she has not been cropped.

As you watch a Miniature Schnauzer move, the forelegs should reach well out, the hindlegs

Ch. Blythewood National Acclaim, by Ch. Blythewood National Anthem ex Valharra Prize O'Blythewood, had sired 18 champions as of 1983. Pictured winning one of 17 Specialty Bests in Show, which record is unbroken as of March 1984. An all-breed Best in Show winner. This handsome dog is handled by Joan L. Huber, pictured winning the Mt. Vernon Miniature Schnauzer Specialty, October 1979.

Geri Kelly smiles with pleasure as her black Miniature Schnauzer, Am., Can., and Ber. Ch. Kelly's K.E. Ebony Show Stopper poses for the photographer following Best in Show. By Ch. Kelly's Black Onyx ex Cayla's Sugar Babe, this is the top winning black Miniature Schnauzer of the decade, who finished at age seven months and is a National Specialty as well as an all-breed Best in Show winner.

Ch. Blythewood Ricochet of La May, by Ch. Fancway's Pirate, Jr. of La May ex Ch. La May's Bonanza Babe illustrates a most excellent head and front. Photo courtesy of Joan L. Huber.

heel, the hock extending beyond the tail. Hindquarters should NEVER appear lacking in angulation or overbuilt. Remember that the topline should SLOPE slightly from withers to tail, never be HIGHER behind than at the withers.

Since this is one of the breeds where clothes DO help to make the man, a Miniature Schnauzer to be considered in show condition should be presenting correct texture, in good furnishings, and well-groomed. Too soft or smooth a coat or lack of coat are serious flaws in a show Miniature Schnauzer. Much of the condition of your Schnauzer's coat will depend on your care of it. We have tried to give all the assistance possible in telling you how best to

Ch. Blythewood Ricochet of La May illustrating the correct rear view of a Miniature Schnauzer. Photo courtesy of Joan L. Huber.

flex nicely and powerfully at stifle and hock joint. Forelegs and hindlegs should travel in the same planes as each other, neither too close nor too far apart. And remember that the correct speed at which to judge Miniature Schnauzer movement is the trot, NOT the gallop.

As the Miniature Schnauzer stands before you, forelegs should be straight and parallel with strong pasterns. The brisket must be deep, and the angulation of the shoulders well laid back. As you walk around the dog, the hindquarters should look nicely "let down" (good bend of stifle and low placed hock), straight from hock to

Ch. Blythewood's Ricochet of La May taking Best of Breed at the 1968 South Florida Miniature Schnauzer Club Specialty. Mrs. Joan L. Huber, owner-handler.

handle Schnauzer coats, and hope that you will find our grooming chapters as helpful as we have tried to make them. Schnauzer grooming is a very great art nowadays, with many people doing it with fine expertise. It just makes no sense to face a competition with a dog who does not look dressed for the part, so do take your show dog's coat very seriously in order to do justice to his other assets in the ring.

Do not pass judgment on a Miniature Schnauzer without carefully examining him with your hands. Feel for musculation in neck, for correct placement of withers, and for desired angulation of the shoulders. Make certain that nice deep looking brisket actually IS brisket, not just hair that has been permitted to grow down to give the appearance of depth where actually

shallowness exists. Feel for musculation and angulation of hindquarters. Feel for good spring of rib. This is where judges in the ring have the advantage over ringside experts; for in coated dogs, there is much the hands feel that is not revealed to the eye!

Ideally, a Miniature Schnauzer should measure 13½ inches height at the withers. Dogs in question should be measured, since both over 14″ and under 12″ are disqualifications. It is interesting to note the gain in Miniature Schnauzer size over the years, the MAXIMUM having been raised from 12″ to 14″ since the early days, and under 12″ now to be disqualified.

Remember that all three colors—salt and pepper, black and silver, and solid black are all acceptable colors and should be judged without partiality.

Miniature Schnauzer Colors
by Gloria Lewis

The traditional Miniature Schnauzer, in the minds of many people, is a salt and pepper color, to the extent that some novices consider this to be the ONLY color for the breed, and that all others are atypical which definitely is NOT the case. Miniature Schnauzers come in black and silver, too, and in solid black, the latter having actually been the leading color of the early breed in Germany and highly favored there over the years. Dogs of both solid black and black and silver have earned prestige and popularity here in the United States and are regarded with admiration by a number of dedicated breeders.

The salt and pepper Miniature Schnauzer is a dog of shaded gray, darkest on the back and sides, fading out to light gray or silver white on the eyebrows, whiskers, cheeks, under throat, across chest, under tail, leg furnishings, under body and inside the legs. This light hair should not rise higher on the sides of the dog than the front elbows. The soft undercoat of the salt and pepper is of light to dark gray.

This same pattern applies to the black and silvers, the salt and pepper area being solid black with black undercoat.

The black Miniature Schnauzer is a true deep black from the roots out, including the undercoat, with black furnishings and whiskers. There must be no brownish tinge (except possibly where the whiskers may have become discolored by food), and no gray hairs. A small white spot on the chest is permissible.

The degree of darkness of a salt and pepper is created by the shading of the individual hairs, which upon close scrutiny, one finds to be "banded" in shades of black and white and brown, each hair ending in a band (or tip) of black. It is the depth of this black band that largely determines the darkness or lightness of the coat in this area, which is one of the reasons why using clippers on the coat of a show Schnauzer should never be resorted to under any circumstances. The harm done in this manner is two-fold: in addition to creating a lighter colored coat the result is also a softer one, most undesirable in dog show Schnauzer competition. But this will be further discussed in the grooming chapter.

The above are the three allowed colors for Miniature Schnauzers under the breed standard. Occasionally a white puppy will occur in some strains. Such puppies, although eligible for

Kelly's C.C. Stevie Wonder owned by Geri Kelly, North Falmouth, Massachusetts.

registration with the American Kennel Club so long as both parents are registered, would be disqualified in the show ring, and should be spayed or altered if a good home can be found.

Other unacceptable colors, seldom seen in modern times, although in the early days they did occasionally appear, include cream, wheaten, yellow, or parti-color (the latter a white dog with colored spots).

Salt and pepper Miniature Schnauzer puppies are born black or black with tan shadings or with brown or fawn colored flanks. As they grow, at a few weeks' age, one notices gray or brownish hair starting to show at the roots. The head may be black or black with tan on the ears, a light tan spot under the nose and on the chin where whiskers will follow. Future eyebrows are indicated by light spots over each eye. Many puppies have white beneath their tails, and, in some cases, there is a trace of white or tan chest hair. Beard, eyebrows and furnishings put in their first appearance at around six weeks of age, with the body coats either black or brownish black. As the puppy matures, this puppy coat changes, so do not be disconcerted at its somewhat scrubby appearance along the way. This is all quite natural.

Ch. Gretchen's Black Tulip, owned by Gloria Weidlein, by Ch. Walters' Black Topper ex Stuart's Gretchen.

Landmark's Black N Blue, by Ch. Skyline Blue Spruce ex Ch. Gretchen's Black Tulip, one of the handsome Schnauzers bred and owned by Gloria Weidlein. Photo courtesy of Dolores Walters.

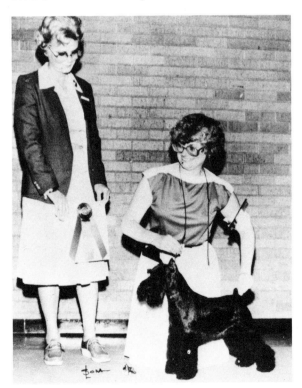

Black and silver puppies are born black apart from eyebrow spots and beard and cheek areas.

Black Miniature Schnauzers are born solid black right to the skin and with no tan shadings anywhere.

Breeding for color is not a common practice in the modern Miniature Schnauzer Fancy, and when attempted it is always done with great consideration for type as well. Over-emphasis on color can lead to other problems if entered into carelessly. It is the total dog which always should be considered in the planning of a litter: its type, quality, faults and assets, and the compatibility of the pedigree.

Some Schnauzer breeders like to occasionally introduce an outstanding black into their salt and pepper breeding program in the hope of darkening color and improving pigmentation. Generally speaking, salt and peppers bred to salt and pepper reproduce salt and pepper, except in the case of both the dog and the bitch carrying the black gene, in which case part of the litter may be black. Usually such a bred puppy when mated to a black stud will produce an entire black litter, we are told, while ordinarily a black and salt and pepper breeding combination will produce anything from an entirely black litter, an entirely salt and pepper litter, or some of each color.

153

Ch. Arbury Gay Matthew, by Ch. Blythewood Main Gazebo ex Arbury Gay Angel, was the fifth champion by Gazebo to finish in 1968. Joan Huber, handler. Clay Matthew, owner. Anna K. Nicholas, judge.

CHAPTER NINE

Selection of a Miniature Schnauzer

Ch. Cedarock's Up-N-Attm, a winning Miniature Schnauzer of the late 1960's.

Once you have made the decision that the Miniature Schnauzer is the breed of dog you wish to own, the next important step for you is to determine the right Miniature Schnauzer to best satisfy your needs. Do you prefer to start out with a puppy, with an adult dog, or with one partially mature? Do you prefer a male or a female? What type of dog do you wish—one for show or for competition in obedience? Are you looking for a Miniature Schnauzer for breeding, possibly as the foundation for a kennel? Do you simply want one for companionship, to be a family pet?

A decision should be reached about these matters prior to your contacting breeders; then you can accurately describe your requirements and the breeder can offer you the most suitable dog for your purposes. Remember that with any breed of dog, as with any other major purchase, the more care and forethought you invest when planning, the greater the pleasure and satisfaction likely to result.

Referring to a dog as a "major investment" may possibly seem strange to you; however, it is an accurate description. Generally speaking, a sizable sum of money is involved, and you are assuming responsibility for a living creature, taking on all the moral obligations this involves. Assuming that everything goes well, your Miniature Schnauzer will be a member of your family for a dozen or more years, sharing your home, your daily routine, and your interests. The happiness and success of these years depend largely on the knowledge and intelligence with which you start the relationship.

Certain ground rules apply to the purchase of a dog, regardless of your intentions for its future. Foremost among these is the fact that no matter what you will be doing with the dog, the best and most acceptable place at which to purchase a Miniature Schnauzer is a kennel specializing in that breed. Even though pet shops occasionally have Miniature Schnauzer puppies for sale, they are primarily concerned with *pet* stock, puppies with meaningless pedigrees. When you buy from a breeder you are getting a dog that has been the result of parents very carefully selected as individuals and as to pedigree and ancestry. For such a breeding, a dog and a bitch are chosen from whom the breeder hopes to achieve show type dogs that upgrade both his own kennel's quality and that of the breed generally.

Ch. Black Watch Sunny Side Up, by Ch. Black Watch of Blythewood ex Blythewood Gazebo Maiden, was bred by Jean L. Heath, co-owner with Ruth Quire. A splendid example of the superb quality raised at Black Watch Kennels whose dogs Jean Heath has made famous. Photo by Dan Kiedrowski.

Much thought has been given to the conformation and temperament likely to result from the combination of parents and bloodlines involved, for the breeder wants to produce sound, outstanding dogs that will further the respect with which he is regarded in the Miniature Schnauzer world. A specialist of this sort is interested in raising *better* dogs. Since it is seldom possible to keep all the puppies from every litter, fine young stock becomes available for sale. These puppies have flaws so slight in appearance as to be unrecognizable as such by other than the trained eye of a judge or a specialist on Miniature Schnauzer. These flaws in no way affect the strength or future good health of these Miniature Schnauzers; they simply preclude success in the show ring. The conscientious breeder will point them out to you when explaining why the puppy is being offered for sale at "pet price." When you buy a Miniature Schnauzer like this, from a knowledgeable, reliable breeder,

you get all the advantages of good bloodlines with proper temperament, careful rearing, and the happy, well-adjusted environment needed by puppies who are to become satisfactory, enjoyable adults. Although you are not buying a show dog or show prospect, puppies raised in the same manner have all the odds in their favor to become dogs of excellence in the home and in obedience.

If you are looking for a show dog, obviously everything I have said about buying only from a specialized Miniature Schnauzer breeder applies with even greater emphasis. Show-type dogs are bred from show-type dogs of proven producing lines and are the result of serious study, thought, and planning. They do *not* just happen.

Throughout the pages of this book are the names and locations of dozens of reliable Miniature Schnauzer breeders. Should it so happen that no one has puppies or young stock available to go at the moment you inquire, it

Ch. Kelly's Im-Per-Ial Black, owned by Richard and Geri Kelly, handled by Geri, finished with five majors, including Westminster, when eight months old. By Kelly's Ebony Von Prince ex Ch. Kelly's Super Star. Judge, Dr. J. Duebler.

Ch. Blythewood Chief Bosun winning 5 points for Best of Winners at the American Miniature Schnauzer Club Specialty in 1967 from the puppy class when only seven months of age. Owned and handled by Mrs. Joan L. Huber, Blythewood Kennels.

would be far wiser to place your name on the waiting list and see what happens when the next litter is born than to rush off and buy a puppy from some less desirable source. After all, you do not want to repent at leisure.

Another source of information regarding recognized Miniature Schnauzer breeders is the American Kennel Club, 51 Madison Avenue, New York, NY 10010. A note or phone call will bring you a list of breeders in your area.

Information can also be obtained from professional handlers. They have many contacts and might be able to put you in touch with a breeder and/or help you choose a dog.

The moment you even start to think about purchasing a Miniature Schnauzer, it makes sense to look at, observe, and study as many members of the breed as possible prior to taking the step. Acquaint yourself with correct type, soundness, and beauty before making any commitments. Since you are reading this book, you have already started on that route. Now add to your learning by visiting some dog shows if you can. Even if you are not looking for a show dog, it never hurts to become aware of how such a dog appears and behaves. Perhaps at the shows you will meet some breeders from your area with whom you can discuss the breed and whom you can visit.

If you wish your Miniature Schnauzer to be a family dog, the most satisfactory choice often is a bitch (female). Females make gentle, delightful companions and usually are quieter and more inclined not to roam than males. Often, too, they make neater house dogs, being easier to train. And they are of at least equal intelligence to the

Ch. Luvemal's Copy Right at Twin Brooks K.C., July 1969. Owned by Robert L. Crews, Somerville, New Jersey and Joseph E. Fiala.

Ch. Unser's Joeby von Hildale, owned by Robert L. Crews and Joseph E. Fiala, taking Best of Breed under judge Mrs. Winifred Heckmann. Robert Crews handling.

Ch. Sky Rocket's Bound to Win taking Best of Breed at the Mt. Vernon Miniature Schnauzer Specialty in October 1972 from the 6-9 months puppy class over Specials and an entry of 60. Handled by Joan L. Huber for owners Homer and Isabelle Graf.

males. In the eyes of many pet owners, the principal objection to having a bitch is the periodic "coming in season." Sprays and chlorophyll tablets that can help to cut down on the nuisance of visiting canine swains stampeding your front door are available; and, of course, I advocate spaying bitches who will not be used for show or breeding, with even the bitches who are shown or bred being spayed when their careers in competition or in the whelping box have come to a close. Bitches who have been spayed, preferably before four years old, remain in better health later on in life, because spaying almost entirely eliminates the dangers of breast cancer. Spaying also eliminates the messiness of spotting on rugs

and furniture, which can be considerable during her periods and which is annoying in a household companion.

To many, however, a dog (male) is preferable. The males do seem to be more strongly endowed with true breed character. But do consider the advantages and disadvantages of both males and females prior to deciding which to purchase.

Ch. Unser's Bravo Brava owned by Robert L. Crews and Joseph E. Fiala.

Ch. Sycamore Esprit, bred by M. Heiden, owned by H. De Luca, handled by Gloria Lewis.

Ch. Blythewood Rocket Man, owned by Garry and Karen Clausing, handled by Dora Lee Wilson, winning Best of Breed from judge Vincent Perry.

If you are buying your Miniature Schnauzer as a pet, a puppy is usually preferable, as you can teach it right from the beginning the ways of your household and your own schedule. Two months is an ideal age at which to introduce the puppy into your home. Older puppies may already have established habits of which you will not approve and which you may find difficult to change. Besides, puppies are such fun that it is great to share and enjoy every possible moment of their process of growing up.

When you are ready to buy, make appointments with as many Miniature Schnauzer breeders as you have been able to locate in your area for the purpose of seeing what they have available and discussing the breed with them. This is a marvelous learning experience, and you will find the majority of breeders are willing and happy to spend time with you, provided that you have arranged the visit in advance. Kennel owners are busy folks with full schedules, so do be considerate about this courtesy and call on the telephone before you appear.

If you have a choice of more than one kennel where you can go to see the dogs, take advantage of that opportunity instead of just settling for and buying the first puppy you see. You may return to your first choice in the long run, but you will do so with greater satisfaction and authority if you have seen the others before making the selection. When you look at puppies, be aware that the one you buy should look sturdy and big-boned, bright-eyed and alert, with an inquisitive, friendly attitude. The puppy's coat should look clean and glossy. Do not buy a puppy that seems listless or dull, is strangely hyperactive, or looks half sick. The condition of the premises where the puppies are raised is also important as you want your puppy to be free of parasites; don't buy a puppy whose surroundings are dirty and ill kept.

One of the advantages of buying at a kennel you can visit is that you are thereby afforded the opportunity of seeing the dam of the puppies and possibly also the sire, if he, too, belongs to the breeder. Sometimes you can even see one or more of the grandparents. Be sure to note the temperament of these Miniature Schnauzers as well as their conformation.

If there are no Miniature Schnauzer breeders within your travelling range, or if you have not liked what you have seen at those you've visited, do not hesitate to contact other breeders who are recommended to you even if their kennels are at a distance and to purchase from one of them if you are favorably impressed with what is offered. Shipping dogs is done with regularity nowadays and is reasonably safe, so this should not present a problem. If you are contacting a well-known, recognized breeder, the puppy should be fairly described and represented to you. Breeders of this caliber want you to be satisfied, both for the puppy's sake and for yours. They take pride in their kennel's reputation, and they make every effort to see that their customers are pleased. In this way you are deprived of the opportunity of seeing your dog's parents, but even so you can buy with con-

Walters' Black Marble represents four generations of Dolores Walters' breeding. By Am. Ch. and Japanese Grand Ch. Walters' Ebony Snow Man ex Walters' Printed in Black. Handled here by Wood Wornall to Winners Dog, then Best of Breed from the classes under Schnauzer breeder-judge Mrs. Jean Fancy, Prescott K.C. 1980.

fidence when dealing with a specialized breeder.

Every word about careful selection of your pet puppy and where it should be purchased applies twofold when you set out to select a show dog or the foundation stock for a breeding kennel of your own. You look for all the things already mentioned but on a far more sophisticated level, with many more factors to be taken into consideration. The standard of the Miniature Schnauzer dog must now become your guide, and it is essential that you know and understand not only the words of this standard but also their application to actual dogs before you are in a position to make a wise selection. Even then, if this is your first venture with a show-type Miniature Schnauzer, listen well and heed the advice of the breeder. If you have clearly and honestly stated your ambitions and plans for the dog, you will find that the breeders will cooperate by offering you something with which you will be successful.

There are several different degrees of show dog quality. There are dogs that should become top flight winners which can be campaigned for Specials (Best of Breed competition) and with which you can hope to attain Terrier Group placements and possibly even hit the heights with a Best in Show win. There are dogs of championship quality which should gain their titles for you but are lacking in that "extra something" to make them potential Specials. There are dogs that perhaps may never finish their championships but which should do a bit of winning for you in the classes: a blue ribbon here and there, perhaps Winners or Reserve occasionally, but probably nothing truly spectacular. Obviously the hardest to obtain, and the most expensive, are dogs in the first category, the truly top grade dogs. These are never plentiful as they are what most breeders are working to produce for their own kennels and personal enjoyment and with which they are loathe to part.

A dog of championship quality is easier to find and less expensive, although it still will bring a good price. The least difficult to obtain is a fair show dog that may pick up some points here and there but will mostly remain in class placements. Incidentally, one of the reasons that breeders are sometimes reluctant to part with a truly excellent show prospect is that in the past people have bought this type of dog with the promise it will be shown, but then the buyer has changed his mind after owning the dog awhile, and thus the dog becomes lost to the breed. It is really not fair to a breeder to buy a dog with the understanding that it will be shown and then renege on the agreement. Please, if you select a dog that is available only to a show home, think it over carefully prior to making a decision; then buy the dog only if you will be willing to give it the opportunity to prove itself in the show ring as the breeder expects.

If you want a show dog, obviously you are a person in the habit of attending dog shows. Now this becomes a form of schooling rather than just a pleasant pastime. Much can be learned at the Miniature Schnauzer ringside if one truly concentrates on what one sees. Become acquainted with the various winning exhibitors. Thoughtfully watch the judging. Try to understand what it is that causes some dogs to win and others to lose. Note well the attributes of the dogs, deciding for yourself which ones you like, giving full attention to attitude and temperament as well as conformation. Close your ears to the ringside "know-it-alls" who have only derogatory remarks to make about each animal in the ring and all that takes place there. You need to develop independent thinking at this stage and should not be influenced by the often entirely uneducated comment of the ringside spoilsports. Especially make careful note of which exhibitors are campaigning winning homebreds—not just an occasional "star" but a series of consistent quality dogs. All this takes time and patience. This is the period to "make haste slowly;" mistakes can be expensive, and the more you have studied the breed, the better equipped you will be to avoid them.

As you make inquiries among various breeders regarding the purchase of a show dog or a show prospect, keep these things in mind. Show-prospect puppies are less expensive than fully mature show dogs. The reason for this is that with a puppy there is the element of chance, for one never can be absolutely certain exactly how the puppy will develop, while the mature dog stands before you as the finished product—"what you see is what you get"—all set to step out and win.

There is always the risk factor involved with the purchase of a show-type puppy. Sometimes all goes well and that is great. But many a swan has turned into an ugly duckling as time passes, and it is far less likely that the opposite will occur. So weigh this well and balance all the odds before you decide whether a puppy or a mature dog would be your better buy. There are times, of course, when one actually has no choice in the matter; no mature show dogs may be available for sale. Then one must either wait awhile or gamble on a puppy, but please *be aware that gambling is what you are doing.*

If you do take a show-prospect puppy, be guided by the breeder's advice when choosing from among what is offered. The person used to working with a bloodline has the best chance of predicting how the puppies will develop. Do not trust your own guess on this; rely on the experience of the breeder. For your own protection, it is best to buy puppies whose parents' eyes have been certified clear and who have been O.F.A.-certified free of hip dysplasia.

Although initially more expensive, a grown show dog in the long run often proves to be the far better bargain. His appearance is unlikely to change beyond weight and condition, which depend on the care you give him. Also to your advantage, if you are a novice about to become an exhibitor, is that a grown dog of show quality almost certainly will have been trained for the ring; thus, an inexperienced handler will find such a dog easier to present properly and in winning form in the ring.

If you plan to have your dog campaigned by a professional handler, have the handler help you locate and select a future winner. Through their numerous clients, handlers usually have access to a variety of interesting show dogs; and the usual arrangement is that the handler buys the dog, resells it to you for the price he paid, and at the same time makes a contract with you that the dog shall be campaigned by this handler throughout the dog's career.

If the foundation of a future kennel is what you have in mind as you contemplate the purchase of a Miniature Schnauzer, concentrate on one or two really excellent bitches, not necessarily top show bitches but those representing the finest producing Miniature Schnauzer lines. A proven matron who has already produced show type puppies is, of course, the ideal answer here, but, as with a mature show dog, a proven matron is more difficult to obtain and more expensive since no one really wants to part with so valuable an asset. You just might strike it lucky, though, in which case you will be off to a flying start. If you do not find such a matron available, do the next best thing and select a young bitch of outstanding background representing a noted producing strain, one that is herself of excellent type and free of glaring faults.

Great attention should be paid to the background of the bitch from whom you intend to breed. If the information is not already known to you, find out all you can about the temperament, character, and conformation of the sire and dam, plus eye and hip rating. A person just starting in dogs is wise to concentrate on a fine collection of bitches and to raise a few litters sired by leading *producing* studs. The practice of buying a stud dog and then breeding everything you have to that dog does not always work out. It is better to take advantage of the availability of splendid stud dogs for your first few litters.

In summation, if you want a family dog, buy it young and raise it to the habits of your household. If you are buying a show dog, the more mature it is the more certain you can be of the future. If you are buying foundation stock for a breeding program, bitches are better than dogs, but they must be from the finest *producing* bloodlines.

Regarding price, you should expect to pay up to a few hundred dollars for a healthy pet Miniature Schnauzer puppy and more than that for a show-type puppy with the price rising accordingly as the dog gets older. A grown show dog can run well into four figures if of finest quality, and a proven brood matron will be priced according to the owner's valuation and can also run into four figures.

When you buy a purebred Miniature Schnauzer dog or puppy that you are told is eligible for registration with the American Kennel Club, you are entitled to receive, from the seller, an application form that will enable you to register your dog. If the seller cannot give you the application, you should demand and receive an identification of your dog consisting of the breed, the registered names and numbers of the sire and dam, the name of the breeder, and the dog's date of birth. If the litter of which your Miniature Schnauzer is part has been recorded with the American Kennel Club, then the litter number is sufficient identification.

Do not accept a verbal promise that registration papers will be mailed to you. Demand a registration application form or proper identification. If neither is supplied, do not buy the dog. These words are to be especially heeded if you are buying show dogs or breeding stock.

Britmor Sunnymeade Frost receiving a 4-point major en route to the title under judge Langdon Skarda, Nebraska K.C., 1980. Karen J. Brittan, owner, St. Louis Park, Minnesota.

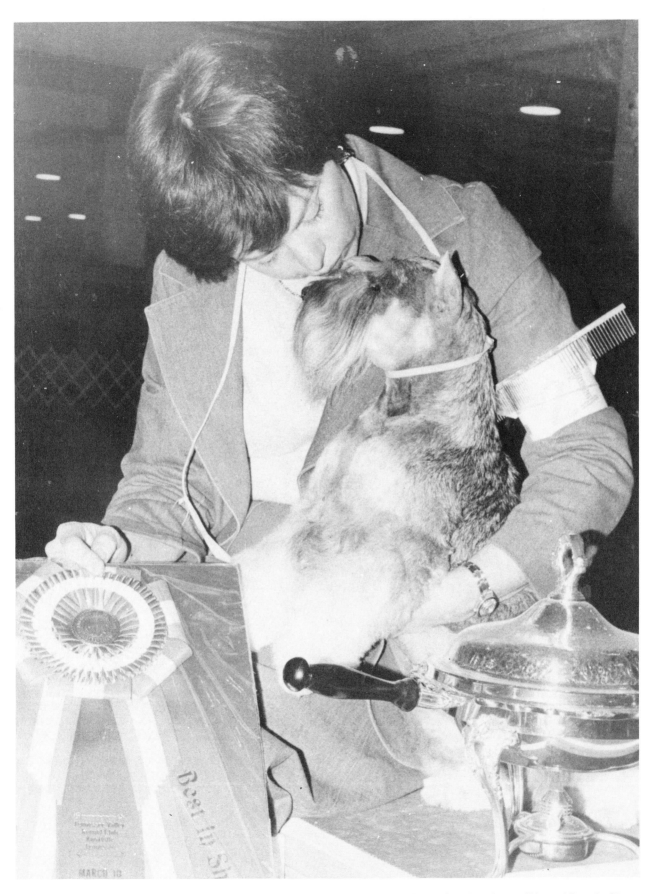

Ch. R-Bo's Victory Flash, by Ch. Shorlaine Dynamic Flash ex Ch. Shalom's Silver Shadow, is an all-breed Best in Show winner, with 14 Specialty Bests of Breed, and 12 Group Firsts. Sire of the Top Bitch for 1983, Ch. R-Bo's Devil Flash, also a Group winner. Handled by Claudia Seeberg for owner Mary Ann Ellis, Atlanta, Georgia.

CHAPTER TEN

Caring for a Miniature Schnauzer

A Tomlen Miniature Schnauzer puppy owned by Mrs. Helen Clifford, Clearfield, Pennsylvania.

Ownership of a dog entails a great deal of responsibility. You must be willing and prepared to provide your pet with shelter, food, training, and affection. With proper attention and care, your pet will become a loving member of the family and a sociable companion to be enjoyed for many years to come.

Advance Preparation

The moment you decide to become the owner of a Miniature Schnauzer puppy is not one second too soon to start planning for the new family member in order to make the transition period more pleasant for yourself, your household, and the puppy.

The first step in preparation is a bed for that puppy and a place where you can pen him up for rest periods. I am a firm believer that every dog should have a crate of its own right from the very beginning. This will fill both of the previously mentioned requirements, and the puppy will come to know and love this crate as his special haven. Crates are ideal, for when you want the puppy to be free, the crate door stays open. At other times, you securely latch it and

know that the puppy is safe from harm, comfortable, and out of mischief. If you plan to travel with your dog, his crate comes along in the car; and, of course, to travel by plane, the dog must be put in a crate. If you show your dog or take him to obedience trials, what better place to keep him when you are not working with him than in his crate? No matter how you look at it, a crate is a very sensible, sound investment in your puppy's comfort, well-being, and safety—not to mention your own peace of mind.

The crates we prefer are the sturdy wooden ones with removable side panels. These wooden crates are excellent for cold weather, with the panels in place, and they work equally well for hot weather when the solid panels are removed, leaving just the wire sides for better ventilation. Crates made entirely of wire are all right in the summer, but they provide no protection from drafts or winter chills. I intensely dislike solid aluminum crates due to the manner in which aluminum reflects surrounding temperatures. If it is cold, so is the metal of the crate. If it is hot, that too is reflected, sometimes to the point that one's fingers can be burnt when handling it. For this reason I consider them unsuitable.

Shirley's Miniature Schnauzer puppies, owned by Dick and Shirley Willey, Simi, California.

When you choose the puppy's crate, be certain that it is roomy enough not to be outgrown as your Miniature Schnauzer matures. He should have sufficient height in which to stand up comfortably and sufficient area to stretch out full length when relaxed. When the puppy is young, give him shredded newspapers as his first bed. In time, the newspapers can be replaced with a mat or turkish towels. Carpet remnants are great for the bottom of the crate as they are inexpensive and in case of accidents can be easily replaced. Once the dog has matured past the chewing stage, a pillow or a blanket for something soft and comfortable is an appreciated luxury in the crate.

Sharing importance with the crate is a safe area where the puppy can exercise and play. If you have a yard of your own, then the fenced area in which he can stay outdoors safely should be ready and waiting upon his arrival. It does not need to be a vast area, but it should have shade and be secure. Do have the fenced area planned and installed *before* bringing the puppy home if you possibly can do so; this is far more sensible than putting it off until a tragedy occurs. As an absolute guarantee that a dog cannot dig his way out under the fence, an edging of cinder blocks tight against the inside bottom of it is very practical protection. If there is an outside gate, a key and padlock are a *must* and should be *used at all times*. You do not want to have the puppy or dog set free in your absence either purposely or through carelessness. I have seen people go through a fence and then just leave the gate ajar. So for safety's sake, keep the gate locked so that only someone responsible has access to its opening.

The ultimate convenience, of course, is if there is a door in your house situated so that the fence can be installed around it, thereby doing away with the necessity for an outside gate. This arrangement is ideal, because then you need never be worried about the gate being left unlatched. This arrangement will be particularly appreciated during bad weather when, instead of escorting the dog to wherever his fenced yard is, you simply open the house door and he exits directly into his safe yard. In planning the fenced area, do give serious thought to the use of stockade fencing for it, as it really does work out well.

When you go to pick up your Miniature Schnauzer, you should take a collar and lead with you. Both of these should be appropriate for the breed and age of the dog, and the collar should be one that fits him now, not one he has to grow into. Your new Miniature Schnauzer also needs a water dish (or two, one for the house and one for outside) and a food dish. These should preferably be made from an unbreakable material. You will have fun shopping at your

This three-month-old Schnauzer puppy is owned by Mrs. Gloria Lewis, Closter, New Jersey.

the dog. But again, do not go off and leave them to be chewed in privacy.

Too many changes all at once can be difficult for a puppy. Therefore, no matter how you eventually wind up doing it, for the first few days keep him as nearly as you can on the routine to which he is accustomed. Find out what brand of food the breeder used, how frequently and when the puppies were fed, and start out by doing it that way yourself, gradually over a period of a week or two making whatever changes suit you better.

Of utmost precedence in planning for your puppy is the selection of a good veterinarian whom you feel you can trust. Make an appointment to bring the puppy in to be checked over on your way home from the breeder's. Be sure to obtain the puppy's health certificate from the

Nylabone ® comes in several sizes, shapes, and flavors. As many as 25 style varieties of Nylabone for dogs and puppies are available.

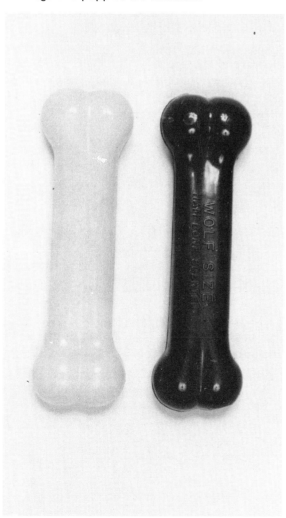

local pet shop for these things, and I am sure you will be tempted to add some luxury items of which you will find a fascinating array. For chew things, either Nylabone or real beef bones (leg or knuckle cut to an appropriate size, the latter found as soup bones at most butcher shops or supermarkets) are safe and provide many hours of happy entertainment, at the same time being great exercise during the teething period. Rawhide chews can be safe, too, if made under the proper conditions. There was a problem, however, several years back owing to the chemicals with which some of the rawhide chew products had been treated, so in order to take no chances, avoid them. Also avoid plastic and rubber toys, *particularly* toys with squeakers. If you want to play ball with your Miniature Schnauzer, select a ball that has been made of very tough construction; Miniature Schnauzers have strong jaws. Even then do not leave the ball with the puppy alone; take it with you when you finish the game. There are also some nice "tug of war" toys which are fun when you play with

Ch. Abington Authority, who was owned by George and Edna Hendrickson, holds the Best in Show record for a Schnauzer in the continental United States of nine times Best in Show. Sire of Ch. Kazels Favorite and an all-champion litter. Photo courtesy of Mrs. K.L. Church, Kazel Schnauzers, Imperial, Missouri. Larry Downey handling.

This important and beautiful dog, winning the Terrier Group at Virginia K.C. in 1979 handled by Sue Baines for owner Jacqueline Hicks, is Ch. Irrenhaus Blueprint, son of Ch. Skyline's Blue Spruce ex Ch. Irrenhaus Fancy Finish. The sire of 18 champions, Blueprint is a Multiple Group winner and a Specialty winner.

This darling Miniature Schnauzer puppy is owned by Mrs. Helen Clifford, Clearfield, Pennsylvania.

Ch. Royalcourt Ball Player and two offspring. The one in the center became Ch. Royalcourt Name of the Game. Mrs. Gloria Lewis, owner, Closter, New Jersey.

strangeness wears off before bedtime. You will find it a more peaceful night that way, I am sure. Allow the puppy to investigate his surroundings under your watchful eye. If you already have a pet in the household, carefully watch that things are going smoothly between them, so that the relationship gets off to a friendly start; otherwise, you may quickly have a lasting problem. Be careful not to let your older pet become jealous by paying more attention to the newcomer than to him. You want a friendly start. Much of the future attitude of each toward the other depends on what takes place that first day.

If you have children, again, it is important that the relationship start out well. Should the puppy be their first pet, it is assumed that you have prepared them for it with a firm explanation that puppies are living creatures to be treated with

breeder, along with information regarding worming, shots, and so on.

With all of these things in order, you should be nicely prepared for a smooth, happy start when your puppy actually joins the family.

Joining the Family

Remember that as exciting and happy as the occasion may be for you, the puppy's move from his place of birth to your home can be a traumatic experience for him. His mother and littermates will be missed. He will perhaps be slightly frightened or awed by the change of surroundings. The person he trusted and depended on will be gone. Everything, thus, should be planned to make the move easy for him, to give him confidence, to make him realize that yours is a pretty nice place to be after all.

Never bring a puppy home on a holiday. There just is too much going on, with people and gifts and excitement. If he is honoring "an occasion" (a birthday, for example), work it out so that his arrival will be a few days before or, better still, a few days after the big occasion. Then he will be greeted by a normal routine and will have your undivided attention. Try not to bring the puppy home during the evening. Early morning is the ideal time, as then he has the opportunity of getting acquainted, and the first

At eight weeks old, this Miniature Schnauzer puppy is just about impossible to resist! Gloria Lewis, owner, Closter, New Jersey.

Ch. Skyrocket's Upswing, six and a half months old, taking Winners Dog and Best of Winners at Montgomery County in 1971 under Gene Simmonds after taking Best in Sweepstakes at the same event, handled by Judie Ferguson. Now owned by D.L. and Judy Smith, Jadee Kennels, Swinger was their first champion, and became a multiple Specialty winner, Group, and all-breed Best in Show winner. He is the sire of 16 champions, including Ch. Skyline's Blue Spruce.

gentle consideration, not playthings to be abused and hurt. One of my friends raised her children with the household rule that should a dog or puppy belonging to one of the children bite one of the children, the child would be punished, not the dog, as Mother would know that the child had in some way hurt the dog. I must say that this strategy worked out very well, as no child was ever bitten in that household and both daughters grew up to remain great animal lovers. Anyway, on whatever terms you do it, please bring your children up not only to *love* but also to *respect* their pet, with the realization that dogs have rights, too. These same ground rules should also apply to visiting children. I have seen youngsters who are fine with their own pets unmercifully tease and harass pets belonging to other people. Children do not

always realize how rough is too rough, and without intending to, they may inflict considerable pain or injury if permitted to ride herd on a puppy.

If you start out by spoiling your new puppy, your puppy will expect and even demand that you continue to spoil it in the future. So think it out carefully before you invite the puppy to come spend its first night at your home in bed with you, unless you wish to continue the practice. What you had considered to be a one-night stand may be accepted as just great and expected for the future. It is better not to start what you may consider to be bad habits which you may find difficult to overcome later. Be firm with the puppy, strike a routine, and stick to it. The puppy will learn more quickly this way, and everyone will be happier as a result.

Socialization and Training

Socialization and training of your new baby Miniature Schnauzer actually starts the second you walk in the door with him, for every move you make should be geared toward teaching the puppy what is expected of him and, at the same time, building up his confidence and feeling of being at home.

The first step is to teach the puppy his name and to come when called by it. No matter how flowery or long or impressive the actual registered name may be, the puppy should also have a short, easily understood "call name" which can be learned quickly and to which he will respond. Start using this call name immediately, and use it in exactly the same way each time that you address the puppy, refraining from the temptation to alternate various forms of endearment, pet names, or substitutes which will only be confusing to him.

Using his name clearly, call the puppy over to you when you see him awake and looking about for something to do. Just a few times of this, with a lot of praise over what a "good dog" he is when he responds, and you will have taught him to come to you when he hears his name; he knows that he will be warmly greeted, petted, and possibly even be given a small snack.

As soon as the puppy has spent a few hours getting acquainted with his new surroundings, you can put a light collar on the puppy's neck, so that he will become accustomed to having it on. He may hardly notice it, or he may make a great fuss at first, rolling over, struggling, and trying to rub it off. Have a tasty tidbit or two on hand with which to divert his attention at this period, or try to divert his attention by playing with him. Soon he no longer will be concerned about that strange new thing around his neck.

Mutual admiration! Bob Hope and a silver and black Miniature Schnauzer puppy from Gas Light Kennels gaze fondly at one another during the puppy's guest appearance on NBC Television.

At the Denver Specialty in 1966, Jean and Glenn Fancy scored a double victory with their Ch. Fancway's Pirate, Jr., Best of Breed; and his daughter, Ch. Walter's Country Girl, Best of Opposite Sex. Gene Simmonds is the judge.

The next step in training is to have the puppy become accustomed to the lead. Use a lightweight lead, attached to the collar. Carry him outdoors where there will be things of interest to investigate; then set him down and see what happens. Again, he may appear hardly to notice the lead dangling behind him, or he may make a fuss about it. If the latter occurs, repeat the diversion attempts with food or a toy. As soon as the puppy has accepted the presence of the lead, pick up the end of it and follow after him. He may react by trying to free himself, struggling to slip his head through the collar, or trying to bite at the lead. Coax him, if you can, with kind words and petting. In a few moments, curiosity regarding his surroundings and an interesting smell or two should start diverting him. When this takes place, do not try at first to pull on him or guide his direction. Just be glad that he is walking with the lead on and let him decide where to go. When he no longer seems to resent the lead, try gently to direct him with short little tugs in the direction you would like him to travel. Never jerk him roughly, as then he will become frightened and fight harder; and never pull steadily or

attempt to drag him, as this immediately triggers a battle of wills with each of you pulling in an opposite direction. The best method is a short, quick, gentle jerk, which, repeated a few times, should get him started off with you. Of course, continue to talk encouragingly to him and offer him "goodies" until he gets started. Repetition of the command "Come" should accompany all of this.

Once this step has been mastered and walks are taken on the lead pleasantly and companionably, the next step is to teach him to remain on your left-hand side. Use the same process as you used to teach him to respond correctly while on the lead, this time repeating the word "Heel." Of course, all of this is not accomplished in one day; it should be done gradually, with short work periods each time, letting the puppy know when he pleases you. The exact length of time required for each puppy varies and depends on the aptitude of each individual puppy.

Housebreaking a puppy is more easily accomplished by the prevention method than by the cure. Try to avoid "accidents" whenever you can rather than punishing the puppy once

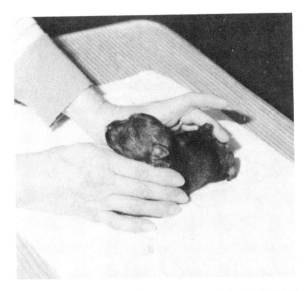

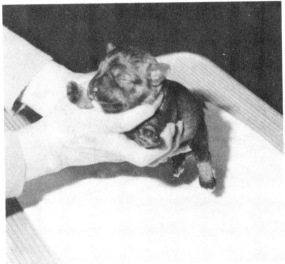

Miniature Schnauzer puppies bred and owned at Royalcourt Kennels, Mrs. Gloria Lewis, Closter, New Jersey. *top,* newly born baby Miniature Schnauzer; *center,* Miniature Schnauzer puppy at ten days; and *bottom,* Orca and Buster at three weeks. Photos by Jil Lewis.

they have occurred. Common sense helps a great deal. A puppy will need to be taken out at regularly spaced intervals: first thing in the morning directly from his bed, immediately after meals, after he has napped, or whenever you notice that he is "looking for a spot." Choose roughly the same place outdoors each time that you take the puppy out for this purpose, so that a pattern will be established. If he does not go immediately, do not just return him to the house as chances are that he will go the moment he is back inside. Try to be patient and remain out with him until you get results; then praise him enthusiastically and both of you can return indoors. If you catch the puppy having an "accident," pick him up firmly, sharply say, "No!" and rush him outside. If you do not see the accident occur, there is little point of doing anything beyond cleaning it up, as once it has happened and been forgotten, the puppy will likely not even realize why you are angry with him.

Your Miniature Schnauzer puppy should form the habit of spending a certain amount of time each day in his crate, even when you are home. Sometimes the puppy will do this voluntarily, but if not, he should be taught to do so. Lead the puppy by the collar over to the crate, and then gently push him inside firmly saying "Down" or "Stay" as you fasten the door. Whatever command you use, always make it the same word for each act every time. Repetition is the big thing in training, and the dog must learn to associate a specific word or phrase with each different thing he is expected to do. When you mean "Sit," always say exactly that. "Stay" should mean that the dog should remain where he was when you gave the command. "Down" means something else again. Do not confuse the dog by shuffling the commands, as you will create confusion for him and a problem for yourself by having done so.

As soon as he has received his immunization shots, take your Miniature Schnauzer puppy with you wherever and whenever possible. Nothing else can equal this close association for building up self-confidence and stability in a young dog. It is extremely important that you spend the time necessary for socialization, particularly if you are planning on the puppy becoming a show dog.

Take your Miniature Schnauzer in the car, so that he will learn to enjoy riding without becoming carsick, as can happen to a dog unused to the car's motion. Take him everywhere you go, provided you are certain he will not be unwelcome or create any difficulties by his presence: visiting friends and relatives (if they like dogs and do not have house pets of their own who will consider your puppy an intruder), to busy shopping centers (always keeping him on his lead), or just walking around the streets of your town. If someone admires him, as always seems to happen under these circumstances, encourage that person to pet or talk with him; becoming accustomed to people in this manner always seems especially beneficial in instilling self-confidence. You want your puppy to develop a relaxed, happy canine personality and like the world and its inhabitants. The most debilitating thing for a puppy's self-confidence is excessive sheltering and pampering. Keeping a growing puppy always away from strange people and strange dogs may well turn him into a nervous, neurotic dog— surely the last thing anyone can enjoy in a pet.

Make obedience training a game with your puppy while he is extremely young. Try to teach him the meaning of and expected responses to the basic terms such as "Come," "Stay," "Sit," "Down," and "Heel," along with the meaning of "No" even while he is still too young for formal training, and you will be pleased and proud of the good manners that he will exhibit.

Feeding

There was a time when providing good, nourishing food for our dogs involved a far more complicated routine and time-consuming process than people now feel is necessary. The old belief was that the daily rations should consist of fresh beef, vegetables, cereal, egg yolks, and cottage cheese as basics, with such additions as brewer's yeast and other vitamin supplements.

During recent years, however, many attitudes have been changed regarding the necessity, or even the desirability, of this procedure. We still give eggs, cottage cheese, and supplements to the diet, but the basic methods of feeding dogs have changed; and the changes are definitely for the better in the opinion of many an authority. The school of thought now is that you are doing your dogs a definite service when you feed them some of the fine commercially prepared dog foods in preference to your own home-cooked concoctions.

Ch. Mutiny Uproar, son of Ch. Landmark's Masterpiece, finished in Arizona. Purchased by Joan Huber after completing his title, he won a number of Groups thus becoming the Top Winning Miniature Schnauzer for 1969. Photo courtesy of Gloria Weidlein, Sun City, California.

The reasoning behind this new outlook is easy to understand. The production of dog food has grown to be a major industry, participated in by some of the best known, most highly respected names in the dog fancy. These trusted firms do turn out excellent products. People are feeding their dogs these preparations with confidence, and the dogs are thriving, prospering, and keeping in top condition. What more could we want or ask?

There are at least a half dozen absolutely splendid dry foods which can be mixed with water or broth and served to your dog, either "as is" or with the addition of fresh or canned meat. There is a variety of canned meat preparations for your dog, either 100% meat to be mixed with kibble or complete prepared dinners, a combination of both meat and cereal. There are several kinds of "convenience foods," these in packets which you open and dump out into the dog's dish. It is just that simple. The "convenience foods" are neat and easy for you when travelling, but generally speaking we prefer to feed a dry food mixed with hot water, to which we usually add canned meat (although leftover meat scraps or ground beef are sometimes added instead of the canned meat). Actually we feel that the canned meat, with its added fortifiers, is more beneficial to the dogs than the fresh meat. However, the

One of the Miniature Schnauzers at Wa-Han-Ka Kennels owned by Mr. and Mrs. George Roberts, Hornell, New York, getting settled in a favorite chair.

two can be used alternately or, if you prefer and your dogs do well on it, by all means use ground beef.

Dogs enjoy variety in the meat part of their diet, which is easy to provide with the canned meat. The canned meats available include all sorts of beef (chunk, ground, stewed, and so on), lamb, chicken, liver, and numerous concoctions of several of these blended together.

There also is prepared food geared to every age bracket of your dog's life, from puppyhood on through old age, with special additions or modifications to make it especially nourishing and beneficial. The dogs of yesteryear never had it so good during the canine dinner hour because these foods are tasty and geared to meet the dog's gastronomical approval.

Additionally, contents and nutritional values are clearly listed on the labels, and careful instructions for feeding exactly the right amount for the size and weight of each dog are also given.

Eleven weeks old Miniature Schnauzer puppies, photo courtesy of Dolores Walters, Burbank, California.

With the great choice of dog foods available today, we do not feel that the addition of vitamins is necessary; but if you do, there are several highly satisfactory vitamin products available at pet shops. These products serve as tasty treats along with being beneficial.

Of course there is no reason not to cook up something for your Miniature Schnauzer's dinner if you would feel happier doing so, but it seems to us superfluous when such truly satisfying rations are available at so much less expense and trouble.

How often you feed is a matter of how a schedule works out best for you and for your dog or dogs. Many owners prefer to feed their dogs once a day. Others feel that twice daily is better for the digestion and more satisfying to the dog, particularly if he is a family member who stands around and watches the preparation of family meals. The important thing is that you *do not overfeed*, as overfeeding can bring on many canine problems.

Until they are about twelve weeks old, fully weaned puppies should be fed four times daily. Each morning and evening, a Miniature Schnauzer pup needs a meal of kibble soaked in hot water, broth, or soup to which either canned or fresh raw beef has been added. At noontime and bedtime, condensed milk mixed with an equal amount of water to which a bit of dry kib-

Shirley's Sugar 'n' Spice, C.D. owned by Shirley's Schnauzers, Dick and Shirley Willey.

Homebred puppies owned by Shirley's Miniature Schnauzers, Simi, California. Shirley's Sunday Matinee is on the left.

ble has been added can be given. The amounts should be adjusted to the individual puppy's weight and appetite.

As the pup grows older, from three to six months of age, cut back to three meals, increasing the size of each. At six months of age, the pup should be fed twice daily, and at twelve months, if you wish, you may cut back to one daily feeding with a biscuit or two morning and evening. If you do feed just once daily, it should be given by early afternoon.

Remember that fresh, cool water should always be available for your dog. This is of utmost importance to his good health throughout his lifetime.

Baby Schnauzers, by Ch. Richlene's Top Billing, bred by the Wyndwood Kennels of Barbara Hall.

Royalcourt Miniature Schnauzer puppies owned by Mrs. Gloria Lewis, Closter, New Jersey.

The all-champion litter following ear cropping: *On the left,* Ch. Kazels Challenge; *middle,* Ch. Kazels Favorite; and *right,* Ch. Kazels Pretty Cute, C.D. Owned by Mrs. K.L. Church, Kazel, Imperial, Missouri. These collars are used after the ears are cropped to prevent the puppies from scratching them. Corrugated cardboard was cut to fit around each puppy's neck and then after having been put in place taped closed with masking tape. To keep the wounds clean, paper plates were set on the necks in the same fashion as the cardboard, and changed regularly just as though they were bandages or dressings. The colored plates, or some with designs on them, are also excellent for keeping track of the identity of each puppy from each one's color code used from birth.

Tail Docking and Ear Cropping

Miniature Schnauzer puppies are born with long tails which should be "docked" (shortened) when the puppy is three or four days old. This process is simple and painless if done by a knowledgeable person. If this is your first experience with it, better get a breeder-friend who is practiced in the art, or your veterinarian, to show you how by doing it for you as you watch the first time.

Ear cropping is done at eight weeks of age, by some one qualified and experienced as the manner in which this is done can make or break a future show dog. The ears should match perfectly and stand firmly erect at the tips. This definitely is NOT the job for an amateur! Care must be taken that the ears heal completely and properly. Instructions for after-care will be given to you by whoever does the job.

Ch. Royalcourt Get Up and Go in a lovely portrait with Mrs. Gloria Lewis, Closter, New Jersey.

CHAPTER ELEVEN

Grooming Your Miniature Schnauzer

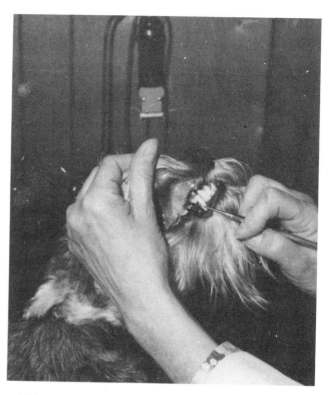

This is how tooth scaling is done, demonstrated by Gloria Lewis and Ch. Royalcourt Ball Player. A very important part of grooming for both the health and beauty of your dog.

Grooming of a Miniature Schnauzer is an important part of your enjoyment of him, whether as a show dog or a pet. A well groomed terrier is a joy to behold; quite a contrast to the shaggy, unkempt appearance of a neglected Miniature Schnauzer. If your dog is a pet, the coat care need not be so sophisticated as in a show dog; but still it should be attended to regularly, under which circumstances it consumes little time and more than rewards you with the pleasure of a smart, well turned-out canine companion.

Since coat care must be done on a steady basis, it is tremendously important that the puppy become accustomed to it as a baby, so that it will come to seem quite usual and not to be dreaded.

How to Groom Your Miniature Schnauzer by Gloria Lewis

Gloria Lewis, well-known breeder/owner/handler whose Royalcourt Schnauzers are known and admired throughout the fancy, gives us some suggestions to pave the way for you in making the most of your dog's appearance.

To begin with, one needs equipment. The most important single item is probably the grooming table, a table measuring approximately 18 × 30 inches is the appropriate size for a Miniature Schnauzer, and this is topped with a non-skid surface to prevent slipping. These are usually equipped with fold-away legs for ease of storage when not in use, and some types have holes and posts in them to which a "noose" can be attached to slip over the dog's head and around his neck to restrain him as you work, which is a helpful device.

Two metal combs will be needed, one in which the teeth are closely spaced, the other more widely spaced, a pin brush, barber's shears to be reserved for cutting hair ONLY (to maintain their sharpness), nail clippers, thinning shears, and an Oster Clipper; Gloria Lewis notes Model A2 or A5, with # 8½, # 10 and # 15 size blades. The higher the number of the blade, the smaller the "teeth" are; therefore a # 15 blade would remove more hair than a # 10.

By the time the puppy has reached three months of age, it will have become apparent which way he is to go—whether as a show prospect or as a pet. If the latter he should be clippered. If, however, he is a show prospect, he should NOT be clippered but instead hand-stripped. Please bear in mind that once you start clippering your puppy it will become almost impossible to hand strip the coat back to its desirable harshness or to regain the darker coat brought about by the black tips removed by the clippers.

To hand strip the coat, one simply plucks out the hairs from the body firmly with one's fingers. Start with just a tiny area at first, since the ease and cooperation of the puppy is important. But this is not a painful process if done properly. Get someone who knows how it's done to show you, and you will acquire the art more quickly and easily than you might assume. As a beginning, work briefly pulling out with the fingers all the long, blackish puppy fuzz around the neck, head, shoulders, body and tail. Quick firm motions are the most effective, those one would use in tweezing one's own eyebrows, but with the fingers as your "tool." Gloria Lewis says these sessions should be spaced about one week apart, and that after all the outer puppy fuzz has been removed, and about two weeks after removel of the head coat, one should take out the remainder of the undercoat densely covering the neck and body. This will leave the puppy quite undressed, but within a few weeks the new hard coat will start to come, breaking through the skin, followed by another approximately ten week period for the complete growth of the new coat.

Hand-stripping is not nearly as complicated as it may seem to the novice owner; and if you have a show prospect puppy, it is to your advantage to try to master the art personally. Although time-consuming, the results are worth it if you take pride in your dog. And if you try to have the coat done at a grooming parlor, you will find them extremely reluctant to undertake this amount of work as the clippering is much quicker.

In hand stripping an adult Miniature Schnauzer, his coat must have reached the length of two to three inches. Stripping is easier if the dog has not just been bathed, slightly soiled hair, Gloria Lewis points out, being easier to grip and pull than very clean hair. On difficult areas, application of powder or chalk will help you achieve a firmer grip.

We quote Gloria Lewis below on the subject of several different methods of hand stripping. She says, "Basically the coat must be removed from the body, tail, shoulders and head with the fingers in a pattern sequence that will permit the hair to regrow to its proper length in ten weeks'

time. Some truly double-coated Schnauzers should have the harsh wiry coat pulled out in a pattern designed for that individual dog, with the entire undercoat being removed ten days after the head coat. Other dogs with little or no undercoat can be stripped to the skin, again following a pattern designed for the dog. Each stripping session should include a thorough combing of the legs and beard. A medicated bath is suggested upon completion of the stripping of the undercoat, as it is inadvisable to bathe the harsh coat once it has grown in. I do not advise the use of so-called stripping knives as their tendency is to cut the hair off at the root rather than pulling it out."

Gloria continues, "After several weeks of new coat growth, the undercoat must be constantly worked out either with the fingers or with a "Magnet" stripper, to reveal the true harsh coat growing underneath. The dog's cheeks and throat may be clippered as well as the rear 'butterfly' and the belly. Two weeks prior to the first show date, the legs, beard and eyebrows should be chalked and trimmed into the correct shape, which should be repeated every week the dog is shown."

Returning, now, to the clippering method, if that is what has been selected for the puppy. The first time this is done can be a traumatic experience for both the puppy and the owner as the sound of the clippers is frightening to many young dogs until they have become accustomed to hearing it. Perhaps if you are a new owner it would be best to seek the help of the puppy's breeder or of a professional groomer for the first session with the clippers. If you decide to undertake it personally, be very gentle (but firm) in your approach, for if this session goes badly, the clippering of the dog may become a major problem throughout his lifetime.

Turn the clipper on a bit in advance of actually starting work, giving time for the noise to be accepted. Bring it, then, close to his head without actually touching him, at the same time talking to him in a reassuring manner and keeping a firm hand on him lest he decide to bolt off. Encourage him to sniff at the clipper. In other words, try to make him understand that it will not hurt him, and that it is really nothing to be feared. Again we quote Gloria Lewis as she directs the clipping be started (with the puppy standing on the grooming table) with an 8½ blade or a # 10 blade away from the head, as the puppy will more easily relax this way. The en-

Paxon's Pandemonium winning Best of Breed at North Western Connecticut in 1971. Jane Forsyth handling for Paxon Kennels, Robert A. Santo, Port Washington, New York. Photo courtesy of Mrs. Forsyth.

tire body should be clippered, following the lay or grain of the hair (in other words, as the coat lies). A # 15 blade can be used under the belly, around the rear parts and on the ears and throat. Care should be taken not to injure the tender skin in these parts, and a heavy touch should not be used. The shaping of the head requires considerable dexterity. The eyebrows must be shaped in exact proportion to each other, the beard must be left long, and the cheeks, throat and chest should be clippered clean. The leg furnishings are left on, and the body should be clipped to the elbow on the front legs and around the stifle to a few inches above the hock on the rear legs. Ears should be clipped close on the outside, and excess hair should be removed from within the ear with blunt tweezers, both for neatness and to guard against ear infections. The legs and beard should be brushed with the pin brush to remove mats, excess dirt and hair. Now the dog is ready to be bathed.

Bathing a Miniature Schnauzer is not a difficult task. For equipment you will need a good mild dog shampoo, a spray with nozzle attachment, or a small cup for dipping water, and use of either a utility sink or the kitchen sink. Place the dog in the sink and thoroughly wet down

with warm water, tipping the head up and back to assure water reaching under the neck area and head. Squirt shampoo on each leg, thoroughly lathering. If you wish, feet can be scrubbed with a rubber shampoo brush or if especially soiled a small nail brush. Using the shampoo brush, thoroughly shampoo the dog, including his underneath and rear. When he has been completely lathered and washed, thoroughly spray with clear water, again tipping head up and back to be sure of not skipping over those parts. Be very certain that the dog is THOROUGHLY rinsed, as soap traces left behind in the coat can cause itching, scratching, and skin irritations.

Wrap a towel around the dog as you remove him from the sink, with which you blot out all excess moisture prior to placing him on the grooming table. If you are working alone, it helps steady him to slip the noose around his neck before starting to comb through all four legs and beard, making certain that all mats are entirely removed. Should tangles persist, use balsam or a tangle-free conditioner (available from your pet supplier) letting it remain on for a few moments before continuing to comb and separate. This should make the job easier. Always comb the legs and beard when wet.

Ch. Royalcourt Bound To Be Happy stands groomed and ready for competition with his owner-handler Mrs. Gloria Lewis keeping a watchful eye. Happy went reserve winners at the New York Miniature Schnauzer Club Specialty Show.

This is an excellent time to attend to the toenails, as they are softer and easier to cut when the dog has just been bathed. Remember to take care NOT to cut below the "quick" as that causes bleeding.

Use your pin-brush as you blow-dry the dog. Leg hair should be combed in an upward direction; beard and eyebrows down and forward. When the dog is thoroughly dry, re-comb the legs and scissor them as nearly as you can to look like those "barber pole" appearing forelegs you admire on the champions in the magazines. Bear in mind that scissors should never be used on dirty hair, so make the most of the opportunity following bathing. For doing the legs, scissors should be held pointing downwards. In shaping eyebrows, slant them towards the ear. Work slowly and carefully, combing out every few moments to see how you are doing. Use thinning shears on the hair between the eyes. If you like, some grooming powder may prove useful on the legs and beard. Gloria Lewis receives many compliments on the fluffy, immaculate appearance of legs and beards of her dogs. Her secret? "Legs and beard must be combed, brushed and conditioned and kept CLEAN, never allowed to mat."

Remember, prevention is the best treatment of all for mats; but if they form and are caught in the EARLY stages they are not so serious a problem as when neglected and permitted to remain once discovered.

Final touches on grooming are to make sure that all hairs have been tweezed or hand pulled out from the inside of the ear, and that the ears are swabbed out to remove any wax accumulation with a cotton swab dipped in alcohol. The teeth should be checked for tartar accumulation, which can be removed with a scraper either by you or your groomer or your veterinarian. This, too, is not difficult if attended to regularly.

It will take a bit of practice to perfect your clippering job, as it is not all that easy in the beginning. If you become discouraged, remember there is always the professional groomer. But also remember that hair DOES grow back in quickly, and that it is worthwhile to stick to it until you can look upon your job with pride!

Rolling a Coat: For the Broken-Coated Terrier
by Mrs. K. L. Church

It is with pride and pleasure that we bring you on the following pages the process known as "rolling" the coat of a broken-coated terrier which has been used with great success by the famous owner of Kazel Miniature Schnauzers, Mrs. K.L. Church. Mrs. Church is noted for the impeccable presentation of her Schnauzers, which she credits to this method of coat care. Please note that by this method a Schnauzer is always in presentable coat; thus the periods of missing shows as his coat "makes up" between strippings are eliminated.

Numerous successful Schnauzer fanciers around the country have written to me of their own successful use of this method. We feel that the information is extremely valuable to those who are interested in maintaining show coats on their Miniature Schnauzers which are ring-ready at all time. And so our thanks to Mrs. Church for allowing us to share the knowledge of her method with our readers.

A.K.N.

The art of maintaining a broken coat is virtually lost. This type of coat is not unique to the Miniature Schnauzer, nor is it limited to the Terrier breeds. It is an important skill for any person to develop who is involved in the care, grooming and exhibiting of breeds requiring stripping and development of the harsh wiry coat that grows perpetually. The subject of "working" a broken coat will be specifically presented herein as it is related to the Miniature Schnauzer.

In recent years it has become a nearly universal fad to "section" or use "stages" in the stripping procedure. This is not "rolling" a coat. "Sectioning" requires setting aside specific days on a calendar at precisely spaced periods of time prior to the arbitrary date selected as "show time." During the series of calendar dates, various patterned shapes and sizes of body coat are plucked, and again four weeks after that the body is "defuzzed." In other words, the soft undercoat which surfaces more rapidly, but belongs underneath the hard coat, must again be plucked away to make a clean appearance. Sectioning is used to produce a smooth outline or picture, and may also establish shorter growth in areas which can become shaggy if pulled too early. This can detract from the clean-cut lines of

the jacket toward the end of its coat life. At that point, the only alternative is to begin scissoring the coat in the offending areas. There may be as few as two sections and as many, or more, than seven or eight sections or stages to achieve a finished jacket. With the spacing of three to four days between each of the sections, the work required to develop a show coat that will last from four to possibly ten weeks with luck, is certainly not time-efficient. Two-stage sectioning might achieve the desired show look if a dog were perfectly formed or well put together. Adding more sections is used to fill low places (by pulling earlier) and level out high places (by pulling later). The more steps you have in a sectioned stripping, the more you would send out a message that you are dealing with a multiplicity of faults, and pointing them out. If you must begin with a small patch stripped out in the middle of the back (dip in the back); or in front of the shoulders (poor blend of neck), there is always a tell-tale line or slight change of color between sections, perceptible to the practiced eye. Would you then resort to tinting? Examination of such a coat is similar to reading a precise road map of the animal's faults, determined by visual perception of the lengths.

We will not concern ourselves with sectioning a coat, as it is merely a technique developed in an attempt to shortcut the correct way. It is only important that you, as the reader, recognize the differences which will provide understanding of the correct method, should you decide to try it. The original and correct method, *rolling a coat,* is actually much easier to implement and maintain, with many additional benefits over sectioning, for both the domestic and show scenes. The drawback is it requires one to think and to develop a skill.

Before the demand grew for thick cottony furnishings and *their* usual companion, softer coats, a broken coat had the natural characteristics for "rolling," and grooming it could be done automatically. Yet, ironically, the poorer quality of the non-wiry, smoother hard coat variety makes the ability to roll a coat even more imperative.

How would you establish a rolled coat? Perhaps it would be more useful to describe in depth the technique for developing a rolled coat from a blown coat rather than a puppy coat. It is first important to be familiar with the structure of the coat hair. Salt and pepper Schnauzer coats are unique because they are "banded."

Skyline's Fallen Angel, by Ch. Skyline's Striking ex Ch. Orbit's Lift Off, C.D.X., was born March 1975. This was the first venture of her owner in showing an uncropped Miniature Schnauzer, and she earned 12 points including three majors owner-handled, as well as reserve at the American Miniature Schnauzer Club National in June 1976 although she never completed her title. She is a litter sister to Ch. Skyline's Sally Forth. Carol A. Parker, Vail, Arizona.

A puppy coat begins its growth in three natural layers or phases and can be promoted into a rolling coat from these layers easily by the age of six months if begun, gently, at six weeks, as part of its grooming training. One dog, for example, Champion Kazels Favorite, began his rolled coat at that age and wore it for *ten years.* In fact, all the four-legged residents in his home were maintained and shown in rolled coats. The quality of the hair varied from dog to dog.

As hair grows out, the appearance and substance of it changes. A very soft coat will change more quickly and more radically than the harsher coat quality. Some hard hairs will remain hard throughout, but become of poorer quality as they grow longer. The straighter, less harsh coat hair, which feels smooth when grown to a true show length is, of course, the least desirable quality. The requirement as stated in the Standard for the Breed is: The hair need only be "of sufficient length to determine texture." By some interpretations, the statement can mean one need only feel the bristly stubble or tips newly emerged. However, that length would misrepresent itself as a "harsh" or hard coat at that extremely short length. This coat may not be representative of the true hard, harsh, wiry feel when it has grown to an acceptable show length. Rolling this type of coat can assist it in producing a slightly harder feel, and possibly, with the different lengths present in a rolled coat, can provide a rougher feeling texture to the coat's surface. It will not, however, do anything to transform it into the correct wiry or broken coated quality. No method will do that. Additives might help "fake" the feel of it, but it will still look straight, visually. Therefore, as stated, if any coats were to benefit from this technique it would be those which are frequently defended, and erroneously so, as not lending themselves well to the rolling method. A natural harsh wiry coat does not need to be "beefed up" further; it is correct regardless of whether it is sectioned or rolled.

With the exception of the all-black hair, "banding" occurs. There are also occasional white or brown hairs, but we will concentrate on the usual coat characteristics. When the hair emerges at the skin's surface, the tips are a shade of gray, dark gray or black. This darker growth may be only a trace, an eighth of an inch, or extend along the shaft for an inch or more. The latter produces the darker looking coats. Next, the color of the shaft changes to white, gray, silver,

tan or brownish shades. This section of growth also may vary in length. As it continues to grow out, the shaft of hair begins to thin and soften, and most lose the ability to maintain the body that conveys the feel of "hardness." The color also fades, becoming washed-out looking, into some shade of grayness, ranging from almost silvery white to very dark charcoal shades. This overall shade of grayness is what one sees when the coat is clipped. In order to reverse the process, the shaft must be pulled out by the root. This is called stripping. Apparently, the follicle is irritated, causing it to produce the harder shaft when it begins to grow back.

A rolled coat is a perpetual coat. There is always fresh hard hair to be found under the surface layer. If it is implemented correctly, this is easily accomplished. To preserve this plan, you must only pull the very top hair each time. You will pull only the longest hair. Hair grows in varying lengths. As the coat continues to grow, there is always a layer or row of longer hairs. Those which were shorter before you pulled the top off, have now become the longest ones, and will be cleared off during the next stripping session. Do not break or cut off the hair. It must be pulled from the skin. What is broken or cut off becomes only leftover dead and soft hair and the growth cycle will not be started for it to grow back as hard coat. This will also result in a mixed coat surface after the layers are established. Resist the urge to trim up the blown long coat during the period of time needed to pull the layers down. If you do scissor it to even it up or tidy it up, it will make all the hairs the same length destroying the advantage you had from the naturally grown lengths which were to be used in setting your "layers." There seems to be a common temptation to "tidy up" the dog during the time the layers are being developed. When it is all the same length, it becomes a more difficult task to decide what to pull and what to leave for the next time.

Rule: Do not alter the coat length while developing the rolled coat, except for the periodic strippings themselves.

When removing a layer, the fingers should not do more than lightly brush against the tips of the longest hair on the coat to raise them up. You are literally skimming the outer surface. You will be pulling only a few hairs with each pass of the fingers or the stripping knife and thumb.

Rule: At each sitting, coat must be "worked" over the entire surface which is to produce hard hair.

The lengths may need to vary on different areas, as demonstrated by the shorter length on the top of the head and longer on the back, but every area must be pulled at the same time. If you do not follow this rule, you will have "blank" spaces on your dog when that layer grows back in and becomes the top coat. You will subsequently be pulling off hair that should be left for the layer beneath it, just to make up for your earlier omission. You are creating a vicious circle, and will find it difficult to keep track of where and when you expect the hair to grow in in any particular area or spot without some kind of detailed calendar. It defeats the very purpose and simplicity of rolling a coat. This same problem can arise if one is careless or heavy-handed, pulling too deeply into any area. If this heavy-handedness occurs over the entire jacket, more than one complete layer could be removed at one time, and more than one cycle of growth becomes combined into a single thicker layer for the next growth period.

Visually, it is a matter of working over the entire surface until it is just slightly shorter. This is true whether you are working on a blown coat, trying to establish a rolled coat, or maintaining a closely worked rolled hard coat.

The tool used to strip the coat is important. The edge has a row of small grooves to assist in holding hair firmly against it. If the blade or edge is too sharp, there will be a tendency to cut off the hair rather than to brace it against your thumb while pulling it; and the possibility exists that you may damage ends of the layer beneath it as well. If the shaft tends to produce only an eighth of an inch of black tip, you could be cutting off the color of the coat you plan to show that weekend. Result: A white or gray coat.

Rule: Do not cut or break coat by twisting the stripping blade against the shaft, or with your fingernails. Pull the hair shaft with a straight, sharp tug.

Logically, keeping the coat pulled to the optimum length at which the shaft is its hardest and the coloring of the banding is primarily its darkest, would produce a more handsome show coat. This is not theory. The writer had done this with many different qualities of coat and found that these facts are borne out in practical application.

We must begin by agreeing with the premise there is no perfect dog, so another advantage of having several layers of coat available to the groomer is being able to "sculpt" the outline of the body. The lengths and blending needed to hide whatever fault any dog might be endowed with are not left up to the whims of the calendar, and environmental influences, of the sectioning approach, when the rolling method is used. If you are rolling your coat, you would be setting up a well-blended surface coat. The color is richer and there are no misleading lines.

In younger dogs, there is often a lot more "down" in the coat. As the rolling coat is developed and matures, this "down" decreases. The soft undercoat remains, but there seems to be less of it if the practice is continued. You will have enough to qualify under the breed standard on any one layer, but it is easily managed in the process of working the coat. The more you pull on the hair, the more it seems to keep the follicles producing harder coat. With a "bad" coat it becomes even more important than ever to try rolling it, because it promotes hair growing in hard, never letting it revert back to the softer quality seen in between strippings.

A practiced hand need spend only from a half hour to an hour a week on a rolled coat, depending on the level of perfection desired. This may be planned on an every other week or more basis, if it is more convenient that way. However, just as with the furnishings, a top show coat should be worked weekly.

Rule: After the layers are established and before any stripping is done, the coat must always first be thoroughly "raked." The appropriate tool for raking out the undercoat is called a magnetic stripping comb.

The blade is held perpendicular to the body and combed with medium pressure in the direction of the growth, not against it. This action will lift up the undercoat and remove it. Do not slant the blade or cutting may occur. You must clean it out down below the level of the layer you intend to reveal with your current stripping job. If this is not done, the coat surface will be mixed with the soft hair, look dull and feel soft. If you follow this practice faithfully, you will not find undercoat accumulating into a large unsightly

"Twas the night before Christmas----." Santa, Schnauzer babies, and the household. The Schnauzers all are in rolled coats. An excellent example of the art. Owned by Mrs. K. L. Church, Kazel Kennels, Imperial, Missouri.

Int., Mex., Can., and Am. Ch. Kazels Favorite. A Tauskey portrait of this great and magnificent dog. Mrs. K.L. Church, owner, Kazel, Imperial, Missouri.

Ch. Richlene's Big Time, the sire of 13 champion offspring. Bred and owned by Rich and Arlene Smith, Fort Wayne, Indiana. Handled by Rich Smith.

mass periodically. This is the main problem which seems to plague the faint of heart at some time during the process of rolling a coat. If this happens, do not decide that the coat cannot be rolled, pulling it all out to "clean it up." You would have ruined your master plan then, not earlier, as you had originally thought.

When working from a blown coat, some of the undercoat should come off with each pulling of the layers as you progress. Do not avoid it. If you do not spread out the lengths of this undercoat too, you will not always have the desired coat quality called for in the Standard, "Double, with hard wiry, outer coat and close under coat," from week to week. The remaining undercoat is dealt with as you roll the coat later on, just as described earlier. It is removed during each layering of the coat kept up in show condition. As mentioned, some of the soft coat found in a blown coat, and the soft coat from clippering does turn hard as you pull it. This is one of the advantages of rolling a coat. The truly harsh, wiry ideal coat can be kept in top condition continuously, and the softer, straighter hair can be developed into a harder texture.

Learning to work swiftly comes through practice. Raising and pinching (lightly) the skin upward between your thumb and forefinger and rolling it along as you skim off the longest tips is the fastest method, especially for the beginner. It does not require constantly brushing the hair upright to line it up before pulling. This alternate method is brushing the hair upright with the thumb, completing the motion by pressing the thumb against the hair and the stripping knife blade and pulling it with a quick jerk. This does not yield an even coat unless you are either well practiced or move very slowly, watching precisely what you are about to pull. It is the swiftest method when you become quite skillful.

It is possible to time a rolled coat. If you are pulling weekly, there is little need for too much preplanning. However, if you are using a two or three week schedule, it is better to project ahead on your calendar for the optimum results of a planned layering. You may want to pull that layer a week or so sooner than normally scheduled if the calendar indicates a special show is listed in eight or ten weeks. You would not want the coat to look great on the Tuesday after that show. You should be familiar with each dog's own unique coat cycle. Some are six week coats, some may be as much as twelve weeks to a short

show coat from a stripping date. Therefore, you will develop anywhere from six to twelve different layers, and logically, six to twelve different coats.

This coat cycle time is important in planning your coat layers. A slower growing coat may lend itself to a bi-weekly layering plan, whereas a fast growing coat can get away from you if it is not worked weekly. A coat "let go" for a few weeks, cannot be caught up by pulling it down harder. You will destroy your layers. You must still pull only the longest layer. If you want to work it back under control more quickly, then you may pull the layers down every four days until you are again working with a closer, tighter coat, gradually extending the time periods, then resume your normal layering schedule, weekly, bi-weekly, and so on. Remember, if you run too few layers too close together in pulling time, you will ultimately have a blank period until the coat breaks the surface at its natural time.

Deciding to develop a rolled coat, you must consider the frequency you wish to use in rolling it and the exact cycle of that coat. Coat planning varies with the intended purpose. Perhaps you are planning a campaign with a Special, and want the coat to always be in top condition. Perhaps you enjoy showing a properly groomed dog regularly in Obedience. Or perhaps you just enjoy having a nice looking dog at home that never has to visit the groomer. If you have an eight week coat cycle from pulling to a desirable show length, you may wish to roll or layer it regularly on a weekly basis. The weekly plan produces the best show coat. You have two options. For example, you may plan to develop a six week coat in six stages, or may want to have backup growth later on by extending the layers to seven levels, planning the first show in seven weeks. You would be doubling up on coat at the end to protect against any errors you might have made as a beginner. Never yield to the temptation of thinking that a coat looks so great that you will try to hold it over for the next week. You should always have a fresh coat coming on and you will be defeating your plan if you do not follow it as you have set out to do.

If the coat cycle is twelve weeks, you will then plan your entries following the twelve weeks figured from the first pull. After this initial waiting period, if you have done a good job, you should be able to feel free to plan attending most shows that appeal to you. Whether six layers or

Ch. Sisterce of Sole Baye at eleven years of age winning the Veteran's Class at the American Miniature Schnauzer Club Specialty. Owner-handled by Yvonne B. Phelps, El Monte, California. Judge, on right, Mrs. Winifred Heckman.

up to as many as twelve, that decision will determine the amount of hair you will pull out at any one sitting. You will literally be dividing the body coat into six, eight or twelve parts. The number is governed by the number of weeks you have decided you will need to grow the first layer of coat. In other words, each week you will pull only one-twelfth or up to one-sixth of the hair, another alternative for planning would include pulling more hair each time, but only every other week. Some of us have jokingly referred to this as pulling every sixth, eighth or twelfth hair. This may convert to either pulling lightly or us-

ing a medium heavy touch. Remember, you are only to skim the surface on each pull or layering. Throughout, you should develop a sense of planning and awareness of what you are trying to achieve in those six, eight or twelve weeks. This does require a knowledge of the Breed Standard and an objective assessment of your dog.

Narrow areas located along the lines between the clipped and trimmed sections (legs, cheeks, tail, etc.) and the hard coat might be worked additional times between the regular pulling sessions. This will produce many very short hairs to be used in *blending*.

All nicely stacked on the table, waiting for the judge. Ch. Royalcourts Bound To Be Happy with owner-handler Mrs. Gloria Lewis.

Rule: Before any scissoring takes place, always pluck in that area *first*.
Rule: Never scissor the jacket.
Rule: Never do any scissoring to blend.

The only time this might become necessary is the day of a show if you have pulled a spot down as far as you can without revealing bare skin. You may trim lightly with the thinning shears to blend into the clipped areas, and then only in a very narrow line. The ideal length for the hair to be maintained along the line of the face, chest hair and furnishings is approximately one-eighth of an inch. This maintains a sharp edge to the jacket. It is similar to drawing a pencil line around the entire edge of the hard coat.

A final word might be offered on the subject of "cleaning-" or "tidying-up." It would be appropriate to clean up the "garbage" at the end of the initial stages of layering. It should be done between two layering dates. It may also be done very prudently if your timing is found to be off periodically every sixth, eighth, etc., week, but you should really try to spread this undercoat out among the layers to eliminate this problem.

As you work, you will discover that, with understanding of what a stripped coat is really like, you will also develop your own personal skills for using it to its best advantage.

Aberdovey's Go Bananas at nine months of age. By Ch. Paxon Pacesetter ex Ch. Paxon's Stage Struck. Bred and owned by Sally Critchlow, Morristown, New Jersey.

Am., Can., and Ber. Ch. Kelly's Ebony Show Stopper, an all-breed Best in Show winner, National Specialty Best in Show winner, Top Winning Black Miniature Schnauzer of the decade. Stopper finished at the age of 7 months, and has the additional distinction of being the only black of his breed to have produced champions in all three colors. Top Producing Black as of mid-1984. By Ch. Kelly's Black Onyx ex Cayla's Sugar Babe. Owned by Geri Kelly, North Falmouth, Massachusetts.

CHAPTER TWELVE

Showing Your Miniature Schnauzer

The suspension trot, so important in the breed, is beautifully illustrated here by Int., Mex., Can., Am. Ch. Kazels Favorite. Mrs. K.L. Church, owner, Kazel's Schnauzers, Imperial, Missouri.

The groundwork for showing your Miniature Schnauzer has been accomplished with your careful selection and purchase of your future show prospect. If it is a puppy, we assume that you have gone through all the proper preliminaries of good care, which actually should be the same whether the puppy is a pet or a future show dog, with a few extra precautions in the case of the latter.

General Considerations

Remember that a winning dog must be kept in trim, top condition. You want him neither too fat nor too thin, so do not spoil his figure and his appearance, or his appetite for proper nourishing food, by allowing family members or guests to be constantly feeding him "goodies." The best "treat" of all is a small wad of ground raw beef or one of the packaged dog "goodies." To be avoided are ice cream, potato chips, cookies, cake, candy, and other fattening items which will cause the dog to gain weight. A dog in show condition must never be fat, nor must he be painfully thin to the point of his ribs fairly sticking through the skin.

The importance of temperament and showmanship cannot possibly be overemphasized. These two qualities have put many a mediocre dog across, while lack of them can ruin the career of an otherwise outstanding specimen. So, from the day your dog or puppy arrives home, socialize him. Keep him accustomed to being with people and to being handled by people. Encourage your friends and relatives to "go over" him as the judges will in the ring, so that at the shows this will not be a strange, upsetting experience. Practice showing his "bite" (the manner in which his teeth meet) deftly and quickly. It is quite simple to spread the lips apart with your fingers, and the puppy should be accustomed and willing to accept this from you or from the judge, without struggle. Some judges ask the exhibitors to handle the mouths, showing them bite and jaws, rather than doing it themselves. These are the considerate judges who prefer not to risk spreading any possible virus infections by taking their hands from one dog's mouth to another's; but the old-fashioned judges still persist in doing the latter, so the dog should be prepared for either.

Take your future show dog with you in the car, so that he will love riding and not become carsick when he travels. He should associate going in the car with pleasure and attention. Take him where it is crowded: downtown, shopping malls, or, in fact, anywhere you go where dogs are permitted. Make the expeditions fun for him by frequent petting and words of praise; do not just ignore him as you go about your errands or other business.

Do not overly shelter your future show dog. Instinctively you may want to keep him at home, especially while a young puppy, where he is safe from germs or danger; but this can be foolish on two counts. To begin with, a dog kept away from other dogs or other environments builds up no natural immunity against all the things with which he will come in contact at the dog shows. Actually it is wiser to keep him well up-to-date on all protective "shots" and then allow him to become accustomed to being among other dogs and dog owners. Also, a dog who never goes among people, to strange places, or among strange dogs, may grow up with a timidity of spirit that will cause you deep problems when his show career gets under way.

Keep your Miniature Schnauzer's coat in immaculate condition with daily grooming (which takes only a few minutes) and baths when the lat-

Ch. Gough's Ebony Polo Player, Best of Breed over Specials at Windham County 1981. Gloria Lewis handling for owners, Neil and Nancy Gallagher. Breeder, Alice Gough.

ter are necessary. For the latter, use a mild baby shampoo or whatever the person who bred your puppy may suggest. Several of the "brand name" products do an excellent job, and there are several which are beneficial toward keeping the dog free of fleas. Look for them at your pet supplier's. Be sure to rinse the dog thoroughly, leaving no traces of soap which may cause itching or skin irritation. It is a wise precaution to put a drop of castor oil in each eye to ensure no soap irritation. Use warm water (be sure it is not uncomfortably hot or chillingly cold) and a good spray. An electric hair dryer is a great convenience; use it after first blotting off the excess moisture with a Turkish towel. Do not let water find its way into the ear cavity. A wad of cotton in the ear guards against this possibility. Toenails also should be watched and trimmed every few weeks. It is important not to let nails grow too long as they can become painful and ruin the appearance of foot and pastern.

Assuming that you will be handling the dog personally, or even if he will be professionally handled, it is important that a few moments of each day be spent practicing dog show routine. Practice "stacking," or "setting him up," as you have seen the exhibitors do at the shows you've attended, and teach him to hold this position once you have him stacked to your satisfaction. Make the learning pleasant by being firm but

A leading breed and Group winner, Ch. Fancway's Gorgeous George and Ch. Fancway's Jillett, winning Best Brace in Show at San Gabriel K.C. in 1963. Handled by Jean Fancy, owned by Jean and Glenn Fancy, Fancway Kennels.

Ch. Black Watch of Blythewood with handler Joan Huber is winning here the Terrier Group at Twin Brooks K.C. in 1970 for owner, Ruth I. Quire, Pleasanton, California.

Ch. Cyngar's Ultimatum, bred and owned by Cynthia C. Garton, Lincoln, Nebraska, moving along nicely in the ring.

lavish in your praise when he behaves correctly. Work in front of a mirror for setting up practice; this enables you to see the dog as the judge does and to learn what corrections need to be made by looking at the dog from that angle.

Teach your Miniature Schnauzer to gait at your side. When you have mastered the basic essentials at home, then look for and join a training class for future work and polishing up your technique. Training classes are sponsored by show-giving clubs in many areas, and their popularity is steadily increasing. If you have no other way of locating one, perhaps your veterinarian may know of one through some of his clients; but if you are sufficiently aware of the dog show world to want a show dog, you will probably be personally acquainted with other fanciers who will share information of this sort with you.

Accustom your show dog to being in a crate (which you should be doing, even if the dog is to be only a pet). He should be kept in the crate "between times" for his own well-being and safety.

A show dog's teeth must be kept clean and free of tartar. Hard dog biscuits can help toward this. If tartar does accumulate, see that it is removed promptly by your veterinarian. Bones are not suitable for show dogs once they have their second teeth as they tend to damage and wear down the tooth enamel (bones are all right for puppies, as they help with the teething process).

Beyond these special considerations, your show-prospect Miniature Schnauzer will thrive under the same treatment as accorded any well-cared-for family pet. In fact, most of the foregoing is applicable to a pet Miniature Schnauzer as well as to a show Miniature Schnauzer, for what it boils down to is simply keeping the dog at his best.

Japanese Ch. Shirley's Sky Rocket going Best in Show at an important Japanese event. Owned and handled by Akio Kuroki.

Ch. Penlan Promissory winning Best in Show, Illinois Valley, May 1982. Owned by Lanny and Penny Hirstein, Washington, Illinois.

Joan L. Huber with Ch. Blythewood National Accord, a Specialty Best in Show winner by Ch. Blythewood National Anthem ex Valharra's Prize O'Blythewood. Owner, Margaret Pratt, Vienna, Virginia.

Ch. Penlan Paper Boy gaining his first points from the 6-9 months puppy class under Alva Rosenberg at the Autumn Specialty Show of the American Miniature Schnauzer Club in 1972. This was one of the many great dogs Alva Rosenberg discovered and started during his illustrious judging career. Owned by Landis and Penny Hirstein, Penlan Kennels, Washington, Illinois.

Match Shows

Your Miniature Schnauzer's first experience in show ring procedure should be at match show competition. There are several reasons for this. First of all, this type of event is intended as a learning experience for both the puppies and for the exhibitors; thus you will feel no embarrassment if your puppy misbehaves or if your own handling technique is obviously inept. There will be many others in that same position. So take the puppy and go, and the two of you can learn together what it is like actually to compete against other dogs for the approval of the judge.

Another reason for beginning a show career at match shows is the matter of cost. Entries at the point shows nowadays cost over ten dollars. True, there are many clubs who reduce this fee by a few dollars for the Puppy Classes (but by no means do all of them), but even so it is silly to throw this amount away when you know full well your puppy will not yet have the ring presence to hold his own. For the match shows, on the other hand, the entry fee is usually less, [than five dollars] so using those shows as a learning ground for you and your puppy certainly makes better sense. Another advantage of match shows is that advance entries for them are seldom necessary, and even those clubs having them usually will accept additional entries the morning of the show. If you wake up feeling like taking the puppy for an outing, you can go right ahead. The entries at point shows, however, close about two and a half weeks in advance.

You will find the judges more willing to discuss your puppy with you at a match show than during the day of a full and hectic point show; one of their functions, when officiating at a match, is to help new exhibitors with comments and suggestions. We might wish that we could do so at the point shows; but, generally speaking, our schedules do not permit this time to be taken. Unless you stay until the judge's working day is ended, it is often difficult to get even a few words with him. The informality of match shows makes it far easier to get a judge's verbal opinion there; and since judges at these events are usually professional handlers or already licensed judges who are working toward applying for additional breeds, the opinions should be knowledgeable and helpful.

As with training classes, information regarding match shows can be obtained from breeders in your area, your local kennel club if there is one, your veterinarian, or, of course, the person in charge of your training class, if you belong to one. The A.K.C. can also furnish this information; and if your local newspaper carries a pet column, announcements of such coming events will almost certainly appear there.

Ch. Skyline's Smoke Signal is the little dog who was campaigned as a Special starting in September 1983. Between then and the end of the year became No. 1 Miniature Schnauzer for the entire year or 1983! Of considerable help in achieving this was his unprecedented sweep of the entire Montgomery County weekend, during which he won the breed all four days in entries well above a hundred on each occasion. By Ch. Skyline's Signature ex Skyline's Valley Forge, born in April 1982. Carol A. Parker, Owner, Skyline, Vail, Arizona.

This is the famed Ch. Blythewood Main Gazebo winning the American Miniature Schnauzer Club Specialty in February 1965, judged by the late Louis Murr. By Ch. Phil Mar Lugar ex Ch. Blythewood Sweet Talk, Gazebo was the sire of 32 champions, and held the breed record for Best of Breed wins, with 105 such victories, over many years. Bred, owned and handled by Mrs. Joan L. Huber, Green Lane, Pennsylvania.

Ch. Blythewood Chief Bosun owned by Mrs. Joan L. Huber, Blythewood Kennels, Green Lane, Pennsylvania.

←Overleaf:
This gorgeous headstudy is of Am. and Can. Ch. Britmor Sunnymeade
Frost, Am. and Can. C.D., at two years of age. Karen J. Brittan, Owner,
St. Louis Park, Minnesota

1. Miniature Schnauzer puppies from Blue Skies Kennels, Marilyn Cooper, St. Louis, Missouri. Photo by Barbara Von Hoffman.

2. Ch. Travelmor's From U.S. To You, Top Schnauzer in England, all three sizes, in 1982, and 3rd Ranking in Utility Group. Owned by Pam Radford and Dori Clarke in England. Bred in the United States by William E. Moore, Trenton, New Jersey.

3. Ch. Skyline's Forever Blue in October 1982 at 18 months. Carol A. Parker, Vail, Arizona.

4. Ch. Regency's Equal Rights, the first uncropped champion Miniature Schnauzer in the United States since 1934, homebred owned by Beverly J. Verna, Regency Kennels, Santa Clara, California.

5. Skyline Royalcourt Lucy, taking Best of Winners, April 1983. Owned and handled by Gloria Lewis, Closter, NJ.

6. Ch. Jilmar's Allstar owned by Lisa M. Grames, Winter Springs, Florida.

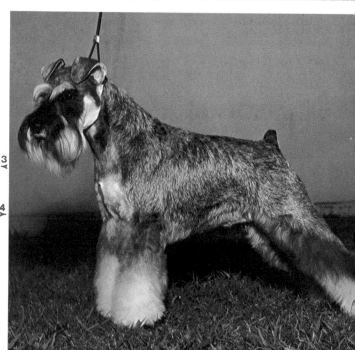

1 ▶

2 ▶

3 ▶

4 ▶

5 ▶

6 ▶

BE
OF
WINNERS

17, 1983

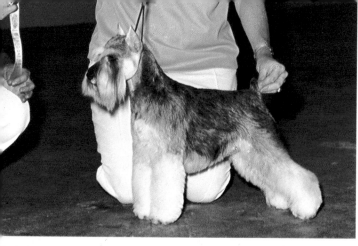

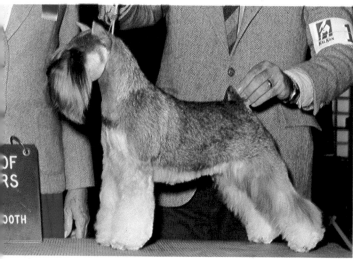

WINNERS

GREENWICH
KENNEL CLUB

1980

SHERRY PHOTO

WINNERS

WALLKILL
KENNEL CLUB

JAN 1983

← **Overleaf:**

1. Ch. Black Watch Sunny Side Up belongs to Capt. Jean L. Heath, USN (Retired), Pleasanton, California.

2. Ch. Skyline's Frostflower, by Ch. Sky Rocket's Upswing ex Ch. Skyline's Summertime, was the dam of three champion sons before having to be spayed at the youthful age of three. Carol A. Parker, owner, Vail, Arizona.

3. How a very promising young Miniature Schnauzer should look! This is Ch. Jilmar's Allstar who at the age of six months has just won a Major under judge Evelyn Kirk. Lisa M. Grames, owner, Jilmar Schnauzers, Winter Springs, Florida.

4. Kajons Holocaust (sired by Ch. Kazels Favorite) has 5-points, the second from a litter of three en route to the title. Handled by Mrs. K.L. Church. Owned by Mrs. C. Muhlenkamp.

5. Specialty Show winner Ch. Merry Maker's Bo Kay, by Ch. Bardow Bounty Hunter ex Merry Maker's Ms. Tillie, is one of the beautiful Miniature Schnauzers owned by Mabel M. (Jinx) Gunville, Deerfield, Illinois.

6. The black and silver bitch Ch. Sycamore's Esprit bred by Margo Heiden and owned by H. De Luca. Handled by Gloria Lewis.

7. The No. 2 Miniature Schnauzer Dog in 1978, Ch. Twin Tree Posh Josh, a multiple Specialty winner, bred and owned by Jacquie and Fred Schnebeli. Handled exclusively by Judy Smith, Bettendorf, Iowa.

8. Ch. Mi-Sher's Mystic Moment, by Ch. Linalee's E Z Lovin' of Mi-Sher ex Ch. Regency's Right On Target, taking Winners Bitch at the Dog Fanciers of Greater Oregon in 1983. Owned by Sheryl Stump, Clackamas, Oregon.

Ch. Irrenhaus St. Nicholas, by Ch. Irrenhaus Blueprint ex Ch. Irrenhaus Flights of Fancy, a homebred multiple Group winner owned and bred by Jacqueline Hicks, Woodford, Virginia and handled by Sue Baines. Started show career with Winners Dog at Montgomery County from the puppy class. Photo by Sue Baines.

Overleaf: →

Can. Ch. Frontenac's Arielle, C.D.X., by Can. Ch. Le Conquerant de Frontenac ex Can. Ch. Frontenac's Pirate Gris-Sel, bred by Jacline and Armand Gratton, owned by Gail King. This was the No. 1 Schnauzer in obedience in Canada for three consecutive years, and No. 3 Terrier. Arielle, 13″ tall, was born in January 1978. She is the dam of Can. Ch. Frontenac's Star Dust who is sired by Can. Ch. Frontenac's Footprint. Frontenac Kennels are at Les Cedres, Quebec.

Travelmor's Friendly Sky, by Ch. Sky Rocket's Travel More ex Ch. Reflections Lively Image. One of the many splendid winners bred by Bill and Olive Moore.

← **Overleaf:**
Spring-along Dark Smoke, a Ch. Carolane's Gangbuster son, with his friend Kim Spring. This fine dog is producing progeny of exceptional quality. Mary E. Spring, owner, Landenberg, Pa.

Overleaf: →

1. Ch. Bokay Dandy Lion winning the breed. Handled by Clay Coady for Ruth and Dorothy Anderson, Dor-Ru Kennels, Santa Ana Heights, California.

2. Ch. Irrenhaus Stamp of Approval, homebred belonging to Jacqueline Hicks, Woodford, Virginia, winning the Terrier Group at Charlottesville-Albemarle. Handled by Sue Baines.

3. One of the fine young Schnauzers of David Kirkland winning Best of Breed under Ron Krohne at Glens Falls K.C. in 1982. This is Ch. Daland's Disco Dancer, second champion bred by David.

4. Sole Baye's Landoluce owned by Yvonne B. Phelps, El Monte, California.

5. Ch. Aberdovey's Happy To Be of Paxon, by Ch. Paxon Pacesetter ex Royalcourt Happy Returns, C.D., placing Winners at South Jersey in October 1981. Bred and owned by Sally Critchlow, Morristown, New Jersey.

6. Ch. Carolane's Moonraker in November 1980. This handsome Schnauzer is one of those by Ch. Penlan Peter Gunn ex Carolane Heaven Sent. Owned by Carl and Carol Beiles. Handled by Claudia Seaberg.

7. Ch. Penlan Pride's Pageantry pictured winning points from the puppy class. This dog is a champion producer owned by Penny and Landis Hirstein, Penlan Schnauzers, Washington, Illinois.

8. Ch. Kelly's Flam-Boy-Ant Black, by Charmar's Johann ex Ch. Kelly's Im-Pec-Cable Black, taking Best of Opposite Sex at Westminster in 1982. Judge was Dr. Josephine Deubler. Bred, owned and handled by Geri Kelly.

GROUP
FIRST
CHARLOTTESVILLE
ALBEMARLE
1980
ASHBEY

BEST OF
BREED
NS FALLS
KENNEL CLUB
1982
ASHBEY

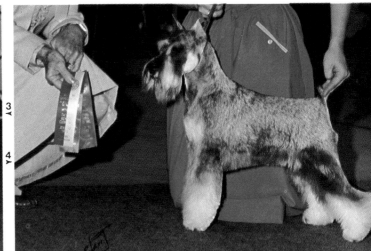

WINNERS
SOUTH JERSEY
KENNEL CLUB INC
JOE C   OCT 1981

BEST OF
WINNERS
SAVANNAH
KENNEL CLUB
NOVEMBER 1980
Graham   PHOTO BY BONNIE

BEST OF
OPPOSITE SEX
PHOTO
BY   K. BOOTH

BES
OPPOSITE
WESTMINSTER
KENNEL CLUB
1982
GILBERT PHOTO

BEST IN SHOW

FOREST CITY KENNEL CLUB

BEST OF BREED

ASHBEY PHOTO

EST of WINNERS

TAMPA BAY
NNEL CLUB INC.
AN 15=78   KLEIN

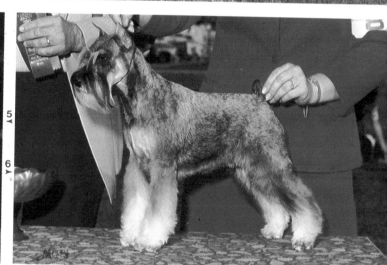

BEST OF WINNERS

ASHBEY PHOTO

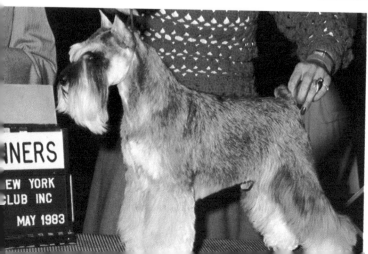

NERS

EW YORK
CLUB INC

MAY 1983

BEST OF BREED

MEDINA KENNEL CLUB INC.
KLEIN   JULY 198

← **Overleaf:**

1. Canadian Ch. Massawippi Troubadour, Canada's All Time Top Winning Miniature Schnauzer, all systems, winning one of his Bests in Show for owners Mr. and Mrs. S.L. Clark, Hillsburgh, Ontario, Canada.

2. Ch. Jadee's Jump Up winning Best of Breed at the Penn Ohio Specialty, June 16, 1975. Owners, D.L. and Judy Smith. Handler, Judy Smith.

3. Ch. Sparks Woerwag, by Ch. Luremi Winsome Jester ex Ch. Reflections Sparkler, owned by Priscilla Deaver Kelley, Fort Washington, Pennsylvania. Handled by Joan L. Huber.

4. Ch. Penlan's Promise, No. 2 Miniature Schnauzer in the U.S. for 1980. He is the sire of Ch. Penlan Promissary and is a Group and Specialty winner. Landis and Penny Hirstein, Penlan Kennels, Washington, Illinois.

5. Ch. Sim-Cal's Personality Plus, by Ch. Blythewood His Majesty ex Blythewood Naughty Kelly, owned by Theresa Klemencic, Bridgeville, Pennsylvania. Joan L. Huber, breeder-handler.

6. Wy-O's Right Answer, by Ch. Regency Right On ex Wy-O's Terrible Tilly, pictured on October 8, 1983. She started out with a 4-point major and a Group First. Owner-handled by Wyoma Clouss.

7. Ch. Pen-dots Mighty Moe, by Ch. Blythewood National Anthem ex Pen-Dots Afternoon Delight, owned by Penni Shipley, Bridgeville, Pennsylvania. Handled by Joan L. Huber.

8. Ch. Dixie Farms Prime Time, sired by Ch. Richlene Big Time, was bred by owners Mel and Joyce Garno and handled by Rich Smith.

Overleaf: →

1. Ch. Jadee's Hush Up, by Ch. Sky Rocket's Upswing ex Ch. Jadee's Juju, was bred by Don and Judy Smith and finished in March 1980. Won a Group First and a Third from the classes. Specialed by Wyoma Clouss, he won 34 Bests of Breed with two more Group Firsts, a Group Second, three Group Thirds and four Group Fourths. Owned by Wyoma and Owen Clouss, Wy-O's Miniature Schnauzers, Boise, Idaho.

2. Ch. Travelmor's Triumph, the last son of Ch. Sky Rocket's Bound To Win, is proving to be a popular and successful stud. Owned by William E. Moore, Travelmor Kennels, Trenton, New Jersey.

3. Ch. Bo-Nanza's Frosty R Jr, handsome black and silver from Bo-Nanza Kennels, Bob and Nancy Berg, Excelsior, Minnesota.

4. Ch. R-Bo's Victory Flash, by Ch. Shorlaine Dynamic Flash ex Ch. Shalom's Silver Shadow, winning Best of Breed at Montgomery County in 1979. He was No. 1 Miniature Schnauzer *Kennel Review* System that year, and No. 1 Knight System for 1979. Handled by Claudia Seeberg for owner Mary Ann Ellis, Atlanta, Georgia.

5. Classic Imperial Sky Jumper, now a champion, winning Best Puppy in Sweepstakes at the Gateway Specialty as a youngster, March 1977. This brother to Ch. Twin Tree Posh Josh, an Uproar son, is owned by Classic Imperial Miniature Schnauzers, Bill and Dorothy Culley, Evansville, Indiana. Photo courtesy of Judy Smith, Sweepstakes judge.

6. Ch. Tel-Mo's Top Cat was bred by Lynda Lucast and is co-owned with Bill Arnold. At the youthful age of 20 months, "Topper" accomplished an all-breed Best in Show, three Specialty Bests of Breed, two firsts in the Terrier Group, and numerous additional Group placements. His first offspring in the ring, Tel-Mo's Ain't She Amazing, took Winners Bitch twice and Best of Breed over specials as she started her show career, all from the puppy classes. Lynda Lucast, breeder-owner, Tel-Mo Kennels, Shakopee, Minnesota. Handled by Kurt Garmaker.

7. Ch. Richlenes Barbie Doll, bred and owned by Richlene Miniature Schnauzers. Handled by Rich Smith.

8. Ch. Sky Rocket's Bound to Win is owned by Homer and Isabelle Graf, Glen Gardner, New Jersey. Handled by Joan L. Huber.

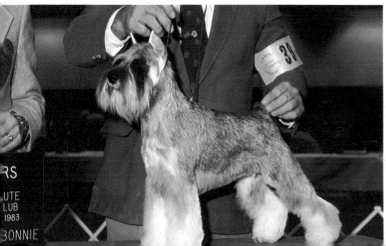

1 ▸
2 ▸

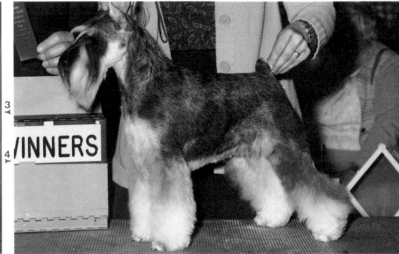

3 ▸
4 ▸

WINNERS

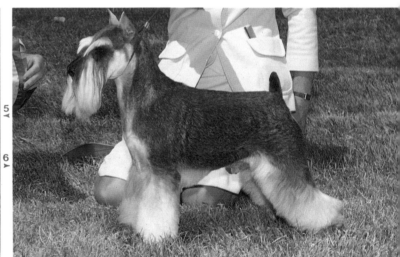

5 ▸
6 ▸

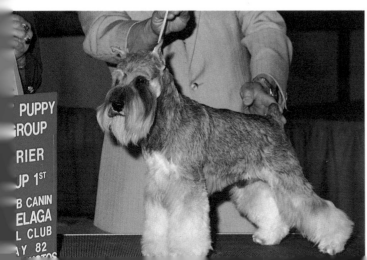

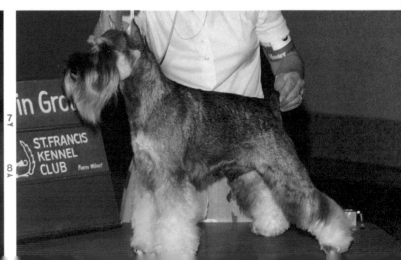

7 ▸
8 ▸

PUPPY
GROUP
RIER
UP 1ST
B CANIN
ELAGA
L CLUB
AY 82

ST. FRANCIS
KENNEL
CLUB

←Overleaf:

1. Int. and Netherlands Ch. Bo-Nanza's Frosted Queen, now owned by Mme. L. Huwaert, Brussels, Belgium.

2. Can., Danish, Ger., and Am. Ch. Frontenac's Peppy Countessa, by Can. Ch. Onontio Scout ex Frontenac's Fancy Hot Pants, was bred by Jacline Gratton. She was Best of Breed, 2nd in Group, and Best Puppy in Show her first time out, at seven months old, finishing her title undefeated in two weekends. Sold to Mrs. L. Carlsen in Denmark when one and a half years old, and took Best of Breed the month after her arrival when shown in Germany. Born in July 1974, Peppy is only 12½ inches tall.

3. Spanish and Club Champion V82 Beauty of Maidenhead, by Dengarse Yankee Spinoff ex Dengarse Pirates Silver, bred by F. Martinez-Guijarro. Owned by J. Martinez-Solano. Handled by C. Alonso Martinez, Madrid, Spain.

4. Ch. Skyline's Cactus Candy, by Ch. Regency's Right On ex Ch. Skyline's Fern of Winrush, has been exported to Japan. Carol A. Parker, breeder, Vail, Arizona.

5. Ch. Beauty of Maidenhead and daughter, Enriqueta de C'an Jack, the latter owned by J. Soler Segoviano. J. Martinez-Solano, Madrid, Spain, is Beauty's owner and was Enriqueta's breeder.

6. Am., Can., and Bda. Ch. Blythewood National Newsman owned by Dr. Martin E. De Forest, Toronto, Ontario, Canada. Newsman is an all-breed Best in Show winner, a National Specialty winner, and No. 1 Miniature Schnauzer in Canada for 1983. Breeder-handler, Joan L. Huber.

7. Can. Ch. Fronsen Gypsy, by Can. Ch. Frontenac's Footprint ex Can. Ch. Frontenac Cleopatra's Pearl, was bred by J. Gratton and I. Wessler and is owned by J. and A. Gratton, Les Cedres, Quebec. He is 13½ inches tall, was born in 1981, became No. 2 Schnauzer in Canada, and was Best Puppy in Show at Hochelaga, May 1982. In his first litter, sired Ch. Frontenac's Heidi Ho!, Ch. Frontenac's Sensation, and Ch. Frontenac's Philomene (uncropped).

8. Can. Ch. Frontenac's Cannon, by Am. Ch. Penlan Peter Gunn ex Can. Ch. Frontenac's Big Deal, was bred and is owned by Armand and Jacline Gratton, Les Cedres, Quebec. He was Best Puppy in Show at the Canadian National Sportsmens; Best Terrier at Quebec; several times Group First; and No. 3 Schnauzer in Canada. Sire of the following champions to date: Ch. Frontenac You're A Doll, exported to E. DeBlander in Belgium; Ch. Frontenac Here Comes Trouble; Ch. Sensation's Trapper John, Ch. Sensation Tribute to Frontenac; and Bahamas Ch. Frontenac's Star Trek who is close to Canadian title.

Overleaf:→

1. Ch. Skyline's Lasting Luv To Baws, by Ch. Regency's Right On Target ex Ch. Skyline's Everlasting, was born December 1981 and is one of four sisters who should finish from this litter. Owned by Vi and Bob Baws, of Baws Kennels. Handled by Beverly Verna.

2. Mione Random Sketches, by Ch. Andrel's Satellite, C.D. ex Hil-D's Proud Pudding, was bred by Hilda Dailey. Owner-handled by Robert Crews.

3. Spring-along Country Cheer, the Springs' latest winner, at a year old already has eight points. He is a son of Dark Smoke and a grandson of Gangbuster, going back to Mrs. Spring's original bitch on the dam's side. Owner-handled by Mary E. Spring, Good Hope Farm, Landenberg, Pennsylvania.

4. Ch. Avalanche Hat Chequer, bred and owned by Gretchen Wilson, handled by Gloria Lewis, winning Best of Breed in 1981. Judge was Ken McDermott.

5. Ch. Kelly's Ebony Top of the Line winning Best of Breed at Central Maine in 1983. Owner-handled by Geri Kelly, North Falmouth, Massachusetts.

6. Ch. Charmar Copy Cat, by Ch. Penlan Paper Boy ex Ch. Charmar Checkberry, was No. 1 Top Producing Male Miniature Schnauzer for 1983 and is the sire of 16 champions as of December 1984. Owned by F. Joseph Williams, New Hartford, New York.

7. O.T.Ch. Pepperhaus Pfiesty Pfritz owned by Marilyn and Bill Oxandale, Crestwood, Missouri. Pfritz is the third Miniature Schnauzer owned by the Oxandales to have gained this title at the time of this writing.

8. Ch. Ruedesheim's Landmark, by Ch. Ruedesheims Entrepeneur (by Ch. Penlan Peters Son) ex Ch. Ruedesheims Free Spirit (by Ch. Landmarks Masterpiece), owned by Gas Light Kennels, Burbank, California.

1 ▶

2 ▶

Best of Breed
Greater Lowell
Kennel Club
1982
Ashbey

3 ▶

4 ▶

Best of Breed
Del-Otse-Nango
Kennel Club Inc.
Klein   June 1981

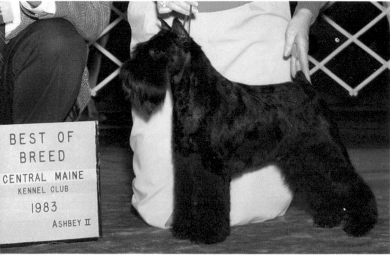

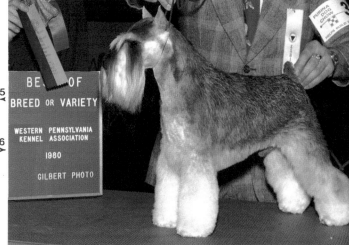

5 ▶

6 ▶

Best of Breed or Variety
Western Pennsylvania
Kennel Association
1980
Gilbert Photo

Best of Breed
Central Maine
Kennel Club
1983
Ashbey II

7 ▶

8 ▶

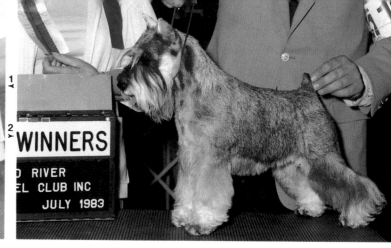

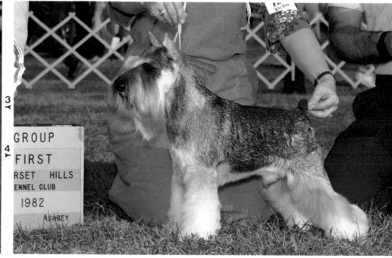

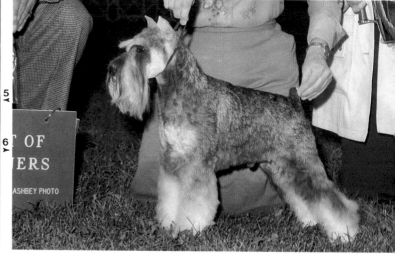

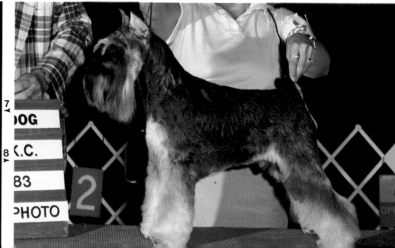

←**Overleaf:**

1. Kajon's Spartan, sired by Ch. Kazel's Favorite, bred and owned by Mrs. C. Muhlenkamp. Shown by Mrs. K. L. Church, Imperial, Missouri.

2. Ch. Richlene's Raisinette, bred and owned by Richlene Kennels, handled by Rich Smith, Ft. Wayne, Indiana.

3. This is the very famous Ch. Valharra's Double Extra, known to his friends as "Marvin," making one of his numerous Group wins. Owned by Robert Baws, Rosemead, California. A splendid example of the breeding program at Valharra Kennels.

4. Ch. Bandsman's Prophecy winning the Terrier Group at Somerset Hills in 1982. Carole Luke, owner, Bandsman's Kennels, Silver Springs, Maryland.

5. Walters Windstorm, by Walters Windjammer ex Linalee's Lil Echo v Van Dyke, taking Best of Opposite Sex in Sweepstakes at New Orleans in May 1982. Bred and owned by Dolores Walters, Burbank, California. Handled by Barbara Wysocki.

6. Ch. Carolane's Fancy That taking Winners Dog and Best of Winners at Montgomery County K.C. for Carl and Carol Beiles, Carolane Kennels, Brookville, New York.

7. Ch. Angler's Allure of Ansu, by Ch. Penlan Checkmate ex Ch. Richlene's Linette, was bred by Sandra Nagengast and Arlene Smith. Owners, Anthony Postemski and Sandra Nagengast. Making her ring debut at ten months of age, she was Winners Bitch from the puppy class. The judge was Mrs. Eve Whitmore from Canada.

8. Ch. Jadee's Royal Supershot, by Ch. Regency's Right On Target ex Jerry O's Kissn Angel Jadee (an unconfirmed champion, points being disputed), shown taking the points at Hawkeye in 1983. This No. 2 Miniature Schnauzer for 1984 bred and owned by D. L. and Judy Smith, co-owned by Robert Hawkins.

Overleaf:→
1. Ch. Shirley's Solo winning the Terrier Group from the Classes at Idaho Capital City in May 1982 when Solo was just a couple of weeks over one year old. Owned by Shirley and Dick Willey, Shirley's Miniature Schnauzers, Simi, California.

2. Ch. Travelmor's Tartar and Ch. Travelmor's Tantrum II, both dams of three champions including Specialty winners, taking Winners Bitch and Reserve Winners Bitch respectively at Devon 1976. Tartar was also Best of Opposite Sex in the Sweepstakes at Montgomery County in the National and Best of Winners at the Specialty at Rock Creek. William E. Moore, owner, Travelmor Kennels, Trenton, New Jersey.

3. Ch. Walters' Black Topper, by Ch. Walters' Black Bonus ex Walters' Black Out, bred and owned by Dolores Walters. Handled by Wood Wornall.

5. Ch. Avalanche Ho Ho Ho, born Christmas Eve 1981, owned and bred by Gretchen Wilson, winning the breed at Springfield 1983. Handled by Gloria Lewis.

6. Ch. Wyndwood Back Packer, by Ch. Richlene's Top Billing ex Wyndwood Run Around Sue, pictured at his first show. "Packy" gained his title with three majors, earning two of them as a puppy, and was Best of Breed over specials at Westchester and Elm City. Owned by Barbara A. Hall, Amston, Connecticut.

7. Ch. Blythewood Gazebo Maiden, by Ch. Blythewood Main Gazebo ex Abingdon Image of Blythewood, was bred by Joan L. Huber and is owned by Captain Jean L. Heath, USN (retired), Black Watch Miniature Schnauzers, Pleasanton, California.

8. Ch. Angler's Top Drawer, by Ch. Richlene's Top Billing ex Ch. Richlene Angler's Keepsake, was Best of Opposite Sex at the Sweepstakes at the American Miniature Schnauzer Club Specialty, February 1982. Bred, owned and handled by Sandra Nagengast. The judge was Janice Rue (Suelen Miniature Schnauzers). The trophy was presented by Mrs. Mabel "Jinx" Gunville (Merry Makers), President of the American Miniature Schnauzer Club.

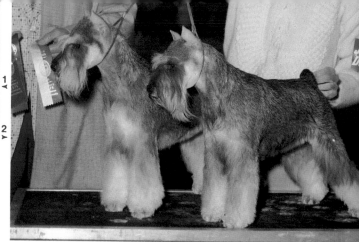

TERRIER
GROUP

CH. CHRISAN'S
IRISH IMP

BEST
OF WINNERS
RIVERHEAD
KENNEL CLUB INC
KLEIN   APRIL 1983

BEST OF
BREED
PRINGFIELD
KENNEL CLUB
1983
ASHBEY

ST OF
NERS
WTOWN
NEL CLUB
1982
HAM PHOTO

W. B.
Photo

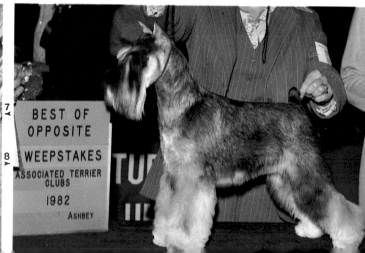

BEST OF
OPPOSITE
SWEEPSTAKES
ASSOCIATED TERRIER
CLUBS
1982
ASHBEY

WINNERS

KANADASAGA
KENNEL CLUB INC
EIN   MAY 1983

ERS DOG

OINES K.C.

T. 11, 1983

SON PHOTO

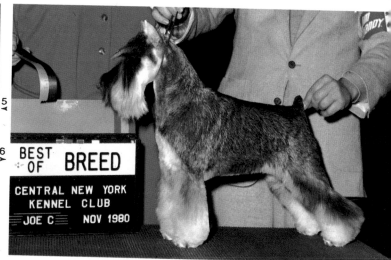

BEST
OF   BREED

CENTRAL NEW YORK
KENNEL CLUB
JOE C   NOV 1980

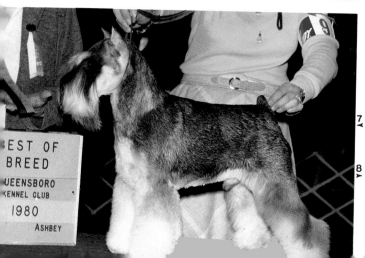

EST OF
BREED

UEENSBORO
KENNEL CLUB
1980
ASHBEY

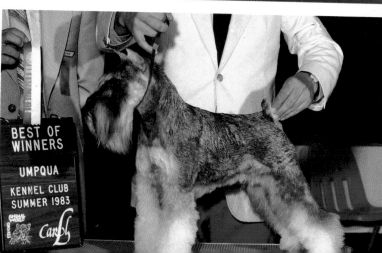

BEST OF
WINNERS

UMPQUA

KENNEL CLUB
SUMMER 1983
Carbh

← **Overleaf:**

1. Ch. Irrenhaus Most Precious, by Ch. Irrenhaus Stand Out ex Ch. Irrenhaus Bluet, handled by Sue Baines for Breeder-owner Jacqueline Hicks, Irrenhaus Kennels, Woodford, Virginia.

2. Ch. Sole Baye's Modus Vivendi owned by Yvonne B. Phelps, El Monte, California. Handled by Joan Huber.

3. Ch. Penlan Pageboy, by Ch. Penlan Paperboy ex Ch. Penlan Pride's Pageantry, is Penlan's latest champion as we are writing, having completed his title out of the Bred-by-Exhibitor Class in just three weekends. Owned by Penlan Schnauzers, Penny and Landis Hirstein, Washington, Illinois.

4. Ch. Johnny O of Dor-Ru, owned by Ruth and Dorothy Anderson, Dor-Ru Kennels, Santa Ana Heights, California, finishing here at 13 months by taking Best of Breed from the classes. Judge was Mrs. Margaret Young.

5. Ch. Regency's Right On, the sire of Ch. Regency's Right On Target, is owned and handled by Beverly J. Verna, Santa Clara, California.

6. Ch. Daland Dazzling Debut was David Kirkland's first homebred champion at his Daland Kennels, East Brunswick, New Jersey. Here winning Best of Breed at Central N.Y. in 1980. This owner-handled champion was also No. 3 Schnauzer bitch for that year.

7. Ch. Royalcourt Name of the Game, Best of Breed, Queensboro 1980. Gloria Lewis handled.

8. Ch. Shirley's September Morgan, Winners Dog and Best of Winners at Umpqua Kennel Club, his first of three majors. Morgan finished on his first coat at a year and one week old. Eddie Boyes handled for Shirley and Dick Willey, Shirley's Schnauzers, Simi, California.

Overleaf:→

1. Ch. Contempra Foolish Pleasure, by Ch. Sky Rocket's Bound To Win ex Ch. Tare Misty Morning, a Group winner, has 36 Bests of Breed and 12 additional Group placements. Owned by Homer and Isabelle Graf, Glen Gardner, New Jersey. Handled by Joan L. Huber.

2. Ch. Britmor Sunnymeade Frost, C.D. at two years of age. Owned by Karen J. Brittan, St. Louis Park, Minnesota.

3. Ch. Bardon Dear Abby, by Ch. Penlan Paper Boy ex Bardon Born A Star, another Specialty winner from the Merry Makers Miniature Schnauzers, Mabel M. Gunville, Deerfield, Illinois.

4. Ch. Blythewood National Accord, by Ch. Blythewood National Anthem ex Valharra's Prize of Blythewood, owned by Margaret Pratt, Vienna, Virginia. Handled by Joan L. Huber.

5. Ch. Carolane's Gangbuster, a Ch. Penlan Peter Gunn son, finished in 11 shows owner-handled, and along with Spring-along Black Pony is the main stud dog at the Springs' Kennels. Mary E. Spring, owner, Landenberg, Pennsylvania.

6. Ch. Bandsman's Capitol Flash, by Ch. R-Bo's Victory Flash ex Ch. Repitition's Renaissance, Best of Breed at the Columbus Kennel Club 1984. Bred by Carol Luke and owned by Mary Ann Ellis and Carol Luke.

1 ▶

2 ▶

3 ▶

4 ▶

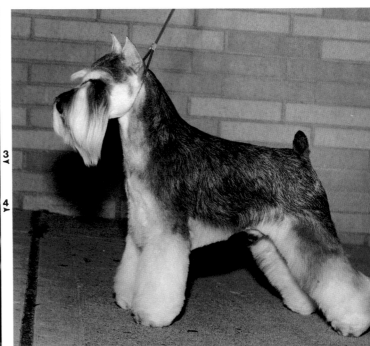

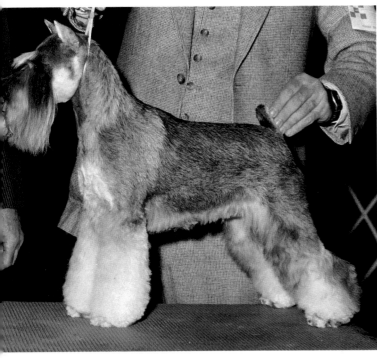

5 ▶

6 ▶

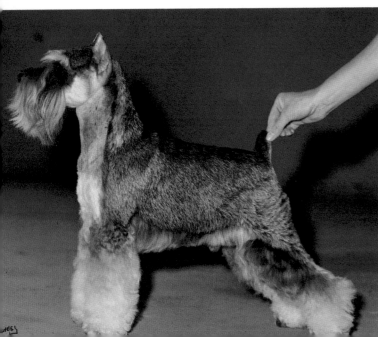

BEST OF
OPPOSITE

MARYLAND
KENNEL CLUB
1983

LEASH TO LENS PHOTO
BY SHERRY

1 ▸

2 ▸

BEST OF
POSITE SEX

HOTO
BY *Graham*

3 ▸

4 ▸

BEST OF
BREED

ASHBEY PHOTO

5 ▸

6 ▸

NNERS

TMINSTER

NEL CLUB

984

ASHBEY

BEST
WINNERS

ROCK CREEK
KENNEL CLUB
1979

SHERRY PHOTO

BEST OF
BREED

7 ▸

8 ▸

←Overleaf:

1. This is the exciting Best in Show winning Ch. Valharra's Extra taking Best of Breed at the Chicago International. One of Enid Quick's great favorites and a splendid example of the quality for which Valharra Miniature Schnauzers are renowned.

2. Aberdovey's Five Card Stud, by Ch. Masterman's Mr. Black Jack ex Aberdovey's Slap Happy, was bred by Sally Critchlow and is owned by Mr. and Mrs. Ron Williams, Summit, New Jersey. Pictured taking Best of Opposite Sex at Maryland Kennel Club en route to the title in 1983.

3. Ch. Carolane's Christy Love owned by Carl and Carol Beiles, Carolane Kennels, Brookville, New York.

4. Ch. Bo-Nanza's Frosty City Slicker owned by Bo-Nanza Schnauzers, Bob and Nancy Berg, Excelsior, Minnesota.

5. Ch. Andrel's Satellite winning Best of Breed at Carroll County in 1975. Jane Forsyth handled for owners, Elinor and Andrew Czapski, Andrel Kennels.

6. Ch. Bobette's Go Go Boy, C.D. won points towards his title under judge Ann Stevenson. Handled by Joe Waterman. Owned by Bobette Gowan Tomasoff.

7. Richlene's Marathon II, by Ch. Richlene's Big Time ex Ch. Richlene's Hearts and Lace, taking the points en route to title at Westminster Kennel Club in 1984. Bred and owned by Arlene Smith. Handled by Richard Smith.

8. Ch. Irrenhaus Stand Out, by Ch. Imperial's Stamp O'Kharasahl ex Ch. Irrenhaus Flights of Fancy, is a homebred owned by Jacqueline Hicks and handled by Sue Baines. This all-breed Best in Show, a multiple Group, and Specialty winner is here taking points towards the title in 1979.

Overleaf:→

1. Ch. Masterman's Midnite Charisma, owned by N. Gallagher, was handled by Gloria Lewis to Best of Opposite Sex in Sweepstakes of the Delaware Valley Miniature Schnauzer Club in 1981.

2. Dardane What's Up O'Blythewood, by Ch. Penlan Checkmate ex Bardane Verity, a full litter sister to top producing Ch. Dardane Wagonmaster, was the dam of Ch. Blythewood National Refrain. Owned by Joan L. Huber, Blythewood Schnauzers, Pennsylvania.

3. Ch. Spring-along Dark Lily finishing her championship at the American Miniature Schnauzer Club National Specialty in 1979 by going Best of Winners over 100 Schnauzers, judged by Dale Miller. She is a homebred, owner-handled by Mary E. Spring, Good Hope Farm, Landenberg, Pennsylvania.

4. Ch. Landmark's Masterpiece at seven years of age won the Miniature Schnauzer Club of Southern California Specialty. Judge was Henry Stoecker and Barbara Baymiller handled for owner Gloria Weidlein, Sun City, California.

5. Tomlen Ka Ka Ka Katie, by Sercatep's Midnight Blue ex Ch. Sercatep's Sweet Melody. Breeders-owners, Helen and Tom Clifford, Clearfield, Pennsylvania. Marcia Foy was the judge and Dennis Kniola, the handler.

6. Ch. Wyndwood Big Spender, by Ch. Richlene's Top Billing ex Wyndwood Sweeter Than Honey, finished his title with three majors at 16 months of age and was the first champion for his sire and dam. Owned by Barbara A. Hall, Amston, Connecticut.

7. Ch. Travelmor's Double Check, by Ch. Penlan Checkmate ex Ch. Travelmor's Tartar, was Best in Sweepstakes and Best of Winners at the New York Miniature Schnauzer Club Specialty and Best in Sweepstakes at Montgomery County. He is the sire of Ch. Travelmor's Check Your Temper. William E. Moore, owner, Travelmor Kennels, Trenton, New Jersey.

8. Ch. New Horizons Spark Plug, by Ch. Royalcourt Name of the Game, a homebred owned by Jackie Hinczynk. Handled by Gloria Lewis.

BEST OF
OPPOSITE
SWEEPSTAKES

1981

ASHBEY II

BEST OF
WINNERS

GILBERT PHOTO

1 ►
2 ►

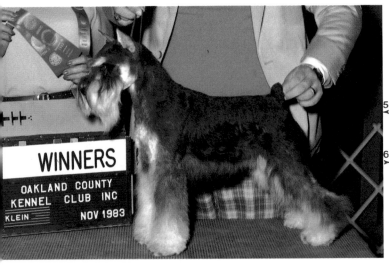

BEST OF
WINNERS

ASSOCIATED TERRIER
CLUB

1979

GILBERT PHOTO

3 ►
4 ►

WINNERS

OAKLAND COUNTY
KENNEL CLUB INC

KLEIN   NOV 1983

BEST OF
BREED

SOUTH WINDSOR
KENNEL CLUB

1982

ASHBEY

5 ►
6 ►

WINNERS

ROCKLAND COUNTY
KENNEL CLUB

EIN   MARCH 8 1980

WINNERS

CATONSVILLE
KENNEL CLUB

1981

ASHBEY

7 ►
8 ►

Ch. Carolane's Flying High taking Best of Winners at a Miniature Schnauzer Club of Michigan Specialty. Owners, Carl and Carol Beiles, Carolane Kennels, Brookville, New York.

Point Shows

Entries for American Kennel Club licensed or member point shows must be made in advance. This must be done on an official entry blank of the show-giving club and then filed either in person or by mail with the show superintendent (or show secretary) in time to reach the latter's office prior to the published closing date and hour or the filling of the advertised quota. These entries should be written out clearly and carefully, signed by the owner of the dog or his agent (your professional handler), and must be accompanied by the entry fee; otherwise they will not be accepted. Remember, it is not when the entry blank leaves your hands or is postmarked that counts but the time that the entry arrives at its destination. If you are relying on the postal system, bear in mind that it is not always reliable, and waiting until the last moment may cause your entry to arrive too late for acceptance. Leave yourself a bit of leeway by mailing *early*.

A dog must be entered at a dog show in the name of the actual owner at the time of entry closing date for that specific show. If a registered dog has been acquired by a new owner, the dog must be entered in the name of that new owner at any show for which entries close following the date of purchase, regardless of whether or not the new owner has actually received the registration certificate indicating that the dog is registered in the new owner's name. State on the entry form whether or not the transfer application has been mailed to the American Kennel Club, and it goes without saying that the latter should be promptly attended to when you purchase a registered dog.

When you fill out your entry blank, be sure to type, print, or write legibly, paying particular attention to the spelling of names, correct registration numbers, and so on. Sign your name as owner *exactly*—not one time as Jane Doe, another as Jane C. Doe, and another as Mrs. John Doe.

Puppy Classes are for dogs or bitches that are six months of age and under twelve months, were whelped in the United States, and are not

Ch. Blythewood Touch of Silver taking Best of Opposite Sex under Bill Kendrick at the American Miniature Schnauzer Club National Specialty, Feb. 1961. Owner-handled by Mrs. Joan L. Huber, Green Lane, Pennsylvania.

Richlene's Calico, bred and owned by Arlene and Rich Smith, Richlene Miniature Schnauzers, Fort Wayne, Indiana.

champions. The age of a puppy is calculated up to and inclusive of the first day of a show you are entering. For example, the first day a dog whelped on January 1st is eligible to compete in a Puppy Class at a show is July 1st of the same year; and he may continue competing in Puppy Classes up to and including a show on December 31st of the same year, but he is *not* eligible to compete in a Puppy Class at a show held on or after January 1st of the following year.

The Puppy Class is the first one in which you should enter your puppy, for several reasons. To begin with, a certain allowance for behavior is made in recognition of the fact that they *are* puppies and lack show experience; a puppy who is immature or displays less than perfect ring man-

ners will not be penalized so heavily as would be the case in an adult class such as Open. It is also quite likely that others in the Puppy Class will be suffering from the same puppy problems as your own; all of the puppies will be pretty much on equal footing where age and ring assurance are concerned. A puppy shown in the same class with fully matured Miniature Schnauzers who are experienced in the show ring looks all the more young and inexperienced and thus is far less likely to gain the judge's admiration than in a class where the puppy does not seem out of place. There are many good judges who will take a smashing good puppy right from the Puppy Class on through to Winners, but more often than not, this puppy started the day and was

Ch. Misty's Winagin Charlie, by Ch. Dardane's Wagonmaster ex Blythewood Misty Acclaim, is the first homebred champion owned by Keith and Betti Ann Evans, St. Michael's, Maryland. This exciting young dog gained his title in a week plus one weekend! At Bucks County in 1983, Sue Baines is handling him to Best of Winners.

"discovered" by the judge right where it belonged, in the Puppy Class. Another bonus of using Puppy Class is the fact that numerous clubs offer a reduced entry fee to those competing in it; this certainly is beneficial because showing dogs is becoming increasingly expensive.

One word of caution on entering the Puppy Class: carefully check the classification, as in some cases it is divided into a 6-9 months old section and a 9-12 months old section; if this is the case you will have to ascertain that your puppy is entered in the correct section for the age he will be on the day of the show.

The Novice Class is for dogs six months of age and over, whelped in the United States or in Canada, who *prior to* the official closing date for entries have *not* won three first prizes in the Novice Class, any first prize at all in the Bred-by-Exhibitor, American-bred, or Open Classes, or one or more points toward championship. The provisions for this class are confusing to many people, which is probably the reason it is so infrequently used. A dog may win any number of first prizes in the Puppy Class and still retain his eligibility for Novice. He may place second, third, or fourth not only in Novice on an unlimited number of occasions but also in Bred-by-Exhibitor, American-bred, or Open and

still remain eligible for Novice. But he may no longer be shown in Novice when he has won three blue ribbons in that class, when he has won even one blue ribbon in either Bred-by-Exhibitor, American-bred, or Open, or even a single championship point.

In determining whether or not a dog is eligible for the Novice Class, keep in mind the fact that previous wins are calculated according to the official published date for closing of entries, not by the date on which you may actually have made the entry. So if, in the interim, between the time you made the entry and the official closing date, your dog makes a win causing it to become ineligible for Novice, change your class *immediately* to another for which your Miniature Schnauzer will be eligible. The Novice Class always seems to have the fewest entries of any class, and therefore it is a splendid "practice ground" for you and your young Miniature Schnauzer while you both are getting the "feel" of being in the ring.

Bred-by-Exhibitor Class is for dogs whelped in the United States or, if individually registered in the American Kennel Club Stud Book, for dogs whelped in Canada that are six months of age and over, are not champions, and are owned wholly or in part by the person or the spouse of the person who was the breeder or one of the breeders of record. Dogs entered in this class must be handled *in this class* by an owner or by a member of the immediate family of the owner. Members of an immediate family for this purpose are husband, wife, father, mother, son, daughter, brother, or sister. This is the class which is really the "breeder's showcase," the one which breeders should enter with special pride, to show off their achievements. It is *not necessary* for the winner of Bred-by-Exhibitor to be handled by an owner or a member of the owner's family in the Winners Class, where the dog or bitch *may be handled by whomsoever the exhibitor may choose*, including a professional handler.

The American-bred Class is for all dogs excepting champions, six months of age or older, who were whelped in the United States by reason of a mating which took place in the United States.

The Open Class is for any dog six months of age or older (this is the only restriction for this class). Dogs with championship points compete in it; dogs who are already champions can do so; dogs who are imported can be entered; and, of course, American-bred dogs compete in it. This class is, for some strange reason, the favorite of exhibitors who are "out to win." They rush to enter their pointed dogs in it, under the false impression that by so doing they assure themselves of greater attention from the judges. This really is not so; and it is my feeling that to enter in one of the less competitive classes, with a better chance of winning it and then getting a second crack at gaining the judge's approval by returning to the ring in the Winners Class, can often be a more effective strategy.

Ch. Shirley's Strike My Fancy winning the breed from the puppy class at the Portland Miniature Schnauzer Club Specialty, January 23, 1983. Later that day he won a Group 4 under judge Howard Tyler. Specialty judge was Mr. Edward Loebe. Owned by Shirley's Schnauzers, Dick and Shirley Willey, Simi, California.

Ch. Benrook Jewel owned and handled by Florence Bradburn, Temple City, California.

Another Best in Show for the great Ch. Penlan Peter Gunn during 1977. This one at Jupiter – Tequesta Dog Club. Claudia Seaberg handling for owners Carl and Carol Beiles, Carolane Kennels, Brookville, New York.

One does not enter for the Winners Class. One earns the right to compete in it by winning first prize in Puppy, Novice, Bred-by-Exhibitor, American-bred, or Open. No dog who has been defeated on the same day in one of these classes is eligible to compete in Winners, and every dog who has been a blue-ribbon winner in one of them and not defeated in any of the others *must* do so. Following the selection of the Winners Dog or the Winners Bitch, the dog or bitch receiving that award leaves the ring. Then the dog or bitch who placed second in the class, unless previously defeated by another dog or bitch at the same show, re-enters the ring to compete against the remaining first-prize winners for Reserve. The latter award means that the dog or bitch receiving it is standing by "in reserve" should the one that received Winners be disallowed through any technicality when the awards are checked at the American Kennel Club. In that case, the one that placed Reserve is moved up to Winners, at the same time receiving the appropriate championship points.

Winners Dog and Winners Bitch are the awards which carry points toward championship

Arbey Dyna-Mite, imported from the United Kingdom to Australia, came out of quarantine in 1983. Owned by Ms. Marelyne MacLeod-Woodhouse, Schonhardt Kennels, New South Wales.

Am., Can., Ber. Ch. Frontenac's Big Foot is the only Canadian-bred Miniature Schnauzer to have won championship in all three of these countries. The sire of six champions to date, this dog has to his credit two Best Puppy in Show awards, several Group Firsts and many other Group placements, and earned No. 3 Schnauzer in Canada. Bred and owned by Jacline and Armand Gratton, Les Cedres, Quebec.

with them. The points are based on the number of dogs or bitches actually in competition; and the points are scaled one through five, the latter being the greatest number available to any dog or bitch at any one show. Three-, four-, or five-point wins are considered majors. In order to become a champion, a dog or bitch must win two majors under two different judges, plus at least one point from a third judge, and the additional points necessary to bring the total to fifteen. When your dog has gained fifteen points as described above, a certificate of championship will be issued to you, and your Miniature Schnauzer's name will be published in the list of new champions which appears monthly in *Pure-Bred Dogs/ American Kennel Gazette*, the official publication of the American Kennel Club.

The scale of championship points for each breed is worked out by the American Kennel Club and reviewed annually, at which time the number required in competition may be either changed (raised or lowered) or remain the same. The scale of points for all breeds is published an-

Ch. Cosburn's Esquire, the foundation sire at Travelmor Kennels where Bill and Olive Moore have produced so impressive an array of superb champions.

nually in the May issue of the *Gazette*, and the current ratings for each breed within that area are published in every dog show catalog.

When a dog or a bitch is adjudged Best of Winners, its championship points are, for that show, compiled on the basis of which sex had the greater number of points. If there are two points in dogs and four in bitches and the dog goes Best of Winners, then *both* the dog and the bitch are awarded an equal number of points, in this case four. Should the Winners Dog or the Winners Bitch go on to win Best of Breed, additional points are accorded for the additional Miniature Schnauzer defeated by so doing, provided, of course, that there were entries

specifically for Best of Breed competition, or Specials, as these specific entries are generally called. If your dog or bitch takes Best of Opposite Sex after going Winners, points are credited according to the number of the same sex defeated in both the regular classes and Specials competition. Many a one- or two-point class win has grown into a major in this manner.

Moving further along, should your Miniature Schnauzer win the Terrier Group from the classes (in other words, if it has taken either Winners Dog or Winners Bitch, Best of Winners, and Best of Breed), you then receive points based on the greatest number of points awarded to any breed included within that Group during

Ch. Jadee's Stride Rite, by Ch. Jadee's Jump Up ex Ch. Jadee's Very Cherry. Owned by Judy Smith and Ruth Dempster, Bettendorf, Iowa. Best in Sweepstakes at Montgomery County in 1977.

Ch. Dixie Farms Ric-O-Shay, sired by Ch. Richlene's Roundup. Bred and owned by Mel and Joyce Garno, Monroe, Michigan. Rich Smith handler, here winning the Terrier Group at Progressive Dog Club of Wayne County in April 1983.

Panda del Escarambrujo, by Int. and Spanish Ch. Miky Kilimanjaro ex Somni Dolc dels Segadora. Bred and owned by Mr. F. Martinez Guijarro, Spain.

that show's competition. Should the dog's winning streak also include Best in Show, the same rule of thumb applies, and your Miniature Schnauzer receives points equal to the highest number of points awarded to any other dog of any breed at that event.

Best of Breed competition consists of the Winners Dog and the Winners Bitch, who automatically compete on the strength of those awards, in addition to whatever dogs and bitches have been entered specifically for this class for which champions of record are eligible. Miniature Schnauzers, who, according to their owner's records, have completed the required number of points for a championship after closing of entries for the show but whose championships are unconfirmed, may be transferred from one of the regular classes to the Best of Breed competition, provided this transfer is made by the show superintendent or show secretary *prior to the start of judging at the show.*

This has proven an extremely popular new rule, as under it a dog can finish on Saturday and then be transferred and compete as a Special on Sunday. It must be emphasized that the change

Ch. Jadee's Juju, bred and owned by Don and Judy Smith, Bettendorf, Iowa, pictured taking Winners Bitch at Hatboro for a 5-point major in an entry of 42 bitches. Judy Smith handling.

Ch. Valharra's Extra Allaruth standing for the inspection of the judge. Owned by Carol A. Parker, Vail, Arizona.

must be made a half hour *prior* to the start of the day's judging, which means to the start of *any* judging at the show, not your individual breed.

In the United States, Best of Breed winners are entitled to compete in the Variety Group which includes them. This competition is not mandatory; it is a privilege which Miniature Schnauzer exhibitors should value. The dogs winning *first* in each Variety Group *must* compete for Best in Show.

Non-regular classes are sometimes included at the all-breed shows, and they are almost invariably included at Specialty shows. These include Stud Dog Class and Brood Bitch Class, which are judged on the quality of the offspring (usually two) accompanying the sire or dam. The quality of the latter two is beside the point; it is the youngsters that count, and the qualities of *both* are averaged to decide which sire or dam is the best and most consistent producer. Then there is the Brace Class (which, at all-breed shows, moves along to Best Brace in each Variety Group and then Best Brace in Show), which is judged on the similarity and evenness of appearance of the two members of the brace. In other words, the Miniature Schnauzers should look like identical twins in size, color, and conformation and should move together almost as a single dog, one person handling with precision and ease. The same applies to the Team competition except that four dogs are involved and, if necessary, two handlers.

The Veterans Class is for the older dog, the minimum age of whom is usually seven years. This class is judged on the quality of the dogs, as the winner competes for Best of Breed, and, on a number of occasions, has been known to win it. So the point is *not* to pick the oldest looking dog, as some seem to think, but the best specimen of the breed, exactly as throughout the regular classes.

Then there are Sweepstakes and Futurity Stakes, sponsored by many Specialty clubs, sometimes as part of their shows and sometimes as separate events. The difference between the two is that Sweepstakes entries usually include dogs and bitches from six to eighteen months of age, and entries are made at the usual time as others for the show, while for a Futurity the entries are bitches nominated when bred and the individual puppies entered at or shortly following their birth.

Ch. Sole Baye's Sundowner winning Best of Breed (and on to Group 3) from the classes at Santa Barbara K.C. in 1981. Brad Wooldridge handling for owner Yvonne B. Phelps, Sole Baye Kennels, El Monte, California.

Am., Can., and Mex. Ch. Fancway's Pirate Jr. of La May. A top breed, Group and Specialty winner. Sire of more than 30 champions including Ch. Faerwynd of Arador, Top Producing Bitch in the breed of all time. Jean and Glenn Fancy, owners, Fancway Kennels, La Canada, California.

Junior Showmanship

If there is a youngster in your family between the ages of ten and seventeen, I can suggest no better or more rewarding a hobby than having a Miniature Schnauzer to show in Junior Showmanship competition. This is a marvelous activity for young people. It teaches responsibility, good sportsmanship, the fun of competition where one's own skills are the deciding factor of success, proper care of a pet, and how to socialize with other young folks. Any youngster may experience the thrill of emerging from the ring a winner and the satisfaction of a good job done well.

Through the years, the Miniature Schnauzer has always seemed especially popular with Junior showmanship-minded youngsters. Being of such superb intelligence and being easily trainable, they are agreeable dogs for the youngsters to work with; and judging by the success of Miniature Schnauzers with their young handlers which we have noted, the breed seems well suited for this type of competition.

Entry in Junior Showmanship is open to any boy or girl who is at least ten years old and under seventeen years old on the day of the show. The Novice Junior Showmanship Class is open to

Can. Ch. Sylva Sprite Extra Dry, one of the Best in Show winning Miniature Schnauzers owned by Sylva Sprite Kennels, Dr. Dorothy Griggs and Mrs. Joanna Griggs, Guelph, Ontario.

This lovely bitch is Wyndwood Sweeter Than Honey owned by Barbara A. Hall, Amston, Connecticut. She is the dam of Ch. Wyndwood Big Spender.

youngsters who have not already won, at the time the entries close, three firsts in this class. Youngsters who have won three firsts in Novice may compete in the Open Junior Showmanship Class. Any junior handler who wins his third first-place award in Novice may participate in the Open Class at the same show, provided that the Open Class has at least one other junior handler entered in it. The Novice and Open Classes may be divided into Junior and Senior Classes. Youngsters between the ages of ten and twelve, inclusively, are eligible for the Junior division; and youngsters between thirteen and seventeen, inclusively, are eligible for the Senior

Ch. Kazels Favorite in 1974, helping his owner's daughter win Best Junior Handler at Westminster. Miss Leslie Church, Junior Handler, Imperial, Missouri.

division. Any of the foregoing classes may be separated into individual classes for boys and for girls. If such a division is made, it must be indicated on the premium list. The premium list also indicates the prize for Best Junior Handler, if such a prize is being offered at the show. Any youngster who wins a first in any of the regular classes may enter the competition for this prize, provided the youngster has been undefeated in any class at that show.

Junior Showmanship Classes, unlike regular conformation classes in which the dog's quality is judged, are judged entirely on the skill and ability of the junior handling the dog. Which dog is best is not the point—it is which youngster does the best job with the dog that is under consideration. Eligibility requirements for the dog being shown and other detailed informa-

tion can be found in *Regulations for Junior Showmanship*, issued by the American Kennel Club.

A junior who has a dog that he or she can enter in both Junior Showmanship and conformation classes has twice the opportunity for success and twice the opportunity to get into the ring and work with the dog. Miniature Schnauzers and juniors work well together, and this combination has often wound up in the winner's circle. There are no age restrictions on a child showing in breed competition, and a youngster may start at any age his parents think suitable. Of course, much depends upon the individual child, and I hardly need point out the irresponsibility of turning too young a child, or one not yet able to control it, loose at a dog show with a Miniature Schnauzer. Too many totally unexpected things could happen.

Pre-Show Preparation

Preparation of the things you will need as a Miniature Schnauzer exhibitor should not be left until the last moment. They should be planned and arranged for at least several days before the show in order for you to relax and be calm as the countdown starts.

The importance of the crate has already been discussed, and we assume it is already in use. Of equal importance is the grooming table, which we are sure you have already acquired for use at home. You should take it along with you, as your dog will need final touches before entering the ring. If you do not have one yet, a folding table with a rubber top is made specifically for this purpose and can be purchased from the concession booths found at most dog shows. Then you will need a sturdy tack box (also available at the show's concessions) in which to carry your brush, comb, scissors, nail clippers, whatever you use for last minute clean-up jobs, cotton swabs, first-aid equipment, and anything else

Ch. Skyline's Scorcher, by Ch. Skyline's Sonora ex Ch. Regency's Reward, born October 1981, is now the all-time Top Winning Miniature Schnauzer in Japan. From Skyline Kennels, Carol A. Parker, Vail, Arizona.

Ch. Skyline's Seventh Heaven, by Ch. Regency's Right On ex Skyline's Summer Rainbeau. Carol Parker's second venture into natural ears, Shasta finished easily on one coat. She is only the second uncropped Miniature Schnauzer to have finished in the past 50 years, the first being her half-sister, Ch. Regency's Equal Rights.

you are in the habit of using on the dog, such as a leash or two of the type you prefer, some well-cooked and dried-out liver or any of the small packaged "dog treats" your dog likes for use as "bait" in the ring, and a turkish towel.

Take a large thermos or cooler of ice, the biggest one you can accommodate in your vehicle, for use by "man and beast." Take a jug of water (there are lightweight, inexpensive ones available at all sporting goods shops) and a water dish. If you plan to feed the dog at the show, or if you and the dog will be away from home more than one day, bring food from home so that he will have the type to which he is accustomed.

You may or may not have an exercise pen. Personally, I think that one is a *must*, even if you have only one dog. While the shows do provide areas for exercise of the dogs, these are among the best places to come into contact with any illnesses that may be going around, and I feel that having a pen of your own for your dog's use is excellent protection. Such a pen can be used in other ways, too, such as a place other than the crate in which to put the dog to relax and a place in which the dog can exercise at rest areas or motels during your travels. A word of caution: never tie a dog to an exercise pen or leave him unattended in it while you wander off, as the pens are not sufficiently secure to keep the dog there should he decide to leave, at least not in

Ch. Wademar Dee-Eh-Ghin finished in six weeks with four majors. Owned by Margaret Pratt, Vienna, Virginia. Handled by Joan L. Huber.

Ch. Edel v Elfland, one of the important dogs from Florence Bradburn's famous kennel, established back in the 1940's.

most cases. Exercise pens are also available at the dog show concession booths should you not already have yours when you reach the dog's first show. They come in a variety of heights and sizes.

Bring along folding chairs for the members of your party, unless all of you are fond of standing, as these are almost never provided by the show-giving clubs. Have your name stamped on the chairs so there will be no doubt as to whom the chairs belong. Bring whatever you and your family enjoy for drinks or snacks in a picnic basket or cooler, as show food, in general, is expensive and usually not great. You should

always have a pair of boots, a raincoat, and a rain hat with you (they should remain permanently in your vehicle if you plan to attend shows regularly), as well as a sweater, a warm coat, and a change of shoes. A smock or big cover-up apron will assure that you remain tidy as you prepare the dog for the ring. Your overnight case should include a small sewing kit for emergency repairs, headache and indigestion remedies, and any personal products or medications you normally use.

In your car you should always carry maps of the area where you are headed and an assortment of motel directories. Generally speaking, we

Andrel's Importance with handler Jane Forsyth in June 1963. Elinor and Andrew Czapski, owners, Andrel Miniature Schnauzers.

Ch. Sky Rocket's Bound to Win, by Ch. Sky Rocket's Uproar ex Frischer's Wendy of Kringle, was the sire of 28 champions as of 1983, which number will probably have increased by the time you are reading this book. Owned by Homer and Isabelle Graf, handled by Joan L. Huber. Pictured winning the American Miniature Schnauzer Club Specialty, October 1974.

have found that Holiday Inns are the friendliest about taking dogs. Some Ramadas and some Howard Johnsons do so cheerfully (the Ramadas indicate on each listing in their directory whether or not pets are welcome). Best Western usually frowns on pets (not all of them but enough to make it necessary to find out which do). Some of the smaller chains welcome pets. The majority of privately owned motels do not.

Have everything prepared the night before the show to expedite your departure. Be sure that the dog's identification and your judging program and other show information are in your purse or briefcase. If you are taking sandwiches, have them ready. Anything that goes into the car the night before will be one thing less to be concerned with in the morning. Decide upon what you will wear and have it out and ready. If there is any question in your mind about what to wear, try on the possibilities before the day of the show; don't risk feeling you may want to change

when you see yourself dressed a few moments prior to departure time! In planning your outfit, wear something simple that will make an attractive background for your Miniature Schnauzer, providing contrast to his color, calling attention to the *dog* rather than to yourself. Sports clothes always seem to look best at a dog show. What you wear on your feet is important, as many types of flooring are slippery, and wet grass, too, can present a hazard as you move the dog. Make it a rule to wear rubber soles and low or flat heels in the ring, so that you can move along smartly.

Your final step in pre-show preparation is to leave yourself plenty of time to reach the show that morning. Traffic can get extremely heavy as one nears the immediate vicinity of the show, finding a parking place can be difficult, and other delays may occur. You'll be in better humor if you can take it all in your stride without the pressure of watching every second because you figured the time too closely.

Day of the Show

From the moment of your arrival at the dog show until after your Miniature Schnauzer has been judged, keep foremost in your mind the fact that he is your purpose for being there. You will need to arrive in advance of the judging in order to give him a chance to exercise after the trip to the show and take care of personal matters. A dog arriving in the ring and immediately using it for an exercise pen hardly makes a favorable impression on the judge. You will also need time to put the final touches on your dog, making certain that he goes into the ring looking his very best.

When you reach ringside, ask the steward for your arm-card with your Miniature Schnauzer's entry number on it and anchor it firmly into place on your arm with the elastic provided. Make sure that you are where you should be when your class is called. The fact that you have picked up your arm-card does not guarantee, as some seem to think, that the judge will wait for you more than a minute or two. Judges are expected to keep on schedule, which precludes delaying for the arrival of exhibitors who are tardy.

Even though you may be nervous, assume an air of cool, collected calm. Remember that this is

Ch. Helarry's Lolly, by Doren Corsair ex Helarry's Antoinette, whelped in 1961 was the foundation bitch at Penlan Kennels, Penny and Lanny Hirstein, Washington, Illinois.

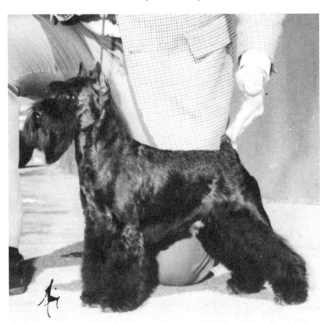

Ch. Walters' Black Bonus, by Walters' Black Coffee from Walters' Irish Spring, taking Best of Winners for a 4-point major on the way to the title at Orange Empire in 1978. Wood Wornall handling for breeder-owner Dolores Walters, Burbank, California.

a hobby to be enjoyed, so approach it in that state of mind. The dog will do better, too, as he will be quick to reflect your attitude.

If you make a mistake while presenting the dog, don't worry about it—next time you'll do better. Do not be intimidated by the more expert or experienced exhibitors. After all, they, too, were once newcomers.

Always show your Miniature Schnauzer with an air of pride. An apologetic attitude on the part of the exhibitor does little to help the dog win, so try to appear self-confident as you gait and set up the dog.

The judging routine usually starts when the judge asks that the dogs be gaited in a circle around the ring. During this period the judge is watching each dog as it moves along, noting style, topline, reach and drive, head and tail car-

Travelmor's Avalanche owned by Bill and Olive Moore, Trenton, New Jersey.

riage, and general balance. This is the time to keep your mind and your eye on your dog, moving him at his most becoming gait and keeping your place in line without coming too close to the dog ahead of you. Always keep your dog on the inside of the circle, between yourself and the judge, so that the judge's view of the dog is unobstructed.

Calmly pose the dog when requested to set up for examination. If you are at the head of the line and many dogs are in the class, do not stop halfway down the end of the ring and begin stacking the dog. Go forward enough so that sufficient space is left for the other dogs. Simple courtesy demands that we be considerate and give others a chance to follow the judge's instructions, too.

Space your Miniature Schnauzer so that on all sides of the dog the judge will have room in which to make his examination; this means that there must be sufficient room between each of the dogs for the judge to move around. Time is important when you are setting up your Miniature Schnauzer, so practice in front of a full-length mirror at home, trying to accustom yourself to "getting it all together" correctly in the shortest possible time. When you set up your Miniature Schnauzer, you want his forelegs well under the dog, feet directly below the elbows, toes pointing straight ahead, and hindquarters extended *correctly*. Hold the dog's head up with your hand at the back inner corner of the lips, your left hand extending the tail to its proper position. You want the dog to look "all of a piece," head carried proudly on a strong neck, correct topline, hindquarters nicely angulated, the front straight and true, and the dog standing firmly on his feet.

Listen carefully as the judge instructs the manner in which the dog is to be gaited, whether it is straight down and straight back; down the ring, across, and back; or in a triangle. The latter has become the most popular pattern with the majority of judges. "In a triangle" means down the outer side of the ring to the first corner, across that end of the ring to the second corner, and then back to the judge from the second corner, using the center of the ring in a diagonal line. Please learn to do this pattern without breaking

at each corner to twirl the dog around you, a senseless maneuver we sometimes have noted. Judges like to see the dog move in an *uninterrupted* triangle, as they get a better idea of the dog's gait.

It is impossible to overemphasize that the gait at which you move your Miniature Schnauzer is tremendously important, and considerable thought and study should be given to the matter. At home, have someone move the dog for you at different speeds so that you can tell which shows him off to best advantage.

Do not allow your Miniature Schnauzer to sidetrack, flop, or weave as you gait him, and do not let him pull so that he appears to lean on the lead as you are gaiting him. He should move in a straight line, displaying strength and power. That is your goal as you work with him on a lead in preparation for his show career.

Baiting your dog should be done in a manner which does not upset the other Miniature Schnauzers in the ring or cause problems for their handlers. A tasty morsel of well-cooked and dried-out liver is fine for keeping your own dog interested, but discarded on the ground or floor, it can throw off the behavior of someone else's dog who may attempt to get it. So please, if you drop liver on the ground, pick it up and take it with you when you have finished.

When the awards have been made, accept yours courteously, no matter how you may actually feel about it. To argue with a judge is unthinkable, and it will certainly not change the decision. Be gracious, congratulate the winners if your dog has been defeated, and try not to show your disappointment. By the same token, please be a gracious winner; this, surprisingly, sometimes seems to be even more difficult.

If you already show your Miniature Schnauzer, if you plan on being an exhibitor in the future, or if you simply enjoy attending dog shows, there is a book, written by me, which you will find to be an invaluable source of detailed information about all aspects of show dog competition. This book is *Successful Dog Show Exhibiting* (T.F.H. Publications, Inc.) and is available wherever the one you are now reading was purchased.

The Miniature Schnauzer Club of Southern California Top Ten Team of 1970. This is the first team the club entered, following which they had a team representation each year up until 1976. Pictured, *left to right,* Dick Willey with Shirley's New Beau, C.D.X.; Sharon Thoener with Mansino's Gay Jubilee, C.D.X.; John Paul with Pirate's Tristan Rah Rah, C.D.; Shirley Willey with Shirley's Sir Prize Package, C.D.X.; Frank McCoy with Cynosure Sam Von Coy, C.D.X.; Loretta Schoellenbach with Sir Jocko of Sierra Madre, U.D.; Bernice Marlo with Frosted Nugget, U.D. and Frosted Sparkle, U.D.; and Lois Barleman with Lady Gretchen Frost, C.D.X. Don Schmidt, team coach.

CHAPTER THIRTEEN

Obedience and the Miniature Schnauzer

One of the two Obedience Trial Champions belonging to the Oxandales, Crestwood, Missouri. O.T.Ch. Pepperhaus Pfiesty Pfritz.

For its own protection and safety, every dog should be taught, at the very least, to recognize and respond promptly and correctly to the basic commands "Come," "Heel," "Down," "Sit," and "Stay." Doing so might at sometime save the dog's life and, in less extreme circumstances, will certainly make him a better citizen, more well-behaved and far more pleasant as a companion.

If you are patient and enjoy working with your dog, study some of the excellent books available on the subject of obedience and start at an early age to teach your Miniature Schnauzer puppy these basic manners. If you need the stimulus of working with a group, find out where obedience training classes are available (usually your veterinarian, your dog's breeder, or a dog-owning friend can tell you) and you and your dog can join. If you have difficulty locating such a class, the American Kennel Club will, upon request, provide you with this information.

As an alternative, you could, of course, let someone else do the training by sending your dog to class, but this is far less rewarding as you then lose the opportunity of working with the dog, developing the rapport and closeness which

the two of you can enjoy by working together. Since there could hardly be found a more intelligent, easily trainable breed of dog than a Miniature Schnauzer, it certainly should prove worth your while to attempt the task yourself.

If the latter has been your decision, there are some basic rules which you should follow. You must remain calm and confident in attitude at all times. You must never lose your temper and frighten your dog or punish him unjustly. Never, ever, resort to cruelty. Be quick and lavish with your praise each time a command is correctly followed. Make it fun for the dog and he will be eager to please you by responding correctly. Repetition is the keynote, but it should not be continued without recess to the point of tedium. Limit the training sessions to ten- or fifteen-minute periods each time.

Formal obedience training can be followed, and very frequently is, by entering the dog in obedience competition to work toward an obedience degree, or several of them, depending on the dog's aptitude and your own enjoyment. Obedience trials are held in conjunction with the majority of conformation dog shows, both all-breed and Specialty, and as separate events as well. If you are working alone with your dog, you will need to obtain information on these from someone local, from a Miniature Schnauzer Club to which you may belong, or from the American Kennel Club. If you have been working with a training class, you will find information readily available regarding dates and locations of trials.

The goals for which one works in the formal American Kennel Club member or licensed obedience trials are the following titles: C.D. (Companion Dog), C.D.X. (Companion Dog Excellent), and U.D. (Utility Dog). These degrees are earned by receiving three qualifying scores, or "legs," at each level of competition. The degrees must be earned in order, with one completed prior to starting work on the next. For example, a dog must have earned C.D. prior to starting work on C.D.X. Then C.D.X. must be completed before U.D. work begins. The ultimate title possible to attain in obedience work is that of Obedience Trial Champion (O.T.Ch.). In order to qualify for this one, a dog must have received the required number of points by placing first or second in Open or Utility after having earned the Utility Dog rating. There is also a Tracking Dog title (T.D.) to be earned at tracking trials and a new, more difficult-to-attain degree, Tracking Dog Excellent (T.D.X.).

When you see the letters "C.D." following a dog's name, you will know that the dog has satisfactorily completed the following exercises: heel on leash, heel free, stand for examination, recall, long sit, and long stay. "C.D.X." means that tests have been passed in all of the exercises for Companion Dog plus heel free, drop on recall, retrieve over high jump, broad jump, long sit, and long down. "U.D." indicates that the dog has additionally passed tests in scent discrimination (leather article), scent discrimination (metal article), signal exercises, directed retrieve, directed jumping, and group stand for examination.

The letters "T.D." indicate that the dog has been trained for and passed the test to follow the trail of a stranger along a path on which the trail was laid between thirty minutes and two hours previously. Along this track there must be more than two right-angle turns, at least two of which are well out in the open where no fences or other boundaries exist for guidance of the dog or handler. The dog wears a harness and is connected to the handler by a lead twenty to forty feet in length. Inconspicuously dropped at the end of the track is an article to be retrieved, usually a glove or wallet, which the dog is expected to locate and the handler to pick up. The letters "T.D.X." indicate that the dog has passed a more difficult version of the Tracking Dog test, with a longer track and more turns to be successfully worked through.

The owner of a dog holding the U.D. title and the T.D. title may then use the letters "U.D.T." following the dog's name. If the dog has gained his U.D. title and his T.D.X. title, then the letters "U.D.T.X." may follow his name, indicating that he is a Utility Dog and Tracker Excellent.

It is only natural that little dogs as bright, teachable and eager to please as Miniature Schnauzers should have an aptitude for obedience work, which has proven to be the case on numerous occasions.

The first Miniature Schnauzer to be shown in obedience was Champion Mussolini of Marienhof, bred and owned by Mrs. Marie Slattery. Mussolini was a member of the litter which also included Champion Mehitabel of Marienhof III who was the first uncropped Miniature Schnauzer Group winner.

Mussolini was really ahead of his time, in that he was shown in obedience prior to the American Kennel Club's recognition of these classes, for the first time in November 1935. With but ten short days of advance training, he won first in a Novice Class of 11 at Philadelphia, then a second in the class at Baltimore that same year. In those days only two qualifying scores were required. However, Mussolini never gained his C.D. title, the American Kennel Club not having started to award them until the following year. Had they done so, he would have been the first of the breed to gain that honor, plus becoming the first combined conformation and obedience title winner on record.

It was Mrs. Marian Shaw who gained the first Companion Dog Degree with a Miniature Schnauzer, the winner being Shaw's Little Pepper, who won first in a class of 19 with a score of 99 among other honors, this in the days when 100 points made a perfect score. As Pepper also became a conformation champion, this was the first Miniature Schnauzer to hold dual titles.

During the following decade, 14 C.D. and two C.D.X. titles were gained by Miniature Schnauzers. The C.D.X. titlists were Dorem Extra and Playboy of Kenhoff, both owned by Mrs. Redmond McCosker. Playboy was sired by Champion Vance of Palawan, and went on, in 1949, to become the first of his breed to gain a U.D.T. Brunhilde v. Stortsburg became the first U.D. bitch during that same year.

Other distinguished obedience Miniature Schnauzers over the years include Fred v. Schonhardt of Crystal, the first black C.D. title holder. This is one of the breeds in which beauty and brains do go well together, and many of the bench show champions hold one to several obedience degrees as well. Among the most distinguished from earlier times were American and Canadian Champion Pocono Rough Rider, Canadian and American U.D.T., the first conformation champion with the tracking degree. Then there were American and Canadian Champion Wildwood's Showboat, American and Canadian C.D.X., Bermudian C.D., and Valentina of Finebrook, American, Canadian and Bermudian C.D.X., with ten High in Trial awards among credits.

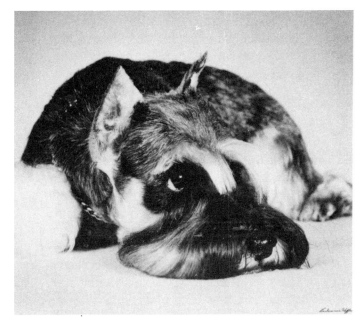

Undoubtedly thinking over the accomplishments of gaining an Obedience Trial Championship, this pensive Schnauzer belongs to Marilyn and Bill Oxandale, Crestwood, Missouri.

Hollywood Dog Obedience Club Top Dog Team, 1982. Second place winners out of 35 participating clubs. Shirley's September Morn is in the middle with Bobette Gowan Tomasoff.

Mrs. Ruth Ziegler, owner of the Allaruth Miniature Schnauzers, started her kennels back in the 1950's with the acquisition of Doman Mehitabel, C.D.X. from Frederick von Huly, and selected Blinken of Mandeville (litter brother to the Best in Show winning Champion Forest Nod of Mandeville) to be the sire of her first litter. This litter produced three bitches, one of them becoming the breed's first Champion Utility Dog, Champion Frevohly's Best Bon Bon, U.D., who along with these honors was also to gain prestige as foundation for the numerous champions to be bred in the future at Allaruth. Certainly this bitch was a splendid example of brains combined with beauty! She produced five champions, becoming the first Western-bred Miniature Schnauzer bitch to do so, holding the record as the West's top producing bitch.

Cinder von Kirche, C.D.X., dam of Ch. Kazels Favorite and of an all-champion litter. Was a top producer and a top scoring obedience dog. Owned by Mrs. K.L. Church, Kazel, Imperial, Missouri.

O.T. Ch. Title Holders Run in the Oxandale Family

At the time of writing, there are three Miniature Schnauzers currently holding the title of Obedience Trial Champion here in the United States. Of these three, Princess Pfeffer II, who was the first to gain the title and her son, Pepperhaus Pfiesty Pfritz, the latest to do so, are owned by Marilyn and William Oxandale of Crestwood, Missouri, who are justifiably proud of this achievement on the part of their dogs.

Pepper was whelped in August 1973 from a breeding of Colomo's Lady Godiva and Cyngar's Cincinnati Kid. She was acquired some eight weeks later by the Oxandales from the breeder, Mrs. Patricia Hartman, purely as a household pet and with no intention of showing her. Not being wise to the ways of properly naming an A.K.C. registered dog, the new owners chose the name "Pepper," prefacing it with "Princess" purely to make it longer. The registration form came back from A.K.C. with the official name having become Princess Pfeffer II.

From the beginning, Pepper exhibited a particularly outgoing personality. This, combined with a more than average intelligence and a liberal sprinkling of energy, were later to be recognized as the ideal mix of traits for obedience work. Unfortunately, obedience was to be the Oxandales' second choice for exhibiting, and with the generous help of the now deceased judge, Maureen Thomann, they entered Pepper in a number of conformation shows during the summer of 1974. Pepper never did badly, but neither did she win, and it became increasingly obvious that while she probably had sufficient quality to finish, the road to a championship would be long and time-consuming.

Thus in the early spring of 1975, Pepper and Bill Oxandale completed a 12-week course offered by a local obedience club. Two weeks later, at Wichita, Kansas, Pepper went High in Trial from the Novice Class, receiving the first of many blue and yellow ribbons. She qualified for her Companion Dog title that weekend, and went on to achieve her Companion Dog Excellent title in September, with her first leg on the Utility Dog Title before the year ended.

After whelping a litter of six puppies the following March, Pepper went on to complete the Utility Dog Title in April 1976. The high point in her obedience career was reached on October 14th, 1978, when she reached the 100 point mark and achieved the A.K.C. Obedience Trial Champion title. Pepper thus became the very first Miniature Schnauzer Obedience Trial Champion in the United States. Although Pepper is still shown occasionally, she has been semi-retired since 1981. Until that time, she was shown in 226 A.K.C. trials, competing in more than 400 classes. Her lifetime record through 1981 included 10 High in Trials, and she placed 136 times as follows:—

48 first placements
40 second placements
26 third placements
22 fourth placements

During the mid-'70's, the Illini Obedience Association of Chicago, under the sponsorship of Gaines Dog Food, instituted a nationwide all-breed obedience competition, this consisting of three class competitions in Novice and Open classes, and six class competitions in Super Class (3 Open and 3 Utility). Dogs are placed according to the highest average score for all classes. Pepper placed in the Gaines Mid-west Regionals three times competing against the best obedience dogs of all breeds in the Central United States. In 1976, in Chicago, she won 9th place in Super Class. In 1977 at Dallas she won 4th place in this class, and in 1978, at Des Moines, 10th place.

In the two recognized obedience rating systems, Pepper placed as Top Terrier nationally four consecutive years in the Shuman System and two years in the Delaney System. Overall she placed in the Terrier Group Top Ten every year from 1975 through 1981.

Now to return to those six puppies which Pepper whelped in the spring of 1976. This litter was from a mating with a well-known sire, Champion Penlan's Paragon's Pride, owned by Penny and Lanny Hirstein, Washington, Illinois. Three of the pups were female and were sold. The three males were kept and shown. Champion Pepperhaus Karbon Kopy, C.D.X., was shown to his championship in 1979 by Lanny Hirstein. Currently he is being shown in obedience for his Utility title. Pepperhaus Watch My Dust, U.D., attained his title in 1983. Pepperhaus Pfiesty Pfritz attained his Utility in 1979, and as we are going to press has just received his certificate from A.K.C. proclaiming him an Obedience Trial Champion. Like mother, like son! What a truly thrilling achieve-

O.T.Ch. Pepperhaus Pfiesty Pfritz, owned by Marilyn and Bill Oxandale, Crestwood, Missouri.

ment for these fanciers to have two of their dogs thus distinguish themselves. Pfritz earned his Obedience Trial Championship (OTCH) on November 25th 1983 at Jonesboro, Arkansas in 48 degree weather at an outdoor show through mud and wet grass. He was the only Utility Dog to pass that day.

Our congratulations to the Oxandales on these accomplishments, along with good wishes for the future.

Shirley Willey Talks about Schnauzers in Obedience

Shirley Willey, owner of the now widely known and highly successful show kennel, Shirley's Miniature Schnauzers, had her start in obedience which she thoroughly enjoyed until 1973 when an injury made it difficult for her to continue the work. Now, however, she is saying "Someday, if I find the dog that I feel will train easily, I may go back into obedience as a challenge to reach my goal."

Ch. Carolane's Fancy That in October 1976, being shown for the first time in California for Shirley's Schnauzers, Dick and Shirley Willey, Simi, California.

Shirley, who lives in Simi, California, was the first Obedience Director of the Miniature Schnauzer Club of Southern California, and organized a Top Dog team for the club in 1970. Top Dog is sponsored by the California Dog Obedience Council and is composed of breed and obedience clubs in the area. Any club who is a member is eligible to enter a team in the competition for Top Ten, and individual dogs who are on the teams are competing for Top Dog.

Her first litter consisted of Champion Shirley's Show Off, C.D., Shirley's Sir Prize Package, and Shirley's Charade, C.D.X. She and husband Dick Willey, started the puppies on leash heeling when they were eight weeks old. "Sir" took to it immediately, the girls going along willingly. They learned to sit-stay with Beau and Gidget (Shirley's New Beau, C.D.X. and Shirley's Sugar 'n' Spice, C.D.), these having been the two preceding them in the Willey household—and with whom Shirley and Dick started out in obedience.

Beau had joined the family following the death of a dearly loved Cocker Spaniel (at age 16 years), in the mid 1960's, a super intelligent little dog who soon had both Shirley and Dick completely sold on his breed. A co-worker of Dick's, impressed by Beau's obvious "smarts," suggested that Shirley and he join an obedience class, the result being their enrollment in the Wright Patterson Air Force Base Obedience Training Club in January 1966. This was where it really began—the Willeys' interest and involvement in the sport. Beau wound up first in his class of ten small dogs, plus a high score for BOTH small and large dogs, a graduation diploma, and a sterling silver charm on which "graduation" was engraved. Need we add that Dick was an extremely proud papa?

That was the beginning! Came the big event in October 1966, the licensed show, Beau had arrived in the advanced class, where he had also distinguished himself.

The Dayton Dog Training Club event took place in October 1966, and Shirley had decided to try Beau out in the big-time competition. 46 dogs competed in Novice A Class, and when the smoke of battle had cleared, Beau was among those who had qualified! That was the day when Shirley and Dick had the opportunity to watch the top obedience Miniature Schnauzer in the country for that period at work, Valentina of Finbrooke, C.D., and watching her intently, they both came to realize that a Miniature Schnauzer COULD make it in obedience, and how it should be done!

From that time on, Beau's scores were consistently higher, leading to his earning his Companion Dog degree (C.D.) in three straight shows, moving from a score of 175 clear up to 191 within three weeks' time, the result of many hours of dedicated work, which certainly paid off!

Gidget was the next to join the Willey family, a real fun dog to train, her first big victory being highest scoring dog at the club match. She

Shirley's September Morn, C.D.X., handled by Bobette Gowan-Tomasoff, at the Ventura County Dog Fanciers Ass'n January 1980. "Ember" qualified here for her C.D.X., and also had a third place in her class.

This lovely black and silver is Ch. Kelly's Ebony Silver Lining pictured with Geri Kelly, handling. Judged by the late Richard Hensel at Springfield in 1981.

Ch. Irrenhaus Flights of Fancy, bred and owned by Jacqueline C. Hicks, Woodford, Virginia. Handled by Sue Baines, here is winning the Terrier Group at Mahoning Shenango in 1978.

gained her C.D. in four shows, starting in the 180's and going up to 195½, with a 192 along the way. Beau and Gidget were the first Miniature Schnauzers in Dayton, Ohio, where the Willeys lived at that time, to gain C.D. titles, and Beau the first for any dog in their club that year. Shirley was ecstatic, for now she had the C.D. dog and C.D. bitch for which she had yearned—and worked!

These two were the parents of the first homebred litter to which we referred at the beginning of this story. Beau and Gidget shared Champion Phil Mar Thunderbolt as a grandsire, so it seemed logical that they should produce well together. They did! Show Off was trained by Dick Willey for a career in conformation (but also earned a C.D.—of course!). Sir had a special talent in obedience, scoring in the high 190's even before reaching six months age, at one year received his C.D. degree, and his C.D.X. when he was two.

Shirley Willey remarks upon the tremendous feeling of elation and satisfaction that accompanies success in obedience, for here is something one has worked for, for many hours and with great patience. Thus victory is sweet since it is directly the result of one's own efforts and the rapport established between master and dog. To quote Shirley,"Obedience is fun and certainly a great experience. Everyone with a Miniature Schnauzer should try for a C.D. When achieved, congratulations! I never said it was easy."

Practicing what they preach, the Willeys have set the routine for their breeding program by which all puppies sold should have some obedience training before leaving to go to new homes, and the new owners should be encouraged to continue this training, taking their puppies to class. So strongly do they feel about this that they have devised the unique practice of offering a refund on the price paid for the puppy if they would put an obedience title on the dog. None of the dogs owned by the Willeys are neglected in this respect; even their top show dogs have their turn, perhaps not until their show careers are finished, but at some time sooner or later. Actually it is often better to wait until after a show career to start obedience so as not to risk the tendency to "sit" each time you stop, as the author has seen happen many times over the years as a judge.

Shirley tells of a tornado, while the Willeys were living in Florida, when Beau and Gidget

The finals in the breed judging at Montgomery County in 1981. In the foreground, Sandra Nagengast (Angler's Schnauzers) with the Best of Breed, Ch. Richlene's Top Billing. Carol Parker of Skyline Kennels with her Winners Dog and Best of Winners, Ch. Skyline's Signature, and Carol Luke, of Bandsman, with the Best of Opposite Sex, Champion Bandsman's Ringside Gossip.

were put into their training collars and left to "down, stay" on the bed. They DID, and when she returned from seeking help, were right where she had left them—safe and dry.

Shirley's goal is to breed a champion that she can take on to U.D. (Utility Degree), and she is constantly watching for the dog who might make this possible. She points out that even dogs who have been highly successful through gaining C.D. and C.D.X. titles are never able to make it through U.D. This is strictly a team effort, which must be thoroughly understood and enjoyed by both the trainer and the dog if success is to follow.

Miss Theresa Klemencic, of the Sim-Cal Miniature Schnauzers in Bridgeville, Pennsylvania, is owner of this 17-year-old bitch, Simmie, whom she believes has the distinction of being the first of her breed and sex to earn a U.D.T. in the United States and Canada. Simmie also has a C.D.X. and a T.D. in Bermuda, having been the first Terrier to gain the latter honor. Simmie passed her T.D. in November 1971, and still alive and going strong as we write these words.

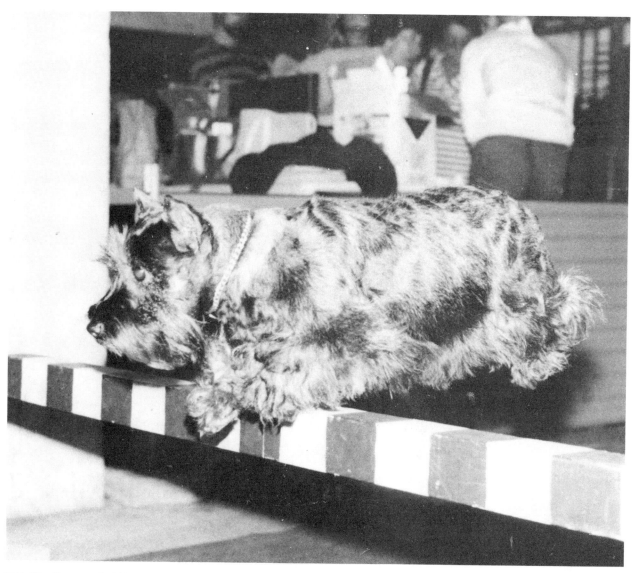

O.T. Ch. Bonanza's Miss Dark Shadow was bred by Bob and Nancy Berg and is owned by Eunice Reusbech, Minnetonka, Minnesota.

Missy in Obedience

Obedience Trial Champion Bonanza's Miss Dark Shadow was whelped on October 19th, 1973 at the Bo-Nanza Kennel of Bob and Nancy Berg. She was the last of the litter to be sold as a pet, her new owner becoming Eunice Reusbech of Minnetonka, Minnesota.

Missy was, and still is, "just a pet." However, in 1975 she earned her C.D. The C.D.X. came in 1976, and the U.D. in 1978. Along the way she was awarded several Highest Scoring Terrier and Highest Scoring Miniature Schnauzer in Trial, and a few times she was Highest Scoring Dog in Trial. Missy has been among the top ten Miniature Schnauzers in obedience for the past eight years. She earned her Obedience Trial Championship in 1980, thus becoming the second Miniature

Schnauzer to do so, and the third Terrier.

Nobody has bothered to tell Missy that she is now ten years old. When people ask her age, and her owners tell them, they are amazed. What Missy may lack in conformation she makes up for in showmanship. There are few dogs in obedience who love to perform the way Missy does; and age has not slowed her down at all. To quote her owner, "I do believe that Missy has been trying to tell the obedience world, 'don't tell me a Miniature Schnauzer cannot be tops' and her flashing dark eyes have certainly told me that. They talk!"

Missy has learned the pattern almost better than some of the judges at this stage of the game. However, she sure has a lot of fun even when she does it her way!

Ch. Skyline's Signature by Ch. Skyline's Blue Spruce ex Ch. Skyline's Frostflower, born September 1973. Currently the second Top Producing sire in breed history with 48 champion offspring. A very outstanding member of the Skyline Kennels owned by Carol A. Parker.

CHAPTER FOURTEEN

Breeding Miniature Schnauzers

Ch. Jadee's Jump Up at age one year. A Top Producer with 36 champions as of early 1984. Bred and owned by D.L. and Judy Smith, Jadee Kennels, Bettendorf, Iowa.

Breeding good dogs requires a lot of hard work. It is not easy to produce dogs who conform as closely as possible to the standard, and it takes years to develop a strain of good and successful dogs. A lot of time and effort must go into choosing the stud dog and brood bitch, and then more time must be spent with the litter once it arrives.

The Stud Dog

Choosing the best stud dog to complement your bitch is not an easy task. The principal factors to be considered are the stud's quality and conformation and his pedigree. The pedigree lists the various bloodlines involved with the ancestry of the dog. If you are a novice in the breed, I would suggest that you seek advice from some of the more experienced breeders who are old-timers in the fancy and thus would be able to discuss with you some of the various dogs behind the one to which you are planning to breed your bitch. Many times such people accurately recall in minute detail the dogs you need to know about, perhaps even having access to photos of them. And do be sure to carefully study the photos in this book, as they show representatives of important Miniature Schnauzer bloodlines.

It is extremely important that the stud's pedigree be harmonious with that of your bitch. Do not just rush out and breed to a current winner, with no regard for whether or not he can reproduce his quality. Take time to check out the progeny being sired by the dog, or dogs, under your consideration. A dog that has sired nothing of quality for others probably will do no better for you, unless, of course, it is a young stud just starting out; such a stud may not have had the opportunity to produce much of anything, good or bad, thus far. Do you want to waste your bitch's time on an unknown quantity? Wouldn't you prefer to use a dog with a good producing record? You may get a little-known or unproven dog for a less expensive stud fee, but is that really sensible?

Breeding dogs is not a moneymaking proposition. By the time you pay a stud fee, take care of the bitch during gestation, whelp the litter, and raise and care for the puppies (including shots, and food, among other things) until they reach selling age, you will be fortunate if you break even on the cost of the litter. Therefore, it is

Ch. Skyline's Striking, by Ch. Sky Rocket's Uproar ex Ch. Skyline's Silver Lining, pictured here at age ten months. He is now the sire of three champions. Carol A. Parker, owner, Vail, Arizona.

foolish to skimp on the stud fee. Let nothing influence your selection except that the dog be best suited to your bitch in background and conformation, with the best producing record, regardless of the cost. It is just as expensive to raise mediocre puppies as good ones, and you will certainly fare better financially if you have show-prospect puppies to sell than if you come up with nothing but pets, which you will probably wind up selling for far less than you had intended or you'll end up giving away to get them good homes. Remember, the only excuse for breeding and bringing puppies into the world is an honest effort to improve the breed. So in choosing the stud you use, remember that the best, most suitable one you can find with an impressive producing record will almost certainly be by far the greatest bargain in the long run.

You will have to decide on one of three courses to follow in planning the breeding of your bitch: inbreeding, line-breeding, or outcrossing. Inbreeding is normally considered to be father to daughter, mother to son, or sister to brother. Line-breeding is combining two dogs belonging originally to the same strain or family of Miniature Schnauzers, descended from the same

Ch. Blythewood His Majesty, sire of nine champions, a son of Ch. Blythewood Main Gazebo ex Ch. Blythewood Crown Jewel, owned and handled by Mrs. Joan L. Huber, Blythewood, Green Lane, Pennsylvania.

ancestors, such as half-brother to half-sister, niece to uncle, granddaughter to grandsire, and so on. Outcross breeding is using a dog and a bitch of completely different bloodlines with no mutual ancestors, or only a few, and these far back, if at all.

Each of these methods has advantages and disadvantages; each has supporters and detractors. I would say that line-breeding is probably the safest, the most generally approved, and the most frequently used with the desired results. Thus, I would say, it is perfect for the novice breeder because it is the easiest to figure out,

especially until one has acquired considerable experience with the breed and the various bloodlines of which it consists.

Inbreeding should be left for the experienced, very sophisticated breeder who knows the line extremely well and thus is in a position to evaluate the probable results. Outcrossing is normally done when you are trying to bring in a specific feature or trait, such as better movement, better head type, superior bone or substance, or better personality or temperament.

Everyone sincerely interested in breeding dogs wants to develop a line of their own, but this is

Ch. Travelmor's Check Your Temper, by Ch. Travelmor's Double Check ex Ch. Travelmor's Tantrum II, taking Best of Breed at Westbury in 1983 for Bill and Olive Moore, handled by Jennifer Moore. One of two victories at the New York Miniature Schnauzer Club Specialty, this Schnauzer also has won Best in Sweepstakes and Best of Opposite Sex at the Miniature Schnauzer Club of America National.

Ch. Hudson's Bold Decision, by Ch. Sole Baye's Bold Impulse ex Fabel's Little Lacy, owned by Luther and Esther Hudson. Handled by Wood Wornall.

Sole Baye's Genuine Risk, stunning young Schnauzer taking Best in Match at the only match she ever entered, with her owner, Yvonne B. Phelps, El Monte, California. A "comer" for the future we are sure! By Ch. Sunshine Sounder ex Ch. Sole Baye's Miss Musket.

not accomplished overnight. It takes at least several generations before you can claim to have done so, and during this time the close study of bloodlines and the observation of individual dogs are essential. Getting to know and truthfully evaluate the dogs with which you are working will go a long way in helping you preserve the best in what you have while at the same time remove weaknesses.

As a novice breeder, your wisest bet is to start by acquiring one or two bitches of the finest quality and background you can buy. In the beginning, it is really foolish to own your own stud dog; you will make out better and have a wider range of dogs with which to work if you pay a stud fee to one of the outstanding producing Miniature Schnauzers available to service your bitch. In order to be attractive to breeders a stud dog must be well known, must have sired at least one champion (and usually one that has attracted considerable attention in Specials competition), and must have winning progeny in the ring; this represents a large expenditure of time and money before the dog begins to bring in returns on your investment. So start out by pay-

ing a stud fee a few times to use such a dog, or dogs, retaining the best bitch out of each of your first few litters and breeding those once or twice before you seriously think of owning your own stud dog. By that time, you will have gained the experience to recognize exactly what sort of dog you need for this purpose.

A future stud dog should be selected with the utmost care and consideration. He must be of very high standard as he may be responsible for siring many puppies each year, and he should not be used unless he clearly has something to contribute to the breed and carries no hereditary disease. Ideally, he should come from a line of excellent Miniature Schnauzers on both sides of his pedigree, the latter containing not only *good* dogs but also ones which are *proven successful producers of quality*. The dog himself should be of sufficient quality to hold his own in competition in his breed. He should be robust and virile, a keen stud dog who has proved that he is able to transmit his best qualities to his progeny. Do not use an unsound dog or a dog with a major or outstanding fault. Not all champions seem able to pass along their individual splendid quality and, by the same token, occasionally one finds a dog who never finished but who does sire puppies better than himself *provided that his pedigree is star-studded with top producing dogs and bitches.* Remember, too, that the stud dog cannot do it alone; the bitch must have what it takes too, although I must admit that some stud dogs, the truly dominant ones, can consistently produce type and quality regardless of the bitch or her background. Great studs like this, however, are few and far between.

If you are the proud owner of a promising young stud dog, one that you have either bred from one of your own bitches or that you have purchased after much serious thought and deliberation, do not permit him to be used for the first time until he is about a year old. The initial breeding should be to a proven matron, experienced in what is expected of her and thus not likely to give the stud a bad time. His first encounter should be pleasant and easy, as he could be put off breeding forever by a maiden bitch who fights and resents his advances. His first

breeding should help him develop confidence and assurance. It should be done in quiet surroundings, with only you and one other person (to hold the bitch) present. Do not make a circus of it, as the first time will determine your stud's attitude and feeling about future breeding.

Your young stud dog must allow you to help with the breeding, as later there will be bitches who will not be cooperative and he will need to develop the habit of accepting assistance. If, right from the beginning, you are there helping and praising him, he will expect and accept this as a matter of course whenever it may be necessary.

Before you introduce the dogs, be sure to have some K-Y Jelly at hand (this is the only lubricant that should be used) and either a stocking or a length of gauze with which to muzzle the bitch should it seem necessary, as you do not want either yourself or your stud dog bitten. Once they are "tied," you will be able to remove the muzzle, but, for the preliminaries, it is best to play it safe by muzzling her.

Ch. Kazels Artful Dodger, son of Ch. Kazels Favorite, is an example of third generation inbreeding Favorite to his daughters. Mrs. K.L. Church, owner, Kazel, Imperial, Missouri.

Ch. Contempra Foolish Pleasure, owned by Homer and Isabelle Graf, winning the Terrier Group at Delaware Water Gap in 1979. Joan Huber handling. The judge, Anna Katherine Nicholas.

Ch. Kelly's Jolee's Top of the Line, born in January 1983, finished at ten months of age. By Ch. Kelly's Im-Per-Ial Black ex Ch. Kelly's Flam-Boy-Ant Black. Geri Kelly owner-handling to Best of Winners at North Western Connecticut in 1983.

The stud fee is paid at the time of the breeding. Normally a return service is offered should the bitch fail to produce. Usually one live puppy is considered to be a litter. In order to avoid any misunderstanding regarding the terms of the breeding, it is wise to have a breeding certificate which both the owner of the stud and the owner of the bitch should sign. This should spell out quite specifically all the conditions of the breeding, along with listing the dates of the matings (usually the bitch is bred twice with one day in between, especially if she is a maiden bitch). The owner of the stud should also at this time provide the owner of the bitch with a copy of the stud dog's pedigree, if this has not previously been done.

Sometimes a pick-of-the-litter puppy is taken instead of a stud fee, and this should be noted on the breeding certificate along with such terms as at what age the owner of the stud dog is to select the puppy and whether it is to be a dog puppy, a bitch puppy, or just the "pick" puppy. All of

this should be clearly stated to avoid any misunderstandings later on.

In almost every case, the bitch must come to the stud dog for breeding. Once the owner of the bitch decides to what stud dog she will preferably be bred, it is important that the owner of the stud be contacted immediately to discuss the stud fee, terms, approximate time the bitch is due in season, and whether she will be shipped in or brought to the stud owner. Then, as soon as the bitch shows signs of coming into season, another phone call to the stud owner must follow to finalize the arrangements. I have experienced times when the bitch's owner has waited until a day or two before the bitch should be bred to contact me, only to meet with disappointment owing to the dog's absence from home.

It is essential that the stud owner have proper facilities for housing the bitch while she is there. Nothing can be more disheartening than to have a bitch misbred or, still worse, to have her get

Ch. Misty's Winagin Charlie taking Best of Winners for William Keith and Betti Ann Evans at Charlottesville-Albermarle in 1983. Sue Baines handling.

Am., Can., and Mex. Ch. Marwyck Pitt Penn Pirate, the sire of 48 champions, was for many years the top breed winner in Schnauzers with his more than 100 Bests of Breed. Also Top Sire for many years. Owned by Jean and Glenn Fancy, Fancway Miniature Schnauzers, La Canada, California.

away and become lost. Unless you can provide safe and proper care for visiting bitches, do not offer your dog at public stud.

Owning a stud dog is no easy road to riches, as some who have not experienced it seem to think; making the dog sufficiently well known is expensive and time-consuming. Be selective in the bitches you permit this dog to service. It takes two to make the puppies; and while some stud dogs do seem almost to achieve miracles, it is a general rule that an inferior bitch from a mediocre background will probably never produce well no matter how dominant and splendid may be the stud to whom she is bred. Remember that these puppies will be advertised and perhaps shown as sired by your dog. You do not want them to be an embarrassment to yourself or to him, so do not accept just any bitch who comes along in order to get the stud fee. It may prove far too expensive in the long run.

A stud fee is generally based on the going price of one show-type puppy and on the sire's record as a producer of winners. Obviously, a stud throwing champions in every litter is worth a greater price than a dog that sires mediocre puppies. Thus a young stud, just starting his career as a sire, is less expensive before proven than a dog with, say, forty or fifty champions already on the record. And a dog that has been used more than a few times but has no winning pro-

Ch. Reflections of Attaway, by Attaway Squire McDuff ex Reflections Jeweled Image. Owners, Isabelle and Homer Graf, Glen Gardner, New Jersey, Handler, Joan L. Huber.

Ch. Kelly's Flam-Boy-Ant Black, bred, owned and handled by Geri Kelly, North Falmouth, MA, winning the Terrier Group at Penobscot K.C. By Charmar's Johann ex Ch. Kelly's Im-Pec-Cable Black.

Ch. Blythewood Chief Bosun winning Best of Breed at the first of the American Miniature Schnauzer Club Specialties to be held in conjunction with the Great Western Terrier Specialties in California in June 1967. By Ch. Blythewood Main Gazebo ex Huber's Cassandra. Bred, owned, and handled by Joan L. Huber, Green Lane, Pennsylvania.

geny should, it goes without saying, be avoided no matter how small the fee; he will almost certainly be a waste of your bitch's time.

I do not feel that we need to go into the actual breeding procedure here, as the experienced fancier already knows how it should be handled and the novice should not attempt it for the first time by reading instructions in a book. Plan to have a breeder or handler friend help you until you have become accustomed to handling such matters or, if this is not practical for you, it is very likely your veterinarian can arrange to do it for you or get someone from his staff to preside.

If a complete "tie" is made, that breeding should be all that is actually necessary. However, with a maiden bitch, a bitch who has "missed" (failed to conceive) in the past, or one who has come a long distance, most people like

to give a second breeding, allowing one day to elapse in between the two. This second service gives additional insurance that a litter will result; and if the bitch is one with a past record for misses, sometimes even a third mating takes place in an effort to take every precaution.

Once the "tie" has been completed, be sure that the penis goes back completely into its sheath. The dog should be offered a drink of water and a short walk, and then he should be put in his crate or kennel somewhere alone to settle down. Do not permit him to mingle with the other males for a while, as he will carry the odor of the bitch about him and this could result in a fight.

The bitch should not be allowed to urinate for at least an hour. In fact, many people feel that she should be "upended" (held with her rear end above her front) for several minutes following the "tie" in order to permit the sperm to travel deeper. She should then be offered water, crated, and kept quiet.

There are no set rules governing the conditions of a stud service. They are whatever the owner of the stud dog chooses to make them. The stud fee is paid for the act, not for the litter; and if a bitch fails to conceive, this does not automatically call for a return service unless the owner of the stud sees it that way. A return service is a courtesy, not something that can be regarded as a right, particularly as in many cases the failure has been on the part of the bitch, not the stud dog. Owners of a stud in whom they take .pride and whom they are anxious to have make records as the sire of numerous champions, however, are usually most generous in this respect; and I do not know of any instances where this courtesy has been refused when no puppies resulted from the breeding. Some stud owners insist on the return service being given to the same bitch only, while others will accept a different bitch in her place if the owner wishes, particularly if the original one has a previous record for missing.

When a bitch has been given one return breeding and misses again, the stud owner's responsibility has ended. If the stud dog is one who consistently sires puppies, then obviously the bitch is at fault; and she will quite likely never conceive, no matter how often or to how many different studs she is bred. It is unreasonable for the owner of a bitch to expect a stud's owner to give more than one return service.

Ch. Manta of Sole Baye, owner handled by Mrs. Yvonne Phelps, El Monte, California.

Ch. Shirley's Show Time winning the breed at Long Beach K.C., January 1977, judge Mrs. Elaine Young. Owned by Shirley's Schnauzers, Dick and Shirley Willey, Simi, California.

Ch. Skyline's Everlasting, by Ch. Valharra's Double Extra ex Ch. Skyline's Fern of Winrush, is the dam of three champions to date with two more close to finishing. Carol A. Parker, owner, Vail, Arizona.

The Brood Bitch

One of the most important purchases you will make in dogs is the selection of your foundation brood bitch, or bitches, on whom you plan to base your breeding program. You want marvelous bloodlines representing top producing strains; you want sound bitches of basic quality, free of any hereditary problems. There is no such thing as a "bargain" brood bitch. If you are offered one, be wary and bear in mind that you need the *best* and that the price will be correctly in ratio to the quality.

Conscientious Miniature Schnauzer breeders feel quite strongly that the only possible reason for producing puppies is the desire to improve and uphold quality and temperament within the breed, certainly not because one hopes to make a quick cash profit on a mediocre litter, which never works out that way in the long run and can very well wind up adding to the nation's shocking number of unwanted canine waifs. The only reason for breeding a litter is the ambition to produce high-quality puppies of intelligence, show potential, and sound temperament. That is the thought to be kept in mind right from the moment you begin to yearn for puppies.

Your Miniature Schnauzer bitch should not be bred until her second period in season; but if she starts her season at an extra early age, say, barely over six months of age and then for the second time just past one year of age, you would be wise to wait until her third heat. The waiting period

Ch. Blythewood Merry Maker taking Best of Breed at the American Miniature Schnauzer Club Specialty, October 5, 1958. By Ch. Dorem Favorite ex Ch. Blythewood Merry Melody. This win over all the top winning male specials of the day has not been repeated by any bitch in the 25 Montgomery County-Miniature Schnauzer Specialties which have followed. Bred and handled by Joan Lea Bauernschmidt (now Mrs. Joan L. Huber). Owned by Delfin Kennels. This is a sister to Ch. Blythewood Sweet Talk, the dam of Gazebo.

can be profitably spent carefully watching for the ideal stud to complement her own qualities and be compatible with her background. Keeping this in mind, attend dog shows and watch the males who are winning and, even more important, siring the winners. Subscribe to *Schnauzer Shorts* and some of the all-breed magazines and study the pictures and stories accompanying them to familiarize yourself with dogs in other areas of which you may have not been aware. Be sure to keep in mind that the stud should be strong in the bitch's weak points; carefully note his progeny to see if he passes along the features you want and admire. Make special note of any offspring from bitches with backgrounds similar to your bitch's; then you can get an idea of how

well the background fits with his. When you see a stud dog that interests you, discuss your bitch with the owner and request a copy of his dog's pedigree for your study and perusal.

You can also discuss the stud dog with other knowledgeable breeders, including the one from whom your bitch was purchased. You may not always get an unbiased opinion (particularly if the person giving it also has an available stud dog), but discussion is a fine teacher. Listen to what they say and consider the value of their comments. As a result you will be better qualified to reach a knowledgeable and intelligent decision on your own.

When you have made a tentative choice, contact the stud's owner to make the preliminary arrangements regarding the stud fee (whether it will be in cash or a puppy), approximate time the bitch should be ready, and so on. Find out, too, the requirements (such as health certificates, and tests) the stud owner has regarding bitches accepted for breeding. If you will be shipping the bitch, find out which airport and airline should be used.

The airlines will probably have special requirements, too, regarding conditions under which they will or will not take dogs. These requirements, which change from time to time, include such things as crate size and type they will accept. Most airlines have their own crates available for sale which may be purchased at a nominal cost, if you do not already have one that they consider suitable. These are made of fiberglass and are the safest type in which to ship a dog. Most airlines also require that the dog be at the airport two hours before the flight is scheduled to depart and that the dog is accompanied by a health certificate from your veterinarian, including information about rabies inoculation. If the airline does not wish to accept the bitch because of extreme temperature changes in the weather but will do so if you sign a waiver stating that she is accustomed to them and should have no problem, think it over carefully before doing so, as you are thus relieving them of any responsibility should the bitch not reach her destination alive or in good condition. And always insure the bitch when you can.

Normally the airline must be notified several days in advance for the bitch's reservation, as only a limited number of dogs can be accommodated on each flight. Plan on shipping the bitch on her eighth or ninth day, but if at all possible arrange it so that she avoids travelling on the weekend when schedules are not always the same and freight offices are likely to be closed.

It is important that whenever possible you ship your bitch on a flight that goes directly to the airport which is her destination. It is not at all unusual, when stopovers are made along the way, for a dog to be removed from the plane with other cargo and either incorrectly loaded for the next leg of the flight or left behind. Take every precaution that you can against human error!

Australian Ch. Guadala Werewolf, owner-handled by John Sullivan, is a well-known winner. Photo courtesy of Guadala Kennels.

Jo Lee's Black Sapphire, by Ch. Jo Lee's Jimmy Rippen, handled by Geri Kelly to Best of Winners at Rhode Island K.C. 1982. Photo courtesy of owner, Joan L. Williams, Colorado Springs, Colorado.

It is simpler if you can plan to bring the bitch to the stud dog. Some people feel that the trauma of the plane trip may cause the bitch not to conceive; others just plain prefer not sending them that way. If you have a choice, you might do better to take the bitch in your own car where she will feel more relaxed and at ease. If you are doing it this way, be sure to allow sufficient time for the drive to get her to her destination at the correct time for the breeding. This usually is any time from the eighth to the fourteenth day, depending on the individual bitch and her cycle. Remember that if you want the bitch bred twice, you must allow a day in between the two services. Do not expect the stud's owner to put you up during your stay. Find a good, nearby motel that accepts dogs, and make a reservation for yourself there.

Just prior to your bitch's season, you should make a visit to your veterinarian with her. Have her checked for worms, make sure that she is up-to-date on all her shots, and attend to any other tests the stud owner may have requested. The bitch may act and be perfectly normal up until her third or fourth week of pregnancy, but it is better for her to have a clean bill of health before the breeding than to bother her after it. If she is overweight, right now is when you should start getting the fat off her; she should be in good hard condition, neither fat nor thin, when bred.

The day you've been waiting for finally arrives, and you notice the swelling of her vulva, followed within a day or two by the appearance of a colored discharge. Immediately call the stud's owner to finalize arrangements, advising whether you will ship her or bring her, the exact day she will arrive, and so on. Then, if she is going by plane, as soon as you know the details, advise the stud owner of the flight number, the time of arrival, and any other pertinent information. If you are shipping the bitch, the check for the stud fee should be mailed now. If the owner of the stud dog charges for his trips to the airport, for picking the bitch up and then returning her, reimbursement for this should either be included with the stud fee or sent as soon as you know the amount of the charge.

If you are going to ship your bitch, do not feed her on the day of the flight; the stud's owner will do so when she arrives. Be sure that she has had access to a drink of water just before you leave her and that she has been exercised prior to being put in her crate. Place several layers of news-

Ch. Sky Rocket's Upswing and Ch. Sky Rocket's Upsweep in 1972. Handled by Judie and Frank Ferguson. Photo courtesy of D.L. and Judy Smith, now the owners of Upswing.

papers, topped with some shredded papers, on the bottom of the crate for a good bed. The papers can be discarded and replaced when she reaches her destination prior to the trip home. Rugs and towels are not suitable for bedding material as they may become soiled, necessitating laundering when she reaches her destination. A small towel may be included to make her feel more at home if you wish. Remember to have her at the airport two hours ahead of flight time.

If you are driving, be sure to arrive at a reasonable time of day. If you are coming from a distance and get in late, have a good night's sleep before contacting the stud's owner first thing in the morning. If possible, leave the children and relatives at home; they will not only be in the way, but also most stud owners definitely object to too many people around during the actual breeding.

Once the breeding has been completed, if you wish to sit and visit for a while, that is fine; but do not leave the bitch at loose ends. Take her to her crate in the car where she can be quiet (you should first, of course, ascertain that the temperature is comfortable for her there and that she has proper ventilation). Remember that she should not urinate for at least an hour following the breeding.

If you have not already done so, pay the stud fee now, and be sure that you receive your breeding certificate and a copy of the dog's pedigree if you do not have one.

Now you are all set to await, with happy anticipation, the arrival of the puppies.

Pedigrees

To anyone interested in the breeding of dogs, pedigrees are the basic component with which this is best accomplished. It is not sufficient to just breed two nice-looking dogs to one another and then sit back and await outstanding results. Chances are they will be disappointing, as there is no equal to a scientific approach to the breeding of dogs if quality results are the ultimate goal.

We have selected for you pedigrees of Miniature Schnauzer dogs and bitches who either are great producers or have come from consistently outstanding producing lines. Some of these dogs are so dominant that they have seemed to "click" with almost every strain or bloodline. Others, for best results, need to be carefully line-bred. The study of pedigrees and breeding is both a challenge and an exciting occupation.

Even if you have no plans to involve yourself in breeding and just anticipate owning and loving a dog or two, it is fun to trace back the pedigree of your dog, or dogs, to earlier generations and thus learn the sort of ancestors behind your own. Throughout this book you will find a great many pictures of dogs and bitches whose names appear in these pedigrees, enabling you not only to trace the names in the background of your Miniature Schnauzer but also to see what the forebears look like.

The following pedigrees are presented to show the lineage of some famous and important Miniature Schnauzers from kennels featured in this book.

Certified Pedigree

Breed: Miniature Schnauzer   Sex: Male   Whelped: May 10-1979
Call Name: "Maris"   AKC No. RA 539264

Great Gr. Grand Parents / Great Grand Parents / Grand Parents

- CH Ruedesheims Entrepeneur (Sire)
  - CH Penlan Peters Son
    - CH Penlan Peter Gunn
      - CH Penlan Checkmate
      - CH Penlan Proud of Me
    - Penlan Practical Viewpoint
      - CH Penlan Portfolio
      - CH Penlan Psychedelic
  - Ruedesheims Splendor
    - CH Valharras Big Sir
      - CH Valharras Dionysos
      - Valharras Artemis
    - Xerxes von Cricket
      - CH Mankit Xer
      - Liebes Maidi von Ruedesheim
- CH Ruedesheims Landmark
  - CH Landmarks Masterpiece
    - CH Mutiny Master Boy
      - CH Mutiny I'm Grumpy Too
      - Bon-ett Ulla
    - CH Allaruths Jasmine
      - CH Allaruths Jericho
      - CH Allaruths Miss Dinah Mite
  - CH Ruedesheims Free Spirit (Dam)
    - CH Alinders Ace of Hearts
      - CH Alpine Cyrus the Great
      - CH Alinders' Atta Girl
    - Ruedesheims Buxzd
      - CH Barclay Square Brat O'Alinder
        - CH Mankits Xer
        - CH Barclay Square Becky Sharp

3058 N Lima St.
Burbank, California, 91504

Gas Light Kennels
MINIATURE SCHNAUZERS

Finished in 15 days

843-4359

300

Certified Pedigree

(202) 447-3557

CAROLE LUKE
12202 LIVINGSTON STREET
SILVER SPRING, MARYLAND 20902

(301) 946-3624

OWNER

ADDRESS

GENERAL DESCRIPTION   Salt and Pepper   Whelped May 19, 1982

SIRE

CH. R-BO'S VICTORY FLASH

REG. NO. ....

- CH. SHORLAINE DYNAMIC FLASH
  - CH. SKY ROCKET'S UPROAR
    - CH. SKY ROCKET'S FIRST STAGE
      - CH. JAY DEE'S SKY ROCKET
      - Miss Little Guys
    - Tessie Tigerlily
      - CH. WID'S VON KIPPER CDX
      - Martin's Countess von Heidi
  - CH. BETHEL'S NEWSFLASH
    - CH. HELARRY'S COLONEL DAN
      - CH. HELARRY's Danny Boy
      - Delsey's Sweet Heidi
    - CH. BETHEL'S LULU
      - CH. HELARRY'S HARMONY
      - CH. BETHEL'S ORIGINAL EMBER
- CH. SHALOM'S SILVER SHADOW
  - CH. SHALOM DUKE OF GLOUCESTER
    - Schnappsetts L.G. Big George
      - CH. BLUE DEVIL SHARPSHOOTER
      - Schnappsett's Little Girl
    - Sophie's Shadow
      - CH. BETHEL'S NEWSBOY
      - Fraulein Erica von Edanbo
  - Heidi's Little Swan CD
    - Simon Willingham
      - Maynard of Forest Hill
      - Pollyanna Sunshine
    - Heidi of Lanier
      - Berry Boy of Briar Patch
      - Dollie's Duchess

DAM

CH. REPITITION'S RENAISSANCE

REG. NO. ....

- CH. SKY ROCKET'S UPSWING
  - CH. SKY ROCKET'S FIRST STAGE
    - CH. JAY DEE'S SKY ROCKET
      - CH. C-TON'S BONFIRE
      - Oh By Jingo
    - Miss Little Guys
      - Ursafell Sandpiper
      - Ursafell Niblet
  - CH. SKY ROCKET'S UPSTART
    - CH. SKY ROCKET'S FIRST STAGE
      - CH. JAY DEE'S SKY ROCKET
      - Miss Little Guys
    - Tessie Tigerlily
      - CH. WIDS von KIPPER CDX
      - Martin's Countess von Heidi
- Muffin XXIV
  - CH. JADEE'S JUMP UP
    - CH SKY ROCKET'S UPROAR
      - CH. SKY ROCKET'S FIRST STAGE
      - Tessie Tigerlily
    - Heather's Windy Weather
      - CH. HELARRY'S COLONEL DAN
      - CH. TASSE KUCHEN
  - Jobie
    - Repitition's Encore
      - Schraeder's Season To Taste
      - Howmor's Replica
    - Repitition's Finale
      - CH. KADOMA'S REPITITION
      - Princess Adelheid

I HEREBY CERTIFY THAT THIS PEDIGREE IS TRUE AND CORRECT
TO THE BEST OF MY KNOWLEDGE AND BELIEF

SIGNED _____

DATE _____ 19_

PEDIGREE

March 8, 1978	MALE		SALT & PEPPER
Date Whelped	Sex		Color

D. L. & Judy Smith   7738 Nina Omaha, NE
Breeder   Address

CH. JADEE'S HUSH UP
Name of Dog

RA481882
Reg. No.

SIRE

CH. SKY ROCKET'S UPSWING
RA887023
Reg. No.

- CH. SKY ROCKET'S FIRST STAGE
  - CH. JAY DEE'S SKY ROCKET
    - CH. C-TON'S BON FIRE
    - Oh By Jingo
  - Miss Little Guys
    - Ursafell Sandpiper
    - Ursafell Niblet
- CH. SKY ROCKET'S UPSTART
  - CH. SKY ROCKET'S FIRST STAGE
    - CH. JAY DEE'S SKY ROCKET
    - Miss Little Guys
  - Tessie Tigerlily
    - CH. WID'S VON KIPPER, CDX
    - Martin's Countess Von Heidi

DAM

CH. JADEE'S JUJU
RA022919
Reg. No.

- CH. SKY ROCKET'S UPROAR
  - CH. SKY ROCKET'S FIRST STAGE
    - CH. JAY DEE'S SKY ROCKET
    - Miss Little Guys
  - Tessie Tigerlily
    - CH. WID'S VON KIPPER, CDX
    - Martin's Countess Von Heidi
- Heather's Windy Weather
  - CH. HELARRY'S COLONEL DAN
    - CH. HELARRY'S DANNY BOY
    - Delsey's Sweet Heidi
  - CH. TASSE KUCHEN
    - CH. HELARRY'S HARMONY
    - CH. SALTY VON BRITTANHOF

Signed: *Wyoma Clouss* (208) 345-5197
3526 Windsor Drive Boise, ID 83705

302

Our Dog's Pedigree

REGISTERED NAME __Blythewood Misty Acclaim__ — INDIVIDUAL REG. NO. __RA504218__ REG LITTER NO. _____ CALL NAME __Misty__

BREED __Miniature Schnauzer__ SEX __Female__ BORN __2/17/79__ COLOR AND MARKINGS __Salt & Pepper__

BREEDER __Joan L. Huber__ ADDRESS __Box 577, R.D. #1__ CITY __Green Lane__ STATE __PA 18054__

Phone: 215-234-8330

LITTER IDENTIFICATION _____ SOLD TO _____ ADDRESS _____

All of the names above are in the father's pedigree

PARENTS	GRANDPARENTS	GREAT GRANDPARENTS	GREAT GREAT GRANDPARENTS
Ch. Blythewood National Acclaim RA 433285 REG NO	Ch. Blythewood National Anthem (SIRE)	Ch. Sky Rocket Bound To Win (SIRE)	Ch. Skyrocket's Uproar
			Fisher's Wendy of Kringle
		Blythewood Symphony (DAM)	Ch. Mutiny Uproar
			Bocaparic Melody
	Valharra Prize of Blythewood (DAM)	Ch. Valharra's Dionysios (SIRE)	Ch. Allaruth's Daniel
			Ch. Faerwind of Arador
		Valharra's Valid Victory (DAM)	Ch. Moore's Max Derkleiner
			Stewart Konigin der Kristen

All of the names below are in the mother's pedigree

Dardane What's Up O'Blythewood RA 327126 REG NO	Ch. Penlan Checkmate (SIRE)	Ch. Penlan Paragon Fanfare (SIRE)	Ch. Penlan Paragon
			Penlan Prissy Cindy
		Orlane's Middle Maid (DAM)	Orlane's Tom Agin
			Orlane's Little Maid
	Dardane Verity (DAM)	Ch. Skyrocket's Bound To Win (SIRE)	Ch. Skyrocket's Uproar
			Fisher's Wendy of Kringle
		Ch. Arnju's Gypsy Serenade (DAM)	Ch. Dardane Priam
			Arnju's Abigail

Signed _____ Date _____ 19____

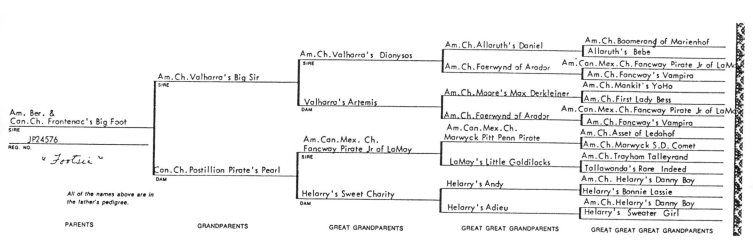

All of the names above are in the father's pedigree.

PARENTS	GRANDPARENTS	GREAT GRANDPARENTS	GREAT GREAT GRANDPARENTS	GREAT GREAT GREAT GRANDPARENTS
Am. Ber. & Can.Ch. Frontenac's Big Foot JP24576 REG. NO. "Footsie"	Am.Ch.Valharra's Big Sir (SIRE)	Am.Ch.Valharra's Dionysos (SIRE)	Am.Ch.Allaruth's Daniel	Am.Ch.Boomerang of Marienhof
				Allaruth's Bebe
			Am.Ch.Faerwynd of Arador	Am.Can.Mex.Ch.Fancway Pirate Jr of LaMa
				Am.Ch.Fancway's Vampira
		Valharra's Artemis (DAM)	Am.Ch.Moore's Max Derkleiner	Am.Ch.Mankit's YoHo
				Am.Ch.First Lady Bess
			Am.Ch.Faerwynd of Arador	Am.Can.Mex.Ch.Fancway Pirate Jr of LaMa
				Am.Ch.Fancway's Vampira
	Can.Ch.Postillion Pirate's Pearl (DAM)	Am.Can.Mex. Ch. Fancway Pirate Jr of LaMay (SIRE)	Am.Can.Mex.Ch. Marwyck Pitt Penn Pirate	Am.Ch.Asset of Ledahof
				Am.Ch.Marwyck S.D. Comet
			LaMay's Little Goldilocks	Am.Ch.Trayhom Talleyrand
				Tallawanda's Rare Indeed
		Helarry's Sweet Charity (DAM)	Helarry's Andy	Am.Ch. Helarry's Danny Boy
				Helarry's Bonnie Lassie
			Helarry's Adieu	Am.Ch.Helarry's Danny Boy
				Helarry's Sweater Girl

303

```
                    CH. ORBIT'S TIME TRAVELER
            CH. GANDALF OF ARADOR
                    CH. FANCWAY'S VAMPIRA
        CH. LADDIN OF ARADOR
                    CH. FANCWAY'S PIRATE JR. OF LAMAY
            CH. FAERWYND OF ARADOR
                    CH. FANCWAY'S VAMPIRA
    CH. SKYLINE'S SILVER LINING (DAM OF 6 CHAMPIONS)
                    CH. MELMAR'S JACK FROST
            CH. ORBIT'S A-OK OF ADFORD
                    ADFORD'S ANYTHING GOES
        CH. ORBIT'S TIME TRAVELER
                    CH. MELMAR'S JACK FROST
            CH. JANHOF'S BON-BON OF ADFORD
                    CH. ALLARUTH'S JEMIMA
```

```
                    CH. JAY-DEE'S SKY ROCKET
            CH. SKY ROCKET'S FIRST STAGE
                    MISS LITTLE GUYS
        CH. SKY ROCKET'S UPSWING
                    CH. SKY ROCKET'S FIRST STAGE
            CH. SKY ROCKET'S UPSTART
                    TESSIE TIGERLILY
    CH. SKYLINE'S BLUE SPRUCE (SIRE OF 48 CHAMPIONS)
                    CH. GANDALF OF ARADOR
            CH. LADDIN OF ARADOR
                    CH. FAERWYND OF ARADOR
        CH. SKYLINE'S SILVER LINING
                    CH. ORBIT'S TIME TRAVELER
            CH. ORBIT'S LIFT OFF, CDX
                    CH. JANHOF'S BON-BON OF ADFORD
```

```
                    CH. SKY ROCKET'S FIRST STAGE
            CH. SKY ROCKET'S UPSWING
                    CH. SKY ROCKET'S UPSTART
        CH. SKYLINE'S BLUE SPRUCE
                    CH. LADDIN OF ARADOR
            CH. SKYLINE'S SILVER LINING
                    CH. ORBIT'S LIFT OFF, CDX
    CH. REGENCY'S REWARD (DAM OF 4 CHAMPIONS)
                    CH. MANKIT'S YO HO
            CH. MARCHEIM POPPIN' FRESH
                    CH. MIRANDA VON BRITTANHOF
        JANA PD
                    CH. HOWTWO'S HIJACKER
```

Certified Pedigree

(2) RL 670 586
(1) RL 636 690 LITTER REG NO

INDIVIDUAL REG. NO.

AKG REGISTERED WITH

CALL NAME

CH. Sole Baye's Sundowner
REGISTERED NAME OF DOG

BREED Miniature Schnauzer **DATE WHELPED** **SEX**

BREEDER Yvonne B. Phelps **ADDRESS** 4526 Baldwin Avenue, El Monte, CA 91731

OWNER **ADDRESS**

GENERAL DESCRIPTION Salt & Pepper

SIRE

CH. Sunshine Sounder
REG. NO. RA 458215

- CH. Valharra's Extra
  - CH. Valharr's Trademark
    - Ch. Moore's Max Derkleiner
      - CH. Mankit's YoHo
      - CH. First Lady Bess
    - Helga Von Mosel
      - CH. Marcheim Shortnin' Bread
      - Florlein Von Mosel
  - Valharra's Annie Fannie
    - CH. Valharra's Dionysos
      - CH. Allaruth's Daniel
      - CH. Faerwynd of Arador
    - CH. Alinders Atta Girl
      - CH. Mankit's Xerxes
      - CH. Orbit's Heaven Sent
- Sky Rocket's Chimney Sweep
  - CH. Sky Rocket's Uproar
    - CH. Sky Rocket's First Stage
      - CH. Jay Dees Sky Rocket
      - Miss Little Guys
    - Tessie Tigerlily
      - CH. Wid's Von Kipper CDX
      - Martin's Countess Von Heidi
  - CH. Sky Rocket's Upsweep
    - CH. Sky Rocket's First Stage
      - CH. Jay Dee's Sky Rocket
      - Miss Little Guys
    - CH. Sky Rocket's Upstart
      - CH. Sky Rocket's First Stage
      - Tessie Tigerlilly

DAM

CH. Sole Baye's Miss Musket
REG. NO. RA 349937

- Sole Baye's Ambassador
  - CH. Sky Rocket's Bound to Win
    - CH. Sky Rocket's Uproar
      - CH. Sky Rocket's First Stage
      - Tessie Tigerlilly
    - Fischer's Wendy of Kringle
      - CH. Orlane's Ringmaster
      - Kandy of Kringle
  - B. J. of Sole Baye
    - CH. Helarry's Colonel Dan
      - CH. Helarry's Danny Boy
      - Delsey's Sweet Heidi
    - Walter's Empress of Swan
      - CH. Fancway's Tom Terrific
      - Walter's Sheer Tweed of Swan
- CH. Manta of Sole Baye
  - Fancway's Daktari
    - CH. Starfire Criterion Landmark
      - Am. & Can. CH. Landmarks Masterpiece
      - Starfire Bonnybell of Ballygar
    - CH. Walter's Country Gal
      - Int. CH. Fancway's Pirate Jr. of La May
      - Pat-Je's Country Bumpkin
  - CH. Sisterce of Sole Baye
    - Am. & Can. CH. Landmarks Masterpiece
      - Am. & Can. CH. Mutiny Master Spy
      - CH. Allaruths Jasmine
    - Hilda V
      - Socrates of San Rafael
      - Liebling Carole of Kenmore

I HEREBY CERTIFY THAT THIS PEDIGREE IS TRUE AND CORRECT
TO THE BEST OF MY KNOWLEDGE AND BELIEF

SIGNED YBP

DATE 1/9 1984

Ch. Kelly's Ebony Dyn-O-Mite, by Ch. Kelly's Black Onyx ex Gough's Black Honey of Knight, handled here by Geri Kelly to a Group placement.

Gestation, Whelping, and the Litter

When your bitch has been bred and is back at home, remain ever watchful that no other male gets to her until at least the twenty-second day of her season has passed. Prior to that time, it will still be possible for an undesired breeding to take place, which, at this point, would be catastrophic. Remember, she actually can have two separate litters by two different dogs, so *be alert and take care.*

In all other ways, the bitch should be treated quite normally. It is not necessary for her to have any additives to her diet until she is at least four to five weeks pregnant. It is also unnecessary for her to have additional food. It is better to underfeed the bitch this early in her pregnancy than to overfeed her. A fat bitch is not an easy whelper, so by "feeding her up" during the first few weeks, you may be creating problems for her.

Controlled exercise is good, and necessary, for your pregnant bitch. She should not be permitted to just lie around. At about seven weeks, the exercise should be slowed down to several sedate walks daily, not too long and preferably on the leash.

In the fourth or fifth week of pregnancy, calcium may be added to the diet; and at seven weeks, the one meal a day may be increased to two meals with some nutritional additives in each. Canned milk may be added to her meals at this time.

A week before she is due to whelp, your Miniature Schnauzer bitch should be introduced to her whelping box, so that she will have accustomed herself to it and feel at home there by the time the puppies arrive. She should be encouraged to sleep there and be permitted to come and go as she pleases. The box should be roomy enough for her to lie down and stretch out in it; but it should not be too large or the pups will have too much room in which to roam, and they may get chilled if they move too far away from the warmth of their mother. Be sure that there is a "pig rail" for the box, which will prevent the puppies from being crushed against the side of the box. The box should be lined with newspapers, which can easily be changed as they become soiled.

The room where the whelping box is placed, either in the home or in the kennel, should be

Wy-O's Secret Testimony and Wy-O's Secret Potion plus a brother at about eight weeks of age. Owen and Wyoma Clouss, owners, Boise, Idaho.

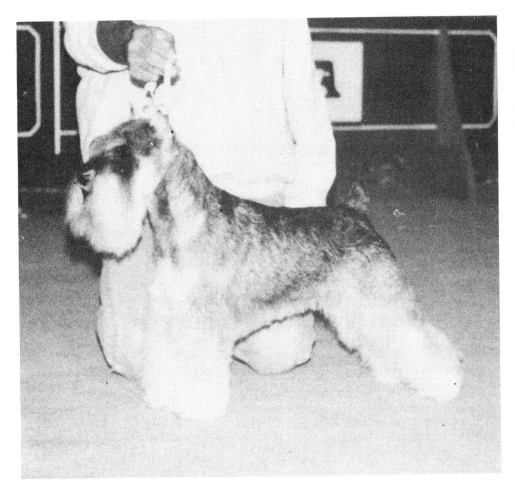

Am. and Jap. Ch. Shirley's September Rain, pictured here qualifying for his Japanese Championship. Owned by Tomai Fujimata of Japan.

Ch. Merwood's Apple Jack, one of the early Schnauzers owned by Arlene and Rich Smith, Richlene Miniature Schnauzers.

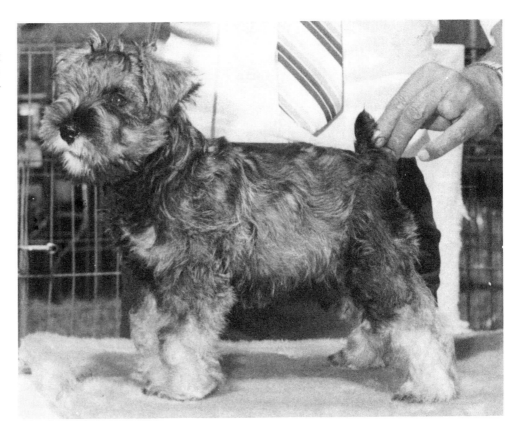

Ch. Shirley's Solo at nine and a half weeks of age. Handled by co-owner Dick Willey.

Ch. Spring-Along Happy Holiday, owned and handled by Kim Spring, is a full brother to Ch. Spring-Along Happy Grunner. Spring-Along Schnauzers, Landenberg, Pennsylvania.

Ch. Mariah's I've Got A Secret with her first litter by Ch. Jadee Jump Up. Crystal is owned by Steve Hayden and Richard Lashbrook, Haybrook Kennels.

free from drafts and should be kept at about eighty degrees Fahrenheit. It may be necessary during the cold months to install an infrared lamp in order to maintain sufficient warmth, in which case guard against the lamp being placed too low or too close to the puppies.

Keep a big pile of newspapers near the box. You'll find that you never have enough of these when there is a litter, so start accumulating them ahead of time. A pile of clean towels, a pair of scissors, and a bottle of alcohol should also be close at hand. Have all of these things ready at least a week before the bitch is due to whelp, as you never know exactly when she may start.

The day or night before she is due, the bitch will become restless; she'll be in and out of her box and in and out of the door. She may refuse food, and at this point her temperature will start to drop. She will start to dig and tear up the newspapers in her box, shiver, and generally look uncomfortable. You alone should be with her at this time (or one other person who is an experienced breeder, to give you confidence if this is one of your first litters). The bitch does not need an audience or any extra people around. This is not a sideshow, and several people hovering over the bitch may upset her to the

point where she may hurt the puppies. Stay nearby, but do not fuss too much over her. Keep a calm attitude; this will give her confidence. Eventually she will settle down in her box and begin to pant; shortly thereafter she will start to have contractions and soon a puppy will begin to emerge, sliding out with one of the contractions. The mother immediately should open the sac and bite the cord and clean up the puppy. She will also eat the placenta, which you should permit. Once the puppy is cleaned, it should be placed next to the bitch, unless she is showing signs of having another one immediately. The puppy should start looking for a nipple on which to nurse, and you should make certain that it is able to latch on and start doing so at once.

If a puppy is a breech birth (*i.e.*, born feet first), then you must watch carefully that it is delivered as quickly as possible and the sac removed very quickly, so that the puppy does not drown. Sometimes even a normally positioned birth will seem extremely slow in coming. Should either of these events occur, you might take a clean towel and, as the bitch contracts, pull the puppy out, doing so gently and with utmost care. If the bitch does not open the sac and cut the cord, you will have to do so. If the puppy shows little sign of life, make sure the mouth is free of liquid and then, using a Turkish towel or terry cloth, massage the puppy's chest, rubbing back and forth quite briskly. Continue this for about fifteen minutes. It may be necessary to try mouth-to-mouth breathing. Open the puppy's jaws and, using a finger, depress the tongue which may be stuck to the roof of the puppy's mouth. Then blow hard down the puppy's throat. Bubbles may pop out of its nose, but keep on blowing. Rub with the towel again across the chest, and try artificial respiration, pressing the sides of the chest together, slowly and rhythmically, in and out, in and out. Keep trying one method or the other for at least fifteen minutes (actual time—not how long it seems to you) before giving up. You may be rewarded with a live puppy who otherwise would not have made it.

If you are able to revive the puppy, it should not be put with the mother immediately, as it should be kept extra warm for a while. Put it in a cardboard box near a stove, on an electric heating pad, or, if it is the time of year when your heat is running, near a radiator until the rest of the litter has been born. Then it can be put in with the others.

The bitch may go for an hour or more between puppies, which is fine as long as she seems comfortable and is not straining or contracting. She should not be allowed to remain unassisted for more than an hour if she does continue to contract. This is when you should call your veterinarian, whom you should have alerted ahead of time of the possibility so that he will be somewhere within easy reach. He may want the bitch brought in so that he can examine her and perhaps give her a shot of Pituitrin. In some cases, the veterinarian may find that a Caesarean operation is necessary, because a puppy may be lodged in some manner that makes normal delivery impossible. This can occur due to the size of a puppy or may be due to the fact that the puppy is turned wrong. If any of the foregoing occurs, the puppies already born must be kept warm in their cardboard box, which should have been lined with shredded newspapers in advance and which should have a heating pad beneath it.

Assuming that there have been no problems, and the bitch has whelped normally, you should insist that she go outside to exercise, staying just long enough to make herself comfortable. She can be offered a bowl of milk and a biscuit, but then she should settle down with her family. Be sure to clean out the whelping box and change the newspapers so that she will have a fresh bed.

If the mother lacks milk at this point, the puppies will need to be fed by hand, kept very warm, and held against the mother's teats several times a day in order to stimulate and encourage the secretion of her milk, which will probably start shortly.

Unless some problem arises, there is little you need do about the puppies until they become three to four weeks old. Keep the box clean with fresh papers. When the puppies are a couple of days old, the papers should be removed and Turkish towels should be tacked down to the bottom of the box so that the puppies will have traction when they move. This is important.

If the bitch has difficulties with her milk supply, or if you should be so unfortunate as to lose the bitch, then you must be prepared to either hand-feed or tube-feed the puppies if they are to survive. We prefer the tube method as it is so much faster and easier. If the bitch is available, it is better that she continue to clean and care for the puppies in the normal manner, except for the food supplements you will provide. If she is unable to do this, then after every feeding, you must gently rub each puppy's abdomen with wet cotton to induce urination, and the rectum should be gently rubbed to open the bowels.

Newborn puppies must be fed every three or four hours around the clock. The puppies must be kept warm during that time. Have your veterinarian show you how to tube-feed. Once learned it is really quite simple, fast, and efficient.

After a normal whelping, the bitch will require additional food to enable her to produce sufficient milk. She should be fed twice daily now, and some canned milk should be available to her several times during the day.

When the puppies are two weeks old, you should clip their nails, as they are needle-sharp

Ch. Blythewood Main Gazebo at age three years with his breeder-owner-handler, Mrs. Joan L. Huber. Gazebo was the result of a successful linebreeding of a Ch. Dorem Favorite daughter to a Ch. Dorem Favorite grandson.

Ch. Aberdovey Ace In The Hole completing her championship under the author at Burlington County in 1984. Handled by Gloria Lewis for owners Neil and Nancy Gallagher, Beacon's Miniature Schnauzers, Beacon, New York. Miss Anna Katherine Nicholas, Judge.

Ch. Kazels Challenge as an adult. One from the all-champion litter of three. Owned by Mrs. K.L. Church, Kazel, Imperial, Missouri.

at this point and can hurt or damage the mother's teats and stomach as the pups hold on to nurse.

Between three and four weeks of age, the puppies should begin to be weaned. Scraped beef (prepared by scraping it off slices of raw beef with a spoon, so that none of the muscle or gristle is included) may be offered in very small quantities a couple of times daily for the first few days. If the puppy is reluctant to try it, put a little on your finger and rub it on the puppy's lips; this should get things going. By the third day, you can mix in ground puppy chow with warm water as directed on the package, offering it four times daily. By now the mother should be kept out of the box and away from the puppies for several hours at a time. After the puppies reach five weeks of age, she should be left in with them only overnight. By the time they are six weeks old, the puppies should be entirely weaned and the mother should only check on them with occasional visits.

Most veterinarians recommend a temporary DHL (distemper, hepatitis, leptospirosis) shot when the puppies are six weeks old. This remains effective for about two weeks. Then, at eight weeks, the series of permanent shots begins for the DHL protection. It is a good idea to discuss with your vet the advisability of having your puppies inoculated against the dreaded parvovirus at the same time. Each time the pups go to the vet for shots, you should bring stool samples so that they can be examined for worms. Worms go through various stages of development and may be present in a stool sample even though the sample does not test positive. So do not neglect to keep careful watch on this.

The puppies should be fed four times daily until they are three months old. Then you can cut back to three feedings daily. By the time the puppies are six months old, two meals daily are sufficient. Some people feed their dogs twice daily throughout their lifetime, while others cut back to one meal daily when the puppy reaches one year of age.

The ideal time for Miniature Schnauzer puppies to go to their new homes is when they are between eight and twelve weeks old, although some puppies successfully adjust to a new home when they are six weeks of age. Be certain that they go to their future owners accompanied by a description of the diet you've been feeding them and a schedule of the shots they have received and those they still need. These should be included with a registration application and a copy of the pedigree.

Ch. Blythewood Merry Melody at six years of age. By Ch. Delfin James ex Mimqua's Blythe Spirit, C.D. This is Blythewood's first homebred champion, owned and handled by Joan Lea Bauernschmidt in the 1950's, who is now Joan Huber, Green Lane, Pennsylvania.

CHAPTER FIFTEEN

You and Your Miniature Schnauzer

At the age of 11 years, Ch. Landmark's Masterpiece. This great dog owned by Gloria Weidlein, Sun City, California.

The Miniature Schnauzer as a Family Dog

If you love an active, busy, handsome little dog who is always on the alert and ready to go, the Miniature Schnauzer definitely is for you. He combines a great deal of "big dog in small package" character, thus making a fun companion, loyal and devoted, to share your daily life.

Miniature Schnauzers are happy at home in the city; in the suburbs; or for country living, if a small dog is preferred. One sees a great many of them in both city and suburbs, attracting admiring glances as they trot briskly along on their leads. They love to go, but at the same time they enjoy being your companion at home, too.

Originally bred as ratters, Miniature Schnauzers are strong and sturdy although small. Their average size is 12″ to 14″ height at the withers, which height nearly squares with the length of the body. Thus, they are an easy dog to manage, being what I frequently refer to as "handy home size." But in that small dog is combined intelligence, alertness and stamina, plus a protective spirit which is second to none.

This little dog loves children who treat him with respect, enjoying running and playing with them whenever asked to do so. He loves to accompany you on your travels, on foot or by car. But he is also quite content to lie by your side or at your feet at home. While he enjoys exercise, the fact that he is a small dog makes him able to stay in good shape with a minimum of it. He does not require miles of walking every day, but fares quite nicely with the run of your apartment or house, a fenced-in yard area, and short walks of a block or two daily. He is not susceptible to cold weather, nor to heat.

As a watch dog, the Miniature Schnauzer is always on guard and quick to sound the alarm at the approach of a stranger or any other event he does not understand. As unnecessary barking can be hard on one's nerves, he should be taught to stop barking when instructed to do so, not too difficult a lesson to put across to a dog this intelligent. You do not want to discourage his barking entirely, and it is smart to investigate if you do not know what has prompted it. Remember, if you are one of the folks inclined to sneer at the protective value of a dog this small, that probably the greatest danger a dog on guard holds for the average thief or house-breaker or person bothering you on the street is noise to

The noted Group winning bitch, Ch. Fancway's Vampira, owned by Margaret Haley, was the dam of seven noted champions, including Ch. Faerwynd of Arador, by Ch. Fancway's Pirate, Jr., Top Producing Bitch in the breed. Bred by Jean and Glenn Fancy, owner handled by Margaret Haley.

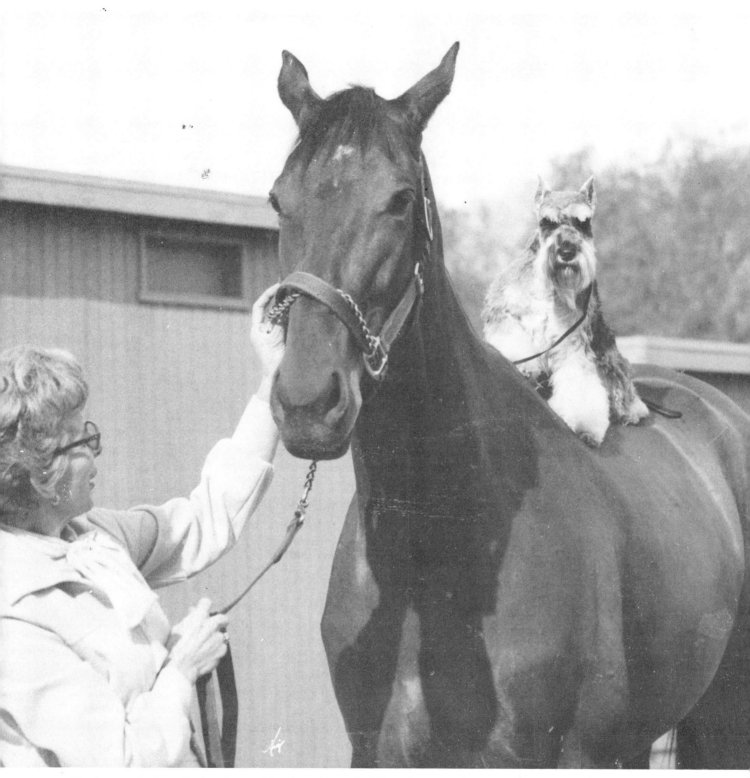

The famous Stakes winning thoroughbred racehorse, Bold Impulse, meets his namesake, Champion Sole Baye's Bold Impulse owned by Yvonne B. Phelps, El Monte, California, who has named several of her Schnauzers after racehorses.

Ch. Regency's Reward, by Ch. Skyline's Blue Spruce ex Jana PD, whelped December 1978. "Mindy" is one of seven champions from this cross of Spruce and PD, and is a Top Producer in her own right as the dam of four champions to date with another close to title. Carol A. Parker, Vail, Arizona.

draw the attention of neighbors or passers-by to what is taking place. Thus, such people, bent on no good, prefer to work where there is not a dog present, especially when said dog is barking up a storm. So appreciate the fact that your Miniature Schnauzer is always on the job in this respect; when he acts as though there is danger, very likely there is something amiss that the dog does not understand, so check it out, tell him "good dog," reassure him, then tell him "that's enough—quiet now" in a firm but friendly voice. After all, it is not Schnauzer temperament to

snooze nearby as someone ransacks your home, a fact for which you should be glad in these times, so do not make him feel that it is wrong for him to bark at all.

The intelligence of the Miniature Schnauzer, and the ease with which these dogs can be trained, is evidenced by their success in obedience, some "stars" of which are described elsewhere in this book. This same intelligence makes Miniature Schnauzers good companions, as they are sensible and quick to learn what is expected of them.

From the time Miniature Schnauzer puppies are a few weeks old, they should be petted and cuddled by their breeder, and as they grow, they should be introduced to neighbors, the children of the neighbors, and family members. This is great for them as it helps to overcome any inclination towards timidity or an anti-social attitude which some puppies can develop if deprived of this human interest. You want your Miniature Schnauzer to mature into a self-confident, even-tempered canine citizen, whether he is to be a loving pet or a self-confident show dog; so plan periods of every day to be spent playing with, fondling, and generally socializing your puppy. Not a bad idea, actually, for puppies of ANY breed, as the more attention these youngsters receive, the more personality they will have as grown dogs.

It has been said that a Miniature Schnauzer's prime interests in life are his food, protection of his home territory, and his family. From this one surmises quite rightly that he is a "good doer," a dog who does not need to be coaxed and teased to eat, a dog who flourishes in his home environment and in the company of the people he loves.

A Miniature Schnauzer is not a hard dog to keep looking his best. As a pet, he must be trimmed periodically with the clippers; and it is wise to keep his whiskers and furnishings combed out every few days if he is to look and feel his best, which actually takes but a few moments of your time, especially if combed frequently so that troublesome mats do not form.

Miniature Schnauzers can be taught to get on amicably with other pets, even cats, if the introduction and early association is handled properly. Better that at least one party be a puppy or kitten rather than a mature dog or cat, although even the latter is not too difficult as long as you are careful how the meeting takes place and are on the lookout for any sign of trouble in the early stages.

Traveling with Your Miniature Schnauzer

When you travel with a dog, you must always remember that everyone does not necessarily share your love of dogs and that those who do not, strange creatures though they may seem, have their rights too. These rights, on which we should not encroach, include not being disturbed, annoyed, or made uncomfortable by the presence and behavior of other people's pets. Owners should have the dog well schooled in proper canine behavior by the time maturity is reached. Your dog should not jump enthusiastically on strangers, no matter how playful or friendly the dog's intentions. We may love having them do this to us, but it is unlikely that someone else will share our enthusiasm, especially in the case of muddy paws on delicate or light-colored clothes which may be soiled or damaged. A sharp "Down" from you should be promptly obeyed, as should be "Sit," "Stay," and "Come."

If you expect to take your dog on many trips, he should have, for your sake and for his, a crate of appropriate size for him to relax in comfortably. In cases of emergency or accident, a crated dog is far more likely to escape injury. Left in a parked car, a crated dog should have the car windows fully open in hot weather, thus being assured sufficient ventilation. For your own comfort, a dog in a crate does not hang from the car window, climb over you and your passengers, and shed hair on the upholstery. Dogs quickly become accustomed to their crates, especially when started with one, as they should be, from puppyhood. Both you and the dog will have a more enjoyable trip when you provide him with this safeguard.

If you do permit your dog to ride loose in the car, see to it that he does not hang from the windows. He could become overly excited by something he sees and jump out; he could lose his balance and fall out should you stop short or swerve unexpectedly; he could suffer an eye injury induced by the strong wind generated by the moving car. All of these unnecessary risks can so easily be avoided by crating!

Never, ever, under any circumstances, should a dog be permitted to ride uncrated in the back end of an open pick-up truck. Some people do transport their dogs in this cruel and shocking

Travelmor Miniature Schnauzers all set to start for the dog show. Bill and Olive Moore, owners, Trenton, New Jersey.

Am., Can., and Ber. Ch. Kelly's Im-Pec-Cable Black handled by owner Geri Kelly to first in the Terrier Group at Central Maine K.C.

Ch. Repitition's Renaissance owned by Carole Luke, Silver Spring, Md., winning first in the Terrier Group at Sioux Empire in September 1978.

Game time! And sometimes Schnauzers play rough! These beauties are owned by Wyoma and Owen Clouss, Boise, Idaho.

manner. How easily such a dog can be thrown out of the car by sudden jolts or an impact! Surely many dogs have jumped out at the sight of something exciting along the way, quite possibly into the path of an oncoming car. Some unthinking individuals tie the dog, probably not realizing that if he were to jump under those circumstances, his neck could be broken, he could be dragged alongside the vehicle or get under its wheels, or he could be hit by another vehicle. If you are for any reason taking your dog *anywhere* in an open back truck, *please* have sufficient regard for that dog to provide a crate to protect him. Also please remember that with or without a crate, a dog riding exposed to the sun in hot weather can really suffer and have his life endangered by the heat.

If you are staying in a hotel or motel with your dog, please exercise him somewhere other than in the parking lot, along the walkways, or in the flower beds of the property. People walking to and from their rooms or cars really are not thrilled at "stepping in something" left by your dog and should not be subjected to the annoyance. Should an accident occur, pick it up with tissues or a paper towel and deposit it in a proper receptacle; don't just let it remain there.

Usually there are grassy areas on the sides or behind motels where dogs can be exercised with no bother to anyone. Use those places rather than the busy, more conspicuous, carefully tended areas. If you are becoming a dog show enthusiast, you will eventually need an exercise pen to take with you to the show. They are ideal to use when staying at motels, too, as they permit you to limit the dog's roaming space and to pick up after him easily. Should you have two or more dogs, such a convenience is truly a "must!"

Never leave your dog unattended in a room at a motel unless you are absolutely, positively, sure that he will stay quiet and not destroy anything. You do not want a long list of complaints from irate fellow-guests, caused by the annoying barking or whining of a lonesome dog in strange surroundings or an overzealous watch dog barking furiously each time a footstep passes the door. And you certainly do not want to return to torn curtains or bedspreads, soiled rugs, or other embarrassing (and sometimes expensive) evidence of the fact that your dog is not really house-reliable.

If yours is a dog accustomed to traveling with you and you are positive that his behavior will be acceptable when left alone, that is fine. But if the slightest uncertainty exists, the wise course is to leave him in the car while you go to dinner or elsewhere and then bring him into the room when you are ready to retire for the night.

When you travel with a dog, it is sometimes simpler to take along his food and water from home rather than to buy food and to look for water while you travel. In this way he will have the rations to which he is accustomed and which you know agree with him, and there will be no problems due to different drinking water. Feeding on the road is quite easy now, at least for short trips, with all the splendid dry prepared foods and high quality canned meats available, not to mention the "just remove it from the packet" convenience foods. And many types of lightweight, refillable water containers can be bought at many types of stores.

If you are going to another country, you will need a health certificate from your veterinarian for each dog you are taking with you, certifying that each has had rabies shots within the required length of time preceding your visit.

Remember that during the summer, the sun's rays can make an inferno of a closed-up car in a matter of minutes, so always leave windows open enough that there is sufficient ventilation for the dog. Again, if your dog is in a crate, this can be done easily and with safety. Remember, too, that leaving the car in a shady spot does not mean that it will remain shaded. The position of the sun changes quickly, and the car you left nicely shaded half an hour earlier may be in the full glare of the sun upon your return. Be alert and be cautious.

When you travel with your dog, be sure to take a lead and use it, unless he is completely and thoroughly obedience trained. Even if the dog is trained, however, using a lead is a wise precaution against his getting lost in strange territory. One often sees in the "Lost and Found" columns the sad little messages about dogs who have gotten away or been lost during a trip, so why take chances?

Responsibilities of Breeders and Owners

Whether you are a one-dog owner, the owner of a show kennel, one involved in obedience, or a breeder, there are definite responsibilities—to your dog or dogs, to your breed, and to the general public—involved which should never be overlooked or taken lightly.

It is inexcusable for anyone to breed dogs pro-miscuously, producing unneeded litters. The only time a responsible breeder plans a litter is when it is *needed* to carry on a bloodline or to provide dogs for which this breeder has very definite plans, including orders for at least half the number of puppies which will probably be born. Every healthy puppy deserves a good and loving home, assuring its future well-being. No puppy should be born to an uncertain future on someone's assumption that there will be no problem selling or otherwise finding a home for it, as very definitely this is not always easy. Overpopulation is the dog world's most heart-breaking tragedy. Those of us who love dogs should not add to it by carelessly producing more. If you have any reason to feel that the puppies may not be assured of homes, don't breed the bitch; wait for a more propitious time. Certainly no dog breeder likes the thought of running around frantically trying to find someone who will take puppies off his hands, even if they must be given away. The latter usually is not a good idea anyway, as many people cannot resist saying "yes" to something which costs nothing, regardless of whether or not they really want it. As the dog grows larger and demands more care, their enthusiasm wanes to the point that the dog soon is left to roam the streets where he is subject to all sorts of dangers, and the owner simply could not care less. If one pays for something, one seems to respect it more.

One litter at a time is all that any breeder should produce, making sure that all those puppies are well provided for prior to breeding for another litter. Breeders should do all in their power to ascertain that the home to which each of his puppies goes is a *good* home, one that offers proper care, a fenced in area, and a really enthusiastic owner. I have tremendous respect for those breeders who make it a point to check carefully the credentials of prospective purchasers, and I firmly believe that all breeders should do likewise on this important point. I am certain that no breeder wants any puppy to wind up in an animal shelter, in an experimental laboratory, or as a victim of a speeding car. While complete control of such situations may not be possible, it is at least our responsibility to make every effort to turn our puppies over to people who have the same outlook as our own where love of dogs and responsibility toward them are concerned and who realize that the ownership of a dog involves care, not neglect.

It is the breeder's responsibility to sell every puppy with the understanding that should the new owner find it necessary to place the dog elsewhere, you, the breeder, must be contacted immediately and given the opportunity to take back the dog or to help in finding it a new home. Many a dog starting out in what has seemed a good home has, under unforeseen circumstances, been passed along to others, only to wind up in exactly the sort of situation we most want to avoid. Keep in touch with what is happening to your dogs after they are sold.

The final obligation every dog owner shares, be there just one dog or many, is that of leaving detailed and up-to-date instructions in our wills about what is to become of our animals in the event of our death. Far too many of us are apt to procrastinate and leave this matter unattended to, feeling that everything will work out all right or that "someone will see to them." The latter is not too likely to happen, at least not to the benefit of the dogs, unless the owner makes absolutely certain that all will be well for them in the future.

If you have not already done so, please get together with your lawyer and set up a clause in your will specifying what is to be done with each and every dog you own and to whom each will be entrusted (after first ascertaining that this person is willing and able to assume the responsibility); also include details about the location of all registration papers, pedigrees, and kennel records, along with ways of identifying each dog. Just think of the possibilities of what might happen otherwise!

It is not wise to count on family members, unless they share your involvement with the dogs. In many cases our relatives are not the least bit "dog-oriented," perhaps they think we're a trifle crazy for being such enthusiasts, and they might absolutely panic at the thought of suddenly having even *one* dog thrust upon them. They might mean well, and they might try; but it is unfair to them and to the dogs to leave the one stuck with the other!

If you travel a great deal with your dogs, another wise idea is to post prominently in your vehicle and carry in your wallet the name, address, and telephone number of someone to be called to take charge of them in case of an accident. Of course, this should be done by prearrangement with the person named. We have

Ch. Unser's Bravo Brava and Ch. Luvemal's Copy Right, father and daughter, owned by Robert L. Crews and Joseph E. Fiala.

Ch. Travelmor's Witchcraft in Olive Moore's arms; Ch. Travelmor's Rango with William E. Moore. Photo of two Travelmor winners from the late 1960's.

such a friend, and she has a signed check of ours to be used in case of an emergency or accident when we are traveling with our dogs; this check will be used to cover her expenses to come and take over the care of our dogs should anything happen to make it impossible for us to do so.

The registration certificates of all our dogs are enclosed in an envelope with our wills, and the person who will be in charge knows each of them, and one from the other, so there will be no identification problem. These are all points to be considered, for which provision should be made.

One also owes an obligation to older dogs who too often are disregarded. It is disgusting that so many supposedly great dog lovers think nothing of getting an older dog, even though well, happy, and enjoying life, out of the way to make room for younger show prospects or additional puppies. Genuine dog lovers are the ones who permit their dogs to live out their lives in comfort as loved, respected members of the household or kennel. How quickly some of us seem to forget the pleasures these dogs have

brought us with exciting wins and the devotion they have shown to us and our families!

So much for our responsibility to our dogs, but we also owe a responsibility to our breed: to keep up its quality and to protect its image. Every breeder should breed only from and for high-grade stock and should guard against the market being flooded with excess puppies. We should display good sportsmanship and concern for the dogs at all times, and we should involve ourselves whenever possible in activities beneficial to the breed.

To the general public we owe the consideration of good dog ownership. Our dogs should not be permitted to run at large and annoy others. Dogs should not be left barking endlessly, tied outside or closed in the house. People should pick up after their dogs, as required in most cities, when exercising them in places where people must walk. We should, in other words, enjoy our dogs without allowing them to infringe on those who may be less enthusiastic.

Ch. Bo-Turn Hizahoney, by Ch. Black Watch of Blythewood ex Bo-Turn Irene, was bred by Mattie Boze and is owned by Capt. Jean L. Heath, USN (Retired), Pleasanton, California. This is the oldest known Miniature Schnauzer to finish his championship, which he did at the age of eight years.

CHAPTER SIXTEEN

The Veterinarian's Corner

Joseph P. Sayres, DVM
Buffalo, New York

This is Peter, full brother to Ch. Black Watch of Blythewood, who made medical history when he received a pacemaker at the age of 12 years, which prolonged his life for an additional two and a half years. It was implanted two months after the loss of Black Watch and as owner of them both, Ruth I. Quire, says "no way could I have lost two dogs in two months—especially these."

By way of introduction to this chapter concerning the medical aspects of the care of the Miniature Schnauzer, I think we should devote a few paragraphs to "how to choose your veterinarian."

Until recent years, there has been a lot of misunderstanding and even animosity between veterinarians and breeders. Some distrust arose on the breeder's part because most veterinarians were not familiar with, nor even interested in learning about, pure bred dogs. Some of the problems encountered were peculiar to certain breeds and some would crop up at inconvenient times. Veterinarians were then beset by breeders who thought that they knew more about the medical problems of their dogs than the vets did. The veterinarians very often were only called for emergencies, or when it was too late to save a sick dog that had been treated too long by people in the kennel. Another problem was that many breeders had never included veterinary fees in their budgets and were slow to pay their bills, if indeed they paid them at all.

Fortunately, these problems have been, to a large extent, solved. Education and better communication between breeders and veterinarians have eliminated most areas of friction.

Today, veterinary education and training have advanced to a point paralleling those of human standards. This resulted from advances in the field of Veterinary Science in the last two decades. Sophisticated diagnostic procedures, new and advanced surgical techniques, and modern well-equipped hospitals all make for improved medical care for our dogs.

Educated breeders now realize that while they may know more about the general husbandry of their dogs, and the unique traits of the Miniature Schnauzer, they should not attempt to diagnose and treat their ailments.

In choosing your veterinarian, be selective. He or she should be friendly, should be interested in your dogs, and in the case of breeders, be interested in your breeding programs. Veterinarians should be willing to talk freely with you. Such things are fees, availability for emergencies, what services are and are not available, should be discussed and understood before a lasting relationship with your veterinarian can be established.

You can expect your veterinarian's office, clinic or hospital to be clean, free of undesirable odors, well-equipped, and staffed by sincere, friendly personnel who willingly serve you at all times. All employees should be clean, neat in appearance and conversant with whatever services you require. You may also expect your dog to be treated carefully and kindly at all times by the doctor and his staff.

Your veterinarian should participate in continuing education programs in order to keep up with changes and improvements in his field. He should also be aware of his limitations. If he doesn't feel confident in carrying out certain procedures, he should say so and refer you to qualified individuals to take care of the problem. Seeking second opinions and consultation with specialists on difficult cases are more the rule than the exception nowadays.

You will know that if your veterinarian is a member of the American Animal Hospital Association, he and his facility have had to measure up to high standards of quality, and are subjected to inspections every two years.

Many excellent veterinarians and veterinary hospitals by choice do not belong to the American Animal Hospital Association. You can satisfy your curiosity about these places by taking guided tours of the facilities, and to learn by word of mouth about the quality of medicine practiced at these hospitals.

So far we have discussed only what you should expect from your veterinarian. Now, let's discuss what the veterinarian expects from his clients.

Most of all, he expects his clients to be open and frank in their relations with him. He doesn't like to be double-checked and second-guessed behind his back. He also wants you to handle your pet so that he, in turn, can examine him. He also expects you to leash your dog, to control him and keep him from bothering other pets in the room. He expects to be paid a fair fee, and to be paid promptly for services rendered. Fees in a given area tend to be consistent, and variations are due only to complications or unforeseen problems. Medicine is not an exact science, therefore things unpredictable can happen.

If you are dissatisfied with the services or fees, then ask to discuss these things in a friendly manner with the doctor. If his explanations are not satisfactory or he refuses to talk to you about the problem, then you are justified in seeking another doctor.

The veterinarian expects to provide his services for your animals during regular hours whenever possible. But he also realizes that in a kennel or breeding operation that emergencies can occur at any time, and that his services will be needed outside office hours. You should find out how these emergencies will be handled, and be satisfied with the procedures.

No veterinarian can be on duty 24 hours of every day. Today co-operative veterinarians group together to take turns covering each other's emergency calls. Some cities have emergency clinics that operate solely to take care of those catastrophes that seem usually to happen in the middle of the night or on weekends.

My conclusion, after thirty years of practice, is that most disagreements and hard feelings between clients and veterinarians are a result of a breakdown in communication. Find a veterinarian that you can talk to and can be comfortable with, and you'll make a valuable friend.

In using veterinary services to their best advantage, I believe that you will find that prevention of diseases and problems is more important than trying to cure these things after they occur. In other words, an ounce of prevention is worth a pound of cure.

Miniature Schnauzers have their share of congenital defects. From publications such as *Current Veterinary Therapy VIII* by Kirk, and *Medical and Genetic Aspects of Pure Bred Dogs* edited by Clark and Stainer, the following conditions are listed as congenital defects in Miniature Schnauzers:

A. Congenital Juvenile Cataracts—Opacity of the lenses of the eyes.
B. Dermatitis—So-called Schnauzer Bumps. Tiny hard scabby lesions (comodomes) along top of the back.
C. Esophageal Achalasia—Failure of esophagus to relax.
D. Fainting Spells—Due to sino-atrial syncope —a heart condition.
E. Legg-Perthes Disease—Lack of blood supply to head of the femur resulting in degeneration.
F. Pulmonary Stenosis—Narrowing of pulmonary artery.
G. Reproductive Disorders:
   1. Cryptorchidism—Failure of testicles to descend.
   2. Sertoli-Cell Tumors—Tumor of the testes.
   3. Pseudo-Hermaphrodism—The existence in the same individual of organs of both sexes.
H. Urinary Tract Problems—Infections and formation of bladder stones.

Ch. Here Comes C C Charlie Chip, the only *known* and *published* carrier of congenital juvenile cataracts to finish his championship. Sire, Ch. Black Watch of Blythewood, tested clear for congenital juvenile cataract. Dam, Woodruff Here Comes Tilly (affected with CJC). Owner-breeder, Capt. Jean L. Heath, USN (Retired), Pleasanton, California. Photo by Dan Kiedrowski.

A test litter for cataracts, all puppies O.K. and all went to loving homes. Owen and Wyoma Clouss, owners, Wy-O's Schnauzers, Boise, Idaho.

By proper and vigilant vaccination programs, the following contagious diseases can be eliminated:

Distemper   Rabies
Hepatitis   Parainfluenza
Leptospirosis   Parvovirus Enteritis

With proper sanitation and the guided use of insecticides and vermifuges, the following conditions can be made extinct or of only minor importance:

Round worm infestation   Fleas
Hook worm infestation   Ticks
Whip worm infestation   Lice
Coccidiosis   Tape worm
                          infestation

These problems will be dealt with individually as our chapter progresses.

The following "shot" schedule should be set up and strictly followed to prevent infectious diseases:

Disease:	Age to Vaccinate:
Distemper	6 to 8 weeks old. Second inoculation to be given at 10 to 12 weeks of age. When given in combination with Parvo vaccine, a third inoculation given at 14 to 16 weeks of age is advisable. Re-vaccinate annually.
Hepatitis (Adenovirus)	Same as distemper.
Parainfluenza (Kennel cough)	Same as distemper.
Leptospirosis	Give 1st vaccine at 9 weeks old. Re-vaccinate with 2nd DHLP (distemper, hepatitis, leptospirosis, para-influenza) at 12 to 16 weeks of age. Re-vaccinate annually.
Parvovirus	Give 1st vaccine at 7 to 8 weeks old. 2nd vaccine 4 weeks later. 3rd vaccine 4 weeks later. Duration of immunity from 3 injections established at one year at the time of this writing. See explanation below. Re-vaccinate annually.
Rabies	1st inoculation at 3 to 4 months old, then re-vaccinate when 1 year old, and at least every 3 years thereafter. If dog is over 4 months old at

the time of the 1st vaccination, then re-vaccinate in one year and then once every 3 years thereafter.

Vaccines used are all modified live virus vaccines except for Leptospirosis which is a killed bacterium. New and improved vaccines to immunize against parvo virus have appeared recently. The long awaited modified live virus vaccine of canine origin was made available. It is safe and should produce immunity lasting one year. Currently there are questions arising concerning the efficacy of combination vaccines as opposed to using single entity vaccines, i.e. giving plain parvo vaccine instead of including it in distemper, hepatitis, parainfluenza, leptospirosis. Some experts think that there is a suppression of immunity when combination vaccines are used. Consult your own veterinarian and be guided by his advice.

Other communicable diseases for which no vaccine has been perfected as yet are:

Canine Brucellosis
Canine Coronavirus
Canine Rotavirus

A brief description of the more common of our infectious diseases follows:

1. *Distemper*—Caused by a highly contagious, airborne virus. The symptoms are varied and may involve all of the dogs' systems. A pneumonic form is common with heavy eye and nose discharges, coughing and lung congestion. The digestive system may be involved as evidenced by vomiting, diarrhea, and weight loss. The skin may show a pustular type rash on the abdomen. Nervous system involvement is common with convulsions, chorea, and paralysis as persistent symptoms. This virus may have an affinity for nerve tissue and cause encephalitis and degeneration of the spinal cord. These changes for the most part are irreversible and death or severe crippling ensues.

We have no specific remedy or cure for distemper, and recoveries when they occur can only be attributed to the natural resistance of the patient, good nursing care, and control of secondary infections with antibiotics.

That's the bad news about distemper. The good news is that we rarely see a case of distemper in most areas today because of the efficiency of the vaccination program. This is proof that prevention by vaccination has been effective in almost eradicating this dreaded disease.

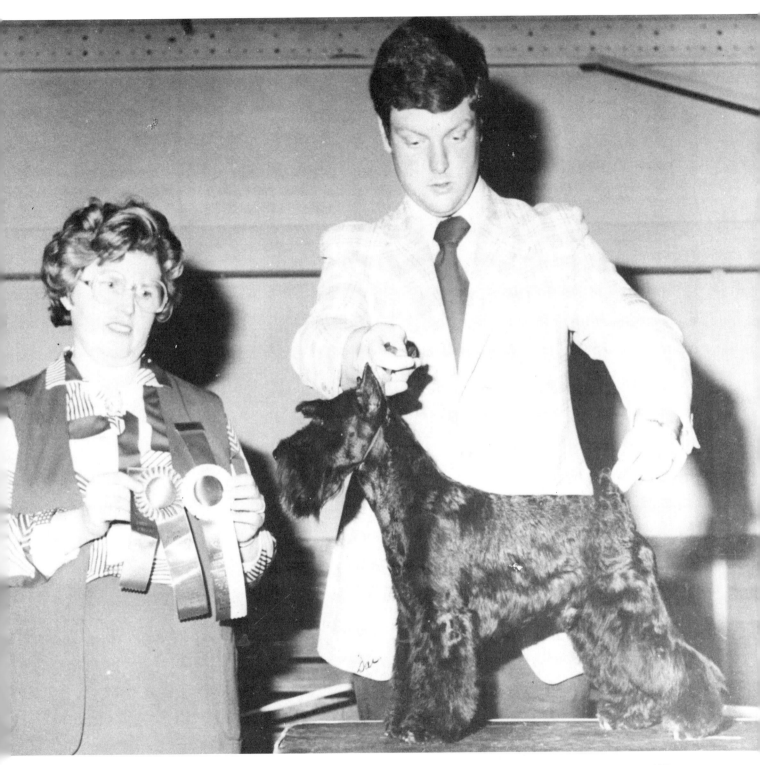

Am., Can., Mex., and Jap. K.C. Grand Ch. Walters' Dazzling Black, by Ch. Walters' Black Topper ex Walters' Ebony Moontide, born in 1978, bred and owned by Dolores Walters, Burbank, California.

Ch. Shirley's String of Pearls, taking Winners Dog, Best of Winners and Best of Opposite Sex under George Pimlott for Dick and Shirley Willey, handled by Eddie Boyes.

2. *Hepatitis*—This is another contagious viral disease affecting the liver. This is not an airborne virus and can only be spread by contact. Although rarely seen today because of good prevention by vaccination programs, this virus is capable of producing a very acute, fulminating, severe infection and can cause death in a very short time. Symptoms of high temperature, lethargy, anorexia, and vomiting are the same as for other diseases. Careful evaluation by a veterinarian is necessary to confirm the diagnosis of this disease.

The old canine infectious hepatitis vaccine has been replaced by a canine adenovirus type 2 strain vaccine which is safer and superior. The new vaccine seems to be free of post-vaccination complications such as blue eye, shedding of the virus in the urine and some kidney problems.

3. *Leptospirosis*—This is a disease that seriously affects the kidneys of dogs, most domestic animals, and man. For this reason, it can become a public health hazard. In urban and slum areas, the disease is carried by rats and mice in their urine. It is caused by a spirochete organism which is very resistant to treatment. Symptoms include fever, depression, dehydration, excessive thirst, persistent vomiting, occasional diarrhea and jaundice in the latter stages. Again, it is not always easy to diagnose so your veterinarian will have to do some laboratory work to confirm it.

We see very few cases of leptospirosis in dogs and then only in the un-vaccinated ones. The vaccine is generally given concurrently with the distemper and hepatitis vaccinations. Preventive inoculations have resulted in the almost complete eradication of this dreaded disease.

4. *Parainfluenza*—This is commonly called kennel cough. It is caused by a throat inhabiting virus that causes an inflammation of the trachea (wind pipe) and larynx (voice box). Coughing is the main symptom and fortunately it rarely causes any other systemic problems. The virus is airborne, highly contagious and is the scourge of boarding kennels. A vaccine is available that will protect against this contagious respiratory disease and should be given as part of your vaccination program, along with the distemper, hepatitis, leptospirosis and parvovirus shots. Pregnant bitches should not be vaccinated against parainfluenza because of the possibility of infecting the unborn puppies. As there may be more than one infectious agent involved in contagious upper respiratory disease of dogs, vaccination against parainfluenza is not a complete guarantee to protect against all of them.

5. *Rabies*—This is a well known virus-caused disease that is almost always fatal and is transmissable to man and other warm-blooded animals. The virus causes very severe brain damage. Sources of the infection include foxes, skunks, raccoons, as well as domesticated dogs and cats. Transmission is by introduction of the virus by saliva into bite wounds. Incubation in certain animals may be from 3 to 8 weeks. In a dog, clinical signs will appear within 5 days. Symptoms fall into 2 categories depending on what stage the disease is in when seen. We have the dumb form and the furious form. There is a change of personality in the furious form, individuals become hyper-sensitive and overreact to noise and stimuli. They will bite any object that moves. In dumb rabies, the typical picture of the loosely hanging jaw and tongue presents itself. Diagnosis is only confirmed by a laboratory finding the virus and characteristic lesions in the brain. All tissues and fluids from rabid animals should be considered infectious and you should be careful not to come in contact with them. Prevention by vaccination is a must because there is no treatment for rabid dogs.

6. *Contagious Canine Viral Diarrheas:*

A. *Canine Coronavirus, CCV*

This is a highly contagious virus that spreads rapidly to susceptible dogs. The source of infection is through infectious bowel movements. The incubation period is 1 to 4 days, and the virus will be found in feces for as long as 2 weeks. It is hard to tell the difference sometimes between cases of diarrhea caused by coronavirus and parvovirus. Coronavirus generally is less severe or causes a more chronic or sporadic type of diarrhea. The fecal material may be orange in color, and have a very bad odor. Occasionally it will also contain blood. Vomiting sometimes precedes the diarrhea, but loss of appetite and listlessness are consistent signs of the disease. Fever may or may not be present. Recovery is the rule after 8 to 10 days, but treatment with fluids, antibiotics, intestinal protectants and good nursing care is necessary in the more severe watery diarrhea cases. Dogs that survive these infections become immune but for an unknown length of time.

To control an outbreak of this virus in a kennel, very stringent hygienic measures must be taken. Proper and quick disposal of feces, isolation of affected animals, and disinfection with a 1 to 30 dilution of Clorox are all effective means of controlling an outbreak in the kennel.

There is no vaccine yet available for prevention of canine coronavirus. Human infections by this virus have not been reported.

B. *Canine Parvovirus, CPV*—

This is the newest and most highly publicized member of the intestinal virus family. Cat distemper virus is a member of the same family but differs from canine parvovirus biologically, and it has been impossible to produce this disease in dogs using cat virus as the inducing agent, and conversely, canine parvovirus will not produce the disease in a cat. However, vaccines for both species will produce immunity in the dog. The origin of CPV is still unknown.

Canine parvovirus is very contagious and acts rapidly. The main source of infection is contaminated bowel movements. Direct contact between dogs is not necessary, and carriers such as people, fleas, instruments, etc., may carry and transmit the virus.

The incubation period is 5 to 14 days. The symptoms are fever, severe vomiting and diarrhea, often with blood, depression, and dehydration. Feces may appear yellowish gray streaked with blood. Young animals are more severely affected, and a shock-like death may occur in two days. In animals less than six weeks old, the virus will cause an inflammation of the heart muscle, causing heart failure and death. These pups do not have diarrhea. A reduction in the number of white blood cells is a common finding early in the disease.

The virus is passed in the feces for one to two weeks, and may possibly be shed in the saliva and urine also. This virus has also been found in the coats of dogs. The mortality rate is unknown.

Dogs that recover from the disease develop an immunity to it. Again, the duration of this immunity is unknown.

Control measures include disinfection of the kennels, animals and equipment with a 1 to 30 dilution of Clorox, and isolation of sick individuals.

Treatment is very similar to that for coronavirus, namely: intravenous fluid therapy, administration of broad spectrum antibiotics, intestinal protectants and good nursing care.

Transmission to humans has not been proven.

Clinical studies have proven that vaccination with three injections of the new modified live virus vaccine of canine origin with four weeks between injections will be over 90% effective. Recent work at the James A. Baker Institute for Animal Health at Cornell University has shown that maternally derived antibodies can interfere with the immunizing properties of our vaccines for as long as 15 to 16 weeks. This means that some of our puppies, especially those from dams with good immunity, will not become susceptible to successful vaccination until they are 16 weeks old. It is also known that the maternal protection afforded these puppies, while enough to prevent successful vaccination, may not be enough to protect them from an exposure to the virus. The best advice is to give our puppies three inoculations of a canine origin modified live virus vaccine four weeks apart, starting when they are eight weeks old. Then, hope for the best and re-vaccinate annually.

C. *Canine Rotavirus, CRV*

This virus has been demonstrated in dogs with a mild diarrhea but again with more severe cases in very young puppies. Very little is known about this virus.

A milder type diarrhea is present for eight to ten days. The puppies do not run a temperature and continue to eat. Dogs usually recover naturally from this infection. There is no vaccine available for this virus.

7. *Canine Brucellosis*—This is a disease of dogs that causes both abortions and sterility. It is caused by a small bacterium closely related to the agent that causes undulant fever in man and abortion in cows. It occurs worldwide.

Symptoms of brucellosis sometimes are difficult to determine, and some individuals with the disease may appear healthy. Vague symptoms such as lethargy, swollen glands, poor hair coat and stiffness in the back legs may be present. This organism does not cause death and may stay in the dog's system for months and even years. The latter animals, of course, have breeding problems and infect other dogs.

Poor results in your breeding program may be the only indication that brucellosis is in your kennel. Apparently, normal bitches abort without warning. This usually occurs 45 to 55 days after mating. Successive litters will also be aborted. In males, signs of the disease are inflammation of the skin of the scrotum, shrunken testicles, and swollen tender testicles. Fertility declines and chronically infected males become sterile.

Ch. Blythewood The Leading Man, by Ch. Blythewood National Anthem ex Dardane What's Up O'Blythewood. Handled by Donald E. Jenner, show assistant at Blythewood, for owners Bill and Sylvia Dwyer, Sarasota, Florida.

Ch. Contempra Foolish Pleasure with handler Joan L. Huber winning the breed at Ravenna in 1979 for owners Homer and Isabelle Graf.

The disease is transmitted to both sexes at the time of mating.

Other sources of infection are aborted puppies and birth membranes and discharge from the womb at the time of abortions.

Humans can be infected, but such infections are rare and mild. Unlike the disease in the dog, the disease in humans responds readily to antibiotics.

Diagnosis is carried out by blood testing which should be done carefully. None of the present tests are infallible and false positives may occur. The only certain way that canine brucellosis can be diagnosed is by isolating the *B. canis* organism from blood or aborted material and, for this, special techniques are required.

Treatment of infected individuals has proven ineffective in most cases. Sterility in males is permanent. Spaying or castrating infected pets should be considered as this will halt the spread of the disease and is an alternative to euthanasia.

At present, there is no vaccine against this important disease.

Our best hope in dealing with canine brucellosis is prevention. The following suggestions are made in order to prevent the occurrence of this malady in your dogs.

1. Test breeding stock annually and by all means breed only uninfected animals.
2. Test bitches several weeks before their heat periods.
3. Do not bring any new dogs into your kennel unless they have two negative tests taken a month apart.
4. If a bitch aborts, isolate her, wear gloves when handling soiled bedding, and disinfect the premises with Roccal.
5. If a male loses interest in breeding or fails to produce after several matings, have him checked.
6. Consult your veterinarian for further information about this disease, alert other breeders and support the research that is going on at the James A. Baker Institute for Animal Health at Cornell University.

This concludes the section on important contagious and infectious diseases of dogs. A discussion on external parasites that affect dogs *is* now in order.

EXTERNAL PARASITES

The control and eradication of external parasites depends on the repeated use of good quality insecticide sprays or powders during the warm months. Make a routine practice of using these products at seven day intervals throughout the season. It is also imperative that sleeping quarters and wherever the animal habitates be treated also.

Fleas

These are brown, wingless insects with laterally compressed bodies and strong legs, and are blood suckers. Their life cycle comprises 18 to 21 days from egg to adult flea. They can live without food for one year in high humidity but die in a few days in low humidity. They multiply rapidly and are more prevalent in the warm months. They can cause a severe skin inflammation in those individuals that are allergic or sensitive to the flea bite or saliva of the flea. They can act as a vector for many diseases and do carry tapeworms. Control measures must include persistent, continual use of flea collars or flea medallions, or sprays or powders. The dog's bedding and premises must also be treated because the eggs are there. Foggers, vacuuming or professional exterminators may have to be used. All dogs and cats in the same household must be treated at the same time.

Ticks

There are hard and soft species of ticks. Both species are blood suckers and at times cause severe skin inflammations on their host. They act as a vector for Rocky Mountain Spotted Fever, as well as other diseases. Hibernation through an entire winter is not uncommon. The female tick lays as many as 1000 to 5000 eggs in crevices and cracks in walls. These eggs will hatch in about three weeks and then a month later become adult ticks. Ticks are generally found around the host's neck, ears, and between the toes. They can cause anemia and serious blood loss if allowed to grow and multiply. It is not a good idea to pick ticks off the dogs because of the danger of a reaction in the skin. Just apply the tick spray directly on the ticks who then die and fall off eventually. Affected dogs should be dipped every two weeks. The premises, kennels and yards should be treated every two weeks during the summer months. The insecticide must be applied to walls and in all cracks and crevices. Frequent or daily grooming is effective in finding and removing ticks.

Lice

There are two kinds of lice, namely the sucking louse and the biting louse. They spend their entire life on their host but can be spread by direct contact or through contaminated combs and brushes. Their life cycle is 21 days, and their eggs, known as nits, attach to the hairs of the dog. The neck and shoulder region, as well as the ear flaps, are the most common areas to be inhabited by these pesky parasites. They cause itchiness, some blood loss, and inflammation of the skin. Eradication will result from the dipping or dusting with methyl carbonate or Thuron once a week for three to four weeks. It is a good idea to fine comb the dogs after each dip to remove the dead lice and nits. Ask your veterinarian to provide the insecticides and advice or control measures for all of these external parasites.

INTERNAL PARASITES

The eradication and control of internal parasites in dogs will occupy a good deal of your time and energy. These pests will be considered next.

Puppies should be tested for worms at four weeks of age, and then six weeks later. It is also wise to test them again six weeks following their last worm treatment to be sure the treatments have been successful. Annual fecal tests are advisable throughout your dog's life. All worming should be done only under the supervision of your veterinarian.

The most common internal parasites encountered will be the following:

1. *Ascarids*—i.e. round worms, puppy worms, stomach worms, milk worms. Puppies become infested shortly after birth and occasionally even before birth. They can be difficult to eradicate. When passed in the stool or thrown up, they look somewhat like cooked spaghetti when fresh, or like rubber bands when they are dried up. Two treatments at least two weeks apart will eliminate ascarids from most puppies. An occasional individual may need more wormings according to the status in its system of the life cycle of the worm at the time of worming. Good sanitary conditions must prevail and immediate picking up of bowel movements is necessary to keep this worm's population down.

2. *Hookworms*—This is another troublesome internal parasite that we find in dogs. They are blood suckers and also cause bleeding from the site of their attachment to the lining of the intestine when they move from one site to another. They can cause a blood-loss type of anemia and serious consequences, particularly in young puppies. Their life cycle is direct and their eggs may be ingested or pass through the skin of their host. Treatment of yards and runs where the dogs defecate with products available from your veterinarian is said to kill the eggs in the soil. Two or three worm treatments, three to four weeks apart, may be necessary to get rid of hook worms. New injectable products administered by your veterinarian have proven more effective than remedies used in the past. Repeated fecal examinations may be necessary to detect the eggs in the feces. These eggs pass out of the body only sporadically or in showers, so that it is easy to miss finding them unless repeated stool testing is done. As with any parasite, good sanitary conditions in the kennel and outside runs will help eradicate this worm.

3. *Whipworms*—These are a prevalent parasite in some kennels and in some individual dogs. They cause an intermittent mucousy type diarrhea. As they live only in the dog's appendix, it is extremely difficult to reach them with any worm medicine given by mouth. Injections seem to be the most effective treatment, and these have to be repeated several times over a long period of time to be effective. Here again, repeated fresh stool samples must be examined by your veterinarian to be sure that this pest has been eradicated. Appendectomies are indicated in only the most severe chronic cases. Always remember that cleanliness is next to Godliness and most important in getting rid of this parasite!

4. *Tapeworms*—They are another common internal parasite of dogs. They differ in their mode of transmission as they have an indirect life cycle. This means that part of their cycle must be spent in an intermediate host. Fleas, fish, rabbits, and field mice may act as an intermediate host for the tapeworm. Fleas are the most common source of tape worms for dogs, although dogs that live near water may eat raw fish, and hunting dogs that eat the entrails of rabbits may get them from those sources.

338

FIRST IN GROUP
SIOUX VALLEY K.C.
SEPT. 12, 1976
OLSON PHOTO

Ch. Cyngar's Light Up, owned by D.J. and Ruth Dempster, handled by Judy Smith. Photo courtesy of Judy Smith.

Ch. Penlan Paper Boy, by Ch. Penlan Paragon's Pride ex Penlan Portrait, one of the splendid Miniature Schnauzers from the Penlan Kennels, Landis and Penny Hirstein, Washington, Illinois. A Best in Show winner pictured here scoring one of these victories.

Ch. Jadee's Jump Up, Best of Breed under Mrs. Anne Clark and on to Group IV at Las Vegas, Nevada, handled by owner Judy Smith.

Another distinguishing feature of the tapeworm is the suction apparatus which is part of the head, enabling the tapeworm to attach itself to the lining of the intestine. If, after worming, just the head remains, it has the capability of regenerating into another worm. This is one reason why they are so difficult to get rid of. It will require several treatments to get the entire tapeworms out of a dog's system. These worms are easily recognized by the appearance of their segments which break off and appear on top of a dog's bowel movement or stick to the hair around the rectal area. These segments may appear alive and mobile at times, but most often are dead and dried up when found. They look like flat pieces of rice and may be white or brown when detected. Elimination of the intermediate host is an integral part of any plan to rid our dogs of this worm. Repeated wormings may be necessary to kill all the adult tapeworms in the intestine. An injection to rid dogs of tapeworms is now available.

5. Less commonly occurring parasitic diseases such as demodectic and sarcoptic mange should only be diagnosed and treated by your veterinarian. You are wise to consult your doctor whenever any unusual condition occurs and persists in your dog's coat and skin. These conditions are difficult to diagnose and treat at best, so that the earlier a diagnosis is obtained, the better the chances are for successful treatment. Other skin conditions such as ringworm, flea bite allergy, bacterial infections, eczemas, hormonal problems, etc. all have to be considered.

Before leaving the topic of internal parasites, it should be stressed that all worming procedures be done carefully and only with the advice and supervision of your veterinarian. The medicants used to kill the parasites are to a certain extent toxic, so they should be used with care.

We have all been alerted to the dangers of heartworm disease in most sections of our country. This chapter would not be complete without a comprehensive report on this serious parasitic disease.

HEARTWORM DISEASE IN DOGS

Just as the name implies, this disease is caused by an actual worm that goes through its life cycle in the blood stream of its victims. It ultimately makes its home in the right chambers of the heart, and in the large vessels that transport the blood to the lungs. They vary in size from 2.3 inches to 16 inches. Adult worms can survive up to five years in the heart.

By nature, this is a very serious disease, and can cause irreversible damage to the lungs and heart of its host. Heart failure and lung pathology soon result in serious problems for the dog.

The disease is transmitted and carried by female mosquitos that have infected themselves after biting an infected dog, and then passing it on to the next dog that it comes in contact with.

The disease has been reported wherever mosquitoes are found, and now cases have been reported over most of the United States. Rare cases have been reported in man and cats. It is most prevalent in warmer climates where the mosquito population is the greatest, but hot beds of infection exist in the more temperate parts of the United States and Canada also.

Concerted effort and vigorous measures must be taken to control and prevent this serious threat to our dog population. The most effective means of eradication I believe will come through annual blood testing for early detection, by the use of preventative medicine during mosquito exposure times, and also by ridding our dog's environment of mosquitoes.

Annual blood testing is necessary to detect cases that haven't started to show symptoms yet, and thus can be treated effectively. It also enables your veterinarian to prescribe safely the preventative medicine to those individuals that test negative. There is a 10 to 15% margin of error in the test, which may lead to some false negative tests. Individuals that test negative but are showing classical symptoms of the disease such as loss of stamina, coughing, loss of weight, and heart failure should be further evaluated with chest X-rays, blood tests, and electrocardiograms. Newer, more accurate tests have recently been approved for use by veterinarians.

Serious consequences may result when the preventative medication is given to a dog that has heartworm already in his system. That is why it is so important to have your dog tested annually before starting the preventative medicine.

In order to be most effective, the preventative drug diethylcarbamazine should be given in daily doses of 2.5 mg. to 3 mg. per lb. of body weight or 5 mg. per kilogram of body weight of your dog. This routine should be started 15 days prior to exposure to mosquitoes, and be continued until 60 days after exposure. Common and trade names for this drug are Caricide, Styrid-Caricide, and D.E.C. It comes in liquid and tablet forms.

This drug has come under criticism by some breeders and individuals who claim that it affects fertility and causes some serious reactions. Controlled studies have shown no evidence that this drug produces sterility or abnormal sperm count or quality. Long term studies on reproduction when the drug was given at the rate of 4.9 mg. per lb. of body weight (2 times the preventative dose level) for two years, showed no signs of toxic effects on body weight maintenance, growth rate of pups, feed consumption, conception rate, numbers of healthy pups whelped, ratio of male to female pups, blood counts, and liver function tests. It is reported as a well tolerated medication, and many thousands of dogs have benefitted from its use. From personal experience, I find only an occasional dog who will vomit the medicine, or get an upset stomach from it. The new enteric-coated pills have eliminated this small problem.

However, if you still don't want to give the preventative, especially to your breeding stock, an alternative procedure would be to test your dogs every six months for early detection of the disease, so that it can be treated as soon as possible.

Heartworm infestation can be treated successfully. There is a 1 to 5% mortality rate from the treatment. It can be expected that treatment may be completed without side effects if the disease hasn't already caused irreversible problems in the heart, lungs, liver, kidneys, etc. Careful testing, monitoring, and supervision are essential to success in treatment. Treatment is far from hopeless these days and if the disease is detected early enough, a successful outcome is more the rule than the exception.

In conclusion, remember that one case of heartworm disease in your area is one too many, especially if that one case is your dog. By following the steps mentioned in this article, we can go a long way in ridding ourselves of this serious threat to our dogs.

HOME REMEDIES

You have repeatedly read here of my instructions to call your veterinarian when your animals are sick. This is the best advice I can give you. There are a few home remedies, however, that may get you over some rough spots while waiting for professional help.

I think it is a good idea to keep some medical supplies on hand, for example, a first aid kit. The kit should contain the following items:

Roll of cotton	Rectal thermometer
Tincture of metaphen	Tweezers
Gauze bandages	Adhesive tape
Cotton applicator swabs	Jar of petroleum jelly
Hydrogen peroxide	Boric acid ointment
BFI powder	and crystals

A word here on how to take a dog's temperature may be in order. Always lubricate the thermometer with petroleum jelly and carefully insert it well into the rectum. Hold it in place for 2 to 3 minutes and then read it. The thermometer should be held firmly so that it doesn't get sucked up into the rectum.

My favorite home remedies are as follows:

1. *To stop vomiting.* Mix one tablespoon of table salt to one pint of water and dissolve the salt thoroughly. Then given one tablespoonful of the mixture to the patient. After waiting one hour repeat the procedure and skip the next meal. The dog may vomit a little after the first dose but the second dose works to settle the stomach. This mixture not only provides chlorides but acts as a mild astringent and many times, in mild digestive upsets, will work to stop the vomiting.

To administer liquid medicines to dogs, simply pull the lips away from the side of the mouth, making a pocket for depositing the liquid. Slightly tilt the dog's head upward and he will be able to swallow the liquid properly. Giving liquids by opening the mouth and pouring them directly on the tongue is an invitation to disaster because inhalation pneumonia can result. Putting it in the side of the mouth gives the dog time to hold it in his mouth, and then swallow it properly.

Tablets are best administered by forcing the dog's mouth open, and pushing the pill down over the middle of the tongue into the back of his mouth. If put in the right place, a reflex tongue reaction will force the pill down the throat to be swallowed. There is no objection to giving the pills in favorite foods as long as you carefully determine that the medicine is definitely swallowed with the food.

2. *For diarrhea:* In the case of adult Miniature Schnauzers, give one or two tablespoons of Kaopectate or Milk of Bismuth every four hours. Use one third of this dosage for puppies.

Ch. R-Bo's Victory Flash finished his championship at the New York American Miniature Schnauzer Club Specialty in February 1978 under Robert Moore. His first time out as a Special, at Knoxville, he went Best in Show under Robert Wills. This made eight consecutive generations of Best in Show winners on his sire's side and six on his dam's. Winning here under Ed Bracey. Handled by Claudia Seeberg for owner Mary Ann Ellis, Atlanta, Georgia.

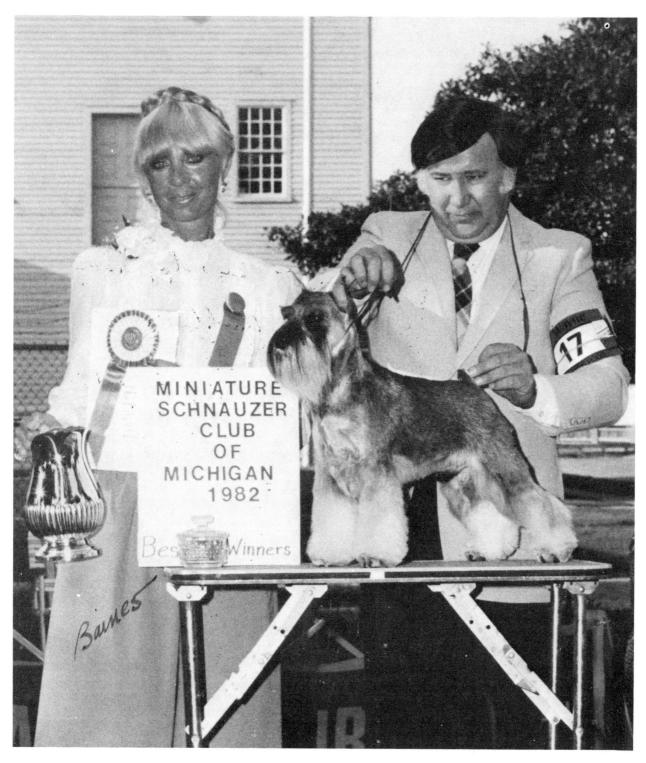

Ch. Richlene's Nutcracker was co-bred by Sandra Nagengast and Arlene Smith and was handled and conditioned by Arlene and Rich Smith. Owned by Jean Kriegbaum. Pictured taking a major en route to the title at the Miniature Schnauzer Club of Michigan 1982 Specialty judged by Enid Quick.

Skip the next meal, and if the bowels persist in being loose, then start a bland diet of boiled ground lean beef and boiled rice in the proportions of half and half. Three or four doses of this medicine should suffice. If the diarrhea persists and, particularly, if accompanied by depression, lethargy and loss of appetite, your veterinarian should be consulted immediately. With all these new viral-caused diarrheas floating around, time is of the essence in securing treatment.

3. *Mild Stimulant:* Dilute brandy half and half with water, add a little sugar, and give a teaspoonful of the mixture every four to five hours. For puppies over three months old, reduce the dosage to half a teaspoonful of the mixture every four to five hours.

4. *Mild Sedative:* Dilute brandy half and half with water, add a little sugar and give a teaspoonful of the mixture every 20 to 30 minutes.

Using brandy for both sedation and stimulation is possible by varying the time interval between doses. Given every four to five hours, it's a stimulant but given every 20 to 30 minutes it acts as a sedative.

5. *Treatment of minor cuts and wounds:* Cleanse them first with soap and water, preferably Tincture of Green Soap. Apply a mild antiseptic such as Bactine or Tincture of Metaphen two or three times daily until healed. If the cut is deep, and fairly long and bleeding, then a bandage should be applied until professional help can be obtained.

Whenever attempting to bandage wounds, first apply a layer or two of gauze over the cleaned and treated wound. Then apply a layer of cotton and then another layer or two of gauze. The bandage must be snug enough to stay on but not so tight as to impair circulation. Adhesive tape should be applied over the second layer of gauze to keep the bandage as clean and dry as possible until you can get your dog to the doctor.

Tourniquets should be applied only in cases of profusely bleeding wounds. They are applied tightly between the wound and the heart, in addition to the pressure bandage that should be applied directly to the wound. The tourniquets must be released and reapplied at 15 minute intervals.

6. *Burns:* Application of ice or very cold water and compresses is the way to treat a skin burn. Apply cold packs as soon as possible and take the dog immediately to your Vet.

7. *Frost bite:* A rare problem. The secret in treating this condition is to restore normal body temperature gradually to the affected parts. In other words, use cold water, then tepid water, to thaw out the area slowly and restore circulation. In cases of severe freezing or shock due to bitter cold temperature, take the animal to the veterinarian as soon as possible.

8. *Abscesses and infected cysts:* Obvious abscesses and infected cysts that occur between the toes may be encouraged to drain by using hot boric acid packs and saturated dressings every few hours until professional aid can be secured. The boric acid solution is made by dissolving one tablespoon of crystals to one pint of hot water. Apply frequently to the swollen area. Further treatment by a veterinarian may involve lancing and thoroughly draining and cleaning out the abscess cavity. As most abscesses are badly infected, systemic antibiotics are generally indicated.

9. *Heatstroke or Heat Exhaustion:* A word about the serious effects of heat on a dog is timely. It never ceases to amaze me how many people at dog shows have to be warned and advised not to leave their dogs in cars or vans on a warm day.

A dog's heat-regulating mechanism is not nearly as efficient as ours. Consequently, they feel the heat more than we do. Keep them as cool and as well-ventilated as possible in hot weather. Another possibility for shock is taking your dog out of a cool air-conditioned vehicle and exposing him immediately to the hot outdoors. Make that change as gradual as you can because a rapid change can cause a shock-like reaction.

In cases of suspected heat stroke which manifests itself with very high body temperatures (as high as 106-107-108 °F. sometimes), severe panting, weakness, shaking and collapse, act quickly to get him into a cold bath or shower or put ice cold compresses on his head. Then, again without delay, rush him to the nearest veterinarian for further treatment. Prevention is the key here and with a little common sense, heat stroke and exhaustion can be avoided.

10. *Poisons:* Many dogs are poisoned annually by unscrupulous people who hate dogs. Many others are victims of poisoning due simply to the careless use of rat and ant poisoning, insecticides, herbicides, anti-freeze solutions, drugs and so forth. Dogs also frequently insist on eating poisonous plants either in the house or outdoors which can lead to serious consequences. Common sources of these toxic products are named in the following section.

Plants that can be a source of poison for dogs are listed here. This list contains only the most common ones: daffodils, oleanders, poinsettias, mistletoe, philodendron, delphiniums, monkshood, foxglove, iris, lilies of the valley.

Vegetables: rhubarb, spinach and tomato vines, and sunburned potatoes can be harmful.

Trees and shrubs: rhododendron, cherry, peach, oak, elderberry and black locust, Jack in the Pulpit, Dutchman's breeches, water hemlock, mushrooms, buttercups, poison hemlock, nightshade, jimson weed, marijuana, locoweed and lupine.

Also, grain contaminants can exist in dog food. The most common ones are ergot, corn cockle and grotolaria.

Poisonous species of animal origin are such snakes as vipers, rattlesnakes, copperheads, water moccasins and the coral snake. Lizards like the Gila monster and Mexican beaded lizard are bad. Some toads, spiders, insects and fish also are potential sources of trouble.

Chemicals comprise perhaps the largest and most common source of poisoning in our environment. These are hazards that our dogs may be exposed to everyday. Careful handling and protection of these products are essential.

Toxic materials are found in all of the following groups of materials:

Arts and crafts supplies, photographic supplies, automotive and machinery products such as: anti-freeze and de-icers, rust inhibitors, brake fluids, engine and carburetor cleaners, lubricants, gasoline, kerosene, radiator cleaners, and windshield washers. Cleaners, bleaches and polishes, disinfectants, and sanitizers all contain products that are potentially dangerous.

Even health and beauty aids may contain toxic materials if ingested in large enough quantities: some bath oils, perfumes, corn removers, deodorants, anti-perspirants, athlete's foot remedies, eye make-up, hair dyes and preparations, diet pills, headache remedies, laxative, linaments, fingernail polish removers, sleeping pills, suntan lotions, amphetamines, shaving lotions, colognes, shampoos, and certain ointments.

Paints and related products also can be dangerous. Caulking compounds, driers, thinners, paints, paint brush cleaners, paint and varnish removers, preservatives, and floor and wood cleaners all fit into the category.

Pest poisons for birds, fungi, rats and mice, ants and snails can all be toxic and sometimes fatal to dogs.

Miscellaneous items like fire extinguishers and non-skid products for slippery floors can be unsafe. Almost all solvents like carbon tetrachloride, benzene, toluene, acetone, mineral spirits, kerosene, and turpentine are bad.

The previous paragraphs only serve to illustrate how many products in our everyday environment exist which can be hazardous or fatal to our dogs.

In cases of suspected poisoning, one should be aware of what to do until professional help can be obtained.

1. Keep the animal protected, quiet and warm.

2. If the contact is on the skin, eye, or body surface, cleanse and flush the area with copious amounts of water. Do this also if the dog gets something in his eye. Protect him from further exposure.

3. Inducing vomiting may be dangerous and should be done only on the advice of a veterinarian. Giving peroxide may induce vomiting in some cases. It is better to allow the animal to drink as much water as he wants. This will dilute the poison. Giving milk or raw egg whites is helpful many times to delay absorption of the toxic products.

Do not attempt to give anything by mouth if the patient is convulsing, depressed or unconscious.

Work fast in getting veterinary service. Take any vomited material, or suspected material and their containers with you to the Vet. When the suspected product is known, valuable time can be saved in administering specific treatment. The suspected specimens should be uncontaminated and be put in clean containers.

A word to the wise should be sufficient: keep all potentially harmful products away from your dog.

11. *Whelping:* We cannot leave the subject of emergencies without considering the subject of whelping. Most bitches whelp without any problems. It is wise, however, to watch them closely during this time. I feel that no bitch should go more than two hours in actual labor without producing a puppy. This includes the time before the first one as well as between puppies. If more than two hours elapse, then the dam should be examined by a veterinarian. It will then be determined if she is indeed in trouble or is just a slow whelper. This rule of thumb gives us time to find out if there is a problem, what it may be, and have time to save both dam and puppies in most cases.

It is good practice to have your bitches examined for pregnancy three-and-a-half weeks after mating, as well as at term around the 58th or 59th day. These procedures will enable the veterinarian to discover any troubles that may occur during pregnancy, as well as alerting him as to when the whelping is going to take place. Knowing this, he can plan to provide service if needed outside office hours.

Bitches that are difficult to breed, miss pregnancies, or have irregular reproductive cycles should have physical exams including laboratory tests to determine the cause of the trouble. These tests may be expensive but a lot of breeding and sterility problems due to sub-par physical condition, hormonal imbalances or hypo-thyroidism can be corrected. If a valuable bitch is restored to her normal reproductive capacity, the reward more than offsets the medical costs.

Another important thing to remember about whelping and raising puppies is to keep them warm enough. This means a room temperature of 80° to 85°F. for the first ten days to two weeks until the puppies are able to generate their own body heat. Be sure the dam keeps them close and leave a light burning at night for the first week so she won't lose track of any of them or accidentally lie on one of them. Chilling remains the biggest cause of death of newborn puppies. Other causes are malnutrition, toxic milk, hemorrhage, viral and bacterial infections. Blood type incompatibilities have been understood lately as causes of trouble.

Consultation with your veterinarian concerning these and any other breeding problems you've had in the past may result in the solution of these problems. This may result in larger litters with a higher survival rate.

Providing medical services from cradle to grave is the slogan of many veterinarians, and rightly so.

The average life expectancy for our dogs these days is about 13 years; with proper care your Miniature Schnauzers should be expected to reach this age.

12. *Approaching Old Age:* This, then, is a good time to speak about approaching old age and some of the problems we can expect during that time. Arthritis, kidney disease, heart failure, and cataracts are probably the most common ailments in older dogs. When our pet has trouble getting up in the morning, jumping up, or going upstairs, you can bet that some form of a joint problem is starting. Giving one enteric coated aspirin tablet three times a day for five days very often will help these individuals. This dosage is for adult dogs. This is relatively free of side effects and as long as nothing else is wrong, your dog will get a bit of relief.

Signs of kidney weakness are excessive drinking, inability to hold urine through the night, loss of weight, lack of appetite, and more than occasional bouts of vomiting and diarrhea. If any of these signs present themselves, it would be worthwhile to have a check-up. Very often corrective measures in diet and administering some medicine will prolong your dog's life.

Some form and degree of heart failure exists in a lot of older animals. Symptoms of chronic congestive heart failure consist of a chronic cough, especially after exercise, lack of stamina, lethargy, abdominal enlargement and labored breathing at times. If diagnosed and treated early in the disease, many heart patients live to a ripe old age.

Cataracts form in the lenses of most, if not all, old dogs. They are a part of the normal aging process. Total blindness from cataracts generally does not result for a long time. Distant and peripheral vision remain satisfactory for the expected life span of the dog. Rarely is total blindness produced by these aging cataracts before the dog's life expectancy is reached. There is no effective treatment for cataracts other than their surgical removal which is not recommended in the older patient that has any vision at all left.

A few words about canine nutrition may be in order at this time.

It is generally agreed that great strides have been made in canine nutrition in the past few years, and that most of our well-known commercial dog foods provide all the essential ingredients of a well balanced diet for our dogs. Probably the greatest problem is providing good quality protein in proper proportions. It is advisable to read dog food labels and to know what we are feeding, and how much is necessary to provide the requirements for a lean healthy individual. The tendencies in our society today are to overfeed and under exercise both our dogs and ourselves.

We must know the energy content or caloric value of the foods we are feeding. Then we must determine the energy requirements of our dogs. These will vary with time and circumstances. Your adult Miniature Schnauzer requires about 25 to 30 calories per pound of body weight daily.

Generally speaking for the average adult Miniature Schnauzer house dog, a diet consisting of 16% protein of high quality, 10% fat, and 44% carbohydrates is a good mix. For the working dog, or those being shown, or pregnant bitches, increase the protein and fat percentages by about 25% and decrease the carbohydrate proportion by 25%. To meet the needs of the increased stress of growth in young puppies and nursing bitches, the protein and fat components should be increased yet another 10 to 15%, decreasing the percentage of carbohydrates by the same percentage. Any stress situation means a rise in caloric requirement; for example, in the case of pregnancy, it is advisable to increase the amount of food intake by 20% after four weeks of gestation and by 75% after six weeks of gestation, etc.

We are assuming that the vitamins and minerals in the foods used are complete and balanced.

You may have to combine, mix or juggle various types and brands of food to attain the desired diet, but don't despair, it can be done. Prescription and special diet foods are available through your veterinarian. These probably cost more initially but may pay off in the long run.

As to exactly how much to feed each individual dog, no one can give you a magic formula that works in all cases. My best advice is to use common sense and a scale. The guidelines on dog food containers have a tendency to be over-inflated. It is better to err on the low side than to overfeed. Remember, keep your dog slim and fit with a proper diet and plenty of exercise. That's not a bad idea for your own well-being also.

This concludes our chapter concerning the medical problems and care of the Miniature Schnauzer. I hope it has been of interest and of some value to you. It should help you to understand some of the problems that may occur in your dog's lifetime.

Glossary

To the uninitiated, it must seem that fanciers of purebred dogs speak a special language all their own, which in a way we do. The following is a list of terms, abbreviations, and titles which you will run across through our pages which may be unfamiliar to you. We hope that this list will lead to fuller understanding and that it will additionally assist you as you meet and converse with others of similar interests in the world of purebred dogs.

A.K.C. The commonly used abbreviation of American Kennel Club.

Albino. A deficiency of pigmentation causing the nose leather, eyerims, and lips to be pink.

Almond eye. The shape of the tissue surrounding the eye, which creates the almond-shaped appearance required by some breed standards.

American Kennel Club. The official registry for purebred dogs in the United States. Publishes and maintains the Stud Book and handles all litter and individual registrations, transfers of ownership, and so on. Keeps all United States dog show, field trial, and obedience trial records; issues championships and other titles in these areas as they are earned; approves and licenses dog show, obedience trial, and field trial judges; licenses or issues approval to all championship shows, obedience trials, and recognized match shows. Creates and enforces the rules, regulations, and policies by which the breeding, raising, exhibiting, handling, and judging of purebred dogs in the United States are governed. Clubs, not individuals, are members of the American Kennel Club, each of which is represented by a delegate selected from the club's own membership for the purpose of attending the quarterly American Kennel Club meetings as the representative of the member club, to vote on matters discussed at each meeting and to bring back a report to the individual club of any decisions or developments which took place there.

Angulation. The angles formed by the meeting of the bones, generally referring to the shoulder and upper arm in the forequarters and the stifle and hock in the hindquarters.

Apple head. An exaggerated roundness of the top-skull.

Apron. Frill, or longer hair, below the neck.

Bad bite. Can refer to a wryness or malformation of the jaw, or to incorrect dentition.

Bad mouth. One in which the teeth do not meet correctly according to the specifications of the breed standard.

Balance. Symmetry and proportion. A well-balanced dog is one in which all of the parts appear in correct ratio to one another: height to length, head to body, skull to foreface, and neck to head and body.

Beefy. Overmusculation or overdevelopment of the shoulders or hindquarters or both.

Benched Show. Dog show at which the dogs are kept on benches while not being shown in competition.

Best in Show. The dog or bitch chosen as the most representative of any dog in any breed from among the group winners at an all-breed dog show. (The dog or bitch that has won Best of Breed next competes in the group of which its breed is a part. Then the first-prize winner of each group meets in an additional competition from which one is selected the Best in Show.)

Best of Breed. The dog that is adjudged best of any competing in its breed at a dog show.

Best of Opposite Sex. The dog or bitch that is selected as the best of the opposite sex to the Best of Breed when the latter award has been made.

Best of Winners. The dog or bitch selected as the better of the two between Winners Dog and Winners Bitch.

Bitch. A female dog.

Bite. The manner in which the upper and lower jaws meet.

Bloom. The sheen of a coat in healthy, lustrous condition.

Blue-ribbon winner. A dog that has won

first prize in the class for which it is entered at a dog show.

Bone. Refers to the girth of a dog's leg bones. A dog called "good in bone" has legs that are correct in girth for its breed and for its own general conformation. Well-rounded bone is round in appearance, flat bone rather flattish. Light bone is very fine and small in diameter, almost spindle-like in appearance; legs are extremely slender. Heavy bone refers to legs that are thick and sturdy.

Brace. Two dogs, or a dog and a bitch, closely similar in size, markings, color, and general appearance, moving together in unison.

Breed. Purebred dogs descended from mutual ancestors refined and developed by man.

Breeder. A person who breeds dogs.

Breeding particulars. Name of the sire and dam, date of breeding, date of birth, number of puppies in the litter, their sex, and name of the breeder and of the owner of the sire.

Brisket. The forepart of the body between the forelegs and beneath the chest.

Brood bitch. A female dog used primarily for breeding.

CACIB. A Challenge Certificate offered by the Federation Cynologique Internationale towards a dog's championship.

Canine teeth. The four sharp pointed teeth at the front of the jaws, two upper and two lower, flanking the incisors; often referred to as fangs.

Canines. Dogs, jackals, wolves, and foxes as a group.

Carpals. Pastern joint bones.

Castrate. To neuter a dog by removal of the testicles.

Cat foot. The short-toed, round tight foot similar to that of a cat.

C.D. An abbreviation of Companion Dog.

C.D.X. An abbreviation of Companion Dog Excellent.

Ch. Commonly used abbreviation of champion.

Challenge Certificate. A card awarded at dog shows in Great Britain by which championship there is gained. Comparable to our Winners Dog and Winners Bitch awards. To become a British champion a dog must win three of these Challenge Certificates at designated championship dog shows.

Champion. A dog or bitch that has won a total of fifteen points, including two majors, the total number under not less than three judges, two of which must have awarded the majors at A.K.C. point shows.

Character. Appearance, behavior, and temperament considered correct in an individual breed of dog.

Cheeky. Cheeks which bulge out or are rounded in appearance.

Chest. The part of the body enclosed by the ribs.

Chiseled. Clean-cut below the eyes.

Choke collar. A chain or leather collar that gives maximum control over the dog. Tightened or relaxed by the pressure on the lead caused by either pulling of the dog or tautness with which it is held by the handler.

Chops. Pendulous, loose skin creating jowls.

Cloddy. Thickset or overly heavy or low in build.

Close-coupled. Compact in appearance. Short in the loin.

Coarse. Lacking in refinement or elegance.

Coat. The hair which covers the dog.

Companion Dog. The first obedience degree obtainable.

Companion Dog Excellent. The second obedience degree obtainable.

Condition. General health. A dog said to be in good condition is one carrying exactly the right amount of weight, whose coat looks alive and glossy, and that exhibits a general appearance and demeanor of well-being.

Conformation. The framework of the dog, its form and structure.

Coupling. The section of the body known as the loin. A short-coupled dog is one in which the loin is short.

Cow-hocked. Hocks turned inward at the joint, causing the hock joints to approach one another with the result that the feet toe outward instead of straight ahead.

Crabbing. A dog moving with its body at an angle rather than coming straight at you; otherwise referred to as side-wheeling or side-winding.

Crest. The arched portion of the back of the neck.

Crop. Cut the ear leather, usually to cause the ear to stand erect.

Crossing action. A fault in the forequarters caused by loose or poorly knit shoulders.

Croup. The portion of the back directly above the hind legs.

Cryptorchid. An adult dog with testicles not normally descended. A dog with this condition cannot be shown and is subject to disqualification by the judge.

Cynology. A study of canines.

Dam. Female parent of a dog or bitch.

Dentition. Arrangement of the teeth.

Dewclaws. Extra claws on the inside of the legs. Should generally be removed several days following the puppy's birth. Required in some breeds, unimportant in others, and sometimes a disqualification—all according to the individual breed standard.

Dewlap. Excess loose and pendulous skin at the throat.

Diagonals. The right front and left rear leg make up the right diagonal; the left front and right rear leg the left diagonal. The diagonals correctly move in unison as the dog trots.

Dish-faced. The tip of the nose is placed higher than the stop.

Disqualification. A fault or condition which renders a dog ineligible to compete in organized shows, designated by the breed standard or by the American Kennel Club. Judges must withhold all awards at dog shows from dogs having disqualifying faults, noting in the Judges Book the reason for having done so. The owner may appeal this decision, but a disqualified dog cannot again be shown until it has officially been examined and reinstated by the American Kennel Club.

Distemper teeth. Discolored, badly stained, or pitted teeth. A condition so-called due to its early association with dogs having suffered from this disease.

Divergent hocks. Hock joints turn outward, creating the condition directly opposite to cow-hocks. Frequently referred to as bandy legs or barrel hocks.

Dock. Shorten the tail by cutting it.

Dog. A male of the species. Also used to describe collectively male and female canines.

Dog show. A competition in which dogs have been entered for the purpose of evaluation and to receive the opinion of a judge.

Dog show, all-breeds. A dog show in which classification may be provided, and usually is, for every breed of dog recognized by the American Kennel Club.

Dog show, specialty. A dog show featuring only one breed. Specialty shows are generally considered to be the showcases of a breed, and to win at one is a particularly valued honor and achievement, owing to the high type of competition usually encountered at these events.

Domed. A top-skull that is rounded rather than flat.

Double coat. A coat consisting of a hard, weather-resistant, protective outer covering over soft, short, close underlayer which provides warmth.

Down-faced. A downward inclination of the muzzle toward the tip of the nose.

Down in pastern. A softness or weakness of the pastern causing a pronounced deviation from the vertical.

Drag. A trail having been prepared by dragging a bag, generally bearing the strong scent of an animal, along the ground.

Drive. The powerful action of the hindquarters which should equal the degree of reach of the forequarters.

Drop ear. Ears carried drooping or folded forward.

Dry head. One exhibiting no excess wrinkle.

Dry neck. A clean, firm neckline free of throatiness or excess skin.

Dual champion. A dog having gained both bench show and field trial championships.

Dudley nose. Flesh-colored nose.

Elbow. The joint of the forearm and upper arm.

Elbow, out at. Elbow pointing away from the body rather than being held close.

Even bite. Exact meeting of the front teeth, tip to tip with no overlap of the uppers or lowers. Generally considered to be less serviceable than the scissors bite, although equally permissible or preferred in some breeds.

Ewe neck. An unattractive, concave curvature of the top area of the neckline.

Expression. The typical expression of the breed as one studies the head. Determined largely by the shape of the eye and its placement.

Eyeteeth. The upper canine teeth.

Faking. The altering of the natural appearance of a dog. A highly frowned upon and unethical practice which must lead, upon recognition by the judge, to instant dismissal from the show ring with a notation in the Judges Book stating the reason.

Fancier. A person actively involved in the sport of purebred dogs.

Fancy. The enthusiasts of a sport or hobby. Dog breeders, exhibitors, judges, and others actively involved with purebred dogs as a group comprise the dog fancy.

Fangs. The canine teeth.

F.C.I. Abbreviation of the Federation Cynologique Internationale.

Feathering. The longer fringes of hair that appear on the ears, tail, chest, and legs.

Federation Cynologique Internationale. A canine authority representing numerous countries, principally European, all of which consent to and agree on certain practices and breed identifications.

Feet east and west. An expression used to describe toes on the forefeet turning outward rather than directly forward.

Fetch. Retrieving of game by a dog, or the command for the dog to do so.

Fiddle front. Caused by elbows protruding from the desired closeness to the body, with the result that the pasterns approach one another too closely and the feet toe outward. Thus, resembling the shape of a violin.

Field champion. A dog that has gained the title field champion has defeated a specified number of dogs in specified competition at a series of American Kennel Club licensed or member field trials.

Field trial. A competition for specified Hound or Sporting breeds where dogs are judged according to their ability and style on following a game trail or on finding and retrieving game.

Finishing a dog. Refers to completing a dog's championship, obedience title, or field trial title.

Flank. The side of the body through the loin area.

Flat bone. Bones of the leg which are not round.

Flat-sided. Ribs that are flat down the side rather than slightly rounded.

Fld. Ch. Abbreviation of field champion, used as a prefix before the dog's name.

Flews. A pendulous condition of the inner corners of the mouth.

Flush. To drive birds from cover. To spring at them. To force them to take flight.

Flyer. An especially exciting or promising young dog.

Flying ears. Ears correctly carried dropped or folded that stand up or tend to "fly" upon occasion.

Flying trot. The speed at which you should *never* move your dog in the show ring. All four feet actually briefly leave the ground during each half stride, making correct evaluation of the dog's normal gait virtually impossible.

Forearm. The front leg from elbow to pastern.

Foreface. The muzzle of the dog.

Front. The forepart of the body viewed head-on. Includes the head, forelegs, shoulders, chest, and feet.

Futurity Stakes. A competition at shows or field trials for dogs who are less than twelve months of age for which puppies are nominated, at or prior to birth. Highly competitive among breeders, usually with a fairly good purse for the winners.

Gait. The manner in which a dog walks or trots.

Gallop. The fastest gait. Never to be used in the show ring.

Game. The animals or wild birds which are hunted.

Gay tail. Tail carried high.

Get. Puppies.

Goose rump. Too sloping (steep) in croup.

Groom. To bathe, brush, comb, and trim your dog.

Groups. Refers to the variety groups in which all breeds of dogs are divided.

Gun dog. One that has been specifically trained to work with man in the field for retrieving game that has been shot and for locating live game.

Guns. The persons who do the shooting during field trials.

Gun-shy. Describes a dog that cringes or shows other signs of fear at the sound or sight of a gun.

Hackney action. High lifting of the forefeet in the manner of a hackney pony.

Ham. Muscular development of the upper hind leg. Also used to describe a dog that loves applause while being shown, really going all out when it occurs.

Handler. A person who shows dogs in competition, either as an amateur (without pay) or as a professional (receiving a fee in payment for the service).

Hard-mouthed. A dog that grasps the game too firmly in retrieving, causing bites and tooth marks.

Hare foot. An elongated paw, like the foot of a hare.

Haw. A third eyelid or excess membrane at the corner of the eye.

Heat. The period during which a bitch can be bred. Also referred to as being "in season."

Heel. A command ordering the dog to follow close to the handler.

Hindquarters. Rear assemblage of the dog.

Hie on. A command used in hunting or field trials, urging the dog to go further.

Hock. The joint between the second thigh and the metatarsus.

Hocks well let down. Expression denoting that the hock joint should be placed quite low to the ground.

Honorable scars. Those incurred as a result of working injuries.

In season. *See* **Heat.**

Incisors. The front teeth between the canines.

Int. Ch. An abbreviation of international champion.

International champion. A dog awarded four CACIB cards at F.C.I. dog shows.

Jowls. Flesh of lips and jaws.

Judge. Person making the decisions at a dog show, obedience trial, or field trial. Judges residing in the United States must be approved and licensed by the A.K.C. in order to officiate at events where points toward championship titles are awarded; residents of another country whose governing body is recognized by the A.K.C. may be granted special permits to officiate in the United States.

Kennel. The building in which dogs are housed. Also used when referring to a person's collective dogs.

Knee joint. Stifle joint.

Knitting and purling. Crossing and throwing of forefeet as dog moves.

Knuckling over. A double-jointed wrist, or pastern, sometimes accompanied by enlarged bone development in the area, causing the joints to double over under the dog's weight.

Layback. 1) Describes correctly angulated shoulders. 2) Describes a short-faced dog whose pushed-in nose placement is accompanied by undershot jaw.

Leather. The ear flap. Also the skin of the actual nose.

Level bite. Another way of describing an even bite, as teeth of both jaws meet exactly.

Level gait. A dog moving smoothly, topline carried level as he does so, is said to be moving in this manner.

Lippy. Lips that are pendulous or do not fit tightly.

Loaded shoulders. Those overburdened with excessive muscular development.

Loin. Area of the sides between the lower ribs and hindquarters.

Lumber. Superfluous flesh.

Lumbering. A clumsy, awkward gait.

Major. A win of either Winners Dog or Winners Bitch carrying with it three, four, or five points toward championship.

Mane. The long hair growing on the top and upper sides of the neck.

Match show. An informal dog show where no championship points are awarded and entries can usually be made upon arrival, although some require pre-entry. Excellent practice area for future show dogs and for novice exhibitors as the entire atmosphere is relaxed and congenial.

Mate. To breed a dog and a bitch to one another. Littermates are dogs which are born in the same litter.

Maturity Stakes. For dogs who the previous year had been entered in the Futurity Stakes.

Milk teeth. The first baby teeth.

Miscellaneous Class. A class provided at A.K.C. point shows in which specified breeds may compete in the absence of their own breed classification. Dogs of breeds in the process of becoming recognized by A.K.C. may compete in this class prior to the eventual provision of their own individual breed classification.

Molars. Four premolars are located at either side of the upper and lower jaws. Two molars exist on either side of the upper jaw, three on either side below. Lower molars have two roots; upper molars have three roots.

Monorchid. A dog with only one properly descended testicle. This condition disqualifies from competition at A.K.C. dog shows.

Muzzle. 1) The part of the head in front of the eyes. 2) To fasten something over the mouth, usually to prevent biting.

Nick. A successful breeding that results in puppies of excellent quality.

Non-slip retriever. A dog not expected to flush or to find game; one that merely walks at heel, marks the fall, then retrieves upon command.

Nose. Describes the dog's organ of smell, but also refers to his talent at scenting. A dog with a "good nose" is one adept at picking up and following a scent trail.

Obedience trial. A licensed obedience trial is one held under A.K.C. rules at which it is possible to gain a "leg" towards a dog's obedience title or titles.

Obedience trial champion. Denotes that a dog has attained obedience trial championship under A.K.C. regulations by having gained a specified number of points and first place awards.

Oblique shoulders. Shoulders angulated so as to be well laid back.

Occiput. Upper back point of skull.

Occipital protuberance. A prominent occiput noted in some of the Sporting breeds.

O.F.A. Commonly used abbreviation for Orthopedic Foundation for Animals.

Orthopedic Foundation for Animals. This organization is ready to read the hip radiographs of dogs and certify the existence of or freedom from hip dysplasia. Board-certified radiologists read vast numbers of these files each year.

O.T. Ch. An abbreviation of obedience trial champion.

Out at elbow. Elbows are held away from the body rather than in close.

Out at shoulder. Shoulder blades set in such a manner that joints are too wide and jut out from body.

Oval chest. Deep with only moderate width.

Overshot. Upper incisors overlap the lower incisors.

Pacing. A gait in which both right legs and both left legs move concurrently, causing a rolling action.

Paddling. Faulty gait in which the front legs swing forward in a stiff upward motion.

Pad. Thick protective covering of the bottom of the foot. Serves as a shock absorber.

Paper foot. Thin pads accompanying a flat foot.

Pastern. The area of the foreleg between the wrist and the foot.

Pedigree. Written record of dog's lineage.

Pigeon chest. A protruding, short breastbone.

Pigeon-toed. Toes point inward, as those of a pigeon.

Pile. Soft hair making a dense undercoat.

Plume. A long fringe of hair on the tail.

Poach. To trespass on private property when hunting.

Pointed. A dog that has won points toward its championship is referred to as "pointed."

Police dog. Any dog that has been trained to do police work.

Put down. To groom and otherwise prepare a dog for the show ring.

Quality. Excellence of type and conformation.

Racy. Lightly built, appearing overly long in leg and lacking substance.

Rangy. Excessive length of body combined with shallowness through the ribs and chest.

Reach. The distance to which the forelegs reach out in gaiting, which should correspond with the strength and drive of the hindquarters.

Register. To record your dog with the American Kennel Club.

Registration Certificate. The paper you receive denoting that your dog's registration has been recorded with the A.K.C., giving the breed, assigned names, names of sire and dam, date of birth, breeder and owner, along with the assigned Stud Book number of the dog.

Reserve Winners Bitch or **Reserve Winners Dog.** After the judging of Winners Bitch and Winners Dog, the remaining first prize dogs (bitches or dogs) remain in the ring where they are joined by the bitch or dog that placed second in the class to the one awarded Winners Bitch or Winners Dog, provided she or he was defeated only by that one bitch or dog. From these a Reserve Winner is selected. Should the Winners Bitch or Winners Dog subsequently be disallowed due to any error or technicality, the Reserve Winner is then moved up automatically to Winners in the A.K.C. records, and the points awarded to the Winners Bitch or Winners Dog then transfer to the one which placed Reserve. This is a safeguard award, for although it seldom happens, should the winner of the championship points be found to have been ineligible to receive them, the Reserve dog keeps the Winners' points.

Roach back. A convex curvature of the topline of the dog.

Rocking horse. An expression used to describe a dog that has been overly extended in forequarters and hindquarters by the handler, *i.e.*, forefeet placed too far forward, hind feet pulled overly far behind, making the dog resemble a child's rocking horse. To be avoided in presenting your dog for judging.

Rolling gait. An aimless, ambling type of action correct in some breeds but to be faulted in others.

Saddle back. Of excessive length with a dip behind the withers.

Scissors bite. The outer tips of the lower incisors touch the inner tips of the upper incisors. Generally considered to be the most serviceable type of jaw formation.

Second thigh. The area of the hindquarters between the hock and the stifle.

Septum. The vertical line between the nostrils.

Set up. To pose your dog in position for examination by the judge. Same as "stack."

Shelly. A body lacking in substance.

Shoulder height. The height of the dog from the ground to the highest point of the withers.

Sire. The male parent.

Skully. An expression used to describe a coarse or overly massive skull.

Slab sides. Flat sides with little spring of rib.

Soundness. Mental and physical stability. Sometimes used as well to denote the manner in which the dog gaits.

Spay. To neuter a bitch by surgery. Once this operation has been performed, the bitch is no longer eligible for entry in regular classes or in Veterans Class at A.K.C. shows.

Special. A dog or bitch entered only for Best of Breed competition at a dog show.

Specialty club. An organization devoted to sponsoring an individual breed of dog.

Specialty dog show. *See* **Dog show, specialty.**

Stack. *See* **Set up.**

Stake. A class in field trial competition.

Stance. The natural position a dog assumes in standing.

Standard. The official description of the ideal specimen of a breed. The Standard of Perfection is drawn up by the parent specialty club, usually by a special committee to whom the task is assigned, approved by the membership and by the American Kennel Club, and then serves as a guide to breeders and to judges in decisions regarding the merit, or lack of it, in evaluating individual dogs.

Stifle. The joint of the hind leg corresponding

to a person's knee.

Stilted. The somewhat choppy gait of a dog lacking correct angulation.

Stop. The step-up from nose to skull; the indentation at the juncture of the skull and foreface.

Straight behind. Lacking angulation in the hindquarters.

Straight-shouldered. Lacking angulation of the shoulder blades.

Stud. A male dog that is used for breeding.

Stud book. The official record kept on the breeding particulars of recognized breeds of dogs.

Substance. Degree of bone size.

Swayback. Weakness, or downward curvature, in the topline between the withers and the hipbones.

Sweepstakes. Competition at shows for young dogs, usually up to twelve or eighteen months of age; unlike Futurity, no advance nomination is required.

Tail set. Manner in which the tail is placed on the rump.

T.D. An abbreviation of Tracking Dog.

T.D.X. An abbreviation of Tracking Dog Excellent.

Team. Generally consists of four dogs.

Thigh. Hindquarters from the stifle to the hip.

Throatiness. Excessive loose skin at the throat.

Topline. The dog's back from withers to tailset.

Tracking Dog. A title awarded dogs who have fulfilled the A.K.C. requirements at licensed or member club tracking tests.

Tracking Dog Excellent. An advanced tracking degree.

Trail. Hunt by following a trail scent.

Trot. The gait at which the dog moves in a rhythmic two-beat action, right front and left hind foot and left front and right hind foot each striking the ground together.

Tuck-up. A natural shallowness of the body at the loin creating a small-waisted appearance.

Type. The combination of features which makes a breed unique, distinguishing it from all others.

U.D. An abbreviation of Utility Dog.

U.D.T. An abbreviation of Utility Dog Tracker

Unbenched show. Dog show at which dogs must arrive in time for judging and may leave anytime thereafter.

U.D.T.X. An abbreviation of Utility Dog and Tracker Excellent.

Undershot. The front teeth of the lower jaw reach beyond the front teeth of the upper jaw.

Upper arm. The foreleg between the forearm and the shoulder blade.

Utility Dog. Another level of obedience degree.

Utility Dog and Tracker. A double title indicating a dog that has gained both utility and tracking degrees. Also known as Utility Dog Tracking.

Utility Dog and Tracker Excellent. A double title indicating a dog that has gained both utility and advanced tracking degrees.

Walk. The gait in which three feet support the body, each lifting in regular sequence one at a time off the ground.

Walleye. A blue eye, fish eye, or pearl eye caused by a whitish appearance of the iris.

W.C. An abbreviation of Working Certificate.

Weedy. Lacking in sufficient bone and substance.

Well let down. Short hocks, hock joint placed low to the ground.

Wet neck. Dewlap, or superfluous skin.

Wheel back. Roached back with topline considerably arched over the loin.

Winners Bitch or Winners Dog. The awards which are accompanied by championship points, based on the number of dogs defeated, at A.K.C. member or licensed dog shows.

Withers. The highest point of the shoulders, right behind the neck.

Working Certificate. An award earned by dogs who have proven their hunting ability and are not gun-shy.

Wry mouth. Lower jaw is twisted and does not correctly align with the upper jaw.

Index

This index is composed of three separate parts: a general index, an index of kennels, and an index of persons mentioned in the text and captions.

General Index

Index of Kennels

Index of Persons